LOEB, Edwin M. **Sumatra; its history and people.** **Oxford, 1973, c1972 (orig. pub. in Vienna in 1935). 350p bibl (Oxford in Asia paperbacks). 10.50 pa.**

A welcome reissue of an ethnographic study. Straightforward, concise, and readable in style, the volume offers a detailed survey of the customs of the Bataks, the Minangkabau, the Achehnese, and the other peoples of the Indonesian island. Loeb has drawn upon his own field work in Indonesia (1926-27) as well as upon a wealth of Dutch language scholarship on Sumatra. More than 30 years after its first publication, *Sumatra* remains the principal English-language source on the ethnography of the Indonesian island. The plates included in the original 1935 edition have unfortunately been omitted from the reprint edition. For a more up-to-date, but much less detailed, survey of the peoples of Sumatra, the relevant section of Frank Lebar's *Ethnic groups of insular Southeast Asia* (CHOICE, Nov. 1973) is highly recommended.

SUMATRA

SCALE

District boundaries ● Chief cities

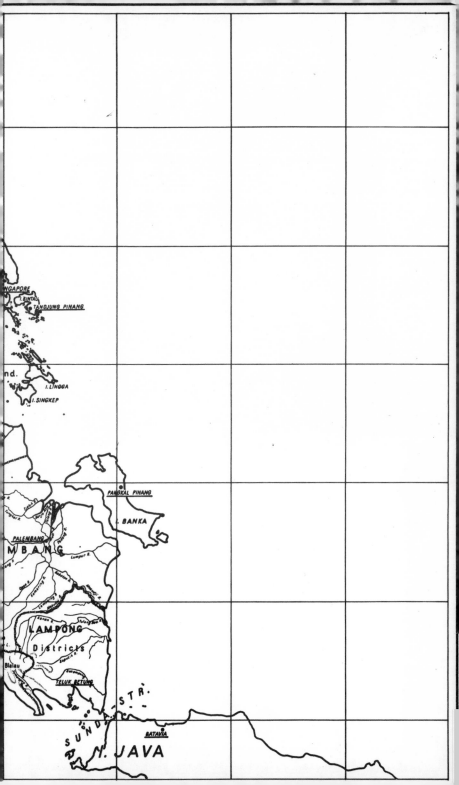

SUMATRA
ITS HISTORY AND
PEOPLE

EDWIN M. LOEB

With an additional chapter by
ROBERT HEINE-GELDERN

KUALA LUMPUR
OXFORD UNIVERSITY PRESS
JAKARTA

Oxford University Press, Ely House, London W.1

GLASGOW NEW YORK TORONTO MELBOURNE WELLINGTON
CAPE TOWN IBADAN NAIROBI DAR ES SALAAM LUSAKA ADDIS ABABA
DELHI BOMBAY CALCUTTA MADRAS KARACHI LAHORE DACCA
KUALA LUMPUR SINGAPORE JAKARTA HONG KONG TOKYO.

Bangunan Loke Yew Kuala Lumpur
● *Oxford University Press 1972*

Reprinted in Oxford in Asia Paperbacks 1972
Second Impression 1974

Reprinted by kind permission of
Verlag des Institutes fur
Volkerkunde der Universitat, Wien
First published in 1935

Printed lithographically in Malaysia by
ART PRINTING WORKS, KUALA LUMPUR

TABLE OF CONTENTS.

Edwin M. LOEB

VI

R. HEINE-GELDERN

* * *

PREFACE.

A book dealing with the history and people of Sumatra can no longer be offered as a novelty. Yet it is true that the only book on the subject which we have in English, that by Marsden, published in 1783, can at the present time be regarded as somewhat of an antiquity. Everything that Marsden set down is reliable. On the other hand, most of Sumatra and the western islands were as yet unexplored in the 18th century, and the technique of an observer was not as well developed then as now.

In quite recent years we have been fortunate enough to have two new general summaries on the people of Sumatra, the first in Dutch and the second in French. I refer to the books by Lekkerkerker and Collet. These have proven invaluable in the present English compilation. The first work is sound, solid, and a treasure mine of digested information. The second combines the scholarship of the first with brilliancy, wit, and a mastery of French diction.

However, ethnology is unending in its exactions and no work is so good that it cannot be bettered by the addition of further pertinent details. Then, also, it is desirable to have as many theoretical thinkers as possible write their conclusions on the same group of facts. Many, perhaps most, of our present theories will prove wrong, perhaps even puerile, to the philosophers of the future. But even these men of clearer vision and fuller knowledge will be glad to read the opinions of workers in the field who were able to observe the last remnants of primitive culture.

In most of our present general works on comparative ethnology the Dutch East Indies have been either entirely or partially neglected. This has not been due to lack of material, for Dutch scientific ethnological journals date back over two centuries in comparison with the average twenty-year life of many similar German and English publications. Nor has there been entire lack of general books on the Dutch possessions from the time of the great comparative Dutch ethnologist Wilken onwards. Furthermore, this neglect has not been due to the non-importance of the region, for no writer should consider himself

1

competent to speak of Asiatic traits in Oceania unless he has more than superficial knowledge of intervening Malaysia.

The neglect of Dutch ethnographic material has arisen from two main causes. First, the fact that relatively few ethnologists have a reading knowledge of Dutch, and secondly because there has been insufficient compilation of Dutch sources. As an example of the second point I may refer to our material on Batak social organization. These people have a surprisingly well developed primitive social system, and it has been fully described by German and Dutch missionaries who have spent a great part of their lives in the region. Yet this material has been allowed to remain undigested in journal form, often in periodicals difficult to obtain outside of Leiden.

The present book, therefore, is written in the hope that it will stimulate further research on the same lines, and that other Indonesian islands, such as Borneo, may receive like attention. Field work then, always so dependent on compiled material, will doubtlessly take a new lease of life.

The author of a book of compilation should, if the book be of merit, take a position far in the background. The interest of the reader is directed to the facts under discussion, and often he will look at the preface, which explains why and how these facts are presented, last or not at all. Yet the correct presentation of ethnological facts is so dependent on the previous training and experience of the compiler that I cannot forbear adding a word concerning my competency and the manner in which this task was accomplished.

My actual field work in Indonesia was performed in the years 1926—1927, when under a grant by the Guggenheim Brothers of New York City, I spent five months in the Mentawei Islands. In the course of these years I likewise became acquainted with Christianized Bataks, and had the pleasure of a brief trip to the Minangkabau Highlands.

In 1928—1929 I was granted a fellowship by the John Simon Guggenheim Foundation for the purpose of working in Austria and Holland and completing a book on Sumatra. Due to the magnitude of the task, and the fact that other work, which I had previously started, had first to be finished, the actual completion of the present book was delayed until the end of the year 1933.

As a result of my field work in Mentawei I gained sufficient knowledge of Malay and the Malaysian languages to verify their usage among other peoples of Sumatra. A writer on Indonesia should also be acquainted with Arabic and Sanskrit. In this regard, however, I have for the most part relied on the works of the Dutch writers.

While I have not written this book for the purpose of proving any particular doctrine, and have at all times emphasized cultural fact rather than theories of culture, yet facts must be interpreted according to one theoretical bias or another, unless they are left totally uninterpreted. In theory I have chosen from the evolutionary school, which I came into contact with at Yale University under Prof. Keller; from the Americanist school, having lectured for nine years at the University of California under Prof. Kroeber and Prof. Lowie; and finally from the Kulturkreise school, since the writing of the book was done in Vienna in contact with Prof. Schmidt, Prof. Koppers, and Prof. Heine-Geldern. The last named ethnologist has been of the greatest help in the present undertaking, and indeed is a pioneer in modern Indonesian comparative ethnology.

Without wishing to estimate the comparative values of these three schools of thought, I may briefly say that from the evolutionists I learned to think in terms of nomenclatures, such as totemism, clans, avoidance customs. In short, to see similarities behind all differences. From the Americanists I learned to look at culture as being to a certain extent localized to areas, and to re-examine certain catchwords such as "matriarchate", dividing them into their component parts. From the Kulturkreise school I learned again to regard cultural facts as occurrences of world-wide distribution. I consider, for example, the underlying principles of tribal initiation to be the same, whether the custom is studied in California, Australia or Ceram.

In the preparation of the present volume I wish to acknowledge my thanks to Prof. J. P. B. de Josselin de Jong for his aid during my stay in Holland, to the Colonial Institute of Amsterdam for most of the illustrations used. Certain of the Mentawei pictures, however, were taken by myself and then presented to the Institute. The topographical map I have taken from Lekkerkerker, and the linguistic map from Collet. Most of my information regarding the social organization of Minangkabau comes from Willinck, as well as a chart of genealogical organization. To the American Anthropologist I am indebted for permission to make use of articles I wrote on Mentawei and on the social organizations of the Bataks and the Minangkabau.

1*

INTRODUCTION.

The geography and geology of Sumatra. — Sumatra is the westermost, and next to Borneo, the largest of the great Sunda Islands in the Malay Archipelago. If we do not consider Greenland as an island, Sumatra is, according to its area, the fourth largest island of the world. Its length is about 1,060 miles, its extreme breadth 248 miles, and its area, including the neighboring islands, except Banka and Billiton, is 180,380 square miles. Thus Sumatra is nearly four times as large as Java, almost as large as Spain, and thirteen times the size of the Netherlands.

The northern half of Sumatra runs roughly parallel to the Malay Peninsula, from which it is separated by the Strait of Malacca, and the southern end is separated by the narrow Sunda Strait from Java. Unlike Java, Sumatra has a series of considerable islands arranged like outworks in front of the west coast, which faces the open Indian Ocean.

In relief Sumatra consists of a high mountain chain, which runs along the western coast, descending eastwards to a huge tract of flat, alluvial land, seamed with many large rivers and their scores of tributaries. The chain extends for a distance of over 1,000 miles and contains numerous volcanic peaks of heights from 5,000 to over 12,000 feet. The whole system is known as the Barisan Mountains, and consists in general of two or more folded chains running parallel to each other with an intervening valley. Along this valley lies a string of mountain lakes; from south to north, Ranan, Kurintji, Singkaran, Maninjau and Toba. Lake Toba is the largest, and in its midst the large island, Pulau Samosir, is situated.

The river system of Sumatra is extensive and of great value to the country. Owing to the proximity of the mountains to the west coast, the rivers there run in valleys with a steep slope, have a very short lower course, and are in general unnavigable except near the mouth. The eastern rivers, however, run through alluvial plains, have extensive drainage areas, and form the principal and often the only means of communication. They are of such value to the community that many of the districts they water are named after them.

South of three degrees north, the following are the important rivers, in the order named. The Asahen drains Lake Toba. The Panei, with its two tributaries, the Bila and the Barumun, and the Rokan, flow into the Strait of Malacca. Then comes the Djambi, the largest and most beautiful river of Sumatra. Below this flows the Musi, the only other river of the island which compares in size to the Djambi. Below Palembang, the Musi splits up into a number of channels which spread out amidst a vast unhealthy swamp covering an area of some 4,600 square miles.

The entire east coast of Sumatra is of such low formation, that it is difficult to say in the case of many broad stretches whether they belong to the land or to the sea. But there are no bare mud flats and banks as in Holland. All is overgrown with tropical plants. Viewed from the sea one can only distinguish the land from the water by the thickets of long evergreen mangrove trees which sprout out of the mud. This low alluvial coast grows rapidly. The rivers bring down mud and the tree roots hold it fast. At the river mouths round banks are formed, which hinder navigation. Often the rivers overflow inland discharging their muddy contents over the swampy land.

Sumatra, like Java and Borneo, is formed largely of strata of the Tertiary period, although it contains also two schistose formations, one of which is anterior to the Carboniferous period. The Tertiary series are more complete than in Java. The numerous volcanoes, so characteristic of the whole archipelago, are due to the Quaternary period.

Climate. — The climate of Sumatra resembles that of Java and is hot and extremely moist. The wind system of North Sumatra differs from that of the great part of the Dutch East Indies, the northeast monsoon blowing from December to March, and the southwest monsoon from May to October.

Southern Sumatra has the highest temperatures, and the mean annual temperature for the lowlands is about 80 degrees. At Toba, at an elevation of 3,772 feet, this is 69.6 degrees, and higher altitudes show a corresponding reduction. On the whole, the temperature of Sumatra is slightly higher than that of Java. March, April, and May are the hottest months; January and February are the coolest, but the difference does not exceed two degrees. The different wind distribution causes a variation of the seasons. Thus in North Sumatra, October is the wettest month and February and March are the driest, whilst elsewhere the wettest months are December, January and February, and the dry period extends from July to September. Accordingly the rainfall varies considerably. The normal average rainfall for North Sumatra is 95.71, for East Sumatra 106.27, and for West Sumatra 122.32 inches. The west monsoon gives the heavier rainfall, and the fall is accentuated in West Sumatra by the high mountains.

Fauna. — Notwithstanding the proximity of Sumatra to Java the fauna of Sumatra shows a greater resemblance to that of Borneo than to that of Java, this being especially noticeable with regard to the fauna of the east coast, while that of the west coast and the adjacent islands is more allied to the Java fauna.

The orang-utan, common to Sumatra (in the northeast) and Borneo, is unknown in Java, the siamang (Hylobates syndactylus) is found in Sumatra only; there also are ape species common to Borneo and Sumatra. Both Sumatra and Borneo have elephants, tapirs, the Malayan bear, and a two-horned variety of rhinoceros, all of which are not to be found in Java. The one-horned rhinoceros and the wild ox or banteng (Bos sundaicus), frequent in Java, are unknown in Sumatra. A species of antelope (kambing-utan) lives in the loneliest mountain districts of this island. Though tigers are common in Sumatra and Java there are none in Borneo.

The Sumatrean fauna also includes the black baboon (Cynocephalus niger) and the hog deer or babi rusa, which animals likewise are to be found in Nias and Mentawei to the west of Sumatra. Other animals native to the main island include the fox-nosed monkey (Tarsius); the slow loris (Nycticebus); the lemur (Galeopithecus volans); the flying fox; the civit cat; the Sumatrean hare (Lepus netscheri); and the wild dog and pig. Species of birds exist in Sumatra which are unknown in Java.

There is a difference between the fauna of North and South Sumatra. The orang-utan, the rhinoceros, and the hog deer are present only in the north, while the tapir and certain varieties of monkeys are to be found only in the south of the island. There even is a difference in the bird world between the north and the south. Volz is of the opinion that the boundary between the two territories should be sought for in the stretch between Padang Lawas and Sibolga, where one can go from coast to coast without ascending over 1,200 feet, and along a young Tertiary formation. This writer believes that a sea channel existed here until the end of Tertiary times separating North and South Sumatra, and that in this time the two sections received the greater part of their present day fauna.

Tigers are found everywhere in Sumatra and are very numerous in some districts. On the whole they are useful animals, as they keep down the number of boars, which are very harmful to cultivated fields. But when the tiger is old and no longer fleet enough to catch wild pigs, deer, and apes, it has to be satisfied with poorly armed human beings. Such a man-eater spreads terror in the neighborhood and is a hindrance to social intercourse.

The crocodile is much more dangerous to man than the tiger. These animals live chiefly at the mouth of the rivers and only sporadically in their upper stretches. Even where the crocodiles are the most abundant the natives bathe without taking proper precautions, and hence these animals, while less feared than the tigers, claim more victims.

History. — The pre-European history of Sumatra is of great importance for the understanding of the complex native cultures of European contact. Unfortunately no uniformity exists in the interpretation of original sources, even among such competent scholars as Krom and Ferrand. Ferrand was one of the first historians to show that it was Sumatra and not Java which gave an early impetus to the expansion of Hindu civilization in Insulinde.

Śrîvijaya in the Palembang River valley in Sumatra was colonized by Hindus at an early date; perhaps between the first and second century A. D. At any rate like Cambodia and Champa, this empire was in full cultural development in the seventh century.

Actually the first Hindu kingdom mentioned in Sumatra was that of Malayu (Malay-Land) in Djambi in 644 A. D. A short time afterwards, however, the kingdom of Śrîvijaya was powerful enough to conquer Malayu and Banka, gain a foothold on the Malay Peninsula and come into close contact with Java. The Chinese royal edict of 695 mentions ambassadors of Śrîvijaya. This kingdom was already the chief one of Sumatra, and held Malayu as a subject state.

The first use of the name Sumatra occurred in 1017. The man who at that time was king of Sumatra (Śrîvijaya) sent ambassadors, a letter, and slaves to China. The treasures consisted of clothing, ivory, and Sanskrit books. The Chinese called this king "haji Sumatra bhūmi", the king of the land of Sumatra. Krom does not accept any of the explanations as yet given for this name. Most writers believe that the word "Sumatra" is derived from the word "Samudra", which is the Sanskrit name for the sea, and also for a later kingdom in Atjeh. In this case Sumatra is "Sea-land". But Krom claims that it is peculiar to call an island Sea-land, and besides, that this name is of later use than the name Sumatra.

The initial cause of the fall of Śrīvijaya is said by Krom to have been two expeditions of conquest sent by Candrabhana, then king of Śrīvijaya. Candrabhana landed in Ceylon in the year 1251. He pleaded friendship, stating "We are all Buddhists". Then, treacherously, he reduced the native cities to ruins. Some years later the conqueror returned again to the island, but this time he was forced to flee, leaving his harem behind. Among the treasures which the vanquished were forced to leave in Ceylon were mentioned: royal insignia, shell trumpets, parasols, and kettle drums.

Due to this weakening of the power of Śrīvijaya, Krtanagara, king of Singasari in Java, thought that the auspicious moment had arrived to conquer his rival kingdom in Sumatra. So he sent an army for this purpose in 1275.

Traditions of the Malays ascribed a defeat of the forces of Java, due to a trial combat by karabau. But an inscription of King Krtanagara himself has been found engraved in stone, on the upper Batang Hari River on the present site of Minangkabau. This inscription calls for the recognition of the sovereignty of the king of Java, and is addressed to all the subjects of the land of Malayu, whether Brahmans, Ksatriyas, Waiśyas, or Śūdras.

Krom believes that this stone gives evidence that the ancient kingdom of Malayu was revived by Java in opposition to Śrīvijaya, not as an independent state, however, but as an outpost of Javanese influence. As the Javanese influence on Sumatra increased, the boundaries of Malayu became further and further extended, until the name Malayu stood for the entire island.

Already in 1281 Malayu sent its own ambassadors to China, and remarkable to say, made use of two Mohammedan men for this mission, their names being Sumayman and Chamsu'd-din.

At about this time (1281) the Islam kingdoms began to form on Sumatra's north coast. They recognized the higher power of Śrīvijaya as they did later that of Madjapahit, but because of the differences in religion the bond could not have been a very close one. These kingdoms included Samudra, which was founded some time before 1286, and Perlak which was founded even earlier, and according to Marco Polo's account, was Mohammedan in 1292.

Marco Polo was the first European to visit Sumatra, travelling there in 1292. In the sixth chapter of his third book he mentioned Java as being ruled by a great king, and as being heathen. It was an unusual kingdom, and rich, trading in pepper and all kinds of spices.

Marco Polo knew Sumatra, or rather the northern portion of Sumatra, much better than he knew Java. In spite of the comparative sizes of the two islands, he called Sumatra Java Minor. In North Sumatra he found eight small kingdoms, of which he named six. The first he called Ferlec (naturally Perlak) converted through Mohammedan merchants to Islam; that is to say, the city dwellers, although in the interior the people still lived as "beasts". Neighboring this was located Basma, and then Samara, each under its own king. In the last-named kingdom Marco Polo remained five months. The natives of these kingdoms were still "wild heathen", as well as the inhabitants of the two following kingdoms, Dagroian and Lambri. Lambri is none other than Lamuri (Great Atjeh), and Basma is Pasè. Samara is Samudra. Dagroian remains uncertain, although Marsden believes that it was Indragiri.

From this account Krom concludes that the small states had not as yet been converted in 1292, and that Samudra was converted between 1292 and 1297, the latter date being the year of the death of its Mohammedan founder.

It is noteworthy that Marco Polo mentions a visit to Malayu, but not to Śrívijaya. He sailed from the north and came to Malayu, which he considered a separate island. This mistake (as Krom and other scholars now believe it to be) of Marco Polo's remains uncorrected in the commentaries on his book of travel. Marco Polo described Malayu as a kingdom with its own king, language, and trade.

In 1292 troops were sent from Malayu to support Java against the Chinese. The troops brought two princesses with them, and one of them was taken as a wife by the king of the newly founded kingdom of Madjapahit. This princess became the mother of the king of Malayu, Tuhan Janaka. After this Malayu commenced to assume the most important rôle in Sumatra instead of Śrívijaya. In 1299 and

1301 she sent ambassadors to China, and colonized in the Malay Peninsula where Malays who still adhered to Śrivijaya were expelled.

In 1347 king Adityawarman of Malayu extended his kingdom northwest, for stones bearing his inscription are found near Fort v. d. Capellen in the Minangkabau Highlands. It is in this same district, the center of the later Minangkabau, that all the later inscriptions of Adityawarman are to be found.

From a Chinese account of 1349 we gather that Śrivijaya was still a kingdom, but no longer a sea empire. Its ruler no longer bore the title of Maharaja. Likewise in 1370, Śrivijaya still sent mercantile ambassadors to the Ming dynasty of China. In 1377, however, Śrivijaya was definitely conquered by Java, and the old naval rivalry was at an end. The chief city had its name changed to Kieu-kiang, and the land became poorer and poorer.

As Palembang waned in importance, Minangkabau and Malacca reaped the benefit. This change of sites gave rise to the founding of a true Malay nation, and the ultimate dispersion of the Malays through the archipelago.

Malacca was established as a kingdom probably in the 14th century. Earlier migrations of natives from Minangkabau had settled on the east coast of the island. From there, in 1160, they founded the city of Singapore. This was destroyed by a general of the king of Java, and its inhabitants fled up the peninsula and founded the state of Malacca.

In the meantime Minangkabau also was becoming an independent Malay state. A stone found at Fort v. d. Capellen, and dated 1356, is inscribed in Old Malay, but with a mixture of Sanskrit and Old Javanese. The king now no longer considered himself a subject of Java, but took the name of "King of the Goldland". In 1375 this kingdom in Minangkabau was still in power and had gained much of the influence which Śrivijaya had lost.

Malacca, which in the later part of the fourteenth century began to predominate as a sea power, was converted to Islam in the beginning of the fifteenth century. Thus Islam took a foothold on the peninsula somewhat more than a century after the founding of Mohammedan kingdoms in North Sumatra. As Snouck Hurgronje has shown, Mohammedanism was conveyed to Insulinde by merchants from South India and not directly from Arabia.

The great period of Madjapahit as an empire lasted only about

orty-five years, from 1335 to 1380. The date 1478 is usually given
by historians for the conquest of Madjapahit by a Mohammedan
coalition, and this year thus supposedly marks the fall of Hindu-
Javanese power in Insulinde. Krom points out, however, that the
Portuguese in later years came into contact with a heathen king of
Madjapahit. Perhaps Madjapahit was first conquered by other Hindus,
and later by Mohammedans.

The Portuguese first came into Insulinde in 1509. Everything
in the east was still in the hands of the heathen, with the exception
of the kingdom of Malacca, a part of the sea coast of Sumatra, and
some harbors of Java and the Moluccas, which belonged to the Moors.
Sumatra's north coast had been Mohammedanized a long time before.

The Portuguese seized Malacca in 1511. Albuquerque, the leader
of the expedition, came to the north coast of Sumatra, where he
dropped anchor off Pedir and Pasè. At first he was well received,
but eventually twenty sailors were seized by the Mohammedans. In
July, 1511, Albuquerque was in front of Malacca, and in August
the city was in his hands. The fall of Malacca marks the beginning
of European rule in the Indies.

With the downfall of the independent Malay States in the
Moluccas, Malacca, and Minangkabau, the Hinduized Malays (now
converted to Mohammedanism) spread everywhere in Insulinde, pene-
trating as far as New Guinea, and converting the coastal peoples to
Islam. With Islam went the Malay dialect of the Malaysian languages.
These Mohammedan Malays are often called deutero-Malays to distinguish them from the Malaysian indigenes of the archipelago.

The European history of Sumatra consists of the struggle between
the English and the Dutch for the possession of the island, of the
victory of the Dutch, and of the long-drawn struggle which this nation
had to obtain control over the natives, especially in Atjeh.

At first it seemed that the Portuguese were to be the rulers over
Insulinde, for having conquered the important mercantile center of
Malacca, they hastened to transform this harbor into a fortress for
their fleets. Rightfully, according to the views of the day, this portion
of the world belonged to them, for it had been conceded in 1454 by the
famous bull of Pope Nicolaus Episcopaus, who had divided the globe
and all its lands, discovered and undiscovered, between the Spanish
and the Portuguese.

The Dutch fleet first arrived on the scene in 1596. They sighted

Engano on the 5th of June. The internal situation of Sumatra wa
at this moment most favourable for the foundation of a Europea
commercial establishment. The entire island was almost without govern
ment. In the north, however, the sultanate of Atjeh lived its hour
of glory, and counterbalanced the powers of Palembang and Lampong
for a long time Javanese. The central kingdom of Minangkabau wa
in full decadence. The débris of this power, which at one time rule
over a greater part of the Malay Peninsula and almost all of Sumatra
now merely included Indragiri, Kurintji, and the territories whic
at present compose the Highlands of Padang.

The Hollanders at once took Malacca from the Portuguese, an
formed the East India Company for trade and rule.

By claim of discovery, the English had rights prior to the Dutc
in the East Indies. Among the early navigators to these waters wer
Drake (1577), Cavendish (1586), and Lancaster (1591). But non
of these explorers had set foot on Sumatra. Finally (1714—1720) th
English built a trading station on the west coast, which they calle
Fort Marlborough, and which, save for brief intervals, remained i
their power until 1825.

The English chiefly extended their rule in the west of Sumatra
They established several trading posts to the north of Padang, a
Natal, and Tapanuli. This trade rivalry between the English and th
Dutch led to constant strife.

Marsden's famous book on Sumatra, the first on that subject
appeared in 1783. The author was secretary for the Britsh possess
ions on the coast of Sumatra.

Raffles was Lieutenant Governor of Java 1811—1816. He wa
Governor of Benkulen in Sumatra 1818—1823. He was instrumenta
in the founding of the city of Singapore in 1819. Since 1818 Malacc
once more belonged to the Dutch. Now the treaty of 1824 was signe
by the British and Dutch, which once and for all put an end to th
rivalry of the two nations in Insulinde. The idea, and one for whic
Raffles was responsible, was to insure the British possessions on th
mainland, the Dutch possessions on the islands. So the Dutch vacate
Malacca, the British left Nias and Sumatra.

Two further wars prolonged the difficulties which the Dutc
encountered in gaining complete possession of Sumatra. One, alread
mentioned, was the prolonged struggle with the fanatical Mohammeda
state of Atjeh. This war, or series of wars, began in 1871 and laste

for thirty years. Its successful conclusion was due mainly to the wisdom and first-hand ethnographical knowledge of Snouck Hurgronje, who acted as adviser to the Dutch.

The Padri War started while the British still occupied the west coast of Sumatra. Certain of the more orthodox people in the Padang Highlands became incensed at the laxity of their lay brethren. Certainly the prevailing matrilineal customs, betting, and the use of opium and strong drink, were not in accordance with a strict interpretation of the Koran.

The word "Padri" is Portuguese, meaning priest, and is used by Europeans and natives for the priests of both orders, Christian and Mohammedan. Persons were called Padris who either were especially zealous in Mohammedan matters, or who held some religious office.

While the English were still in Sumatra they bribed the Padris to remain clear of Padang, so the coastal regions remained quiet while the war raged inland. The Padris gave their cause the appearance of a religious war, and killed or enslaved their adversaries whom they labelled "unbelievers".

In 1820 the Padang Highlands were entirely in the hands of the Padris, and with one exception, Radja Muning Sjah, who knew enough to flee, the princely family was wiped out. While Raffles had constantly refused intervention in the strife, the Dutch were not adverse to rendering aid to the oppressed. Therefore they made terms with a party of chiefs, and in consideration of the annexion of the Minang-kabau kingdom, the Dutch stepped into the fray and defeated the Padris. As the Dutch historians record, the chiefs had no authority to hand over the territory to Holland. On the other hand, the Padris had no right to keep it. The Padris likewise had overrun the southern part of Batakland, forcibly converting the heathen to Mohammedanism. The Dutch now took possession of this territory. Thus the first Batak strip came under European rule.

A final word may be said concerning the eastern islands of Banka and Billiton. While the western islands remained for long almost untouched by civilized nations, Banka and Billiton underwent much the same fortunes as the main island.

Banka and Billiton at one time were part of the Javanese kingdom of Madjapahit, and after the fall of this kingdom they became in-dependent. By turn they belonged to the kingdom of Djohore (on the peninsula) and Minangkabau. Next they were ruled by the

Sultan of Bantam in West Java, and finally, through an alliance by marriage, they came under the Sultan of Palembang in the 18th century. The first contact with the East India Company dated in 1617, while in 1668 officials of the company resided in Banka. The island came into prominence in 1709 when tin was discovered there. In 1812 the English seized Banka while on an expedition against the Sultan of Palembang. In 1816 it was returned to the Dutch. The dominant population at present is Malay and Mohammedan, most of it derived from Palembang.

The races and peoples of Sumatra. — Three races are to be found in Southern Asia; in the order of their probable migration into the region they are: the Negrito, the Veddoid, and the Malaysian.

The most important characteristics of the Negritos are short stature (under 150 cm.), kinky hair, dark skin, black-brown eyes, and brachycephalic skulls. This race is found in the Andaman islands, in the Philippines, and in the Malay Peninsula (the Semangs). No Negritos and little trace of Negrito blood is to be found in Sumatra or the adjacent islands.

The Veddoid race (of which the Veddas of Ceylon are the purest type) is more widespread than the Negrito. The Veddoids are of small stature, 153—158 cm. for the men. They have a brown skin color, but are lighter than the pigmies. They have wavy, coarse black hair, heavy eye ridges and retreating foreheads. Their noses are flat with the roots dipping into the face, while the nostrils are elevated. Their faces are broad, but narrow towards the sharply retreating chin. The mouth-opening is large, but the lips are narrow. The Veddoids are very dolichocephalic and have very small skulls.

The Veddoids of Southern Asia are never unmixed with other blood, nor have they preserved their original language. The Senoi, or Central Sakai, is the purest remnant. Kleiweg de Zwaan believes that the Veddas of Ceylon are the remains of the ancient pre-Dravidian race which at one time was spread over the whole of India. While Sarasin thinks that the Toala of Celebes are related to the Vedda, de Zwaan believes them to be more closely connected with the Senoi. Traces of Veddoid blood are to be found, according to Heine-Geldern, in Further India from the sources of the Irrawaddy to Southwest China, especially among the Moi and the Kha. Very strong Veddoid influence (as noted by pronounced wavy hair) is to be seen among the Shom Pen in the center of Big Nicobar.

In Sumatra, Veddoid blood is most prominent among the Kubu of Palembang, of which two racial types are to be distinguished, and the Sakai of the province of Siak. The latter people bear close racial and cultural resemblances to their namesakes on the Peninsula, and probably are an offshoot of them. Wavy-haired individuals are likewise to be found in Engano and Mentawei, and even among the Bataks. It may be concluded that the more primitive Malaysians of Sumatra show the most Veddoid admixture.

Kleiweg de Zwaan has demonstrated a common Veddoid culture of which the Senoi are typical. These people are nomadic, and live on the products of hunting and fishing. They build very primitive huts and wear tapa cloth. The Senoi use blowpipes and poisoned arrows, but they also have bows and arrows. They are monogamous, and have no actual chieftaincy. They are lacking in agriculture, and have the dog as the sole domestic animal. They lack metal-work, weaving, and pottery.

The Malaysians began migrating into Insulinde from Asia at an early period. Heine-Geldern in his research concerning the origin and early wanderings of the Malaysian (Austronesian), believes that they came from South China somewhat later than 2,000 B. C. In Indonesia the early straight-haired yellow race mixed with or displaced the kinky and wavy-haired races.

Kroeber, following Sullivan, has divided the Malaysians into two types. The first, and earlier type, he calls Indonesian and is dolichocephalic. The second he calls Malayan, and is brachycephalic. The Indonesians are supposed to be the inland mountain dwellers of the Philippines and elsewhere in Indonesia, while the Malayans are the coast dwellers. The Indonesians likewise are supposed to have smaller bodies and broader noses. This distinction has not been followed by later anthropologists. As Heine-Geldern points out, the Malaysians cannot be subdivided according to head form, since some of the oldest Malaysians in the archipelago, as the Punan of Central Borneo, are brachycephalic. As a rule, however, we find dolichocephalic Malaysians in Eastern Indonesia, where there is Papuan influence, in the interior of Borneo, and among some mountain peoples of the Philippines.

The customary distinction now made is between Malaysians and Malays, or Proto-Malaysians and Deutero-Malaysians. Proto-Malaysians are merely those Malaysians who are relatively free from other racial mixtures (Hindu, Chinese, Arabic), and dwell in the interior of the islands. Good examples of the Proto-Malaysians are the Bataks, Dayaks, Toradja of Celebes and the Igorot (mountain dwellers) of the Philippines. The Javanese present a good type of the Deutero-Malaysians. Anthropologically, the Proto-Malaysians are distinguished from the coast Malays by a shorter body, longer head, darker skin, broader and more concave nose, and a broader mouth.

Thus it has been shown that the Indonesians (Austronesians) came to Sumatra probably some time after 2,000 A. D. and certainly long before the Christian Era and the days of Hindu influence. When they arrived they found an aboriginal population composed partly or entirely of Veddoid and Negrito races. The question has often been discussed as to the cultural elements which they brought with them. This has been done by showing that certain fundamental words are found in all Indonesian languages, and that the objects corresponding to these words were therefore brought from the continent.

First come the tropical plants, sugar cane, bananas, bamboo and rotan; the most important in the category is the word for rice, "běras". Běras really means fruit, and elsewhere the word for rice is found signifying food. This cereal, however, at least of the dry variety, actually seems to have been in use in the western part of Indonesia before the days of Hindu influence. It was grown everywhere in Sumatra, but not on the western islands of Mentawei and Engano.

Heine-Geldern believes that the primitive Indonesians had some form of out-rigger canoe, while Krom states that the Indonesian language contains both the words for boat and sail. This would show that the Indonesians came from river country, if not actually from the sea. Even the primitive Mentawei Islanders had large war boats with sails.

Among the primitive Indonesian animals the dog, pig, and chicken may safely be assumed. The karabau, perhaps even the tamed variety, is usually thought to be Indonesian. Cattle again are entirely lacking to Mentawei and Engano.

Iron working was known on the mainland, and was assimilated by the islanders. In most of the languages "pandai", workman, is used especially for a smith. Iron working, however, is unknown in Mentawei and Engano, and the word "pandai" is of recent introduction in Mentawei.

Heine-Geldern adds, on archaeological and ethnographic grounds, he following traits as being probably of primitive Indonesian origin: ion-coiled pottery, mats, bone lance points, bone tools and arrow points, stone and mussel rings as decorations and perhaps as money, stone bead ornamentation, pile dwellings, the cultivation of millet and rice, megalithic monuments, head-hunting, possibly tapa preparation.

I myself have tried to demonstrate that the primitive Indonesian was lacking in all sib forms of family, that is, in unilateral descent and the accompanying exogamy. In other words, the Indonesian social organization was similar in form to that of the Negrito and Veddoid. The sib organization was brought from South India along with other traits of higher culture, but remained foreign to Mentawei, Engano, and the primitive Malaysians of Sumatra. On linguistic grounds this is shown by the lack of a native term for mother's brother in Indonesian.

It seems probable that the earliest waves of Indonesians, as still found isolated in Mentawei, lacked certain cultural traits brought by succeeding waves. Among these traits lacking to the earlier arrivals were: rice, cattle, iron working, and megalithic monuments.

Absence of autocratic monarchs may be postulated for the primitive Indonesians, as well as for all other very primitive peoples, and the Hindus did little to better this condition. The great power enjoyed by the chiefs of Nias may be ascribed to Polynesian concept of divine descent of chiefs.

Political and linguistic divisions. — There are fourteen main dialects of the Malaysian language spoken on Sumatra, together with many sub-dialects. These divisions are shown on the accompanying linguistic map. As is usual among primitive peoples, it is difficult to obtain agreement among authors regarding the sub-dialects. In my map, which I have taken from Collet, the Bataks are arranged according to six sub-dialects. Yet the Batak villages, if they are far apart, each speak a little differently from one another, even though they are placed in the same linguistic group.

Minangkabau is, as we have shown, the mother of the Malay language, since the original Malays migrated from here. The Minangkabau language of to-day varies a bit, in dropping and changing of consonants, from the ordinary spoken Malay. The customary Malay is understood everywhere on Sumatra, regardless of the local dialect spoken, since it is the common language of the schools.

Through Islam the Malays lost their ancient Sanskrit alphabet and took to the Arabic. The Dutch in turn have taught the natives the use of Roman letters in the schools, so that Arabic is becoming less and less used for ordinary purposes. The Latin script is well adapted for all Malayo-Polynesian languages.

Old alphabets, adapted from the Sanskrit, are still to be found among the natives of Lampong, Redjang, and the Bataks. The first two forms are closely related to one another. The written characters are scratched on bamboo, tree bark, or certain forms of leaves.

North Sumatra is the home of the Achehnese, the Gajo and the Alas. The topography of this part of Sumatra is different from that of the remainder of the island. Instead of mountainous regions and long plains, there are here high plateaus with bordering mountains. The chief water sheds lie in the center of the island, and no longer in the west. Hence the races of the northern part of Sumatra are not divided by east and west divisions, mountains and plains, but extend across the island. The lowland and civilized Achehnese occupy the coastal strip, the mountaineer Gajo and Alas are in the center. A later chapter will describe the Achehnese and Gajo, but little at present is known about the Alas.

The north central part of western Sumatra is occupied by the important districts of Tapanuli and Padang Lawas. These districts are inhabited by Bataks. Padang Lawas was acquired by the Dutch in 1838, after the Padri War.

Further south the division of Kurintji is best known and is the most thickly populated of the highland divisions of the districts of Djambi. Most of the people here are Minangkabau in language and custom.

The center of Minangkabau is situated in the Padang Highlands, a short distance by rail from the chief seaport of the west coast, Padang. The Padang Highlands are subdivided into three parts. 1. Padang Pandjang (long plains). 2. The deep-lying, long and narrow valley of the Meer van Singkarak. 3. Tanah Datar (flat lands), which spreads southeast and south from Merapi and Sago.

The province and people of Redjang have received the special attention of Marsden in his book on Sumatra. Redjang came under the Dutch rule in 1860 as a result of a small expedition.

The natives of Lampong, the most southern part of Sumatra, live mostly along the river banks of the Sekampung. But even this region is but scantily inhabited. Lekkerkerker believes that the population was formerly of the same ancient strata as the Bataks, but it is well-known that later the people became much mixed with the Sundanese. From ancient times there has been much trade across the strait of Sunda, and many place names in Lampong are Sundanese or Javanese. The mountaineers of Lampong have a slightly variant dialect and call themselves Orang Abung. The plains-people are called Orang Pablan.

The location and customs of Kubu and other primitive peoples of Sumatra with Veddoid admixture will be treated in a later chapter.

Population. — According to the 14th edition of the Encyclopaedia Britannica, the total population of Sumatra numbers 6,219,000 people, of which 19,259 are Europeans and Eurasians, and 229,775 are Asiatics, including Chinese. One third of the Europeans, and four-fifths of the Chinese live on the east coast. This population could be many times increased, for Java has roundly forty million native inhabitants, in spite of its being one quarter the size. Sumatra has 13.2 people per sq. km., Java has 266.

The main native elements of the population are 1,500,000 Minangkabau; 1,000,000 Bataks; and 650,000 Achehnese.

The religion of Sumatra is predominantly Mohammedan, for of the total population only 170,000 are Christian and 300,000 heathen. Protestant missionary stations are established among the Bataks, in Nias, and in Mentawei. Naturally only the heathen, and not the Mohammedans, can be converted.

_____

CHAPTER I

THE BATAKS.

The People.

Herodotus, perhaps, made first mention of the Bataks, calling them Padaioi, or cannibals. Our first somewhat exact account of Batak custom, however, was made in 1783 by Marsden, who astonished the civilized world by the paradox of a cannibalistic people, who nevertheless possessed a real culture and system of writing. The actual exploration of Batakland started in 1823 when Anderson visited the east coast of Sumatra. In 1853 Van der Tuurk discovered Lake Toba. To-day there are about 1,000,000 Bataks, all of whom are under Dutch rule. During the Padri rebellion of 1815 and subsequently, the southernmost third of these were converted to Mohammedanism, and 80,000 have been converted to Christianity by German missionaries working from 1860 on to the present day. The remainder are still pagan.

The Bataks are divided into a number of linguistic groups, among them the Singkel, Pak-Pak, Dairi, Toba, and Mandheling. The Toba Bataks who live east of Toba Lake are called Timur (east). Actually there are only two main linguistic, as there are only two main ethnographic, divisions: 1. the Dairi, including the Dairi proper, the Pak-Pak, and the Karo; and 2. the Toba, who speak the other dialects. Toba is considered by Ypes to be the mother dialect of all Batak languages.

The origin of the name Batak is not certain, but it was already in use in the seventeenth century. It was probably an abusive nickname given by the Mohammedans and signifying pig-eater. The Bataks have taken up this nickname as an honorary title, thus distinguishing themselves from the Djawi, the Mohammedans, and Malays.

The Bataks were influenced to a considerable extent by Hindu civilization. Direct Hindu influence is said by the natives themselves to have come from the east (Timur). They state that this country was the starting point of indigenous "science" (divination books, magic staves, and magic preparations). The more important Hindu traits

mported into the Batak country were wet rice culture, the horse, the
plow, the peculiar style of dwelling, chess, cotton and the spinning
wheel, Hindu vocabulary, system of writing and religious ideas. Some
of the colonies from India were Dravidian, as has been shown by the
presence of Dravidian sib names among the Pak-Pak, Karo, and even
the Gajo and Alas. Even the Batak term for sib (Toba, marga; Karo,
merga) is Sanskrit in origin. Mohammedan influence came to Sumatra
earlier than to Java and had the effect of stopping Hindu influence
on the Bataks, thus isolating them from contact with higher civilizations.

Economic Life.

Villages and houses. — The Bataks live everywhere in large villages (Toba, huta, Karo, kuta). The villages, especially in Toba, formerly were fortified with earthen and bamboo walls. Entrance to a
village was effected through a narrow doorway in one of the walls.
In Toba the village consists, as a rule, of six or seven houses and
some sopo's, council houses. The houses and the sopo's are placed
in two rows opposite one another, and in the center is a rectangular
enclosed space (alaman). Among the Karo the village is built up
slightly more irregularly, and among the types of houses listed are
dwelling houses (rumah); the young men's houses (djambur); different forms of buildings for the keeping of rice and structures where
women grind the rice. Sometimes there is a smith (perpanden) as well
as a skull house (geriten). Normally there are eight families (djabu)
in a house.

In the northern parts of the country, due to the rigor with which
sexual avoidance customs are maintained, boys above the age of ten
and widowers are forced to spend their nights in the sopo's. In the
south unmarried girls also are either guarded by the radja or sleep
in a separate house (bagas podoman) where they are guarded by a
widow, but are allowed male visitors.

The dwelling houses vary considerably. Like all Batak houses
they are built on piles three to six feet above the ground. Those of
chiefs and wealthy people are usually of wood and are roofed with
sugar palm fibre (idjuk) or with wooden planks. The construction
of the roof is especially involved, and slopes inward towards the center
with a saddle-back bend, the points often being decorated with buffalo

horns. The roomy interior of such a house is not separated into com
partments by walls although it is commonly inhabited by severa'
families. Mats, which are let down at night, form a partial separation
There are from four to six open fireplaces in the larger houses. The
smoke from these is permitted to find its way out through the roof
Since there are no windows or doors to the houses they are very dark
inside and covered with soot. In Karo, however, there is a door at
the front and one at the back. The dwellings of radjas are constructed
from elaborately carved planks which are painted with figures.

In Toba besides the dwelling houses there are rice granaries and
communal or young mens' houses (sopo's). The appearance of the
granaries does not differ from the houses of the common people. Every
village has at least one sopo in its center, and sometimes a second
sopo if the village houses an important radja. These sopo's surpass
the dwellings of the chiefs in size and splendor, especially in the rich
leaf and floral designs carved on their roofs. They differ from the
houses of chiefs in so far as all four walls are open, the house having
side walls from three to three and a half feet high. On both sides of
the entrance of a sopo are raised benches which serve as sleeping
places for the village men and their visitors. All sopo's have an upper
room (söller) which is used as storeroom for harvesting utensils and
as an extra dormitory. Every village which has two sopo's has one
of them dedicated as a religious warehouse, elsewhere the single sopo
serves this additional purpose. In the söller are kept both the village
jewelry and the religious paraphernalia: the skull of a slain enemy,
the jaw bones of a karabau, the ashes of a burnt child preserved in
bamboo cookers, the sacred writings inscribed on bark or bamboo,
and the war standards. The entire safety of the village depends on
the proper safeguarding of these objects. In the lower room of every
sopo is kept the kettle drum, "panken", wich serves to summon the
inmates of the village to feast or council.

The houses of a village are quite barren of furniture. Above each
fireplace there is a scaffolding (para). There are three levels to a
para, one for ground rice, another higher up for cooking pots and
utensils, and on top the firewood is kept. The utensils kept within
the house consist in part of: 1. Earthen pots, of which every family
owns from three to six. 2. Bamboo water reeds, from three to four
feet long, in which the drinking water is kept, and which serve at the
same time as drinking cups. 3. Small knives with wooden hand grips,

whose blades are inserted between two wooden fangs and fastened with string. 4. Small conical baskets woven from fine split bamboo rods serving as containers for cooked rice. 5. Rice pounders made from tree trunks. The trunks have one or two holes in which rice is pounded with wooden rods and thus freed from the husk. 6. Formerly bamboo cookers were kept in the house for cooking rice, and leaves and coconut shells were used instead of dishes. 7. The entire floor of the house usually is covered with mats with the exception of the cooking place. Mats also are hung along the walls and smaller mats are used as chairs. Only the wealthy have chests or trunks, others roll up their possessions in mats. Mats are woven from pandanus leaves, tapa or rotan. 8. Banana wood torches are used for lighting the house.

Prior to Dutch sanitary measures the Batak villages and houses, similar to Indonesian conditions elsewhere, were hardly appetizing places of abode-from the viewpoint of the white man. Chickens lived, or at least brooded, in the house itself in little conical baskets. Pigs roamed freely through the village and served as scavengers. Thus Neumann describes early living conditions among the Bataks:

"No matter what Batak building one sees one obtains a feeling of repugnance. The houses are all equally unclean. Soot covers the walls and ceiling, the corners are full of cobwebs, the walls are smeared with chalk, and the floor is covered with sirih chews and chicken excrement. The houses are like caves into which the openings in the walls scarcely admit a ray of light. When the houses are filled with smoke one asks oneself how human beings can live in them. It is almost impossible for a human being to spend a night in one of them, for centipedes and scorpions wander about freely, ants build their runways and make their way across the natives, cockroaches fly around unmolested, and lice lurk over all. One really cannot sleep in such a house. The Bataks themselves are accustomed to their environment."

Food. — The economic pursuits of the Bataks are more numerous than one would expect among such a primitive people. Agriculture is by far the most important. With few exceptions every Batak is an agriculturist, even though he has other occupations as well, such as smith or lumberman. Rice is the most important crop raised, being cultivated both in flooded and in dry fields. Maize is the second cereal of importance cultivated by the Bataks. This grain plays a prom-

inent part in the agriculture of Padang Lawas. Other cultivate
plants are potatoes, taro, yams, leguminous plants and various othe
vegetables. Coffee, tobacco, coconut, cinamon, sugar cane and indig
also are raised. The Bataks raise crops only for their own needs, an
there is little or no export.

The chief instruments of agriculture are: the plow (tinggala), th
long pointed stick with which one works the ground (engkal), an
the harrow (roka, sabi, sekel). The digging stick (perlebeng), als
is used in the highlands.

A second important means of subsistence is cattle raising. Th
Batak horses are famous, especially those of the Karo highlands. Th
horses are raised for sale, but are not ridden by the Bataks themselves
Buffalo and other cattle are very numerous on the plateaus, bu
Padang Lawas raises the most cattle. Milk is partaken of in Toba
contrary to usual oriental habits, but neither butter nor cheese is pre
pared. Pig breeding by Christian and pagan tribes furnished a shor
while ago a very common source of income.

Hunting and fishing are of lesser importance. The gathering o
brush products, and during modern times, the planting of rubber an
benzoin trees, in some districts is quite prevalent.

The Batak eats twice a day, in the morning and in the evening
Formerly all food was cooked without salt, which was both rare an
dear, and was to be found only in the houses of the richest peopl
carefully wrapped up in leaves. In Toba Spanish pepper (lasiak
almost entirely took the place of salt. The chief food is rice, and unde
normal circumstances this is to be had in abundance. The chief food
of the Bataks are, in order, rice, yams and taro. Taro is as a rul
only eaten by the poor. At times of scarcity the rice is mixed witl
maize and thus eaten. In the complete absence of rice the people hel
themselves to all kinds of root foods, eatable leaves and fruits from
the brush; they especially fall back upon sago.

A regular meat or fish diet is unknown to the Batak. When lucky
they may kill a deer or boar in the hunt, or catch a small fresh wate
fish, a rat, a bat, or perhaps a leguan. Eggs are almost never eate
and chickens are consumed chiefly after a chicken fight. The poore
Batak is then glad to obtain a wing or leg.

Upon special occasions chickens, dogs, pigs, cattle or karaba
are killed and eaten. These festivities include: the leading of the brid
into the home of her future husband, the changing of dwelling plac

the finishing of a new house, the visit of strangers (especially when these include important chiefs), great gatherings, and consultations in the sopo's (in order to start war or conclude peace), and the burial of chiefs. On minor celebrations chickens and dogs are killed, pigs and cattle being reserved for the more important feasts. The meat from the animals slaughtered is never sold or preserved, but is divided among the guests. Everyone receives his or her appropriate share; the poor perhaps only an ear, a tail or a snout. Human flesh has never been consumed at festive occasions nor treated as a regular article of diet.

The Bataks eat frogs, field mice, insect larvae and flying white ants. They are not averse to eating elephants, bears, tigers, apes and even snakes. Junghuhn states that there is no form of animal, as long as it carries meat on its bones, which is not eaten by the Bataks. They even have no horror of putrid meat, and dogs which suffer from skin disease and no longer can walk are killed and eaten.

The customary drink of the Bataks is water. In former times the water source had to lie within the village fortifications and hence usually was poluted by the live stock. Palm wine is also consumed, either sweet or fermented, but not to the point of intoxication. Sirih chewing is universal both for men and women. Tobacco is smoked in considerable quantities, even by children, but the women do not smoke. Among the Karo tobacco is smoked rolled up in leaves; the Toba use copper pipes.

Clothing and decorations. — The clothing of the Bataks has been considerably influenced by the Malays. Formerly the nationality and rank of a Batak could be determined from the color and adornment of his attire, which was made from native cotton, spun, woven and dyed in the homes. The colors used were blue, black and red. Yellow dye was employed only on the coast. Tapa clothing was worn only by the poorest people, and consisted of a girdle around the limbs and a jacket covering the breast. In most places in Batakland the old style of clothing is worn only on festive and official occasions and otherwise handed down as heirlooms.

The chief piece of Batak clothing is a cloth drawn around the limbs and hanging to the feet. Both the men and women among the Karo wear a head covering, but the Toba women go with their heads uncovered. Cloth wrappers were used in former days to protect the upper portion of the body, but now various kinds of jackets are coming more and more into use. Besides these articles of clothing which every one wears irrespective of rank, the Radjas adorn themselves with specially worked tunics decorated with glass beads.

The distinction between Karo and Toba Bataks may be seen at a glance. The national color of the Karo is blue (dark red in war time), while the Toba dye their clothing brown. The women still keep to these colors. The Karo women part their hair and bind it in a knot at the back of their heads, in Toba the knot of hair is allowed to droop down in a loop above one ear. The most distinguishing feature, however, of both Karo girls and married women are the heavy lyre-formed silver ear-rings (padung). While a Karo woman puts aside other jewelry after marriage, she continues wearing these. The weight of these heavy adornments is born chiefly by the head covering.

The Toba radja wears as a mark of rank the elaborate tunic and arm rings made from the giant mussel (Tridaena gigas) or of ivory. Since rank is handed down from father to son many a poor man who no longer owns a square foot of ground nor the allegiance of a single subject still continues wearing these insignia of office. The arm rings are also worn by the radjas of Nias and the Batu islands.

The Toba virgins wore in former days copper wire rings around the neck, the forearm and the ankles. Elderly women, in the rare case that they still were virgins, were not allowed these ornaments. The richer the parents the more numerous were the neck decorations of the daughter, and the higher the bride-price demanded. Male children also were allowed this decoration.

Artifacts. — As among many African peoples, the smith has a peculiar position among the Karo. One cannot say that he belongs to a special rank, but yet he is always diligent and a man of importance. There are gold, silver, and iron smiths.

While anyone may learn the profession it is customary for a son to follow in the footsteps of his father. The instruments only may be inherited and not sold, it is said that they demand the ownership of the son. To deny this claim of the soul (tondi) of the instruments would bring misfortune to the family.

There is a special village smithy (perpanden) for the iron smith (pande), but the silver smith works in an outhouse of his own home. The entire workshop of the iron smith and the implements are objects of religious veneration. There are secret names for the implements which are known only to the smith, and sacrifices are given at times

f sickness by those people who come much into contact with iron. A
ed and a black chicken is the usual sacrifice.

War weapons are very much the same throughout Batakland. In
he wars observed by the whites, the Bataks made use of old model
irearms. Thrusting and striking weapons consisted of lance, spear,
sword and chopping knife (klewang). A wide variety of knives were
used in war, as decorations, and as tools. These weapons, however,
were not very deadly in the hands of the Bataks as hand to hand con-
lict was rare.

In former days the bow (panah) and arrow (sore), the sling
kalim bawang), and the shield (ampang-ampang) were used in
var. These weapons now are either playthings or inherited curiosities.
The blow-pipe (eltep) is used often in hunting small animals, especially
oirds. It was never used by the Bataks in war. The arrows of the
olow-pipe (nangkat) are sometimes poisoned.

The weapons of defense consisted of the usual Indonesian foot
angles (batjur, randjo) of pointed bamboo, and the more or less permanent fortifications (kuban) of embankments and ditches.

While the musical instruments of the Bataks are similar to those
of the Javanese, they are employed mainly for religious purposes and
not for enjoyment as in Java. The Toba instruments are: 1. The drum
(gontang). This consists of skin stretched over wood, and is the most
widely used of all the instruments. It is kept in the sopo. 2. The
copper gongs. These are similar to the Javanese. They are struck
with a wooden hammer. They are used in the orchestra, and also
singly for exorcising evil spirits or to drive off wild animals from
ields. Every chief possesses at least one. 3. A variety of clarinet
(sordam, Malay serdum). 4. A small violin with two strings, which
gives a pure but very harsh sound (harwab, Malay rabab). These last
wo instruments are seen only in Toba. They give musical notes somewhat similar to the Chinese orchestra.

The Karo orchestra, which is not as complete as the Toba
orchestra, consists of three drums (gendang), a large and a small
gong, and a clarinet. The Karo also use a metal mouth harp, a mouth
harp made from the center of the palm leaf, flutes, and string instruments, one being a variety of violin and another of mandolin. In
entral Batakland a wooden xylophone (garantung) is employed.

Music and dancing always go together. The dance as practiced
n Indonesia is chiefly a moving up and down of the body accompanied

by waving and turning of limbs. In Timur masked dances are held at the time of funerals.

The Toba copper pipes are a peculiar Batak artifact. These pipes and the practice of smoking them the entire day, are as characteristic of the natives of the highlands of Toba and as inseparable from their persons, as the kris from the Javanese or the horse from the Mongol. The poorer natives are content with bamboo stemmed wooden pipes, but all other men have copper pipes at least a half foot in length. Radjas own several copper pipes apiece, and one pipe three to four feet long and weighing over a pound. These giant pipes are constructed from several pieces of copper, and are too heavy to hold, being smoked with the bowl setting on the ground. Phallic human figures are carved on the pipes similar in form to the idols of Nias. The copper for the pipe industry is obtained by trade, and the pipes themselves are manufactured in a district of Toba.

In former times money was unknown to the Bataks, the use of money being a non-Indonesian trait, and trade was conducted entirely by barter. As an aid in exchange, use was made of pieces of iron and tin. Scales and weights were not employed by the Bataks or other Indonesians, nor were instruments of measure. Resource was made to the parts of the body. The Bataks were lacking in sundials or other simple devices for determining the equinoxes. The people could tell the time to the half hour by measuring with an arm the angle between the sun and the horizon.

Religious artifacts are everywhere similar both in form and use in Batakland. They owe their origin, at least, to Hindu influence. 1. Pustaka (divination books) are usually written in Timur or Toba dialect. The books are made from the bark of the alim tree, and also of silk. The pages are treated and made smooth with rice water and then glued or sewn together. The writing is done with brush and ink. The books contain various kinds of divination formulae and cabbalistic designs. 2. Tungkat, the so-called "magical staves". These are of two varieties. a) the tungkat malekat, or smooth staff, with only an image on the upper end. b) tungkat panaluan, these are entirely covered with human and animal figures except at the lower end. 3. Perminaken, little pots, some of wood, others of clay, containing a brew, preferably made of parts of the human body, called pupuk. 4. Various divination objects, tablets and figures for the determination of ominous times.

and calendars (perkatan) for the determination of days. 5. Pengulu-balang or stone idols located in the brush near villages.

Games. — Although the Bataks are a merry and joyous people and given to frequent feasting they appear to lack indigenous games. This lack of games apparently is an Indonesian trait, and one which I observed likewise in the Mentawei islanders. The exchange of riddles and puzzles is a favorite form of amusement, and one used also in court-ing. The games played by children are usually those of skill, including sham battles with lances. Fencing, dancing, music and song are the few amusements possessed by the people. Chess, dice games with corn dice, and chicken and bird fights are of foreign origin.

Daily life. — A good description of Toba daily life in the first part of the nineteenth century is furnished by Junghuhn.

"The Batak women rise early before sunrise. They first go to the watering place to fill the empty bamboo reeds with fresh drinking water and also to wash and bathe. On returning with the filled bamboo reeds, which they carry in a bundle under their arms, the business of rice pounding commences. In regions which are poor in rice one half maize is mixed with the rice. The rice pounding is performed by the women at daybreak. It is also at this time that the remainder of the village bestirs itself to life. The men now arise from their mats and go to the bathing place. Soon after sunrise the shelling of the rice is finished and the pots filled with the cereal and water are placed over the fires to cook. The fires are lit with flint and stone and then the men have nothing more to do but light their pipes and go to walk and talk before the house of the radjà. Then they have a bit to eat, or (this only in Toba) a bamboo full of milk. Tobacco smoking in Toba takes the place of sirih chewing, which is only done on the coast where the sirih and betel grow in abundance, and gambir is easily bought. Now at about half past seven the daily work really begins, which, in all regions except Toba, is almost equally divided between the two sexes, for more field work falls to the men while the women are kept busy inside of the village.

"In Toba, however, the women do almost all the work, in the house as well as in the fields. They really are the drudges of the house. The men smoke tobacco out of their big copper pipes, watch the children (really play with them), hold councils in the sopo, and — conduct war. The building of houses and the cutting down of trees for the houses are about the only varieties of work which the men perform in times of peace.

"Among the other divisions of the Bataks the men go at this time out into their fields (ladang) in order to perform the necessary work, especially the heavy work of laying out the plantation, cutting down the trees, charring off the debris left by the fallen timber, digging up the ground, burning off the weeds, building the huts, and planting.

"While the men are occupied in the field, the women (in Toba only those women who are left in the house) occupy themselves with household work of various kinds, with the weaving of fabrics, the plaiting of baskets (karong) or mats (tika) out of banana leaves, or the preparation of dyes. The women also see to the cooking. At seven o'clock the animals, that is, the chickens and pigs, are fed by the women with maize.

"The first real meal is eaten at twelve o'clock. In the morning the Bataks eat only a handful of rice. All the people who do not own houses in the fields come back to the village for this meal. Then the people rest for an hour lying down on mats. At half past four or five the work stops for the day. Rice is put to cook over the fire and a second meal prepared. The people tell stories until seven, when they spend an hour eating.

"Radjas and their wives do no field work, but have their slaves perform all manual labor. Although the rough outdoor work is always done by the men, the women too in most regions do some of the work in the open, such as keeping the fields clean, pulling up weeds, gathering fire wood, and picking ripe fruit. The fruit trees are always planted outside the villages."

War. — The Bataks and the natives of Nias were by far the most warlike of the peoples of Sumatra. To the Batak, as to all very primitive people, strangers and enemies were synonymous, and hence direct contact with the outside world was avoided. So great was the desire to keep away strangers, and so distrustful were the Bataks of one another, that paths were not maintained between villages nor were bridges constructed. Due to this absence of intervillage means of communication the Bataks of the interior lacked many of the necessities of life, especially salt. The natives used even their reputation of cannibalism as a means of defense, for the eating of strangers tended to keep aliens away. So this custom was not without its purpose.

It appears to be the rule among all peoples of the earth that frequency of warfare bears an inverse proportion to the severity of its consequences. Were it not for this wise regulation of providence, or perhaps of human caution, the Bataks long ago would have become extinct, and this present chapter would never have been written. Fortunately, however, these people had very strict rules (adat) governing the conduct of wars; most of the combats had the nature of ordeals in which the first death or serious injury indicated the will of the gods and the rights and wrongs of the parties concerned.

The main restrictions governing war were as follows. Chiefs were not to be killed, and under all circumstances the lives of women and children were to be spared. A declaration of war had to be made before the opening of hostilities. Cultivated fields were considered sacred and were not molested, and among the Karo a captured town was neither sacked nor destroyed. Territory could never be taken away from its rightful owners, even when these had emigrated in order to avoid the yoke of the conquerors.

It was not until the Padri wars, when the fanatical Mohammedanized Minangkabau came up into Batak territory to convert or destroy, that the Bataks learned the real meaning of war. Then for the first time defenseless women and children were killed or sold into slavery, the torch was applied to towns and granaries, and fields, hitherto sacred, were ruthlessly destroyed.

Nevertheless war as practiced by the Bataks themselves was far from being a native form of sport. While war prisoners legally were supposed to be held until ransomed; when bad feeling ran high they were eaten, scalped or beheaded. The skulls and bundles of hair were then kept; the first in the sopo's, and the latter were sold back to the family of the beheaded. This happened when the people became angry at insults offered to their chiefs.

The usual cause which led to war among the Bataks was the contraction of debts, mostly gambling debts. When the debt was not paid within a specified time the creditor had the right to seize the debtor. If the latter belonged to a different town, and his radja refused to surrender him, war followed. The injured Radja formed a federation with his neighboring chiefs, attacked the town of this opponent, and when successful, took their cattle and made slaves of the survivors.

Other causes of war were personal insults to the radjas, village boundary disputes, and especially theft, when the thief belonged to an alien village, and the radja of this village refused to surrender him or make good the damage. The ambition of the various radjas and the jealousy which existed between them, creating envy and hatred, often was the real motivating cause of the incessant warfare which racked Batakland for centuries and kept the population far below the number which could have obtained support on the fertile lands.

War was always declared in a routine manner. After a casus belli had occurred, the aggrieved radja invited the friendly chiefs of the district to a conference in the sopo. A cow or buffalo was slaughtered and all the radjas partook. Every chief who was present at the feast had to break off friendly intercourse with the hostile village under penalty of being treated as a traitor, even though his own subjects took no part in the war. In Toba this conference of chiefs was called pege-pege (pege, ginger), because the meat eaten was seasoned heavily with ginger.

On the day in which the buffalo was slaughtered, and the decision to wage war entered upon, all communication with the hostile village was ended. All the towns concerned in the dispute put themselves in a state of defence, palisades were renewed or bettered, bamboo lances were pointed and distributed among the people, and powder was manufactured. Lookouts were posted and armed guards held themselves in readiness.

War had to be declared in a formal manner. A village was not attacked without warning, this would have been robbery and not war and would have been punished as such. Enough discussion took place beforehand between the opposing and the neutral radjas, so that the oncoming war surprised no one.

The declaration of war took place in one of two ways. The usual way was to hang up the so-called "pulas" in the neighborhood of the hostile village. This pulas consisted of a piece of bamboo on which a letter in Batak characters was written. On the same piece of rope on which the first piece of bamboo was hung, another piece of bamboo cut in the form of a knife, was attached, and also a piece of "keteela" fruit in the form of a human head, and finally a piece of half charred wood, as a symbol of murder and arson. The contents of the letter (the ultimatum) gave the debtor three or four days in which to pay his debt, after that the consequences would be "on his head".

The second way in which war was declared was the so-called

sampahaek. The person entrusted with the declaration cried out the true or pretended grievances in the open, amid the firing of about ten shots. There were no other formalities, and the parties of the opposing side were presumed either to have heard the shots or to have been informed about the matter through a third party. But, as we have said, an oncoming war took no one by surprise.

In consequence of the declared state of war the natives of the hostile villages did not dare venture beyond their fortifications unless armed and in sufficient numbers either to work their fields or visit other villages. Both sides now attempted to cut off stragglers. When these were not killed on the spot they were brought home and put in the block in the sopo. They were kept there as hostages in order to force the opposing side to surrender. Since these unfortunates sometimes were kept in the blocks for years, being neither able to stand up, to sit, or to lie down, their feet wasted away from non-use. Also if the hostile side committed any "atrocity", such as cow stealing or murder, one of the captives was killed and eaten in revenge. As the war progressed through a number of years the number of atrocities increased, as did the retaliations, and affairs became more and more embittered. Finally no one dared any longer work in the fields, large tracts of land became wasted, and the necessities of life were at low ebb. Then, and not until then, was the overthrow of the hostile village decided upon, and all who could bear arms were summoned for the assault.

Attacks on villages took place usually between ten and twelve o'clock at night. The entire adult male population took part in such an assault, leaving only the women and children behind to guard the home town with their bamboo spears. The chiefs carried the war banners which had been preserved for hundreds of years in the sopo. If the village was captured all the inhabitants were killed or taken prisoner and the town itself (in Toba) was burned. Some of the prisoners were killed later and eaten.

Among the Karo, wars seemed seldom, if ever, to have arrived at the point where villages were captured and destroyed. Here the war was more of an ordeal, with both sides being supported by champions who were hired from afar. In a battle first the champions and the especially courageous people fought, and the remainder, armed with sharpened bamboos, joined in only if their side seemed certain of success. Otherwise they fled. The champions seemed to have been more governed by religious emotions than by training as marksmen. A man would first pray and dance. Then a shot was fired at random, and if the cause were just, it was believed that the bullet would attain its mark. As soon as anyone was hit, by chance or otherwise, the conflict was at an end for the time being and the defeated party withdrew. Then the priest who had read the omens for the battle was put on trial for incompetency.

When both parties were tired of war they entrusted arbitration to a pair of neutral chiefs. Whichever party was declared guilty payed a fine, and karabou were killed for a feast of conciliation. An oath of conciliation was sworn on the heart of a karabau.

Cannibalism. — One of the most striking customs of the Bataks, and the one for which they have acquired the most notoriety, is their cannibalistic propensity. The cause of their cannibalism is unknown and its occurrence isolated. No other Asiatic or Indonesian peoples are cannibalistic and it is not until we arrive at New Guinea that we find a recurrence of the custom. It is an ancient custom here, first having been mentioned by Herodotus, later by the Arabs, and Marco Polo relates that the natives of "Little Java" ate their elders when these were too old to enjoy life. Some doubt has been cast upon this statement of the Venetian traveller, yet accounts illustrated with drawings of Pak-Pak shields and coming from the first thousand years of our era show a cannibalistic rejoicing dance. Cannibalism may have persisted as a very old survival from the time in which the dark skinned peoples passed through Indonesia, or it may have developed from the custom of head-hunting. In Nias and elsewhere the attainer of a head frequently takes a bite from the relic of his victim, and in New Guinea the two customs are not entirely disassociated.

Cannibalism persisted into the twentieth century among the Toba, Pak-Pak, and Timor Bataks, but the Karo deny that they ever had the custom. While the Bataks enjoyed human flesh, preferring it to pork, the habit was practiced merely as a severe form of capital punishment, and was not of frequent occurrence. Thus during the one and a half years which Junghuhn spent among the Bataks there were only three cases of public cannibalism.

Cannibalism was practiced for the following causes: 1. When a commoner committed adultery with the wife of a radja. A commoner in this case could not buy his freedom. 2. Traitors, spies, and deserters to the enemy were eaten. These criminals, however, could buy their freedom for 180 guldens. In cases 1 and 2 the adat prescribed that the guilty party be killed by a lance thrust before being eaten. But since the offended party was accuser, judge, and executioner, it often happened that some of the flesh was eaten and some of the blood drunk of before the mortal thrust was given. 3. Enemies were eaten alive when they were caught armed outside the village, and if their weapons had been used against the people of the village. If they were caught in the fields in peaceful occupation they were held for ransom, enslaved, or killed. Women and children were as a ruled spared, and never officially eaten.

Junghuhn witnessed the official practice of cannibalism during his stay in Toba.

"When an enemy is captured the day is set upon which he should be eaten. Then messengers are sent to all allied chiefs and their subjects inviting them to be present at the feast. Hundreds of people stream to the village. The victim usually is taken out of the village, but the feast itself is held in the village, when this is large enough. The captive is now bound to a stake in an upright position. A number of fires are lighted in the vicinity, the musical instruments are struck, and all of the customary ceremonials are observed. Then the chief of the village in which the ceremony takes place draws his knife, steps forward and addresses the people. For among the Bataks nothing is done, no matter of how evident a nature, unless all the reasons for the contemplated action are discussed beforehand. It is explained that the victim is an utter scoundrel, and in fact not a human being at all, but a begu (ghost) in human form, and that the time has come for him to atone for his misdeeds. At this address the people water at the mouth and feel an irresistible impulse to have a piece of the criminal in their stomachs, as they will then rest assured that he will do them no further harm. This is the expression they themselves use to explain their cannibalism. According to their description, the pleasure which they feel in satisfying their revenge in this manner, and the consoling quiet which it gives them, is not to be compared to anything else. All draw their knives. The radja cuts off the first piece, which varies according to his taste, being either a slice of the forearm or a cheek, if this be fat enough. He holds up the flesh and drinks with gusto some of the blood streaming from it. Then he hastens to the fire to roast the meat a bit before devouring it.

"Now all the remaining men fall upon the bloody sacrifice, tear

3*

the flesh from the bones and roast and eat it. Some eat the mea raw, or half raw in order to show off their bravery. The cries of th victim do not spoil their appetites. It is usually eight or ten minute before the wounded man becomes unconscious, and a quarter of a hour before he dies. The remainder of the flesh then is cut from th bones (and eaten that same day) and the skeleton buried outside th village."

Among the Pak-Pak the men cut off the head and hands of th victim and danced around the head, hacking it with their spear The head and hands were then treated and later hung up in the sop Volz has shown that animistic motives here came to the fore. B eating an enemy one obtains his soul qualities; also by eating hi one identifies oneself with him, and so renders him (his soul) powe less to work further damage. Here also, as among other head-hunter of Indonesia, by preserving the head, the soul of the enemy become the servant of the victors.

The Pak-Pak had a definite skull cult, and the skulls of ancestor were preserved in the sopo. These skulls received honor and sacrifice and hence their owners the ghosts were kept happy in the other world But the skulls of enemies received no honor or sacrifice, and henc their ghosts were kept in a state of misery.

In southern Bataklandcannibalism ceased when the peopl became converted to Islam. Formerly when an adulterer or thief wa to be eaten his relatives had to furnish the salt (sira) and lime (assam required to make the human flesh tasty. This was done in order t make the relatives show proper submission and to render certain tha they would not resort to blood revenge. Under native adat wher cannibalism ruled in former times in criminal matters (capital), th blood relatives still have the duty of paying money, which is calle sira-assam.

Time reckoning. — The Toba have harvest years and a moo year. The harvest year is reckoned according to the planting, th growth, and the maturity of the maize and the rice. The harvest perio is called taon djaung, the moon period taon eme. The maize is plante and ripens in three or four months, the rice in six to eight months so that the years have these lengths. In daily life time is reckone by these harvest periods. Under the taon eme, however, the entir lunar year is understood, the time from harvest to harvest, or twelv months.

Thus the Bataks have a year of 360 days, with 30 days to the month. The priest (datu) takes astronomical observations, and determines the position of the moon to the great scorpion (hala na godang) in order to decide upon the beginning of each year. A short month is inserted when necessary into the year under the name of lobi lobi.

The division of the month into weeks and days is due to Hindu influence. The days are named from one to seven, the names being Sanskrit. For the reckoning of days and months an almanac (porhalaän) is made use of. This contains a table of 13 times 30 places, and is engraved on bamboo. The chief use to which the almanac is put is the dermination of lucky and unlucky days, again a Hindu belief.

The day itself is not divided into hours, but time is described relative to the position of the sun or of events which occur at customary intervals of the twenty-four hours. Thus early morning is called "when the cock crows".

While the Bataks evidently once had a good knowledge of astronomy, they have either forgotten it, or else the proper informants have not been examined on the subject. The Pleiades furnish the date for the sowing of rice. The evening star is utilized by palm wine gatherers.

The Toba believe that the eclipse of the sun and moon are caused by the combat which the champion of the sun, the lau, has with the champion of the moon, the hala. As long as the eclipse lasts the Bataks help with loud cries and the firing of guns.

At times of earthquake the word "suhul, suhul" is shouted from village to village. This word means "sword-grip", and is used to remind the gigantic serpent Naga Padoha of the sword by which he is pinned under the earth, and which is intended to hold him a fast prisoner.

Society.

Government and Classes. — Among the Bataks, the government no longer rests in the hands of the sibs (marga's), but the territorial unit or village (huta) is governing unit. Among the Toba this is the only unit of government, whereas among the Karo most of the large villages are subdivided into hamlets, each with its own name. Each of these hamlets has its own chief, territory, and settlements outside of the principal village. Formerly wars between hamlets (kesain) were not infrequent.

As among the people of Minangkabau and Gajo, the Bataks had the institution of divine kingship, unquestionably of Hindu origin. The Singa Maharadja resided among the Pak-Pak, and was a human fetish for all the Batak people, but had no temporal power. All kinds of wonders were related about him. His mother had carried him for seven years under her heart. To look at his sword was certain death. He spoke with a closed mouth and gave his commands in writing. He could remain seven months without food, plunged in deep sleep and attended by spirits. He governed rain and sunshine, and the people prayed to him for their crops. The last Singa Maharadja was killed in battle fighting the Dutch in 1907, and his family became converted to Christianity.

Of more practical importance was the influence exerted by the Hindus among the Timur and Karo Bataks toward state formation. The Timur districts, ruled by radjas and their families, are the only large territorial units. These, however, are often conglomerations of almost independent units and have somewhat the appearance of the feudal states of the Middle Ages. All minor rulers, including the heads of villages, must belong to the family of the radja. Among the Karo confederations of villages often are found, the word "urung" actually meaning "association of villages". Yet the village (kuta) itself remains the true unit of government.

Apart from the Timur Batak the form of government is truly democratic. The actual affairs of state are conducted in the sopo's before the assembled people, and consist, outside of the rare consultations with foreign radjas or with their ambassadors, of the following matters: to settle boundary disputes, to surrender village dwellers who have fled or thieves who have been seized, to conclude peace negotiations, to arrange matters of trade, or to form an alliance against the enemy. Among the people of the village the radja investigates and settles various disputes, he makes known judgements and punishments, whether these consist of fines or the death penalty.

The orders promulgated by the radjas must conform to the adat are then deliberated over by all adult men of the village, and finally decided upon by a majority in a council held in the sopo. A radja probably would be more despotic were it not for fear of losing his constituents. When a village is oppressed by its radja and wrongfully treated, the members leave and place themselves under the protection of a neighboring radja, who always receives them with open arms since they strengthen his power. When these seceding fighters then are demanded back and this is refused, war invariably follows. In fact, this is an important cause of the constant intervillage warfare.

While all Bataks have the right of admittance into the sopo's, as a rule only adult (i. e. married) males have voice in the government. Women, however, often get their opinions into the council house and not only are heard, but, if it happens to be the opinion of an elder shaman, acclaimed.

Outside of the inheritance of their power and decorations, namely the special arm rings and embroidered tunics, the radjas have few prior rights over the people, and since taxes are unknown, have no fixed income. However they obtain the free labor of their subjects in working the rice fields and building their houses. Likewise when a chief goes on a trip he is accompanied free of charge by a number of his subjects who carry his baggage. Chiefs also receive a portion of fines levied and ransoms paid in war, and share the booty obtained by their subjects when hunting, fishing, or gathering wild products in the jungle.

The radjas, however, procure their chief income through trade, especially cattle trade, and thus they become wealthier than their village mates. As soon as they are sufficiently wealthy they purchase slaves to work their fields. The products of the fields form thus their only fixed income, and since they themselves consider manual work undignified, slaves are their chief source of wealth. Many radjas, however, are as poor as their poorest village members, although they have bigger and better houses. Only a few are rich, and this is through trade, which in Batakland is conducted almost entirely by the radjas.

As is usual among primitive people the executive radja of a village is chosen from among members of a certain eligible family. Thus primitive succession to office is a combination of inheritance and election. The family from which the radja is chosen must be a part of a sib which is spoken of as the "ruling sib". The wives of a radja must always be members of a second sib, and the men from this second sib always marry women of the ruling sib. This system has been thought to be a survival of the time when there were but two sibs among the Bataks, that is, when the Bataks had a moiety system of exogamy.

Among the Karo the five main sibs are to be found in every village, although in every district a certain one is in the majority and is generally said to be the oldest one in the region, as well as the ruling one. Irrespective of actual power or following every male representative of this sib calls himself radja or sibajak (rich, illustrious). In some villages there are more radjas than subjects. In Toba, however, the government has cut down the number of radjas considerably. In Timur while there is a ruling sib there appears to be no sib having the function of furnishing wives for the radjas.

Notwithstanding the strife as to precedence within the villages, a united front is maintained in dealing with outsiders. Thus in Toba the chief radja is called radja huta (town radja), and he alone deals with other villages. Sometimes, however, this rank is split between two men, a man and his brother-in-law. One then has charge of the village internal affairs and the other deals with outside communities. The rule passes from father to son or younger brother, according to fitness. The radjas deal with intervillage matters abroad and act as judges at home.

Batak society (before the freeing of slaves) was divided into three ranks, the nobles, the commoners and the slaves. The nobles were members of the ruling sib who were not actual executive radjas. Only the nobles were allowed to own slaves, and, at least in southern Batakland, only the nobles were allowed to practice polygyny. In the criminal code the punishment of nobles was more severe, but they were judged more leniently. An insult to a person was judged according to the rank of the offended person.

Formerly it was not possible for a commoner to improve his position. He was bound to the territory in which he was born, and was not allowed to move out without the consent of his radja. The commoners and slaves had to support the nobility, since these did no work.

Slavery was practiced everywhere in Batakland, and lasted until 1914 in Samosir, when the last of the slaves were freed. Besides slavery people were taken as pawns. In southern Batakland this changed into slavery when the debt could not be paid off in a fixed time. The best description of Batak slavery is furnished by Neumann and treats of southern Batakland.

People became slaves 1. through birth, 2. by contract, 3. through debt, 4. through juridical sentence, 5. by war, 6. by capture.

1. Children born of a slave woman were slaves, of a free woman

were free, irrespective of the status of the father. This adat was the reverse of the customary Batak patrilineal following.

2. People who pawned themselves for a certain period of time and later were unable to redeem themselves. This must have been done as a voluntary contract, and did not include wives and children who had been pawned by the husband.

3. Through debt, other than that contracted to pay the bride-price. When a debt was not paid at the fixed time the creditor had the right to take the debtor in pawn, or as a slave, if the amount was large and of long standing.

4. A person who was unable to pay a fine was made a slave. For severe crimes, such as murder and incest there existed a death penalty. But this could be commuted to slavery.

5. Prisoners of war were sometimes kept after peace had been declared and made slaves. This was done as an act of blood revenge.

6. Before the Dutch rule certain chiefs made their living by being brigands, capturing goods and people, and selling the people as slaves. This happened mostly in the mountain regions.

While the slave was the absolute property of his master in Timur and could be crippled or even killed at will, in southern Batakland he was amply protected by the adat. Here, while he was the property of his master, he also was considered a member of the general community. Wounding, crippling or even the sale of the slave could only be effected by court order. On the other hand, the master could order the slave to do any kind of work and could beat him for disobedience. If the slave committed a crime he had to be brought into court. If the slave ran away he was caught, bound, and placed in the stocks. If he repeatedly ran away, by court orders, he was crippled by having his knee-caps broken to prevent repetition of the offence.

However, the master was compelled to support the slave, was responsible for his debts, and had to pay any fine the slave incurred.

Slaves were divided into two classes: house slaves and field slaves. The house slave fetched the water, cut kindling wood, took care of the children, and accompanied his master on trips. The field slave lived in the field which he made and tilled for his master, gathered the crops and brush products. He lived off the yield of his field, and by having more time than the house slave often was able to acquire sufficient capital to purchase his freedom. The field slave had to be married, thus assuring his master that he would not escape, and his lot was superior to that of the house slave.

A slave could purchase his freedom. Slaves also obtained their freedom at the funeral rites of prominent chiefs. One of the slaves stood under the body of the corpse when it was washed, and if any of the water fell upon him he was declared free. Freed slaves (other than prisoners of war) were obliged to remain in the same village in which they were freed, and likewise their children. Otherwise they had all the rights of the free.

The lot of slaves in southern Batakland was but little worse than that of the commoners. Nevertheless they did not like the name of slaves (hatoban), nor did they enjoy being treated as commodities and having their marriages arranged.

The custom of pawnship was borrowed from the Malays. If a man had a debt he could not pay he was forced to borrow from his chief, since the chief was responsible for the debts of his subjects. The man himself was then held as security, and had to work for the chief, and was not allowed to leave the village. A chief never collected his debts in full, for he valued the possession of his subjects more than wealth or goods. Thus the subjects of a radja were virtually his slaves, in fact, even though not in name. Since interest was reckoned at one hundred percent, if the pawn was not able to pay off a good portion of the debt the first year the amount due was doubled. In two or three years the debt increased sufficiently to equal the price of a slave and then the debtor loses his freedom. The heirs of a Batak inherited debts as well as possessions. The heirs of a pawn, however, were not placed in pawnship.

Land rights. — The Batak sibs formerly were territorial. In Palembang the Batak word for sib, "marga", indicates a district, and among the Garos the sibs still are territorial. In Toba, at the present day, the sibs are above all the owners of the land, which is then called the golat of the marga. Elsewhere it is the community of villages (urung, &c.) or even the village which can be regarded as the land owner.

Evidently there has been a change in recent times and the sibs which primarily were territorial units have now become governmental units. This change is illustrated by the fact that the "ruling marga" in a district is the oldest marga. Formerly there were no other sibs

resent in the district. Now there are, but the ruling marga has kept
ontrol of the land by maintaining control of the rule.

De Boer explains this transition as follows: "Formerly, no matter
how large a marga was, its members lived in a fortified village
(huta) or village complex. Such a Toba village consisted of 1. the
people of the marga, 2. those who married in from other marga's,
3. strangers (dagang), and 4. debtors, mostly slaves (hatoban). The
members of such a marga stayed as near together as possible. When
over-expanded some members left but they remained in the district.
Later on, at the time of the East India Company, for instance, there
were fewer wars and the marga broke up into numerous subdivisions.
New villages were founded as distant from one another as possible.
Under such conditions the people no longer regarded themselves as
being descended from the old marga ancestor (ompu) but from a
much later one, the village founder. Often, as the marriage price
became high enough to be burdensome, men married matrilocally
and this brought about an infusion of alien marga's into the village.
While the first-comers thus kept their rule, the village itself, and
not the sib became the unit of government. Each marga in the village
has its own grounds which it rents out to the members of the sib."

As noted in this discussion, whether a village (i. e. the radja
and the ruling sib) or the various sibs have control of the land, the
question of actual ownership never comes to the fore. There is no true
possession of land, as rated by European concept, for land can neither
be given away, sold or pawned. The right of possession only can
be gained by cultivation of the field. Strangers must obtain permission
to cultivate from the sib or the village chief. The use of land is
inherited within the family of the first cultivator.

Laws. — As is customary among primitive people whose code
of law rests primarily on the demands of an aggrieved family or sib
for blood revenge or weregild, most of the complaints brought forward
are of a civil rather than criminal nature, are torts rather than crimes.
This fact has led many writers on the Bataks to assume that the
Batak knows no distinction between civil and criminal code. This
statement, however, is truer for the Minangkabau than for the Batak,
for the latter were well on the road to the construction of petty states,
and treason not only was a crime, but a capital offence.

According to native Batak-adat the chiefs are the judges and the
aggrieved party the accuser. Every case has to be ferreted back to some

injury (ido). Evidence usually is taken through material token (tanda). In case of doubtful or incomplete evidence a purification oath is required. Formerly the ordeal also was resorted to. The court is held in the sopo or in the open.

Personal disputes, as over land or the payment of a bride-price do not come into court, but are brought before a third party who tries to make the contenders come to terms. If he failed in former days war followed.

The chief crimes are murder, theft, adultery and insult. If a widow marries some man other than a near relative of her deceased husband this also is treated as adultery. The special punishments meted out in time of war have already been noted. The punishments as listed for southern Batakland are as follows:

1. The death of the criminal and his nearest blood relatives.
2. The death of the criminal.
3. The slaying of the criminal and his household.
4. Banning forever.
5. Banning.
6. Paying of graded fines. There are eleven grades.
7. Putting in block.
8. Whipping (for slaves only).
9. Loss of rank or power of franchise.
10. Sira-assam (lime and salt; formerly, being eaten).

The Bataks have three varieties of collective responsibility. The first variety is a natural responsibility, the consequence of the solidarity of relationships. In the same way, a host is responsible for the action of his guest, and a chief for the actions of his subjects in another territory. A chief also is responsible for the actions of the subject of another chief in his own territory.

The second variety of responsibility is one which is voluntarily selected. While all of one's kin are responsible for the actions of a man, certain chosen ones are especially responsible in court, and these are called the anak boru and the senina. This matter will be treated under "kinship usage".

Finally there is the collective responsibility of village mates.

Oath and ordeal. — The oath and ordeal formerly played a large rôle in Batak law cases, especially where material evidence was not of a convincing nature. We already have seen that warfare among he Bataks — and the same thing was true among the Minangkabau — was in itself often a form of ordeal, for the side which lost the irst man was judged the guilty party. Naturally, the oath and rdeal are but two sides of the same psychology, for the oath itself s a form of ordeal in which the perjurer will be punished by the ods. Therefore among the Bataks, as among most primitive people nd even the civilized Greeks and Romans, there often is no unishment in the native adat for perjury.

Oath and ordeal must be considered a part of the Hindu, or more robably pre-Hindu, complex of traits which penetrated to Sumatra, he East Indies, New Guinea, and even to Polynesia. Fire-walking s practiced in India was originally an ordeal ruled over by Agni, od of fire. This same custom in Polynesia however, was no longer n ordeal. The more backward peoples of the earth, as the Andaman slanders, the Australians, and the American Indians lacked the oath nd ordeal. The Africans added a new form of ordeal, the poison rdeal for the detection of witches, which is not found elsewhere. ll the people of Sumatra, including even the primitive Kubu, had he oath and ordeal. Among the natives of the western islands the eople of Nias had the trait, but the Mentawei islanders are without it.

In the Batak law court testimony is not given under oath. If he truth of a statement is doubted, an oath may be demanded of he witness. If this is refused the testimony does not pass as valid.

The Batak is very easy going in his use of the oath of purgation gana). He curses, without the quiver of an eyelash, himself and his ntire family even when he is guilty. There is a considerable list of ath formulas. Usually the oath, which is an attestation invoking he names of ancestors or gods, is accompanied by some symbolical ct of death. Thus one pierces the heart of a slaughtered animal, rushes a frog, or, more simply, swears by an extinguished firebrand r by a grave. Naturally the swearer invokes a like fate upon himself f he commits perjury.

The ordeal is a severer form of oath, and one which a guilty man s loath to undertake. If the ordeal goes against the accused, for xample, if a dying chicken falls on its right side, a confession sually follows.

Among the Toba the institution of hopokwas was formerly a estive affair, to which the priest (datu), the chief of the person rom whom the article was stolen, and the chief of the accused were invited. The hopokwas served as a means of recovering stolen objects but not cattle. The priest, as well as a representative of the family or village of the accused, likewise submitted to the test. No sharpened weapons could be brought to the ordeal, although the accused sometimes challenged the priest to an ordeal with edged weapons.

The time of the trial was determined by the priest with the aid of the magic calendar, and notice given four weeks beforehand. In every case an exorcism formula was chanted by the priest invoking the hopok to set free the innocent and kill the guilty. The gods and ancestors likewise were invoked.

The usual hopok fell into two varieties; eating trials and fire trials. At the eating trials the accused had to take a handful of shelled rice or rice meal and swallow it without the aid of liquid. If the accused preferred he was allowed to swallow Spanish pepper without wincing. In the fire trial the accused stuck his hand in boiling lead or molten iron. Walking over molten iron was another form of the fire trial.

As in the Philippines and elsewhere in Indonesia the ordeal by water also was common. The accused was ducked in a pond and if guilty he drowned.

Inheritance. — Women and children are denied right of inheritance and must be supported by adult males. Where the adat is most strictly observed, the law of ultimogeniture holds and the youngest son has the most rights and then the eldest. Usually both youngest and eldest divide equally in preference to the other sons. No difference is made between the claims of sons of different wives.

In southern Batakland the rule of inheritance has been summarized by Willer as follows. The sons inherit from their father, grandfather, and further grades in the ascending line. At the death of the son, the grandchildren inherit. If anyone dies without leaving male descendants, then his father inherits or, if he is deceased, the brother's sons, or his nephews. If all of these are dead then the head of the "ripe" (family) inherits. As long as there are male descendants, all grades in the ascending or side lines are excluded.

Marriage restrictions. — The Bataks have exogamous patrilineal sibs. These, however, have been so broken down by the altered conditions of Batak life that now it is difficult to state the number of sibs among most of the Batak divisions and the laws of sib exogamy no longer are strictly adhered to.

The Karo Bataks have five main marga, each of which is said to have been founded by a fictitious tribal father. There are no chiefs at the head of the marga or sub-marga. The village chiefs among the Karo cannot produce genealogical records of descent from the marga founders as in Toba and elsewhere.

The five main Karo marga are: — Karo-Karo, Tarigan, Ginting, Perangin-Angin, Sembiring. The marga are divided into sub-marga also called marga and these again are divided into family groups called houses (rumah). It is absolutely forbidden to marry into one's sub-marga or into one's marga, if it is one of the first three of the above-named. In the case of the fourth this restriction is less absolute; in the fifth there are many endogamous marriages.

It is impossible to state accurately the number and names of sibs elsewhere. Tideman, however, writes that the Timur have four main marga: Damanik, Sinaga, Saragih, and Purba. Among the Toba, there is no accurate account of the number of sibs existing. While some authors have claimed that the Toba have five main sibs as have the Karo; Van Dijk, Warneck and Brenner claim only two, thus giving the Bataks moieties. Brenner, in fact writes that the Bataks have two main sibs, the Tartharol and the Teivaliol. These are then subdivided into sub-sibs, each sub-sib possessing a group of villages and taking its name from the chief of these villages. Joustra believes that this statement is correct; and that there are two groups, the one composed of the decendants of Tuan Haringguan Godan and the other of Saribu Radja.

In general, a man must marry a woman of a different sib and both sibs must not be of the same origin. With the exception of cross-cousin marriage a Karo man also is supposed to marry a woman of a different sib than his mother's. Every child is instructed regarding his father's and mother's sib. Joustra writes of the Karo, who call the father's sib "marga" and the mother's "bebere".

"All conversation between two strangers begins with mutual questioning in regard to this point. This ertutur (questioning) is for the purpose of explaining in what family relation the two stand, and then a decision is reached as to whether one can call one another by name or make use of another appellation, such as uncle, aunt, brother-in-law, father, mother, &c.

"A man always begins by addressing a strange man as silih, brother-in-law. A woman addresses another woman as bibi, father's

sister. A woman speaks to a strange man as ama', mother's brother
A woman also can call a strange woman kadih, or teman, friend."

"If two people are of the same marga, even though they be of
different bebere, then the family relationship is very close. According
as to whether they are of the same or different age-groups, they are
siblings, father and child, aunt and nephew (niece), &c. The
relationship is not so close as blood relationship but is more than a
bare name, due to marriage taboos. Sexual intercourse between name
relatives is regarded as incest."

"If the marga differs but the bebere is the same, then the family
relationship is still intimate but not so close. One still can be another
person's brother (senina) but this relation is usually called ersenina
sipemeren. A marriage between a youth and a girl of the same bebere
cannot be made unless they belong to different subdivisions of the bebere."

In Mandheling, in former times, there was no adat rule regarding incest between close blood relatives as this was too exceptional.
Incest between those who called themselves ibotoh, sibling, was punished by death. If a girl fled with a man who was not actually related
to her but was of the same marga, the young man was fined the
amount of her marriage price and the girl was condemned to celibacy
or married beneath her rank and in a distant place.

Totemism. — The Bataks still have strong indications of totemism
connected with their sib organization. Certain sibs are believed to be
descended from certain animals. These animals are said to belong to
the sibs and the sib members are forbidden to eat their flesh. According to Neumann the Southern Batak have the following totems:

Tiger, panther, &c.	to marga	Babijat
Dog	to marga	Tompul
Ape, goat	to marga	Si Regar
Doves	to marga	Harahap
White buffalo	to marga	Nasution
Cat	to marga	Si Pospos (pus-pus)

These sibs are forbidden to eat the above-named animals because
according to many accounts, they are descended from them.

The Karo Bataks have similar food taboos and similar animal
belonging to their margas. A part of the Karo-Karo believe themselves
to be descended from the daughter of a giant snake. Formerly, in the
court of the divine ruler Singa Mangaradja, snakes were fed and were
considered sacred.

Cross-cousin marriage. — A man is supposed to marry his mother's brother's daughter but is not allowed to marry his father's sister's daughter. The woman may be either the daughter of the mother's brother or the granddaughter of the mother's brother's father but the first cousin is chosen by preference. While the specific cross-cousin relation however is called tunanang, the Toba uses this title also for every woman he is allowed to marry.

Due to the fact that no village statistics or family genealogies are available for the Bataks, it is impossible to state the frequency of cross-cousin marriage. Meerwaldt asserts that among the Toba this form of marriage is not frequent. It would be mere chance, he claims, if a man has a daughter and his sister a son, and these two were *api* (rime) to one another. If a man has a suitable cousin and does not marry her but some one else, he taks his maternal uncle a present and tries to conciliate him. There is no law about the matter but a marriage between cross-cousins is considered the proper form of marriage. While I was told that in Angkola a man does not pay a lower marriage price for a cousin, Joustra claims that among the Karo the sum is less than would ordinarily be asked and in some cases no price is demanded at all. Meerwaldt states the same for the Toba.

Marriage with the father's sister's daughter is treated under the criminal code. The Batak explain the prohibition by saying: "How is it possible that water can flow back to its origin?" However, in the third generation a man is allowed to marry a cousin on his paternal side. While at the present time all cousins of the opposite sex who are not daughters of the maternal uncle are avoided as if they were actually sisters, many Bataks claim that formerly, when the people were still few in numbers, it was permitted to marry the father's sister's daughter. This type of union, however, caused the wrath of the gods and the custom was accordingly stopped.

While polygyny is practiced by the Bataks, a man is not allowed to take two full sisters in marriage simultaneously nor is it even permitted for two men of the same mother to take two full sisters as wives. The people say that this would be like putting two whetstones on one ring.

Levirate and sororate. — According to the rigorous patrilineal adat of the Bataks, "a woman is as a child the property of her father, as a woman the property of her husband, and after his death the property of his male relatives".

Upon the completion of the payment of the marriage price, the

woman becomes the property of her husband's sib. Thus a woman
whose marriage is regarded as complete, is not only bound to her husband but, by his death, to his family, so that she is guilty of breaking
the marriage bonds if upon his decease she refuses one of his brothers,
nephews, sons, or nearest male relatives to take the place of her husband. This refusal would have as its consequence that she became the
slave of the village chief. In the absence of male blood relatives, the
woman passes to a sib kin. If the inheritor does not wish to marry the
woman, he has to support her.

Actually a woman is not inherited as if she were merchandise since
she can regain her freedom by repayment of the marriage price. Or, if
she has not the proper amount of money, she at least has the choice as
to which of her husband's relatives she will have in marriage. Among
the Toba, if a woman has a son it is not deemed necessary that she
remarry within the family.

Neumann gives the regulations of the levirate and sororate of
southern Batak as follows:

"At the death of a man his inheritance and also his wives go to
the waris (Arabic, heir) who usually is the younger brother or the
eldest son. If the younger brother is the heir and wishes to take the wife
of his brother in marriage, she must comply. With sons (stepsons) the
adat varies. Marriage with a stepson at the present day is forbidden
but formerly an eldest stepson could marry his stepmother when the
father was dead. The actual mother either remains a widow or is
taken by a younger brother-in-law. If there are no younger brothers-
in-law or they will not have her, she can enter into another marriage
with the consent of her son. In some places a father is waris of his
son and is allowed to marry his daughter-in-law. If the waris does
not wish to marry the widow of his testator he can give her to one of
his brothers. If these also do not wish to marry her, the widow is free
to make her own choice with the consent of the waris.

"If a woman dies childless and the full marriage price has been
paid, the father is obliged to furnish another woman as substitute. The
best substitute is one of the younger sisters of the deceased or another
young girl of her kindred. The widower then pays a small sum in gold
to his father-in-law. If, however, the woman had already given birth to
a child, there is no obligation to do this. In this case the father-in-law
at the birth of the first child would have sent his daughter a small
present as a token that his son-in-law had nothing further to expect

The son-in-law would then return a small present to the father-in-law. Thus the djudjur (marriage price) purchases not only the wife but the wife and one child."

It is general rule among the Bataks that the man who marries a widow assumes all the debts of the deceased husband. A widow or widower must wait a year before remarriage. Failure to do this is not punished, but the hasty party is ridiculed.

The actual and presumably oldest status of marital choice is summed up by the Toba word "poriban". A man should marry his poriban; that is, first his wife's younger sister; secondly his mother's brother's daughter; and thirdly any other woman of his mother's sib and his own age class. All these women a man calls poriban and he is on a joking, or free, relationship with them. On the other hand, a man avoids his sisters, his wife's elder sisters, and his father's sister's daughters, all of whom he regards as sisters.

The younger sister of a wife also calls her brother-in-law poriban; a woman calls her husband's younger brother poriban; and two men whose wives are sisters call one another poriban.

Among the Karo the female child of the mother's brother and the male child of father's sister are called impal. These two are impal to one another and should marry.

Kinship usage. — Among the Bataks avoidances seem to be based solely on the principle that all appearance of wrongdoing should be prevented. If a man and woman are alone together, or if they even exchange a few words, they at once come under suspicion. Incest between family members is a thing to be avoid at all costs, as it would arouse the wrath of the gods and lead to disaster. The taboos therefore are strictest between brothers and sisters. A brother and sister would be embarrassed at being together even when others were present. The rules regulating the actions of parents and children are less strict, but a father should not be alone in the house with his daughter nor a mother with her son. Joustra, who records these taboos, admits that the most of them are very necessary.

In general, people of the opposite sex who may not marry are taboo to one another while those of the opposite sex who may marry and, especially, those who should marry, are on free terms or on joking relationship with one another. There is no avoidance or joking relationship between people of the same sex.

A father-in-law is very polite to his daughter-in-law. If he has

4*

anything to say to her he does it through a third party. He is no
allowed to utter her name, just as he is not allowed to mention the name
of his own wife. He calls her by her sib name or says "daughter o
so-and-so". A daughter-in-law is also very polite to her father-in-law
She does not speak directly to him but makes use of a third party. I
the father-in-law comes her way, she steps aside. On the other hand, a
girl is very friendly with her mother-in-law, who always calls her by
her name. The greatest intimacy arises when the mother-in-law is also
her father's sister.

A man and his mother-in-law are on avoidance terms but a man
is on very intimate terms with his father-in-law. If the father-in-law
also is the man's mother's brother he is called "second father". In
fact, among the Batak, the bond between a man and his parents-in-law
is stronger than the bond between a man and his own family.

In the same way a man avoids the wife of his younger brother and
she avoids him. They may not speak to one another and if they pass on
the way the man steps aside or, if this is not possible, the woman turns
her back. A man also avoids his bao, the wife of the brother of
his wife.

On the other hand, intercourse between proper cross-cousins
is very free and they are said to stand outside the customary law. When
they talk together or appear openly together on the market, no one has
anything to say in opposition. They joke and exchange riddles or play
on words in songs. Usually it is forbidden for an engaged couple to
speak to one another in the house of the girl's parents, but cross-cousins
are not ashamed to do this. They are purposely left alone together so
that they may become better acquainted.

Likewise a younger brother is allowed to speak to the wife of his
older brother and joke with her, for when his brother dies the woman
will become his wife. If the wife of the brother is also a cross-cousin
a still greater liberty in speech may be assumed.

Among the Bataks men and women stand in definite relationship
to both the members of their own sib and to the members of the sib
into which they marry. Men and women of the same sib and of the
same age class are fictitious brothers and sisters. Thus in Ankola al
the men of the same sib and generation call one another sa-marga, and
all women of the same sib and generation paribotoan, sisters. In th
Dairi dialect, people who belong to the same sib call one another
senina, literally "mother members" or "members of common mother"

Among the Toba, the expression dongan saina (ina-mother) is used, but only for those in the same sub-marga.

While theoretically, at least among the Karo, a man should not marry a woman from his mother's marga, all the kinship terms seem in consonance with just this form of marriage, and it is considered proper that a man marry his mother's brother's daughter and a woman her father's sister's son. The Toba man calls the elder relatives of his mother hulahula or bona ni ari ("origin of his life", or "beginning of his days") regardless of whether he has married his cross-cousin or not. But if he married elsewhere, he has a secondary set of hulahula relatives from whom he has actually obtained his wife. The hulahula relatives must always be treated with the greatest respect. Failure to do this is liable to incur the wrath of the gods. One must hold these relatives in high honor, this being shown by presenting them with food and by the manner in which one speaks to them. If the mother's brother asks for a present or for money, this must, if possible, be given, above all if one has married his daughter. If a man has had a fight with his own parents he flees to his mother's brother.

Yet circumstances alter cases and if the hulahula are rich they are very much honored, but if poor they are despised. In the latter case a man avoids marriage with his lawful cousin.

There remains a certain legal and social aspect to the relationship between two intermarrying sibs which requires discussion. In the Toba language when a man marries he becomes the anak boru (male daughter) to the father of his wife and all the male relatives, i. e., anak boru for the entire sib. The reciprocal term is tondong. Tideman has shown that these two terms express a relationship between the two sibs and that while all sib members of the man entering marriage are anak boru to the tondong, the most important is the one called anak boru sikahanan (kaha meaning old).

The tondong, besides having his anak boru, also has the male members of his own sib as attendants, and these he calls senina (of one mother, sada ina). Of his senina, the most important one is his senina sikahanan.

The anak boru is a hostage who has full responsibility for the actions of his tondong. If the tondong does not conform to the adat or does not pay his debts, the anak boru is held responsible. If the anak boru sikahanan must pay a debt and cannot, he calls the other anak boru together and they all share in the payment.

The only advantage the anak boru has, against the many disad
vantages under which he suffers, is that at feasts and certain cere
monials he obtains some cloth and a part of the slaughtered animal
On the other hand, the anak boru must, at marriages and certain
feasts, give a small sum of money.

The anak boru senina come together at all important family
matters, as for instance, a death. Then questions such as inheritance
and succession to office are discussed.

Thus in Toba and Timur the anak boru relationship appears to
have developed from the duties which a nephew owes, among the
Bataks, to his maternal uncle. Among the Karo, however, the choice
of anak boru and senina seems somewhat different. Here also the
senina is a sib brother, but the anak boru is not a member of the sib
into which a man marries; he is usually a man's brother-in-law
that is, a member of the sib into which one's sister marries. According
to Joustra:

"As soon as a youth begins to take part in social and private life
that is, when he marries, he cannot be without an anak boru and a
senina. The anak boru plays the chief part in the trinity. He corre
sponds to the Malay-Arabic word wakil, agent or representative; but
is more useful. The a. b. s. relationship rests entirely on these grounds
1. that for every legal transaction an account must be given; 2. that in
the absence of written records the matter must be witnessed as far as
possible. Punishments, fines, stocks may be exacted from anyone of
the three."

Every ruler among the Batak has his anak boru and his senina
at his side and these aid him in his governmental transactions. The
marga from which the men of the ruling marga (called bajobajo
marga) take their wives is the boru marga.

Marriage and Courtship. — In Indonesia as a whole there is a
wide divergence concerning the demand made on women for prenuptial
chastity. While the generalization has been made that such chastity
is prized in patrilineal areas and not demanded in areas having the
bilateral family, yet even the patrilineal Batak are divided on this
point. Among the northerners, especially the Toba, sexual freedom be
fore marriage is taken for granted, while among many of the people of
the south the girls' houses serve the special purpose of protecting the
chastity of the inmates. Everywhere child betrothals save the virtue of
young girls for their future husbands.

Usually among primitive peoples courtship and marriage have little or nothing to do with each other. The first has for its object the obtainment of sexual gratification, is often aided by magic, and is entirely an affair between the two interested parties, who merely abide by the rules prohibiting incest and adultery. Marriage, on the other hand, is an exchange between families or sibs, is arranged by a third party, and the interested couple are, at the most, asked to give their consent. Among the Bataks, however, courtship frequently leads to marriage, especially where pregnancy occurs.

"There is no dainty cake on which a fly fails to sit", runs a famous Batak saying, and likewise a Batak husband expects his wife to be a hard worker, but does not inquire too closely into her past. Many occasions are given boys and girls by which they can become acquainted. In the course of their work in the rice fields and at the time of feasts they mingle freely with one another. Full license is allowed the young couples, provided they come from different sibs and obey the proper rules of decorum. Among the South Batak these gatherings are called martandang, a name also employed for the visits the youths pay their girls in the women's communal houses. In Toba intercourse between the sexes is especially free and the youths and girls often have a form of competition in which four-line rimed couplets are exchanged. Whoever loses has to pay a forfeit: the boy gives a piece of his clothing, a knife, or some other trinket, the girl gives herself.

The youths have various means which they employ to win the favor of the young women. Courtship takes place within the village enclosure in the evenings and is called tarutaruan by the Toba. The young men sing erotic songs accompanied by the notes of a mouth-flute made from the stalks of large sugar palm leaves. Charms (dorma) also are employed as well as counter-charms taken as prophylaxis by the girls. For it is thought that love charms lead to unhappy marriages when successful. Sacrifices have to be made to the love charms, which are sung over by the makers. Still another method of courtship is more prosaic and is called gambir di toru by the Toba. The youth pays the girl for her favors but obtains a rebate on the marriage price if a wedding between the two climaxes the romance.

In cases where the young couple form a permanent attachment for each other or when the young girl becomes pregnant, a marriage results. Thus among the southern Batak young girls of ten or eleven are called budjing, are considered of marriageable age, and sleep in the women's communal house, bagas podoman, under the charge of a responsible woman. All the unmarried men of the community have the right to enter a padoman. They come in small groups, with lights burning, and speak with the young women, offer them sirih, and remain until the chaperon gives them a signal to depart.

If the visit of one of the courters has been successful, the girl speaks about the matter with her parents and obtains their consent. Then on a following night the young man comes in front of the court of the padoman and calls out the name of the daughter of his choice. She leaves the house with him, and together they go to an empty sopo (communal house, without walls) where they spend the night together, according to the adat, in chastity. This elopement is called mermaijam. After this the young man, accompanied by his relatives, asks the elders of the girl for her hand in marriage. He gives the relatives a pledge (tanda), such as an arm-ring, and then the couple are engaged. While Batak girls are, as a rule, allowed to conduct themselves as they will before they become engaged, they must not become pregnant. If a woman, either as girl or widow, becomes pregnant without being able to marry her lover, all marks of woman hood, such as her hair, are taken from her, or she can be compelled to marry a man of lower rank. Because of the unusual license allowed young men in their treatment of women — it is not only allowed but proper that a young man should attack a young woman if he meet her alone — the women are given legal means whereby they can force their guilty lovers into marriage.

A proposal of marriage on the part of the girl is called mahi jompo. This is done as publicly as possible. The girl takes the greater part of her belongings, walks across the village in broad daylight and climbs up to the house of the elders of the young man. If she is allowed to remain a certain length of time, the young man must marry her. If the girl has no token of the man's guilt, such as a piece of his clothing, or if they have not been seen together by wit nesses, she can be ejected. If she has proof, however, the man must either marry her or pay the bride-price without the marriage. Few Batak men will pay the price and not take their purchase. Often a girl will take the risk of being ejected, since she has no proof but is merely in love with a man upon whom she has happened to cast her eyes. Forcible ejection in this case is very much feared by a girl, since it lowers her repute and with it her bride-price.

There are, however, two forms of mahijompo. One is called manaik and is really an elopement form of marriage. It is done for the purpose of avoiding the trouble and expense of a formal wedding and is entered into with the knowledge of the girl's parents or even after a long engagement. The word manaik merely means to mount up. In this case the full marriage price is paid. In mandakit, however, the parents of the girl are not consulted and the act is often against their will. The girl in this case usually is pregnant or fears that she will be abandoned by her lover. While the marriage price remains the same, only a small portion is paid off and the wedding is complete with the killing of a karabau.

Engagement. — In Toba, as well as elsewhere among the Batak, girls are often sold into marriage before being actually born. The expectant father may be in debt and pressed for immediate money. The custom whereby a man receives the marriage price or a portion of it and as yet has no daughter, is called morboru tapang. As soon as a daughter is born to him, the father of the groom comes with his presents. The village chief is invited, a meal is held, rice strewn on the heads of the boy and girl and both given favorable names. Then the pair are considered engaged, and such contracts often lead later on to marriage.

Between adults engagements can be closed by sending the elders of the girl and slaughtering a karabau. More simply, engagements can be announced by the sending of a piece of cloth or a weapon. After an engagement marriage usually does not take place for a long time. The youth during the period of the engagement is free to live with the girl. He helps the elders in the fields and is fed by them. This custom is followed so that 1. both parties can become well acquainted and accustomed to each other, 2. so that the youth will be certain that the girl will not give herself to another, and 3. in order that the youth, during this period, can perform service in order to be able to pay off the marriage price. In the case of a noble, a slave can be employed for this service, as well as to watch over the girl.

The reverse of this situation can also occur, namely, that during the engagement the girl is taken to live with the parents of the boy. This manner of treatment arises from mistrust on the side of the youth's family who fear that the girl will give herself to other men and if the marriage is very much desired by both families. Such a procedure also only takes place when the groom is too young to marry. The girl steps entirely into the position of daughter-in-law (pa-ruma-en) and performs the usual housework and rice stamping

The bride-price. — The bride-price is the sum of money paid by the man's side to the woman's side. The South Sumatra name djudjur is the best known to Europeans. The Bataks regard the payment of the price as a legitimate purchase and call wives "things bought". Thus Toba, na hu-tuhor, my wife (that which I bought). Nevertheless marriage among the Batak has remained one of exchange and has never fully developed into purchase. The bride-price is merely a token given by one sib to another, to be reciprocated in kind. The price a girl brings does not depend upon her age, beauty or capacity for work, but is the same in size as that paid for the mother and grand mother. The father thus secures back the same amount he paid for his own wife. Possibly the earliest form of sib marriage among the Bataks was one of exchange between two sibs or moieties, as is now the case between the two ruling sibs. Cross-cousin marriage kept the two sibs exogamous and the bride-price maintained an even balance of trade between the moieties.

In Toba the bride-price varies from $ 50 to $ 1,000. The owners (porboru) of the girl get the main share of the money. These are in most cases, the father of the girl and his brothers. If the father is dead, one of the girl's brothers may be her porboru. But all male relatives, even the most distant, receives a certain share. The chief of the village and also the village inmates obtain a portion, thus showing that originally the price was divided among all sib mates. A smaller return present is made to the family of the groom.

As a rule, the bride-price is not demanded in whole. Usually only half the amount is paid. If the two families get along well together the remainder is never asked for. Cancellation of the debt, however is unknown and the grandchildren and great-grandchildren can be held responsible.

If the price be entirely paid, the groom has the right to demand that jewels and clothing be given his wife as dowry. If the woman is of noble birth, these are of considerable value and become the property of the man. If the price is not entirely paid, the children at death or upon divorce remain with the mother, who retires to her family

All these rules are not always obeyed. Sometimes no bride-price is paid because the two families are on good terms with each other The kin of the woman then often turns to the family of the man for nancial assistance and aid in the fields. If then, however, there is divorce or the man dies, matters may be very complicated so far s the children are concerned. Some then insist that the bride-price s as good as paid, others pretend that it is not and the family of ae man have no claim on the widow and children. The usual settlement s to pay the bride-price without making deductions for the settlements 1ade during marriage, so that it would, in fact, have been cheaper) have paid the stipulated amount at the time of the wedding.

Occasionally a marriage is contracted for which there is no 1tention of ever paying the bride-price or its equivalent. This form f marriage is both a disgrace to the woman and her future female escendants, who then also will be forced to marry without the bride-rice. A girl given away in this fashion is called boru mangambe y the Toba. The word mangambe indicates that the arms of the erson in question dangle as she walks. Such a girl may be suffering rom an infectious skin disease; or she may be a girl of noble birth vho has given herself to a slave; or she may be bearing the conse-uences of adultery without wishing or being able to name the man.

A fairly common form of matrilocal marriage occurs among many f the patrilineal peoples of the Indies, such as the Bataks, Gajos, atives of South Sumatra and Ambon in the Moluccas. The native Malay term for this form of marriage is ambil anak, which simply 1eans "to produce children", this being perhaps the main purpose of uch an arrangement. Where this form of marriage exists, the man ives with the family of his wife, pays no bride-price, and the children elong to the wife's family. Naturally, the service marriage is merely temporary form of the ambil anak.

The most common form of the ambil anak marriage is when the ather of the bride has already reached old age and wishes to take he bridegroom into his family as male inheritor. The son-in-law is hen adopted into the house of his father-in-law, lives there at his xpense, and works for him. If the son-in-law ever has sufficient noney to pay the djudjur, after the death of the parent-in-law, he an obtain title to the land.

It thus becomes clear that the bride-price among the Bataks was n important factor in determining the patrilineal reckoning of the ibs. Had there been no bride-price and had marriage remained a natter of exchange between sibs or families, as it was occasionally mong the Lampong people of Sumatra and still is among many of the tribes of New Guinea, then the sibs would have become either matrilineal or patrilineal depending on the ownership of the hand, &c When, however, the bride-price becomes too high, there is a tendenc for the payment to be evaded altogether; for residence to becom matrilocal; for the property to remain in the hands of the bride' family and, perhaps eventually, for the sib to become matrilinea While this last-named event probably has never taken place in Sumatr or elsewhere, matrilocal residence has been frequent enough amon; the Bataks to change the sibs from territorial to genealogical units

Forms of marriage. — The following forms of marriage ar listed by Neumann for the South Batak and are general throughou the Batak country. In all cases, the bride-price or its equivalent mus be paid.

1. After an engagement.

2. After the childless death of the woman; when the father o his heir (waris) is obliged to furnish another daughter, althougl nearly always a younger sister of the deceased.

3. Through inheritance or succession.

4. Through abduction.

5. After the freewill coming of the girl to the man of her choic (mahijompo, maniompo).

6. After "dishonorable treatment", when the girl has the righ to force her lover into màrriage (manaik).

7. When the dishonorable treatment brings visible consequence or becomes public. The girl then can go to the house of her lover an force him into marriage (mandakit).

8. After violation (mamintui).

Abduction is a regular form of marriage according to the adat Its main purpose is to avoid the expense of a wedding. The bride price must be paid in full, however; one-half at once and th remainder in instalments. Marriage in the regular form among th nobility may almost equal in cost the returns from the bride-price It involves not simply the feast, but the parents of the girl mus also furnish her with clothing, decorations, and house utensils. Thu; both sides gain by the abduction — the parents of the youth dela giving half the bride-price, and the parents of the girl avoid giving most of the dowry.

When an abduction is legally performed the youth brings the gir to a town (kampong) other than his own, and she leaves some toke ehind, such as a piece of cloth under her sleeping mat, to show that he has gone of her own accord. The youth sends word to the parents f the girl that he has abducted her and these pretend to be very angry, ut the wedding is gone through as a matter of form by the simple illing of a karabau.

Sometimes the elders of the girl are actually opposed to the match while those of the youth desire it. Even then the matter is legal, rovided that the difference in rank between the couple is not too reat. The elders of the girl must give in to save her reputation. he initial payment on the bride-price is reduced then, but not to half.

Thus actual capture-marriage does not exist among the Bataks, or is the abduction-marriage in any sense a survival of capture-marriage; it is rather an elopement in our sense of the word. Marriage by violation is allowed only in exceptional cases. When a radja, or example, is in love with a woman beneath his rank and she efuses his offer, he is allowed to violate her. However, he must pay he bride-price and marry the woman. If he wrongs the woman in ither of these respects, he is liable to have his subjects swear off heir allegiance to him and complain to another radja. Likewise, if widow shows aversion to her waris, he is allowed to violate her fter having informed his radja of his contemplated action.

Normally marriage takes place when the youth is about eighteen nd the girl fifteen. However, the girl can marry as young as ten, e., before the age of puberty. The man sends a mediator to make he proposal, as it is not thought proper to speak directly concerning he matter. The girl would be ashamed to give in at once and she irst investigates the character, worth, and appearance of the suitor. Upon yielding to the pleas of the mediator, she says: "If so-and-so ishes to make use of the daughter of a poor man, let him ask my arents." This is taken as a sign that she has given her consent. he young man then goes to his sopo (communal house) and seeks dream.

He takes a separate sleeping place, apart from the other youths, ses a pillow of rice, and prays to his ancestors and the gods for guiding dream. If he dreams that he is harvesting rice or drinking lear water, it is considered a favorable omen. It is inauspicious, owever, if he dreams that he is tilling the ground or climbing a ountain. In the later case he avoids the marriage. Some men go o a soothsayer and see if their names fit with those of their brides.

In order to produce children the names of married couples and therefore, the tondi (souls) of the couples, have to be in accord.

If all the omens are auspicious the man gives his future father-in-law and the daughter presents as pledges. The bride-price and the date of the wedding are then arranged. The son-in-law bring meat for the wedding, pays the bride-price, and takes the bride bac to his village.

It can be seen that in all forms of marriage, excepting violatio and inheritance, the choice of the girl is the primary factor. Th bride-price counts for but little, as a marriage will not be delayed i it cannot be paid at once. A Batak girl, when marrying, is suppose to be as favorably inclined towards the family of her husband a she is towards her spouse himself and therefore not to be averse t a second marriage within the family.

The wedding ceremony. — The wedding ceremony is performe by the radja. As a part of his discourse he says: "If the man die he will be replaced; if the woman dies she will be replaced." As sign that the bride and groom from now on belong together, the must eat out of the same plate of rice, which has an egg in th middle, sit on one mat, and allow themselves to be wrapped in th same mat.

Eventually the groom takes his bride home to the house of hi parents. On the way the woman gives vent to her assumed sorrow With deep sobs and tears she sings her songs of lamentation.

After the ceremony the couple is taboo (robu) for four or seve days. This is their honeymoon. During this time they can do n work (with the exception of stamping a little meal), they cannot g to the rice field or cross a river.

The actual marital status of the Bataks is not established unt the first child is born. Before this time it is not thought proper fo them to appear in public together and they would be ashamed t be seen talking or walking with each other. While marriage i usually patrilocal, within a year the married couple must pay a vis to the father of the woman. If the pair are not cousins, the mother' brother (tulang) has the right to demand that the married pair also visit him and fulfils the adat requirements. Presents are exchanged betwee the wife and the tulang to show that the marriage bond is not broke

Polygyny. — The Bataks have no law concerning the number o wives they may have, but due to their cost the common members o the village rarely have more than one. In Toba the chiefs have from three to five wives, never more than eight. The first wife has certain rights over the others. Sometimes a Batak will take a second wife at the urging of his first one, if the first wife can bear no children and would rather share her husband with another woman than be divorced. There are sufficient women in the Batak country to permit the chiefs to have several wives for, in former days, many of the men were sold into slavery and others migrated to East Sumatra or the mainland.

Pregnancy. — When a woman is pregnant she has certain taboos to observe. She cannot, for example, sit long in the doorway; she cannot be present when another woman gives birth to a child, she may not use remains of food nor take food from another. She is not allowed to loosen her hair nor her husband to cut his. No fire can be taken from her hearth for the purpose of kindling other fires. The husband is not allowed to kill any animals. During the last months the husband will not leave his wife alone at nights, for it is during this period that she is plagued by bad dreams. The gods (dibata) or their emissaries visit the unborn children then and give them their future lots in life.

Childbirth. — When a child is to be born, all the men are required to leave the house and the patient is assisted by women only. The mother gives birth to the child in a sitting position.

After the child is born the placenta (called anggi, younger brother or sister) is watched for. A sharpened piece of bamboo is used to cut it. The placenta is buried in the space beneath the house and upon it is supposed to hang the welfare of the child, containing as it does a part of his soul (tondi).

At a difficult childbirth various kinds of sympathetic magic are used, such as untying knots, opening doors, etc. If the woman dies, her body is not given honorable burial but is thrown under the house and burnt. According to the Batak belief, such a woman committed a serious crime and her tondi (soul) no longer wished to remain with her.

After the child is born the woman is laid with her back to the fire and is kept warm for a couple of days. During this time the fire is taboo. In the southern Batak country, as in Atjeh, a steam bath is used. The mother and child are placed in a kind of oven for fifteen or twenty days, under which damp wood is placed.

The Karo and the Toba of Central Batakland have a custom called manuruhon api ni anduhur, "the bringing away from the fir of the turtle-dove". On the fourth or seventh day after the birth o the child, the mother takes the child on her left arm and a stick o burning wood from the fireplace in her right. She extinguishes th wood in the water and throws it into the shrubbery. Then she take a bath, washes the child, and carries it in a cloth back to the village

Names. — Sometimes a child is given a name on the day o which it is taken to the river for its first bath, but often the name giving is delayed and the boy is called by the Karo si tangat and th girl si boru. Usually, however, a name is given on the fourth o eighth day.

A boy is named by the mother, the mother's brother, or th mother's brother's wife. The father's sister names the girl. The fathe or mother give second and third children their names. All name naturally begin with the article "si", and the same names are give both sexes. It is taboo to name children after blood relatives, livin or dead. Rice kernels may be used as lots to determine lucky name or, again, the child may be allowed to choose its own name. In thi case the name-giver slowly pronounces a long list of names and i the child laughs after one of them it receives this name.

Each Batak actually has two names: a proper name and a si name. The sib name is always asked for at greetings. Thus Si Samp is the name of a Karo man who belongs to the sub-marga Buki Therefore the man is called Si Sampei Bukit.

Children of chiefs receive other names than commoners. A for instance, Si Radja Balas, "the chief". Si Anggur, "he who i everywhere known", Si Tagor, "fear or anxiety, such as thunde causes". Circumstances occurring at birth sometimes determine th choice of names as, for instance, Si Perang, "war". Sometimes anim names are given, without however this implying totemism, as in th case of two brothers, Si Gadja, "the elephant" and Si Beruwan "the bear". Opprobrious names may be given to ward off bad lucl such as Si Bengkala, a variety of monkey. Special names may b given to obtain good luck, as when a sick child is named Si Bola "round and fat".

If the parents had previously lost children, a child often is give no name at all. When he is older he either picks out a name fc himself or is called by a nickname which by custom becomes his re name. Examples of such nicknames are: Si Gopok, "fat", Si Keling, "dark as a Singhalese"; &c.

People change their names as often as they wish and for the same reason as is customary in Polynesia, sickness. If a child is sick the parents will change its name in the hope that it will recover. Notice of the change in name must be given to the people of the village.

Teknonomy. — The custom of teknonomy among the Bataks is unquestionably due to the rigid taboo on the utterance of personal names. Neumann believes that the avoidance of names is due to ghost fear, but Tideman writes that there is an adat against the mentioning of names enforced by law. In Timur it is forbidden, even when alone, to pronounce one's own name or that of one's elders loudly. If a man is heard infringing this law, criminal accusation can be brought to the radja by the witness.

Now while it would be highly improper for a child to mention the name of his parents or, as we shall see, for a subject to mention the name of his radja, there is no objection for a person of higher status to mention the name of a person of lower age or status. In the same way, it is improper for a person to mention the name of another of the same status. As a consequence the inconvenience of the situation can be avoided either by the use of relationship terms or by reference to the paternal or grand-paternal status of the individual in question.

A Batak will not tell his own name or that of his father; this would cause misfortune. If one asks a Batak his name he will not answer but will nudge one of his companions to make him give the information. Above all he will not give the name of his grandfather (ompu). If one asks a woman the name of her husband, she will not answer but, pointing to her child, she will reply: "Ama-ni-on, father of this one."

Ama-ni and Ompu-ni, father of and grandfather of so-and-so: all proper names begin this way among the Bataks. They call themselves after their sons and grandsons. The name Ompu-ni is the more honorable, and therefore every Batak longs to have it. Sometimes even young men acquire this title by the following method. A man may choose for his young son a grown-up woman and the son not as yet being old enough to take care of his manly duties, the father will intercede in the marriage and presently have "grand-children". When a man is father and has taken the title of Ama-ni, it would lead to war to call him by his own name.

Among the Toba the word goar means name. One never asks a person his name directly, however, by saying: ise goar, "What is your name?" Instead one says: ise pang-goar-an-mu, "What is the name of the child after whom you are called?" The man then answers for example: Si Dangol pang-goar-an-ku, "My name is Ama ni Dangol". A father and mother name themselves after their first child, and if it dies, after the following. If the first child is a girl and the second is a boy, the father calls himself after the son.

Not only is it forbidden to mention the name of superiors but their names remain taboo after they are dead. It may even be forbidden to make use of words which contain syllables which were part of the name of former radjas. This rule is here, as among certain tribes of North America and North Asia, the cause for changes in the language. Thus in Tanah Djawa, a district in Timur, it is forbidden to use any word which begins or ends in "hor". Formerly a radja called Horpanaluan lived there. One must therefore call karabau (horbo) si ranggas. One dare not use the common word tuhor for "buying" but boli, instead.

Treatment of children. — Children, in former times, were taught mainly by imitating their elders. Only those destined to become priest (datu) received a more formal education, especially in the arts of reading and writing. In Toba, however, all the boys and girls learn enough of the art of writing to exchange love-letters. These were written in native characters on pieces of bamboo one and a half inches in width and one-half to one feet in length.

Children are seldom punished when they are very young. A parent would have to be beside himself with rage before he slapped, cuffed, or dragged a child over the ground. As everywhere in Indonesia there is fear that the child might lose its tondi (soul). A young girl is seldom punished and then always by the mother, not the father. When a girl becomes grown up, she may be much more roughly treated, especially if she refuses to marry a man of the parents' choice, or follows a man against the wishes of the parent. Then she may be cursed, allowed to starve, or whipped with rods.

A girl who marries and runs away from her husband is treated still worse. If the girl persists in her determination to leave her husband the father must pay back the bride-price and the costs of the wedding. In order to make her change her mind the father may beat her with rods, drag her by the hair, or put her in the stocks.

Or again, he may bind her hands and put biting ants on her back. If the husband agrees to take the girl back — which he does by accepting a small present from the father — and the girl promises never to run away again, she is allowed her liberty and loaded down with presents. The punishments which may be inflicted by the father or seller of the girl are so severe that many girls have taken their lives rather than endured them. Often, if a girl threatens to take her life, a father will pay the fine even if he has to borrow the money. The suicide of a daughter would occasion much unfavorable gossip at the expense of the father.

Puberty ceremonies. — Puberty ceremonies are of little importance for either girls or boys in western Indonesia and are probably in the nature of survivals, as in Polynesia. In none of the accounts which I have read of western Indonesia, nor in my experience in Mentawei, is mention made of any restrictions placed on girls at the time of first or subsequent menstruation. The Toba Bataks call a menstruating woman dioro bulan (moon), and there is a folk belief that the moon is her lover.

One puberty ceremony for boys similar to that I have observed in Niue and Samoa is connected with the hair. The hair of a Batak boy cannot be cut before the canine teeth have appeared and then it cannot all be removed, but a lock must remain standing. This is done for fear of losing the soul (tondi).

Filing and blackening of teeth is common among the people of Indonesia. Wilken believes that filing is a substitute for knocking out of teeth as a puberty rite; and blackening of teeth, to indicate their loss, is a substitution for filing. In Oceania the knocking out of teeth at puberty is practiced in Australia, parts of Melanesia, among certain peoples of Celebes, and in Formosa. In Engano a woman has two of her incisors knocked out by her parents at the time of marriage, "in order to show that she is no longer free, but the property of another".

Among the Bataks the filing of teeth (kiku) takes place about the time of puberty or a couple of years earlier for boys, while the teeth of girls are filed when they reach approximately the age of seven. The mutilation is limited to the incisors. Boys have half the crown cut away with a fine file and girls have the entire crown removed. On the same day the mutilated teeth are rubbed with badja, a tar stuff made form the smoke of wood, to make them appear black. After

5*

the boys and girls have had their teeth filed they are considered grow up and are allowed to chew betel.

Among the southern Batak there are certain professional teet filers called baon ipon. Girls are operated on earlier than boys, fo it is believed that if they had already menstruated the filing operatio would cause sickness to the filer. The reason given for the operatio is that a person with unfiled teeth resembles a dog.

After a boy or girl has had his teeth filed he is robu (taboo for seven days or longer, at least until the pain stops and the wound heal. He is not allowed to appear in public or ask for sirih.

Circumcision is an ancient custom among the Bataks, as amon; many of the other primitive people of Indonesia, and is called batotal It is performed on boys in secret. The prepuce is split gradually b squeezing the upper part between two pieces of bamboo. It is no longe a puberty rite nor is it required for all males. Anyone, however, wh is not circumcised is not allowed to kill chickens. Girls are incisec

Among the southern Batak there are two methods of circum cision, an old one in which the prepuce is split and the Mohammeda: one in which it is cut off. Girls also are incised in this region. Th malims (Mohammedan preachers) perform the act on boys, but girl are still incised by women. The girls are operated on before th seventh year, the boys at puberty. A meal is given at the time of th circumcision to which the relatives are invited. The datu (Batak priest or malim who performs the operation is paid. Those operated o: are robu for seven days and cannot appear in public.

Divorce. — Nowhere does the form of social organization show influence in Indonesia more than in the laws of divorce. In a stric patrilineal society divorce can only be obtained at the will of th husband and then is of exceptional occurrence, since the husban would not wish to lose the bride-price. An exception to this rule i made in the case of adultery. Thus in Buru and Aru, if the wif commits adultery the man gets the bride-price refunded. In the sibles or bilateral families of Indonesia (Mentawei excepted) divorce i frequent, and where there is a bride-price the rule almost everywher holds that the bride-price must be paid back if the fault lies with th woman and not paid back if the fault lies with the man. The villag or family head checks too frequent divorces. Among people wit! matrilineal sibs, as the Minangkabau, there is no bride-price an(divorce is very frequent and can be obtained at will by either party

A difference also occurs between the patrilineal and matrilineal peoples of Indonesia regarding the disposition of the children upon the divorce of the parents. Among strictly patrilineal peoples, such as the Bataks and the natives of Nias, all the children remain with the father. An exception is furnished in the case of Buru where the woman sometimes is given a daughter as helper. Among sibless people the children are divided between the parents at divorce, and among matrilineal peoples they naturally remain with the mother.

Opinions are divided among the various authors regarding the possibility of divorce among the Bataks in former times. Joustra, the foremost authority on Batak adat, claims that the old adat knew no divorce and that in no case could the woman seek a divorce. In the same way Van Ophuijsen writes of the South Bataks that apart from very unusual circumstances a Batak marriage was for life. Both of these authors referred probably to the fact that it was almost impossible for a woman to obtain a divorce but, presumably, a man could always send his wife back to her people if he had grounds and was willing to lose the bride-price.

Willer wrote in 1846 of the Mandheling Bataks: "Neither a woman nor her relatives can demand a divorce, even if they are willing to pay back the bride-price. A woman however can request a divorce from a man upon the repayment of the bride-price or part of it. Impotence in the man gave the woman the right to separate from him or go to one of his relatives. The man can repudiate his wife and send her back to her people without recovering the bride-price. He can also repudiate her without sending her back, but in this case he is obliged to furnish her a separate dwelling, food, and clothing, and she must work for him."

Warreck states this for the Toba: "Properly speaking there can be no divorce after the bride-price has been paid. This completes the purchase transaction which afterwards cannot be cancelled. However, 1. a man may be insulted by his wife and send her home. Then he recovers the bride-price after she is sold again. He loses the cost of the wedding and is forced to make a considerable present to the relatives of the woman. 2. If the woman runs away, the man recovers the bride-price and the cost of the wedding. The relatives put the woman in the block."

Junghuhn says practically the same for the Toba in 1847, when their customs were as yet untouched by white influence: "Divorces seldom occur among the Bataks, but they may occur in connection with a special adat, called sei-sei. If the man wishes to drive away his wife nothing is said about the matter, for he has already paid for her. The wife in this case has nothing to get and the children go to the man. If, however, the woman wishes to separate from the man, then the adat sei-sei comes into force. By this adat the parents of the woman are obliged to give back the marriage price of six yards of cloth, slaughter a karabau, and give a feast. The man keeps the children. This makes divorce almost impossible for the woman."

Joustra has described the ceremony of divorce as it took place among the Karo as follows: "If a divorce takes place a public meal is given. This is given by the guilty party as a form of conciliation. If no conciliation follows, however, this meal becomes a method of loosening the bonds of matrimony. After the end of the meal, the custom of kah-kah bohan takes place, i. e., a bamboo-cooker is cut in two and thrown into the air, while the assembled people are told about the divorce. If the two halves fall down alike, either hollow or concave below, this is taken as an omen that conciliation is not excluded. Otherwise divorce is irrevocable."

Naturally a woman cannot divorce a man because of adultery, and a man is absolutely free, provided that he keeps away from married women. A woman can be made to pay for adultery with her life.

Position of women. — The position of women among the Bataks is perhaps the best illustration of the wide variation between the "patriarchate" in fact and in theory. Theoretically the Batak woman is bought and sold as a karabau or some inanimate piece of property over whom the owner has absolute rights and of whom he refers to as "that which I have bought". Being a piece of property herself, she has no right to own any possessions, not even her ornaments, clothing, and live stock (chickens), as among the patrilineal people of Nias. Writing from this viewpoint Neumann says: "Women are purchased and become the complete property of the men. If a woman is guilty of adultery, her husband can slay her. He is only obliged to furnish her with the most necessary things, as a house, clothing, and food. But even this latter she must obtain for herself, the husband only providing the field. The man can illtreat his wife, even treat her as a slave so that after his death she will be included in the property he leaves. The only restriction which the husband has to observe is that he is not allowed to sell his wife outright. Yet he is allowed to pawn er as a pledge for his debts. The greatest right that a woman has, nd her only right, is that her husband cannot withhold sexual inter-ourse from her."

Yet even Neumann does not depicture the position of the Batak oman as entirely in keeping with her status as a piece of merchan-ise. As we have seen, the younger women have the utmost freedom efore marriage, as is general among the bilaterally reckoning Indo-esians. In strict keeping with patrilineal reasoning the bride-price f a woman would suffer were she not a virgin before marriage. Thus a Nias girl who is not a virgin or a woman who is a widow sells t half price. Then, again, it is more often the woman who chooses er future husband than her parents, and the bride-price is of second-ry importance to the inclinations of the girl. Neumann is referring o this divergence in status between the unmarried and the married voman, between the house drudge and the social head of the house, vhen he says: "The lot of a Batak woman is a peculiar one. One 10ment she is the most abused, the next the most protected; now he is bent under the hard yoke of the adat and then, again, she ·ecomes arbiter in the circle of her house companions and nearest elations. On the one hand she is treated as a commodity for sale, n the other she not infrequently stands forth, adorned and jeweled."

The Bataks themselves do not take their own concept of woman s a purchasable commodity seriously, and, when they withhold part f the bride-price, they sometimes say: "She is no karabau that she nust be bought." Furthermore, while, theoretically, married women ave no redress from harsh treatment at the hands of their owners, ·ractically, the Batak women are as well protected from actual physi-al harm as their civilized sisters.

The adat does not see in women objects which one can treat .rbitrarily but the entire population is made responsible for the pro-ection of women. Wounding, shameless conduct, and insult to them .re heavily punished. They can, in fact, demand satisfaction for the east injury done them. In time of war the women are always spared. ˙he missiles of the enemy are not allowed to enter the bathing place ·f the women.

The ultimate position occupied by women in any society depends ·n their part in the economic life of the group and not upon real or ictitious rules of superiority, as implied by the terms "matriar-hate" and "patriarchate". The Bataks and the people of Minangkabau

are neighbors sharing the same civilization and economic conditions.
Hence whatever difference there may be in the legal status of th
women of the two groups, their actual position in the everyday activ
ities is very much the same. The wives of the radjas among th
Bataks had even one advantage denied the Minangkabau women —
they were able to have slaves perform the menial tasks of hom
and field.

Death. — The Bataks usually practice burial. Among the member
of the Sembiring sib of the Karo, however, cremation is the rule. Thi
sib is largely of Dravidian origin. Some years after cremation th
bones of the dead are dug up at the death feast, put in a miniatur
prow, and allowed to drift away.

The normal course of events among the Karo at time of a deat
is as follows. As soon as the death has occurred the loud mournin
cries of the women and children give notice of the fact, and the famil
members living in the village hasten to the place. The body, wrappe
in white cotton, is brought out of the house and laid on a stretcher
A female shaman dances herself into ecstasy and informs the sou
(begu) that he is now dead. The stretcher bearers then pick up thei
burden, carry it around the house an uneven number of times, an
then to the grave, under the accompaniment of the native orchestr
which plays funeral dirges.

When the burial place (pendawawen) is reached the corpse i
laid down and a shallow grave dug. Next the souls of the spectator
have to be driven out of the grave. This is accomplished by firin
muskets and thrashing around with leaves. Now the face of the dea
person is uncovered so that he can have his last glimpse of the su
(so that his soul will go into the next world with the sun?) an
then the burial takes place immediately.

The mourners leave some food and drink by the grave whil
they themselves return to the village, take a bath, and then partak
of food in the death house. Usually the ghost of the dead is summone
that same night to possess a shaman. From this time on communi
cation is available with the deceased.

Bodies of very prominent people are kept for a long time in th
village and sometimes they are not buried at all. In the latter cas
the body is placed in a chest formed by a hollowed out tree trun
and fitted with a cover. Sometimes the chest is boat-shaped. A
opening in the lower portion of the chest allows the fluids to escap

Jsually the casket is not placed in the grave, but is kept above round in a fenced enclosure called kubur.

In many cases a second mourning ceremony takes place after he flesh has decayed from the bones. This second ceremony has the urpose of sending the soul to the land of the dead. Amid the clanging f the orchestra what is left of the body is burnt (pilaspilasi, literally o beautify), and the skull is decorated and set up in the skull house.

Common people have their bodies exposed on platforms and very oung children are either buried under the house, or immediately urned. It is feared that the priest will make use of their bodies in he preparation of the magical substance "pukpuk".

Among the Toba, cremation is unknown and the bodies are either uried, or (in the case of chiefs) preserved with salt and camphor and laced in wooden chests or huge stone sarcophaguses. These stone ombs often are elaborately carved with phallic figures of men and omen. Nowhere else in Sumatra other than Nias do we find traces f phallic worship.

As among the Karo, about a year after the death of an important hief a second mourning ceremony is held and the bones are removed om the coffin. The shamans are possessed by the ghosts of the ead, and the eldest of these take the opportunity to tell their des- endants that from now on they will become nature spirits (sambaon) nd inhabit neighboring woods, mountains, and springs. They direct he people to bring sacrifices to these places. The feast for the dead sts a week, but it may be extended from three months to an entire ear. The invited guests are obliged to bring food to the feast. In mes of disaster, as in epidemics and famines, the bones of the dead re taken out and fed, so that they (the ancestors) cease demanding uman lives. This feast lasts but a day and food is placed between he jaws of the skulls, or, if these are not to be found, it is rubbed n the other skeletal remains. The next morning, amidst the beating f drums, the bones are replaced in their graves or containers.

The use of puppets (si galegale) is found only among the Toba, nd then only in connection with mortuary customs at the death of rich man who leaves no male descendants. A wooden doll is made the likeness of the deceased and dressed in his clothing. The doll equipped with strings and is made to dance with the mourners the market place. Finally the doll is stripped of its clothing and ecorations and, amid the firing of musketry, thrown over the city walls. Hence the Batak proverb, "Rich for a moment like a puppet" This drama is symbolic of the fate of a rich man who leaves n descendants to cater to his ghost in the afterworld.

Masks are used in connection with burial customs by the Timu Bataks. These masks are preserved in special buildings called rumah rumah which also house the bones of former radjas and their families At the death feast of important people a masked performance i enacted by two men. The one has a large wooden mask before hi face, the other wears a variety of box work on his head in th form of the movable head of the hornbill bird. The two men perforr all sorts of comical antics. Joustra believes it probable that formerl two slaves were utilized for the purpose of the play, and during it performance one was seized, killed, and buried with his master.

The Timur Bataks are the only people of Sumatra making us of masks; artifacts which unquestionably originally were connecte with spirit impersonation and secret societies. Among the Kajar Dayaks of Central Borneo masked dances are held at harvest festival and the masked figures are said to represent spirits. Among th Toradja of Central Celebes masked images were used at the deat feast in representation of the dead. It is not until we arrive at Dutc New Guinea, however, that we find masked spirit impersonators i actual secret societies.

It may be suggested that the negroid races while passing throug Indonesia left traces of their tribal initiations and secret societie in the form of puberty mutilations, the bull-roarer, and the maske representation of spirits. Actual tribal initiation is found in the Kakea cult of Ceram. On the other hand, the Indonesians themselves ma have brought tribal initiations and secret societies from the mainlan and have lost the completeness of the traits through contact wit Hindu civilization.

Religion.

Introduction. — The Bataks and the people of Nias have derive practically all of their more advanced forms of religious beliefs fro India, for the most part in post-Hindu times. Certain of these high forms of beliefs, cults, and philosophies have traversed Indones and have passed into Polynesia, and perhaps even, as some ethn logists believe, into the New World. Some of the more striking these Hindu layers of Batak religion include the ideas of creators an e creation, the stratification of the heavens, the raising of the eavens, the fate of the souls of the dead, augury, animal sacrifice, nd true shamanism. The Bataks were more directly affected than the eople of Nias by Hinduism, for true shamanism is lacking in Nias lthough found among the Bataks, many Indonesian peoples and all f the Melanesians and Polynesians. Mentawei not only lacks namanism, but also the idea of higher gods and the creation. Augury nd animal sacrifice, however, are found in Mentawei.

Since the Batak religion contains so many Old World aits which were destined to work their way across the Pacific, a roper understanding of this religion is essential for students of ceanic cultures.

The religious beliefs of the Bataks may be divided into three ain sections.

1. Cosmology and cosmogony. The world of the gods.
2. The native concept of the soul.
3. Beliefs concerning ghosts, demons and ancestors.

Cosmology and cosmogony. — The Bataks like the Brahmans ivide the world into three sections. The upper world has seven pheres and is the home of the gods and their families. The middle orld belongs to man. The underworld is the home of the dead, the hosts, and the demons. The division is not perfect, for there are many hosts in the middle world and the renowned dead ascend to heaven.

Formerly heaven was nearer the earth, and there was regular ommunication between gods and the human beings. But human ride destroyed the road to the upper world. Since the interruption f direct communication the gods lost interest in mankind, and man irns to them only in hour of need.

In truth, since the time when direct communication with Hindu urces was broken, the people ceased their customary worship of e higher gods (debata). The knowledge of these Hindu divinities s well as the few forms of sacrifices and prayers in their honor came the possession of the priests (datu).

The High God of the Bataks is *Mula djadi na bolon,* the great ginner of being, or "He who has his beginning in himself". This d is a personal god, according to Batak concept, and not a bare rinciple. He lives in the highest of the heavens. He is an otiose ity who does not concern himself about the affairs of this earth d receives from it no honor or sacrifice. Yet to this High God are

attributed immortality and omnipotence, and he is the actual creato
of everything including the gods themselves. The Bataks have n
traditions concerning the creation of the universe, but they hav
traditions concerning the origin of the gods.

The Bataks conceive of the High God as an anthropomorphi
figure who possessed a fabulous blue chicken, manuk-manuk, in plac
of a wife. This chicken layed three extraordinarily large eggs ou
of which the three actual world gods came, namely: *Batara Guru*
Soripata and *Mangalabulan*. These three gods live one level lowe
in the heavens than the High God, are always worshipped as
trinity at the sacrifice, and, in fact, are called *Debata na tolu* (th
three gods). However *Batara Guru* is regarded as the creator of th
middle world (the earth), and is considered the most powerful c
the trinity. *Batara Guru* also is considered a culture hero who taugl
the people arts and customs. *Mangalabulan* is considered bot
propitious and cruel, for although he blesses and helps, he is at th
same time the patron of thieves and robbers.

Ködding lists the more important of the second and third ran
Toba gods. They live a bit lower in the heavens then the principa
deities.

1. Datu hasi hasi. The priest (datu) especially implores the bless
   ings of this god, at his magical workings.
2. Radja moget pinajungan, the doorkeeper of the heavens.
3. Radja Indainda. He lives in the clouds above the visible heaven:
   in the first level of the heavens. There he is ruler and thunde
   god. He also is messenger and spy of the gods.
4. Radja Guru. He is the huntsman of the gods. He catches huma
   souls by means of his dogs Soridaudau and Auto Porburu. Thes
   dogs can be heard in the rustling of the air which precedes
   storm. When the souls of people are caught the people then
   selves suddenly die.

Gods and spirits of lower rank, and in part indigenous, also a
worshipped. These include house gods (debata idup), earth spiri
(boraspati ni tano), and water spirits (boru saniang naga).

The Bataks make no idols or representation of their gods othe
than the wooden dolls called debata idup (live gods). These god
are supplicated by childless couples. They are in form male an
female. The husband takes the male doll, feeds it, and treats it a
a child, and the wife the female.

The Bataks have as their principal evil divinity the world serpent Naga Padoha. This god lives in the underworld. The creation concept of the Bataks is limited to the creation of the middle world (the earth) upon the primordial sea. It happened in this manner:

Boru deak pordjar (all knowing), daughter of the god Batara Guru, leaped from the upper world into the limitless sea because of the unwished for courtship of the god Mangalabulan. A swallow informed Batara Guru of the plight of his daughter, and he sent back with the swallow a handful of earth. This handful of earth was set down upon the sea, and growing larger and larger became the earth. As the earth commenced growing it took the light away from Naga Padoha, who being vexed, gave it a shove and allowed it to float off on the waters. Batara Guru, however, sent new earth and also a powerful hero to combat the serpent. The hero sank his sword up to the hilt in the serpent and forced him into an iron block. Naga Padoha now had less room in which to wiggle. His early squirmings, however, caused mountains and valleys to be formed, and at the present day cause earthquakes.

After Batara Guru had created the new earth he scattered upon it all kinds of seeds and created all varieties of animals. Then the hero again appeared as the companion of Boru deak parudjar, and from her begot sons and daughters, the first people. He also, however, married a demon (begu) daughter, begot begu children by her, and finally was killed by her curse. The hero was taken up by the debata and placed in the moon. His wife, Boru deak parudjar, followed him to the moon.

The Bataks believe in the ultimate destruction of the earth, for in the end Naga will make his way loose and destroy the middle world.

Ködding has pointed out the identities between Batak and Hindu mythologies. In the Hindu account, Manu is the first man and like-wise a world creator. Krishna is killed by the curse of a woman and is reincarnated with Vishna, or creates a heaven for himself. Deak Pordjar, the all-knowing, reminds one of Brahman's wife, Sarasvati, the patroness of science and art.

The relationship of the principal gods to Brahmanism is clear. The word "debata" itself is Sanskrit. In Mala djadi na bolon we find Brahma personified as Svayambhu, "he who exists through himself". The golden world egg, in which, or out of which, Svayambhu came as the god Brahma, and as such created the world and the gods, is converted in the Batak myth into three eggs from which the gods arise. The speculative element of Brahmanism is omitted, and the earth rather than the universe is created. The chicken is an afterthought in the Batak legend; there are eggs, and the eggs must have been laid.

The trinity of gods on the second level of heaven likewise are Hindu. The names of the first two are Sanskrit in origin. Batara Guru, like Śiva, is the patron of teachers. Among both peoples they are leaders of the gods and world creators. Soripata is Vishnu who had as a second name Srîpati, husband of Śrî. Both Soripata and Vishnu are blessing, sustaining gods. The third god of the trinity Mangalabulan is of doubtful origin. Ködding believes that the word mangala is derived from bala (Sanskrit wala) meaning companion. Bulan means moon in Batak. If this be true, the god is a moon companion, or lord of the moon. Śiva also had the moon in his possession, and was called lord of the moon. At any rate the dual natures of both gods are in close agreement. The Linga worship which in India is joined to the Śiva cult, is unknown among the Bataks except for tomb engravings.

The soul concept. — Warneck, the most noted authority on Batak religion, defines the word "tondi" in his dictionary as "the spirit the soul of man, his individuality. The tondi originates while the person is still in the body of his mother, and determines at this time his future lot. It exists near the body, which it sometimes leaves This makes the person sick. Therefore one sacrifices to one's tondi and tries to keep it in good humor".

The soul concept in Indonesia is the important factor in religion while the idea of mana, or supernatural power, is almost absent. Thus the word for soul is built into just those compound words where the Melanesians and Polynesians would invoke the idea of mana. For example, the Toba word for fate is "portondion" and the word for luck "portondion na denggan". A trace, however, of the idea of mana is found in the Toba word "sahala". While all people have tondi the power of the various tondi differs. Only the tondi of prominent people have sahala. Good fortune is the basis of all sahala.

The Bataks have received from the Hindus a fatalistic concept of life. Longevity and the fortunes of the unborn child depend entirely upon the demands which the tondi makes before birth. In the topmost heaven in the home of the creator exists the tree of life alled Djambubarus. On each leaf of this tree God has written a word, such as fruitfulness, wealth, &c. Every tondi must beg one of these eaves before departing for the middle world.

The fatalistic attitude of the Bataks, like that of the ancient Greeks, is in direct contradiction to cult procedure. Still when ordinary cult sacrifices and prayer fail, the priests have an excuse. All misortune is predestined and human effort is of no avail. Fatalism in he Orient, as well as its manifestations among peoples exposed to Oriental influence, is a late superimposition on the naive concept of cult efficacy.

While men, animals, and plants have souls, other objects (with he exception of rice, iron, and certain useful instruments) have not. Thus the Bataks place the same distinction as did the classical religions between the animate and the inanimate. Contrary to the ideas of most Indonesians the ordinary Batak believe that a person has but one tondi, and that it is this same tondi which leaves the body temporarily at fright, dreams or sickness, and permanently at death. Some priests teach that people have seven tondi, but this is but scholastic metaphysics.

The entire religious life of the Batak is one of self-seeking; not with an idea of improving one's lot in the next world, but of improving one's lot here and now. This is done by nursing one's tondi. Warneck writes that "the fight with the tondi and around the tondi" is the keynote of animistic (Batak) religion. The well being of a man depends on his keeping his own tondi in good humor; on increasing its efficacy by nourishing it with the tondi of other people (cannibalism), plants, and objects; and on guarding it from other self-seeking tondi's. A person is very intimate with his tondi, he prays to it and curses it. In case of sickness he sacrifices to it, and when frightened he will scatter rice along the ground, make a chuckling sound as if summoning chickens, and appeal for the return of his soul. The tondi enters and leaves the body via the fontanel.

Whether or not the tondi becomes the begu (ghost) after the death of the owner is a moot point among the missionaries in Batakland. Meerwaldt writes that every Toba to whom he placed the question "what is a begu?" answered "tondi ni na mati do i" (a soul which has died). On the other hand Warneck claims that among the Toba the soul and the ghost have nothing to do with one another. For the sake of those readers who desire definite information on this

point, I recommend the following Karo proverb indicating the manne
in which the body returns into its elements.

> The tondi becomes begu,
> The hair becomes idjuk (roofing material),
> The flesh becomes earth,
> The bones become stones,
> The blood becomes water,
> The breath becomes wind.

The Afterlife. — The Batak explain death by stating that a beg
has stolen the tondi of a person. If a man dies in his prime a fema
begu has taken him as husband, if an attractive woman dies a ma
begu. If, however, one dies in battle then it is not a begu, bu
judgement of the gods which has felled the man.

The Batak conception of after life is somewhat vague and n
very different from the present one. All occupations are carried o
as on earth, only in the night and not in the daytime.

The tondi and the begu are very different from one another. Th
tondi, explain the Bataks, is like a man who clings fast to his hous
as long as he lives in order to insure himself sufficient food. Th
begu however, is like someone who wanders around without food o
house. He therefore approaches human beings (through a medium
and demands sacrifice.

The dead are half friend, half enemy. They are considere
jealous of the living, envious of their good fortune. They especiall
hate any innovation, any departure from the adat as they knew i
They (through the words of their mediums) are a powerful for
towards conservatism.

A Batak family consists of both the living and the dead, an
the fortunes of the living depend on the will of the dead, the positio
of the dead in the next world on the wealth and sacrifice of th
living in this world. The dead are given feasts by their descendan
and in this way are made nature spirits (sambaon); or, if the de
cendants are numerous and wealthy enough, they again dig up th
bones of their ancestors, feast them, and make them sumangot.
sumangot is almost on the same rank as a god (debata).

The Shaman and Priest. — The Bataks, as already stated, hav
true shamanism. According to G. A. Wilken, "The conjuring o
spirits into certain people — in order to get the words of the spiri
from these people, — is shamanism, while the person is called

shaman". The shaman among the Bataks is called "si baso" which means "the word". Among the northern Bataks the shaman was almost always a woman, and the office often descended within the family.

Shamanism is lacking in the islands west of Sumatra where the more primitive form of medium still exists, the seer.

The seer is to be found among all primitive peoples who lack shamanism. The essentials of the seer are the obtaining of a vision and, with the vision, a guardian spirit or spirits. The seer is then able to communicate with these spirits, who aid him in curing. In the case of the true shaman the spirits speak *through* the shaman, in the case of the seer the spirits speak *to* the shaman. Both the shaman and the seer are in special rapport with the spirit world, both are especially "elected" by the spirits. A refusal frequently results in death. The shaman receives his election by being possessed, the seer through a vision, which is either sought for or comes involuntarily.

No Batak ever voluntarily becomes a shaman. Likewise there is no special instruction for this profession, but when the proper shaman is dead or delayed the ghost has to pick out a new medium. The ghost enters this person and music is played until the desired result is obtained.

Two varieties of drums, the gondang and the gordang, are used to summon the spirits, and incense is burnt the while. Each spirit has his own melody, to which the shaman dances with wild grotesque movements around the fire. Each spirit likewise has his own color of clothing, and if the shaman wishes to summon more than one ghost, she must wear several colors of clothing.

When the ghost has descended into the medium he displaces her ondi. The music serves partly the purpose of driving the tondi from the shaman, partly to allure the ghost. When the shaman now speaks it is no longer her voice which is heard, but that of the ghost. The language spoken has to be interpreted, as it is ghost language.

The head of the family to which the ghost belongs now asks the name of the particular begu, and the begu asks why he is summoned. Then both sides make known their desires, and an agreement is arrived at. For example, the begu will help relieve family sickness in return for proper sacrifice.

The Batak priest is called the datu. Among primitive peoples the seers and shamans include both sexes, but the priests are practically always men, as is the Batak datu.

It is only those primitive peoples who have been greatly exposed to the influence of higher religions who have a priesthood; elsewhere all of the older men are the custodians of the sacred traditions and rituals, and all are capable of performing the sacrificial ceremonies. The Bataks have no college of priests, nor in fact are the datu priests in the strictest sense of the word, since all adult Bataks perform sacrifices. Still the datu are priests in so far as they hand down to one another the main part of the Hindu esoteric ritual and learning. Naturally before the days of Hindu influence the Bataks had neither shamans nor priests. The datu, in fact, show clearly that they originally were the seers and healers of the people.

After the chief, the datu has the highest standing in the village. Many chiefs also function as datu, in this way increasing their prestige. The duties of the datu are many. In first place he is a physician, and as such has to treat the sick and protect the healthy from sickness.

Sickness is directly determined by "soul loss", but the contributing cause may be the secret influence of a begu, the capriciousness of the patient's tondi, or the power of a hostile magician. The datu therefore must be versed in "white magic". He functions as priest only at a big feast, when it is important to perform the ritual with exactitude. The datu is the sole oracle, soothsayer and clairvoyant. He is also the weather-maker. The people are able to make and drive away rain by magical means, but the datu alone can provide permanent freedom from storms. The datu not only is conversant with "white magic" but also controls the "black" art, and is the sorcerer.

Finally, it is the duty of the datu to have occult knowledge handed down entire from generation to generation. Oral tradition is not deemed sufficient for this purpose, so the first thing a pupil in magic has to learn is the art of writing. The magic books and the calendar are written down by the pupil at the dictation of the datu; the paper bark of a forest tree, a brush, and native ink, serve as writing materials. The books contain oracles, prayers, and exorcisms.

The course of studies for a pupil of magic involves great difficulties and pecuniary sacrifice. The man who can afford it, and who wishes his son to become a datu, invites the chosen teacher to a feast, at which the prospective student ceremonially feeds the master. After this the pupil must board the datu, and frequently his entire family, in order to receive instruction. He must first learn the nineteen

hief signs of the Batak alphabet, next the vowel signs, and finally
ctual reading. Then only follows instruction in the magic art.

Since all beginning is difficult, the tondi of the pupil reacts
gainst the reception of the higher science of reading. In order to
emedy this condition, the teacher now takes energetic measures. He
oes to a river with the pupil. There he stuffs a handful of rice meal
nto the novice's mouth, and ducks him under the water until he
as swallowed the rice. This is done seven times. The datu then
nakes a food offering to the ancestors and the gods, praying that
is pupil will acquire more wisdom and that the instruction will
nter into him. The pupil then is taken back to the village, and his
ondi rewarded with food.

If the pupil still has difficulty in learning the rudiments of the
cience, the datu makes a second and last attempt to cure his stupidity.
he two go at night to a mountain on whose peak the tribal ancestor
bides. There, uttering a spell, the datu recounts the dullness of his
upil over a pot filled with magical implements. He then places the
ot on the swaying point of a bamboo shaft, this being done in order
hat the pupil's stupidity shall escape into the wind. On the return
f the two men into the village, the datu again gives the elders hope
or a successful completion of the course of studies, but only after
ertain necessary presents have been handed over. If, however, this
econd ordeal also fails, the datu gives up the course of instruction.

Winkler, to whom we are indebted for this description of the
raining and duties of the Batak datu, believes these ordeals to be
survival of the initiation of shamans, the ducking representing a
ymbolic death, while the nocturnal visit to the mountain top signifies
he formal communication of the apprentice with the spirits during
is course of training. I myself can see in the ducking of the candidate
othing more than the customary form of the Batak ordeal. This is
common Indonesian test, and the swallowing of dry rice a specific
3atak ordeal. It is probable, however, that the trip to the ancestral
nountain top is a survival of the vision quest of the former Batak seer.

The datu is summoned for all public offerings, which he con-
lucts through the summoning of such ghosts and spirits as are
lesired. He does this in a secret language. After this he moves to
he scaffolding where the sacrifice is to be made and offers it up
mid the burning of petroleum. The offering, which consists of cooked
ice, the heart of an animal, sirih and palm wine, is thrown into the

6*

air by the datu. In the meanwhile the officers, armed with sticks an
weapons, run around the place as if possessed, driving away the ev
ghosts who would make the sacrifice fruitless. This ends the sacrific

Sickness, as before noted, is ascribed to soul loss. Nevertheles
the Bataks are aware that certain forms of sickness are due to natura
causes and treat these forms of disease with proper herbs. Ofte
sickness is ascribed to carelessness in the ancestral cult, or to othe
sins. An epidemic, or any great disaster, is called sumbang by th
Karo, that is, incest. Idols of wood, armed with spears and lance
are sometimes placed before the entrances of villages to keep awa
the begu who cause the epidemics by stealing the souls of the inmate

In the case of a mysterious ailment, if the patient is able t
pay for a cure, a datu often is summoned to recover the lost sou
The datu himself makes various kinds of mysterious movements t
drive away the surrounding begu. In the meanwhile a crowd of th
younger relatives go to a place where it is thought that a hosti
being is keeping the abducted soul prisoner, and beg for its return
Then they return and the datu divines by rice kernels as to whethe
or not they have brought the soul back with them. If they hav
an even number they are reassured, but if the number is odd th
lamentations begin at once. This is done so that the sick perso
might know how he will be cried over after he is dead.

The Toba make use of the sweat-bath as a means of exorcisn
For the sweat-bath (mortup, manajas), the fruit and leaves of variou
kinds of citrus are taken and mixed with assorted herbs in an earthe
pot, which is placed between the outstretched legs of the patien
and is covered by a number of blankets, so that the steam will go ove
the entire body. This form of sweat-bath is used for cases of feve
rheumatism, skin disease, and for the bite of a mad dog. In mar
of the regions of Toba, a complicated form of sweat-bath is used t
cure mental ailments of various kinds. It is supposed to expel th
spirit which causes the disease. Steam is lead into a tent by a clay
covered bamboo pipe. The patient creeps into the tent and allow
himself to be enveloped by the steam.

Usually, in the case of spirit intrusion, the datu is summone
to expel the begu from the patient. This can be done by the use o
leaves, roots, or bark, when accompanied by the proper formula. Ofte
the evil spirit is transferred to some animal, such as a chicken. Aft
this has been done the chicken is killed and the spirit rendered harmles

The datu, as before stated, is a poisoner as well as a healer. While witchcraft is not so prominent a feature of the higher primitive civilizations as it is of the lower, still the Bataks are well known for their skill in mixing deadly potions. I have heard it stated by a member of the German missionary society that one of their early teachers was poisoned in Batakland by eating the fruit from a tree which had been tampered with by a hostile datu.

Unlike the Mentawei Islanders who poisoned through the credulity of their victims, the datu's used real poisons, both animal and plant. As, for example, the poisonous hairs of the bear caterpillar, the liver and sting of poisonous sea fishes, the poisons of snakes and centipedes, poisonous mushrooms, the corroding sap of different trees and herbs, and all kinds of poisonous plants. Arsenic and rat poison furnished a new addition obtainable by trade. The mushroom was considered the most deadly of this array, and while for the others the datu had antidotes, for this there was none. Some poisons resulted in instant death, others in death only after days or weeks, while still others caused a long period of invalidism.

For all healing one says "mortondi do", they have tondi. For all poisons and poisonous preparations and magical means, one says "morbegu do" they have begu. So the poisonous mushroom is classified under the saying "dan ni begu" (mushroom of begu).

Naturally the Bataks use credulity to a large extent as an aid in poisoning. All manner of symbolic action is gone through at the time of mixing lethal preparations. The way in which one chops, pounds, roasts, dissolves, or buries and allows the magic to rot, is imitative of the manner in which the enemy will be destroyed. In the same manner in which one bores through a large toad with a glowing iron, so will the victim be struck with disease.

Naturally the roasting and charring of the poisons weaken or destroy their deadly qualities, but according to the animistic ideas of the Bataks they are rendered more deadly through the process.

Poison named "bisa" is applied externally to the victim, while that called "rasun" is mixed with food or palm wine. It is not even necessary, however, to bring the poison into contact with the person. It is sufficient to bring it into his neighborhood, to his bathing place, or place it under his house. Gangrene and malignant tumors may thus be caused by working from a distance.

Sympathetic magic also is used. The datu obtains a hair of his

chosen victim, or a piece of his chewed betel-nut, a piece torn fror
his clothing, or some earth on which his foot has pressed or hi
shadow fallen. These exuviae are then mixed with the poison. On
the datu may on some propitious occasion, such as at a crowdel
market, measure with a stick the length of the body of his enemy
But it is sufficient for the datu if he only know the *name* of hi
victim. Then he initials the name on a piece of bamboo bark, scrape
the writing off again with his knife, and mixes the peelings witl
the poison.

Finally, the datu is indispensable in time of war, for a conflic
cannot be started without his advice. He must determine a propitiou
time for battle. Sometimes his knowledge, his sorcery books and tables
are not enough. He then consults the pangulubalang, the villag
guardian spirit.

Magic staff. — Every Batak guru must own a magic staf
(tunggal panaluan). This is a stick carved with ancestral figure
and with a hole in the center in which the magical substance pang
ulubalang is placed.

The magic staff is used by the datu to produce rain and t
protect his village against enemies. The spirit of the pangulubalan;
is supposed to combat the hostile pangulubalang's. The datu is abl
to communicate personally with the spirit of the pangulubalang.

The making of a good magical staff takes many months of time
A new one usually is made when a subdivision of a sib parts from it
parent sib and wishes to have a magical staff of its own. The makin;
of such a staff costs much money, as many sacrifices are necessar;
during the progress of the work. According to the legend accountin;
for the origin of magic staffs, each has to be made from the wood o
a special tree.

The Bataks believe that it is a great misfortune to give birth t
twins, and in former days one of the twins was usually put to death
It is a still greater misfortune if the twins are of opposite sex, for then
if they have not already committed incest in the womb, they wil
certainly do so later on in life. Once twins of opposite sex were born
were allowed to live, and did commit incest. As punishment they wer
turned into wood while climbing a tree. Three datu's, one after th
other, were turned to wood on the tree while trying to rescue the twins

The first magic staff was made from the wood of the tree on which
the twins and the datu's had died. The human and animal figures or

ll staffs are said to represent the datu's and the twins, and all are made from the same variety of tree as used in the first staff. Because f the initial wrath of the gods, this wood is especially potent to frighten the enemy in time of war and to produce rain.

Van Ophuijsen, on the other hand, believes that the figures on the ticks represent marriage between heaven and earth, and that the origin of the sticks is in India, where droughts are common. The subject is still in the process of study. The idea of marriage between Father Sky and Mother Earth is Indian, and reoccurs again in eastern Indonesia and Polynesia, although it is lacking in western Indonesia.

The pangulubalang, or spirit within the stick, appears to be a folk-belief of Indian origin. According to Crooke, in northern India a magical substance called momiai is claimed to be distilled from the life juices of a small boy. The medicine thus made is used for healing and renders the owner invulnerable.

The Batak datu must steal a child from a hostile village in order to obtain a pangulubalang. When the chief and the datu have recognized the necessity of the undertaking, the datu consults his calendar and selects a propitious day for the expedition. At the appointed time the warriors assemble. They are entertained and fed in order to strengthen their tondi for the difficult undertaking, their wages being paid beforehand. They set out that same evening. A child is kidnapped either from a field hut or from the hostile village itself. Muffling its cries with a cloth they bring it back to the village sopo (communal house), where it is held prisoner and fed weeks and even months with the best of foods, including gold-colored rice, spiced meat, sour fish, and especially the liver of all kinds of house animals, apes, and other game animals. A "sahan", a buffalo horn with a hole in its end, is used to give the child palm wine. In this manner the tondi of the child is made willing and ready for everything that will be demanded from it. Three or four years is considered the best age for a child to be used in the preparation of the pangulubalang, for such a child is old enough to answer the questions put to it, but young enough to be unsuspecting.

When the tondi of the child has been properly propitiated, the datu says to it, "I am going to send you to destroy my enemy. Wherever I send you, there must you go. You must never, however, reveal either your or my name to anyone, nor the manner of your death." If the child refuses to obey, it continues to be well taken care of until such

time as it is ready to accede to anything asked of it. The child is led
blindfolded out of the village on a day reckoned favorable by the datu.
After placing it in a ditch with earth around it so that only the head
remains above ground, the datu asks once more, "Will you allow
yourself to be sent by me?" If the child answers, "Yes", the datu puts
some food into its mouth and speaks to it kindly, saying, "Here, take
this special meat, take this sour rice, take this ginger, take this roasted
rice kernel, take this palm wine and be obedient." Unsuspectingly the
child answers, "I ma tutu", (Yes, certainly). The datu says, "Open
your mouth, so that I can give you something more." The child obeys
and receives in his mouth the point of the drinking horn from which
he has been accustomed to drink palm wine. Boiling lead is im
mediately poured into the child's mouth, and he dies a quick but
painful death. The vow, however, which the child has taken with his
last words binds his tondi after death. The operation has succeeded
and the village has obtained in the ghost world a willing and obedient
ally for the fight against the enemy.

Since the ghost of the child remains in contact with its body, the
magical substance, pupuk, can be prepared from this. The body is
dismembered, parts are charred with other magical ingredients, and
the whole filtered into a pot. The pupuk is divided among the datu of
the sub-sibs and is used to besoul, or make potent, all images and idols
from which magical power is desired. The magic staff is one of the
most important vehicles for the pupuk.

Sacrifice and prayer. — A religion, in its simplest terms, consists
of a belief in spirits, actions which are appropriate to such a belief
and the emotions which accompany these actions. The belief in spirits
is customarily termed animism, while the actions are labelled the cult
Peoples who are above the most primitive stage of civilization, but who
as yet have not been converted to one of the "higher" religions, have
the sacrifice as the mainstay of their cult. Thus the Bataks call their
own heathen "sipele begu", people who sacrifice to the begu.

The Batak sacrifice clearly shows its Hindu origin, and in the
Hoda Debata, the horse sacrifice, we find in a slightly altered form
the Hindu horse sacrifice.

Kodding believes that the sacrificial system of the Bataks must
have been borrowed in either pre-Brahman times, or else at the earliest
Brahmanistic period. Thus sacrifices are performed by the house
father, and the Bataks lack idols, temples, a caste system and a real

riesthood. However, since much of the Hinduism of the Bataks
oubtlessly came by way of the empires of Crivijaya and Madjapahit
Toba is listed as a dependency or tribute payer of the later empire),
his point is not well taken. The Hindu empires of Sumatra and Java
ad these traits, as do the people of Bali to-day. The primitive Bataks,
owever, merely borrowed what could be adapted, with a certain
mount of alteration, to their own systems. A caste system among the
emocratic Bataks would have been almost as out of place as it would
ave been among the Crow Indians of Montana.

The philosophy of the sacrifice among the Bataks is a simple one.
he ancestral cult furnishes the continuation of the family soul cult.
ne informs the departed concerning all important family matters, one
ill relies on their aid and expects their blessing, since one remains a
ember of the great family, the living and the dead. The forefathers
ho live in the next world have a higher power to help or to injure
an have their living descendants. It is therefore of the greatest
mportance that this power be used correctly to increase the prosperity
the group and to injure all enemies. When the dead are not directly
eeded they are sedulously avoided.

Almost any member of the family may perform the simple sacri-
cial cult. In giving offerings for a deceased father or grandfather
e sisters and daughters alone are excluded. However, at great
cestral sacrifices the oldest member of the family performs the
iestly office. Even women may sacrifice under special conditions,
for example widows and childless women. The women sacrifice
side the house, they must be competent to recite the prayers without
istake, and the sacrifices are intended for near family relatives. It is
ly at great sib sacrifices, at the time of public calamity or when some
rge undertaking is at stake, that the datu, chief, or some professional
crificer is called upon to perform the office.

Sacrifices are made to souls, ghosts and demons, and to the gods.
he fact has already been mentioned that every Batak sacrifices to
s own soul. Otherwise the temperamental tondi would not yield to the
st interests of the owner, would refuse goods given to its master, or
ight even leave its sheltering body entirely. Furthermore one sacri-
es to the tondi of all living relatives. The tondi of the house animals
e not sacrificed to, since they themselves are used in offerings, but
angerous wild animals, such as crocodiles and tigers, receive sacri-
es lest they harm people. Plants, such as rice and coconut trees,

receive offerings to encourage their growth. The more useful o inanimate objects are propitiated. The fisherman sacrifices to hi canoe, the hunter to his gun, and the carpenter to his work tools. Eve the family house receives offerings, via the hearth, after the birth c a son. The house spirit itself is conceived of as being incorporated i the friendly little house lizards, which are spared and fed by all.

The souls of the dead (whether they are simple begu or have bee turned into sumangot) are more important for the living than the soul of the living. The dead are especially sacrificed to at the time of ba dreams, sickness, or misfortune. The sib as a whole sacrifices to th deified ancestors, the sumangot.

Among the nature spirits sacrificed to by the Toba are the wate spirits (saniang naga), the earth spirit (boraspati, incorporated in th lizard), rain spirits (boru deak porudjar, also the creator of th earth), and wind spirits. There also are nature spirits in streams wells, whirlpools, trees, mountains and waterfalls, who everywhe threaten human beings. Occasionally sacrifices are made to the ligh ning, clouds, stars and the new moon. While both the sun and moo are spoken of as being alive in the Batak stories, there is no trace c sun or fire worship.

While special sacrifices to the higher gods are a rarity they ar summoned at many other sacrifices and invited to eat. It is peculiarity of the Bataks that besides the special spirit summoned t receive offering, many others are invited for fear of giving offenc

The usual place of sacrifice is in the house where one ha intercourse with the family dead. The sacrifice is allowed to lie o the balcony. Offerings to the dead also are laid on graves, immediatel after the death and whenever the mourners feel their loss. Larg sacrifices to ancestors are made on bamboo altars in the market plac and in the mountains where the deified ancestors have their dwelling

All varieties of domestic animals are sacrificed, excepting dog Light colored animals are consecrated to the heavenly spirits, and dar animals to those of the underworld. Other sacrificial gifts includ cooked meat, rice, vegetables, fruits, eggs, salt, ginger, betel, mea cakes, palm wine, tobacco, flowers, leaves, ashes, implements, clothe and pieces of red and white cloth. Every ghost receives the good to which he was entitled during life.

The spirits receive the soul of the sacrifice, the worshippers th material portion. The soul goes off as the smell, so cooked food is le

an altar until cold. At the time of certain animal sacrifices the
ul is said to be in the blood. Sometimes blood is allowed to drip
wn on a grave to nourish the recently departed.

As among all people who perform cult sacrifices, the spirits are
emed stupid and easily deceived. Thus one kind of sacrifice is
lled "panulaan" and is given to atone for the sins of the relatives
a woman when she is childless. Three grasshoppers are sacrificed,
d are called cow, buffalo and horse, respectively.

Horses are offered up in a great sacrificial feast for the three
ds of the trinity. Every Toba sib has a sacred horse consecrated
one of these gods. It is the "throne", that is, the symbol of the
esence of the divine tribal father for his descendants. The black
rse is sacred to Batara Guru, the brown horse to Soripada, and
e piebald to Mangalabulan. Each sib, in accordance to which of
e three gods it traces its descent, possesses a black, brown, or
ebald horse. These sacred animals are inviolable and non-alienable.
ey are not confined but graze anywhere with impunity.

When a sacred horse (hoda debata) has grown old in honorable
rvice, it must be replaced by a young beast of the same color.
r this purpose a feast is arranged, at which the old horse is
crificed to the god appropriate to its color. A lucky day is picked
t with the aid of the calendar, and the sib members, including
e women, assemble in the village of the head chief, who, as manager
the feast, has already obtained a black, brown, or piebald young
llion, selected for its beauty. The two sacred horses, the intended
tim and its successor, are now bridled, the ears of the young
rse being decorated with flowers and sweet-smelling herbs. To the
ains of the native orchestra both horses are conducted to the center
the village, where the men entrusted with the duty of slaughter
d evisceration await their office. They kill and skin the old sacred
rse. The pelt is washed and laid over a "rangin", the crudely
t image of a horse, which is simply a tree trunk, hollowed out
the underside and ending in the image of a horse's head. The
ngin covered with the hide is brought to the chief's house, where,
id a food offering of rice, sacrificial cakes, fruit, white flowers,
d the purifying lime juice, the datu offers the hide to the god as
covering for his throne. Sprinkled with the consecrated water the
de is then left in the house for the time being. The people return
the village, where the datu summons the three gods, Mula djadi

(the Batak creator and father of the three gods), the nature god
and the ancestral spirits, for the consecration of the new horse.
man comes forward with a plate of sacrificial cakes and a sma
sack of rice kernels with a chicken's egg or a gambir nut on to
When the datu has summoned both the gods and the ancestors
both sexes up to the seventh generation for the blessing of the peopl
the young horse is sprinkled with lime juice water. The participan
scatter rice kernels over its head, praying, "Our tondi is firm, ma
we remain healthy". The young horse is now led back to its sta
through a further shower of rice. The people return to the hou
of the chief, where the ceremony ends in music and dancing. T
god, stimulated by the orchestra, enters his medium, one of the chief
to inform the people that he has received their sacrifice and will gi
them help. After the feast the horse flesh is divided, and everyo
takes his portion back to his village to eat.

In a manner similar to the Dravidian tribes of India, the Bata
formerly practiced human sacrifice. At the present time the paga
Bataks still sacrifice to the earthgod Boraspati ni tano when th
ram the main pillars of a house into the ground. This is done
atone for having disturbed him. Warneck records that formerly
one of the northeast sections of the country a living slave was buri
beneath each of the house posts.

Human sacrifice, where the life of a slave was not taken, w
usually of a voluntary nature. This sometimes occurred at harve
festivals. An animal was killed and related families shared the me.
Then youths of the sacrificing party divided into two bands, an
armed with reed lances or with stones, fought a sham battle. Passio
arose on both sides, the married men joined with the youths, wh
the women looked on and incited the combatants to fiercer strugg
with cries and clapping of hands. For complete success, blood had
flow and a life be lost on both sides, so that there would be
cause given for blood revenge.

Occasionally a sambaon visited a datu in his sleep and designat
a certain person (one who was hated by the datu) as victim. T
fatal red jacket and white turban were then put upon the sacrifi
In 1864 a sambaon demanded the life of the missionary Nommense
but the natives feared to attack him, although he was alone a
unarmed.

More often the sambaon simply demanded a human sacrifi

without designating the victim. The datu then sent people through all the villages of the district, crying, "Who is tired?" When anyone answered, "I am", he was destined for the sacrifice, whether he were a powerful or a lesser personage. (When someone answers "I am", it is a sign that his tondi has designated him for sacrifice, for the tondi determines the fate of man.)

The next morning the victim and a buffalo were tied to a sacrificial pole. All the people streamed to the place of sacrifice, beat drums, and danced around the pole. With prayers the sacrifice was given over to the sambaon, for the forgiveness of the people. The spectators spat on the bound man, as a sign that they transferred their faults and misdeeds to him. Finally the human scapegoat was released and allowed to run away. But he lived scarcely a month, for he was avoided by all, since his life was given over (sacer facio) to the sambaon and no one would feed him. His death was a sign that the sambaon had accepted him.

Prayer is a necessary element of every sacrifice. The prayers are spoken in stereotyped form and very polite language is used. The longer the prayer the greater the honor to the being addressed, sometimes the supplication extends an entire half day. At great sacrifices the datu recites the prayer. He must be properly attired and decorated for the occasion.

The Batak prayer is not a magical formula, nor is the sacrifice a magical ceremony. The gods and spirits are begged, not forced, by prayer. The Bataks also have magical formulae, but these are not connected with the sacrificial system.

In order that a sacrifice be successful it must be accepted by the spirits. The people decide by omen taking whether or not their plea is heeded, or the datu can test the matter by divination, or the spirit may be allowed to speak for himself through the medium.

Taboo. — A system of taboos is known to extend from the Nagas of Assam through Indonesia, Melanesia and Polynesia. It is from Polynesia, of course, that we have taken over the word "taboo" into our own language. The Romans used the word "sacer" for taboo, indicating that a thing was set apart for the gods, and therefore the opposite of "profanus". Properly speaking the breach of a taboo should be punished by the gods rather than by human agency.

The Karo system of taboos has received special study by Neumann. The three words used by the Karo for taboo: pantang, rebu

(Toba, robu), and kemali, all indicate the prohibition of an act which, if performed, would be a breach of religious law. It has been noted, however, that among the Bataks, as among primitive people in general, all law is religious law. There is no other law than the adat, and the adat is but ghost sanctioned custom. Likewise there is no sin other than innovation, for any innovation is a breach of customary procedure, and therefore taboo.

Kemali does not so much indicate that a thing is forbidden as it does that a thing is strange or unusual. It therefore is set apart because it is dangerous, powerful, or potent of disaster. Kemali always indicates the weird and the extraordinary. It is kemali when a colored cloud is seen over a village in the daytime, for it indicates that a chief of the village or one of his blood relatives will shortly die. If one meets a red snake or a locust with four feet one trembles before the oncoming anger of the gods. Yet the very things which are most dangerous are also the most useful for working magic, and all magic in fact is thought to have originated in the incest of twins as noted in every magic staff.

Pantang (Toba subang) is a prohibition governing routine and expected matters. It is based, however, on ghost fear. Thus the members of certain sibs are not allowed to eat the white karabau since this is their totem. It likewise is pantang for a man to cut his hair, carry dead things, or swear, when his wife is pregnant. Any of these acts would injure the foetus. Things are pantang when they hinder or hold back the working of other things. Thus the datu places certain restrictions on the sick, who are prohibited eating and doing certain things.

Rebu corresponds the most closely to the Polynesian taboo. Rebu is the isolation in which a person or thing is placed, either because the person or thing is sacred or because it is unclean. Contact with a rebu object would be religious desecration and would bring disaster. Persons and things also are isolated for their own sakes, when they are rebu, lest they be contaminated by the profane.

As already noted a newly married pair is rebu. They must spend the first four or seven days in the house, nor may they receive visitors. At the birth of a child nothing can be taken out of the house, and entrance to the house is forbidden to all except those who are needed to help the mother. A building newly completed is rebu for the first seven days. No stranger is allowed entrance to the village, nor may he people of the village come into contact with the outside world. A town also is cut off from contact with the outside world at the ime of epidemic. A fence is made of draconia leaves, and wooden mages with weapons in their hands keep off the disease begu. Chiefs re especially rebu. It is considered, as already noted, sacrilegious o kill a chief or one of his wives in time of war. The house of a hief is rebu, and a criminal can find asylum there. Parents-in-law nd children-in-law of the opposite sexes are rebu to one another nd therefore must avoid mutual conversation. If a death occurs the ntire village is rebu for a day and no work is done in the fields. The taboo lasts for several days at the death of a chief.

One does not use the word rebu with reference to incest, but umbang, a still stronger expression. Mereha indicates merely indecent conduct, punishable by the chief, as when a brother and sister walk together, or when a man sits next to his mother-in-law. Finally embung is the weakest of all terms indicating taboo, and means mbarrassment or shame, as when a large child runs around naked.

Sacrifice involves an especially great number of taboos. The mediums who serve at the sacrifices also have to observe the taboos n their daily life. They can not eat dog meat, or beef if the cow died natural death. They are not allowed to carry unclean objects on heir heads, since the spirits descend there. So many are the taboos hat few people wish to be mediums.

When a sib gives a large sacrifice there is a general state of ebu. On the first day it is forbidden that rice be pounded, water e fetched, except early in the morning or late in the evening, or any eavy work be performed. The rebu lasts seven days. Everything nust be kept quiet, and there should be no quarreling or warfare. Whoever disturbs the rebu, whether purposely or not, incurs the wrath of the spirits until the time of the next sib sacrifice. He also s fined by the chief for having endangered the safety of the entire sib.

Taboos which at one time were purely religious gradually become ecularized. Thus in Hawaii one sees to-day the word "kapu" painted n signs in the grass plots to ward off trespass. Likewise the Toba ave the word "marobu" which primarily indicated a taboo on work or a given period of time, as when rice was being planted. The word now indicates any action prohibited by the adat or the radja, nd for the breaking of such a prohibition there usually is a punishment.

The word "pantang" also has acquired a secular meaning.

Sacred number. — One of the most noticeable traits which ha spread from Asia into the islands of the Pacific is the sacredness o the number seven. In Babylon and India seven was made sacred b the astrologers who counted five planets and the sun and moon As Kroeber has shown, with Babylon as its source, the number seven like hepatoscopy (the reading of livers) and haruspicy (divinatio by the flight of birds), was carried into Indonesia, and, I may add even into Polynesia.

Neumann has listed the main occurrences of the number sever in Batak religion. .

The Bataks have seven important gods. A person has seven soul (according to certain datu's), the soul will die seven times and finall become a sambaon. The human half-god Singa Mangaradja was sever years in the womb. He can go seven months without eating. The rebu for newly married couples lasts seven days, as is also the case with the Arabs. At the birth of a child the house is rebu for sever days. At the building of a town or dwelling, the completed work is rebu for seven days. A child cannot be washed in the river unti it is seven days old, and seven people are appointed to do the washing The filing of teeth takes place on or after the seventh year. Afte this is done the person cannot appear in public for seven days. Circum cision is best performed in the seventh year, and the individual is rebu for seven days afterwards. The body of a dead person is covered with seven cloths. For seven days the grave of the dead must be sprinkled with rice, sirih, and palm wine, for the ghost remain seven days near the grave.

HAPTER II.

MINANGKABAU.

The People.

According to Minangkabau tradition the kingdom was founded
y Alexander the Great. Actually the kingdom of Malayu, which
ater extended to the present site of Minangkabau, was established by
Hindu colonists by the seventh century A. D. The name Minangkabau
irst seems to have appeared in a list dated 1365 A. D., giving the
ames of lands and districts in Sumatra which owed tribute to the
avanese kingdom of Madjapahit.

The folk etymology of the name "Minangkabau" dates from the
ime during which the kingdom was struggling to retain its independence. The legend relates that at one time the Javanese came
vith a great army to conquer the land. The chiefs of both sides
decided to settle the issue by a fight between two karabau. The
Malays thought of a trick, and allowing a calf to hunger for ten
days, bound a sharp iron point to its nose and set it free to run
ull tilt against the belly of the Javanese buffalo. The starving calf
n thus attempting to obtain milk killed its adversary. In commem-
oration of this event the Malay conquerors named their land and
people "Minang Kabau" after the conquering buffalo. The story is
still fully accredited among the people, and the karabau is the symbol
f national unity.

In a more prosaic manner, Van der Tuuk derives the name from
"pinang kabhu", an archaic expression which means "original home".
This derivation seems the more likely, since Minangkabau was in
act the cradle land of the Malays. While about one and a half
million Malays have remained in Minangkabau proper, an equal
number migrated in Hindu times to Malacca and other coastal places
f the archipelago. These Malays, often called the deutero-Malays,
have adopted a patrilineal form of family. Their language is slightly
different, at the present time, from that spoken in the home land,
Minangkabau.

In the fourteenth and fifteenth century the ancient kingdom of

7

Minangkabau covered the whole of central Sumatra. This kingdom was divided into three parts: the three "luhaks", the three "rantaus" and the eight "babs". To the luhaks, or districts, belonged Tanuh Datar, Agam, and the Lima-puluh (15 towns). To-day these district form the environments of Fort van der Capellen, Fort de Kock, and Pajakumbuh. These three luhaks formed the kernel of Minangkabau. The three rantaus, states, stood in loose relation to the central province, although they recognized the supremacy of the maharadj of Minangkabau. These were: Rantau Kampar, Kuantan (Indragiri) and Batang Hari. Once every three years the ruler visited thes provinces. The eight babs, the entrances and exits to the kingdom were the large seaports: Padang, Priaman, Indrapura, Djambi Indragiri, Siak, Painan, and Benkulen. The connection of the bab to the luhaks, or central provinces, was very loose, and at an earl date they became entirely disconnected from the central kingdom.

In the beginning of the seventeenth century, when the Dutch came to Sumatra, Minangkabau was already on its way toward complete disintegration. The kingdom at this time was composed of a collection of petty rajahs who ruled over Lilliputian village states, o negari. The overlord ruler at Palembang, the Jang di Pertuan, wa a mere figurehead. In 1680 when King Alip died without leaving any direct heirs, the kingdom was divided into three parts. In th nineteenth century the rule of the ancient kingdom came entirely t an end, the Padri rebellion giving it its final death blow.

It is impossible to give an exact date for the introduction o Mohammedan law and customs into Minangkabau. According t Willinck, Mohammedan Achehnese pirates roved the coast and upor occasion penetrated into the interior as early as the last half of th fourteenth century. While the middle of the sixteenth century is th date usually assigned for the introduction of Islam, yet Willincl claims that a great part of the Highland still was unconverted in th later part of the eighteenth century. In the beginning of the nineteenth century Mohammedan priests (the Padri) became discontented with the pagan state of the country and resorted to force, killing an enslaving all who resisted the introduction of the strict Mohammedar law. Nevertheless the people persisted in maintaining their matrilineal adat and merely made formal and outward concessions t Moslem promptings. In matters of religion, however pagan the remain at heart, they make pretence of Mohammedan public ceremony

nd prayer. The social and political organization of the people at
resent is a bewildering intermixture of pagan matrilineate, Hindu
nd Mohammedan patrilineate, all functioning under Dutch rule.

The Economic Life.

Houses. — Minangkabau in Hindu times was divided into village
tates or negari (from the Sanskrit nagara, city). All of the negari
ave fixed boundaries supposed to have been established by the first
ettlers, either consisting of natural features, such as rivers, trees,
r large stones, or artificial landmarks. Formerly all the inhabitants
f a negari knew these landmarks and considered them sacred. Wars
ever were fought for the purpose of land seizure, nor could the
oundaries be altered, even with the consent of the land owners.

The town itself, in previous days fortified with hedges, walls, and
ven moats, is the only inhabited portion of the negari. The town
ere, as among the Bataks, is called kota. Evidently the word for
wn, as well as the method of defence, was borrowed from the Hindus.
n Sanskrit the word kuta means a fortified place. This type of
ortification is common in Assam and Western Indonesia, but lacked
ilitary justification in Minangkabau. The pa, or fortifications of
e far off Maori of New Zealand, were built along somewhat the
ame model, but may have had a separate origin.

The first settlers in a kota, belonged to a single family division,
r kampueng. The Malay word kampong, now invariably used for
n Indonesian native town, thus originally had genealogical rather
an territorial significance.

The Minangkabau town consists of a group of family houses
rumah kumanakan) and rice granaries. In each town there is a
uncil and communal house (balai) and a mosque. The balai serves
s sleeping quarters for the youths above the age of eight.

In the Highlands a single family house (rumah-kamanakan)
ometimes lodges seventy to eighty persons descended from the same
ncestral mother. The house itself is built on piles and is of oblong
ape. The roof projects over a long front balcony, is saddle-backed,
nd decorated with buffalo horns. Stone steps lead up to the front
f the house. The back part is fashioned out of small rooms (bilie).
hese are separated from one another by planks, bamboo, or cloth,
nd serve as sleeping quarters for the married and marriageable girls.
he fore room (tangah rumah) contains a large fireplace and serves

as a communal family room, often also slept in by the children and the unmarried. The space beneath the floor of the dwelling lodges the domestic stock, consisting of karabau, cows, horses, chickens and ducks. In general the buildings are made of wood and bamboo various sorts of leaves being used for the roofing.

The house furnishings and utensils are simple. Iron and copper pots and pans are used in the preparation of food. Large and small baskets are woven from bamboo, rotan, or pandanus leaves as receptacles for rice and other objects. Mats serve the dual purpose of beds and chairs.

The rice is stored in granaries alongside the dwelling place Each village likewise has a tabuah house in which is kept the large drum, tabuah. This is fashioned from a hollowed out tree trunk and is used to summon the people on special occasions. The balei, or communal house, is used chiefly as a council house by the chiefs and secondarily as communal sleeping house for the unmarried.

The market (pasa) plays a large rôle in Minangkabau life. The market place is situated on a large plain and is frequented during the week by those who wish to buy or sell.

Graves are situated in the village proper, often in the house plots

Clothing. — The clothing of the Minangkabau varies greatly When the men are at home or at work in the field, they usually wear nothing more than sarongs, and short trousers reaching to the knee.

A man, fully attired, wears a head cloth, a jacket, a sarong, girdle and a pair of trousers. The chiefs on state occasions wear gold plates set with jewels in their girdles.

Weapons. — Among the weapons which are in use among the Minangkabau are European hunting fire-arms, and a great variety of cutting weapons, as krises, lances, swords, daggers, &c. These are native made and very elaborately decorated. A form of sling (umba tali) is still in use. It is made of rope and is used for killing cattle in the field.

Musical Instruments. — The Minangkabau musical instruments include gongs, drums, small flutes and a peculiar model of a three stringed violin. The instruments are used to accompany dances. In the Highlands only the men dance, but in the bordering regions both sexes join in.

Industries. — The Minangkabau people are chiefly engaged in agriculture, trade, especially cattle trading, industries, hunting and fishing

Breeding of animals is less well developed than agriculture, yet of some importance. Buffalo, horned cattle, horses and goats are raised. The people use the buffalo (karabau) both as draught animal and for their milk and meat.

The chief industries are spinning, weaving, lace making, the weaving of mats and baskets, the preparation of silk, washing for gold, cloth dyeing, and pottery. These are especially women's work. Rope making, paper manufacture, carpentry, boat building, wood cutting, decorating and painting wood, mineral mining, smithing, lead pouring, and candle moulding are especially the work of men. Sugar manufacture, chalk making, and the preparation of gambir and tabacco and oil mining are engaged in by both sexes.

A half century ago the spinning wheel and the hand loom were to be found in every house. Nowadays, however, the natives buy the cheap American and European cotton goods. Silk industry is of recent importation from Europe. A variety of paper formerly was made from pounded leaves.

The wet and dry rice fields are worked together by men and women. When cattle are scarce or not to be had, the woman has to work the fields by hand. The man has to lay fences around the field, do the house building and keep it in repair, plant his tobacco, make his fishing utensils and boats, do most of the fishing and all of the hunting, gather wood and brush products in the jungle, and sew the clothing. The woman plants the sugar cane, works on the house garden, and catches crabs and fish in the swamps. She does all of the house work, takes care of the children, cooks, grinds rice, weaves, spins, and prepares palm leaves for the roofing.

The chief who is paid by the government no longer works in the field, and still less do the native chiefs where the local adat is in force. Those also who have a smattering of Mohammedan letters deem themselves too important to work in the swampy rice fields. Preceded by their mothers and their sisters, who carry the heavy loads on their heads, they wander marketward in ornamented clothing, carrying nothing else than bird cages with their favorite doves carefully protected from the heat of the sun by coverings of colored cotton cloths.

In spite of the nominal "matriarchate" Van Hasselt claims that the women really are the servants of the men. They not only prepare the meals for the men in their family, but they also serve them first, they themselves eating later with the children.

Society.

Government. — The government of Minangkabau is essentiall tribal rather than territorial, and the actual rulers of the land ar the sib (suku) heads, the datuq nan berampè. These heads, as wil be explained presently, receive their orders from lower family council and therefore are representatives rather than governors.

Nominally, in Hindu times, the independent village states, o negari, formed one nation with one language and one ruler, the Jan; di Pertuan. Actually, this radjaship was utterly foreign to nativ concept and never integrated into the Minangkabau adat. While i Minangkabau exogamy and matrilineal succession are the rule, th radjas always married within their own family and the eldest so succeeded his father to the throne.

The only authority the radja had was that of intermediary in th petty wars fought between the negari. When such a war had laste a long time without a decisive victory, the radja sent a messenger wit a yellow umbrella to the struggling negaris. This emblem was plante on the battlefield for the purpose of establishing peace. If both partie continued the struggle, however, the radja did nothing further in th matter. He had no army to enforce his power, nor did he try t arbitrate.

The Hindu line of radjas appeared satisfied with the honor pai them, and the taxes. They were kings without soldiers: the poores pretense of monarchs the world has known. With their disappearance the actual government of the negari went on quite as before.

While, then, the negari is the autonomous state, actually thi concept also is apt to be misleading. For in each negari there has t be representatives of the four sibs (suku), and the heads of thes furnish the highest council. The sibs, in fact, could function equall well without the negari, which is but the Hindu idea of territoria government superimposed upon the native genealogical rule. In fac mere residence within a negari does not furnish a stranger with right of citizenship; for this he has to be adopted into a sib.

It is the suku, or rather that portion of a suku which resides i a certain negari, and not the negari, which furnishes the highest uni of government. Unfortunately, the history and significance of th suku is by no means clear. In Malay the word means "leg" or "fourt part". Evidently, however, the word is original to Minangkabau, sinc here the suku corresponds to the sib (marga) of the Bataks. The fac at originally the Minangkabau had four sukus no doubt caused uku to have the meaning of "four" among the deutero-Malays. Certainly the word does not necessarily mean four, for the Gajo sib is called either kuru or suku, and likewise in the Lampong district uku is sometimes the name of relatives in a village.

The Minangkabau themselves believe the sukus to be of Hindu rigin and ascribe their founding to the sons of a mother Indo Djati. Certain Dutch ethnographers, including Willinck and Westenenk, elieve that the sukus were founded by the Hindus for governmental urposes. It appears probable, however, that the Hindus found a sib ystem here, as elsewhere in Sumatra, and made use of it for governental purposes.

Originally the four sukus were the exogamous units of Minangabau. They again were divided into two sections, or moieties, called ras and named after the sukus of which they were composed. Thus ne laras was called Bodi-Tjaniago and the other Koto-Piliang. The ord "laras" is Javanese and means "symmetrical" or "harmonious". he presumption is, therefore, that the Hindu-Javanese found the Minangkabau sukus divided into two unnamed parts, which they alled laras.

The Minangkabau people have two traditions concerning the aras. According to the first, these moieties were instituted in egendary times for the purpose of preventing incest, and later split p into the four sukus. According to the second tradition the laras ere instituted as territorial divisions from which the present negari ave arisen.

＊At the time of the conversion of Minangkabau to Mohammednism the laras already were territorial units, each with slightly ifferent adat. Bodi-Tjaniago had the milder criminal code of the wo. The arrangement of the balais was also different in the two aras; in Bodi-Tjaniago the flooring was level so that all the chiefs at at the same height, while in Kota-Piliang certain chiefs sat on n elevation.

At the present time the four original sukus have split into a large umber of smaller exogamous units, each bearing its own name. Some uthorities state there are twenty-four of these units, while others claim wenty-seven. The divisions of a village, the hamlets, also have been amed suku, since each division would naturally be inhabited by one enealogical family and hence acquire a suku nomenclature. Thus,

104

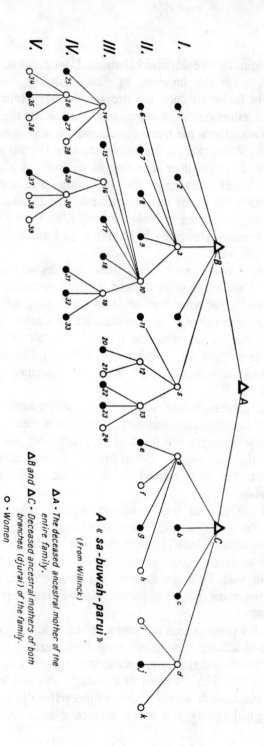

A « *sa-buwah-parui* »

(From Willinck)

A - The deceased ancestral mother of the entire family.

ΔA - The deceased ancestral mother of the entire family.

ΔB and ΔC - Deceased ancestral mothers of both branches (*djurai*) of the family.

○ - Women

● - Men

I.-V. - Surviving generations of both ancestral mothers, ΔB and ΔC, descended from female members of the family.

f a village is inhabited by four of these "large families", it would be
aid to have four sukus or quarters.

The actual smallest indepentent unit of government in Minangkabau is the sa-buah-parui, which consists of all those who have
descended from a common female ancestor. The sa-buah-parui, then,
omprises the children, their mothers, aunts, uncles, cousins, grand-
mothers, grandaunts and granduncles, usually up to the fifth generation. "All those who have the same dwelling district and the same
omb, the same dwelling place and rice fields." The sa-buah-parui
ives in a section of a village and has over it a chief or panghulu
(1 on chart). The chief is chosen from the male relatives of the oldest
woman of the lineage, as the name implies-hulu meaning "to begin"
or "the first".

The lineage again is divided into branches, or families, called
djurai. Each djurai lives in a separate house and is ruled over by
he oldest brother of the oldest woman of the house, providing the
man be fit for the office. Thus 1 and *a* are mamaqs of their respective
houses *B* and *C*. It must be noted that the term mamaq means
mother's brother here as among the Karo Bataks and is Tamil in
origin. The head of the house may be simply a mamaq, or, if he also
s head of the sa-buah-parui, he may have the title of panghulu.

The government of Minangkabau rests primarily on two councils,
first that of the village panghulus, who meet in the village balai, and
secondly on the four heads of the negari sukus, the datuq nan berampè,
who meet in the negari balai. While the actual enforcement of law
rests with the mamaqs and the panghulus, the executive power is in
he hands of the suku chiefs.

The panghulu has a double function. As a mamaq he is a simple
house father, acting upon the advice of his house companions. As a
panghulu he is representative of his family in the state. As such he
s only responsible to the other panghulus and the suku heads. The
panghulu has to take care that his underlings keep the adat and the
Mohammedan law (sjarat), or be punished. He is the *trait-d'union*
between his sa-buwah-parui and the suku, and between his family and
he negari. He also is the repository of family traditions. He sees to
t that the members of his family perform their appointed tasks: the
making of roads, building of balais or mosques, &c. He is also
responsible for the fidelity with which the mamaqs under him perform
heir tasks toward their various djurai.

The panghulu has the duty of bringing the demands of his family to the attention of the suku chiefs and to the other panghulu when they are sitting in council. If he fails to act as just representative, his family may complain over his head, and he may be displaced or even cast out of his family.

The panghulu always must be informed of everything that happens within his family among the anak-buah (members of sa-buwah-parui) No child can be born, no death occur, no marriage contracted, but the panghulu must be informed of it. No contract can be closed by his anak-buah, no money given out, or land given in lease, no important act of trade, but that he must receive word. He keeps account of the harto pusako (the communal property) and the harto pantjarian (the individual property) in his family. Not alone does he know the affairs of his own family, but he also knows the internal history and the anecdotes of the other sa-buwah-parui in the negari. When he becomes aged and feels that the end of his life is close at hand, he hands over these traditions to his younger successors.

The panghulus possess no executive power but are mere representatives of their families. Executive power rests alone in the hands of the suku chiefs. But these act more as advisors than as law makers. They also receive their orders from below and are unable to do anything of their own initiative.

Several important points must be noted in this system of government, which is the most truly democratic form which could be devised 1. The real sovereignty of the state rests with the individual sa mandehs or families. A mamaq never forms decisions on his own account: important questions first are discussed in each household under the direction of the Indua, the oldest woman of the house, and then debated among the masculine members of the family and the mamaqs who carry out their orders. 2. All decisions must be merely interpretations of the dual constitution, the native adat and the Mohammedan law. 3. All decisions must be arrived at by unanimous vote. In Minangkabau there can be no tyranny of a majority over a minority. Dissenting members of a council, however, can be cast out of the family or even out of the community. 4. Minangkabau rule is a true gerontocracy, for the oldest male member of each djurai is eligible for the position of mamaq, the mamaq of the oldest djurai of the sa-buwah-parui should become panghulu, and the oldest branch of the suku in the negari should place its panghulu in the negari council

This system, then, stresses universal suffrage, security of possessions, and immutability of constitution. It is fastened to the traditions of the past and would be ill-adapted to the vicissitudes of war or commerce. It has maintained the average male above the line of poverty and provoked the immigration of the more energetic.

Similar to most primitive communities, accession to office is a matter of inheritance — here through the female line — with the proviso that the successor have the proper qualifications. A candidate for the office of panghulu must be normal, both physically and mentally, and must always have conformed to the adat. He must be capable for the position, neither over or under opinionated, and trustworthy. If he be too young, an older relative performs the functions of the office for him. Before a man is "lifted up" to the position, the consent of his family must be obtained. Then the family candidate must be approved by the head of the suku. If the datuq nan berampè cannot agree on the family choice, another candidate from the same line has to be chosen.

Another primitive factor in the Minangkabau adat lies in the fact that the rewards of office are honorary rather than pecuniary. In the first place, the panghulu inherits an honorary name, galar pusako, which can be freely mentioned in the place of his real and secret name. This honorary name is thought to outdate Hindu times, it cannot be altered, and is handed down in the family with the position. Then again the panghulu is entitled to wear special clothing and the kris as emblems of office. He is only treated as panghulu while wearing those badges of office. Finally, the panghulu has a special place of office at festive occasions.

Both honors and status are pyramided in Minangkabau, and the suku chief receives all the honors and titles of lower positions as well as his own special prerogatives. As mamaq he is simply the house father of the oldest djurai of his family, as panghulu he is an officer of the state in their midst, as datua nan kaämpe he is the highest state head in the complex of families forming his suku, and, finally, in conjunction with the three other suku chiefs he forms the government of the negari.

Social classes. — Unlike the Bataks, the Minangkabau lay but little stress on social classification. Indeed, before the days of Hindu influence, there could have been no other classification between individuals other than an age distinction. At present, the nobility are

called urang bangsa (bangsa from Sanskrit vamca, race). The "noble⟨
are the oldest families in the community and therefore supply the hea⟨
officials. Families endeavor to marry their daughters off to oth⟨
families of equal standing or antiquity.

Likewise, slavery originally was unknown to matrilineal Minan⟨
kabau, although it flourished in the patrilineal communities of Ni⟨
and Batakland. In these countries slavery was primarily due to w⟨
and debt, institutions which were almost foreign to Minangkab⟨
adat. While Hindu civilization introduced the idea of slavery, it w⟨
not until the Padri rebellion that slavery became widespread.

Property. — Minangkabau property at the present time is divid⟨
into two classes: communal property (harto pusako), and priv⟨
property (harto pantjarian). The word pusako is borrowed from t⟨
Sanskrit and means in the original language "those things whi⟨
serve to sustain life". In Indonesian pusako means "inherited thing⟨
It appears probable that at one time all Minangkabau property w⟨
harto pusako.

There is no law of testament in the Highlands of Minangkab⟨
since after the death of an individual his harto pantjarian is simp⟨
joined to the harto pusako of his djurai. Even during his life t⟨
individual has not full control over his own earnings (harto pantjaria⟨
He has full use of his private property and can enter into contra⟨
concerning it without the consent of his mamaq, but so far as ⟨
consists of immovables he cannot give it to strangers or even to ⟨
own wife and children.

The harto pusako may be immovable possessions, such as r⟨
fields, cultivated fields, brush or meadow land, houses, rice granari⟨
and stables. But it may consist equally well of movable goods, ⟨
gold and silver work, costly clothing, weapons, karabau, and catt⟨
The harto pantjarian likewise consists of both movable and immoval⟨
goods. The earnings of the day mechanic and of the merchant ⟨
harto pantjarian. The cultivator of a piece of waste land takes t⟨
land as harto pantjarian. In short, all the property which a pers⟨
possesses as harto pantjarian rests on personal labor.

The oldest harto pusako are known as harto manah and a⟨
inherited from the ancestral mother. All the members of the sa-buw⟨
parui have a claim on this. But the harto pusako which is acquir⟨
later belongs to the various branches (djurai). As property becom⟨
harto pusako, only the succeeding, but not the lateral or precedi⟨

enerations have claim to it. The mamaq is administrator over the
arto pusako which belongs to his djurai, and the panghulu is admin-
strator over the harto pusako which belongs to his djurai and the
arto manah which belongs to the entire sa-buwah-parui.

The property system of Minangkabau acts as a preventative to
he squandering of wealth. Yet there are cases where the harto
antjarian is not sufficient, and the harto pusako has to be loaned
r rented out. It is only sold, however, as a last resort and with the
onsent of the entire family. According to the adat the harto pusako
an be sold for debts which have been contracted in the following manners:

1. The cost of burial of a family member.
2. The cost of marrying out a virgin.
3. In order to prevent the family house falling into decay.
4. In former days to pay weregild (bangun) when the slayer
imself had not sufficient property.
5. At the present time a few families are willing to pay the
xpense of a trip to Mecca for their members out of the harto pusako.

The harto pusako is divided only when a sa-buwah-parui goes
nto division. If, however, a daugther section migrates into another
egari, it loses its share of the harto pusako.

Land. — Real estate in Minangkabau is always privately owned
y a negari in the first place, and then if cultivated given either to a
a-buwah-parui as harto pusako, or to the individual reclaimer as
arto pantjarian.

Land is divided into two categories: tanah mati (dead land) or
ungle land, and tanah hidui (living land) or cultivated land. The
anah mati belongs to the negari, but without being worked it cannot
ecome the private property of families. It belongs to the inhabitants
f the negari as a whole, who have the right to gather jungle products
nd to hunt and fish on it. The tanah hidui consists of wet and dry
ice fields, as well as all pepper, sirih, gambir, coconut, and other
ields. Cultivated land belongs to the original reclaimer and is in-
erited as harto pusako by the children of his sisters.

Cultivated land actually is owned by the negari and the individual
amilies merely enjoy the usufruct. Repeated divisions of the culti-
ated soil are made by the negari chiefs and no family is allowed to
etain more than it needs. In this way an equitable allotment of
anded wealth is attained, and there is no danger of estates becoming
ither too large or too small for economic exploitation.

The women of Minangkabau are the chief cultivators of the soil and through the native system of communistic ownership they control its equitable division by means of their representatives, the mamaqs. Unquestionably it is this factor in the Minangkabau matrilineate which has insured its success and its permanency.

Criminal law. — In Minangkabau there is a code of criminal law (adat siksa) but no civil law. The lack of a civil code must be attributed to the paternal power exerted by the mamaq. When a family member wishes to enter or leave his negari, or when he wishes to enter into a contract concerning his harto pantjarian, he must consult his mamaq. In cases of dispute concerning the fulfilment of contracts, the mamaq decides on the merits of the case, or the matter may be brought before a higher court, even to the negari chiefs. A family member who disobeys the orders of his mamaq can have his share of the harto pusako withheld. If he wishes to obtain this back, he must conciliate his chief and give a feast.

The native criminal code has not progressed beyond the law of blood revenge and weregild. In spite of Hindu and Mohammedan influence, the Minangkabau recognize no crimes against the state or a deity. This backward aspect of Minangkabau law is due to the fact that in the matrilineal regime the family is the state. Among the Batak with their better developed state government treason formerly was the gravest of crimes against the state.

Since in Minangkabau all crimes offend merely the avenger and his family, money compensation can atone for all misdeeds. The fine however, paid by the guilty party goes not only to the wronged party but also to the negari chief, who receives the compensation partly due to the fact that he is head of the wronged party, and partly due to the fact that he is an expert in pronouncing judgment. The negari chief does not seek out the criminal, however, but waits until an accusation is brought before him.

In the case of murder no distinction is made between intentional and unintentional homicide. A distinction is made, however, between the worth of a panghulu and an ordinary man, an adult and a child, a man and a woman, in terms of weregild.

In spite of the matrilineate a husband has the customary Indonesian right of killing a guilty pair if they are caught *flagrant delicto,* and a thief may also be killed if caught in the act.

Judgments are made in court on the basis of material evidence andos or tokens) and the oath and ordeal. On the basis of tando jehe a case can be brought to court but no conviction obtained. Vith tando djemo (as footprints, or when the accused was seen near ie place of crime), the accused must perform a purification oath. Only tando beti convicts, as a piece of cloth cut from the criminal, r where the accused sold stolen goods under price.

Since a family is responsible for the crimes of its members, it, irough necessity, has the power of evicting black sheep from its onds (dibuwang hutang). Women, however, are treated as objects nd not subjects of the law. They have no executive power and no ght of entering into contracts, not even marriage contracts. There-ire they are powerless to commit crime and cannot be cast out of ie community.

Willinck sums up the Minangkabau law by stating that "there here is no real judge, no indictment, and no actual law case".

Kinship usage. — Minangkabau kinship terms are divided into iree groups: the cognate, the agnate, and terms of affinity. While ie last two groups are fairly complete, only the cognate terms are upposed to express actual relationship. This fiction is supported y the local proverb that "a rooster can lay no eggs" and that hildren owe their existence entirely to the mother, by the fact that nly the descendants in the female line live together in the communal ouse, and by the denial of actual forms of marriage. Minangkabau ociety in these respects is quite similar to that of the Jowai branch f the Khasi of Assam.

According to Minangkabau adat a man neither gains possession f a woman by marriage nor a woman a man. By the payment f a certain price the woman rents the services of her husband at ight. The husband then can sleep with his wife in her bilik, the mall sleeping room of the family house, or else with the men 1 the men's house. In the daytime he has access to his own family ouse but is not allowed to enter further than the tangah rumah, ie long front room of the house in which the women ply their work hen they are not out of doors.

The Minangkabau man has no rights over his wife other than demand that she remain faithful to him. He cannot ask her to iake clothes for him, for that is the duty of his mother and sisters. f he obtains any food from her or her family, he is supposed to ay for it. It can even happen that a man and his wife never eat

together. The woman, on the other hand, can always demand tha
her husband come to visit her from time to time and fulfill his marita
function. If he wishes to be agreeable, he can aid her in the manage
ment of the household and the laying out of rice fields. He also ca
give her presents from time to time or even a fixed income for he
maintenance. But this is all liberality on his part, for by the adat h
is not compelled to any of these obligations. In fact if he is to
liberal in sharing his harto pantjarian with his wife, he is liable t
get into difficulties with his own family.

Marriage is more brittle in Minangkabau than elsewhere i
Indonesia, and as soon as the visits of a husband become few i
number and the family sees that he does not care for his wife an
longer, the marriage is broken off. Then both sides remarry as soo
as possible.

Married couples are rakanan, comrades, to one another. The
are spoken of as balaki babini, man and wife, duwo istri, the marrie
couple, and barumah bakanti, house companions. A married woma
is called padusi or paradusi, a maid anak gadis, and a widow o
divorced woman orang rando or barando. To her husband a marrie
woman is the istri or the bini, the wife; while he is her laki, or t
use the more dignified Hindu appellation, her suami. By courtes
the husband is also called the djundjungang, the support, by hi
wife. Whenever a wife speaks of her husband she calls him ajah o
bapa anak hamba, the father of my children. When she speaks t
him she calls him ang, older brother, or paq, father, if he has give
her children. If he has not, she may call him maq (mamaq). Sh
may also call him tuan, or simply label him by his professio
Whatever she does, she must never mention his name in speakin
to him or of him. In like manner, the man speaks of his wife a
his bini and addresses her as adieq, little sister, thus comparin
her to his younger sister.

It is interesting to note that teknonomy takes two forms i
Minangkabau, each of which has as its object the avoidance o
personal names. A man before he has children may be an uncle; i
this case he would be called by his wife mamaq si A. If he ha
children then he is called paq si A. In the same manner the parent
in-law must refer to their son-in-law either in his capacity of uncl
or father of so-and-so. However a mother-in-law can address he
son-in-law as dawan and the son-in-law his father-in-law as angk

Joking and avoidance customs as well as the laws of incest are not so rigorously enforced in Minangkabau as among the Bataks. They are nevertheless of the same nature. A father may not caress his daughter, nor may brother and sister be demonstrative with one another. The law of the family covers the entire suku, and all suku acquaintances of opposite sexes must be very reserved. On the other hand, men and women of different suku may be very forward in their behavior, especially if they are not married. There is one striking point of difference between the Minangkabau and the Bataks: in Minangkabau boys and girls before they become engaged can mingle freely, but once engaged they must rigorously avoid speaking or meeting each other; among the Bataks an engagement is merely one form of trial marriage.

Parents-in-law and children-in-law, regardless of sex, are forbidden to be familiar, cordial, or jest with one another. They are not allowed to sit on the same mat or bench or eat from the same board or banana leaf lest their fingers touch. In the same way siblings-in-law of opposite sex never joke, and avoid one another.

Theoretically the sa-buwah-parui of the husband and that of the wife are brought into no relationship with one another by a marriage between members. Actually, however, marriage has preserved its aspect of group exchange here as among the Bataks. Thus, after the death of one's wife, it is deemed highly desirable to marry one of her sisters "so that the bond between the two families should not be broken". It also is considered desirable that a man marry the widow of his deceased brother for the same reason.

Cross-cousin marriage is not prescribed by the adat, and the kinship nomenclature does not reflect this form of union, yet it is nevertheless the custom for a family to pick out the son of the mother's brother (anak mamaq) or of the father's sister (kamanakan bapa) as the most suitable husband for the daughter. In this way the family believes itself assured of having a son-in-law of the same social standing as themselves.

Marriage restrictions. — Marriage has been shown to be exogamous, and a woman must marry a man not only from a different sa-buwah-parui but also from a different suku. Incest is called sumang and is punished by disowning.

In regard to other restrictions on marriage the Mohammedan law at the present time is followed more closely than the native adat.

Thus, while a woman might marry a half-brother from a differer father according to native adat, this is seldom done. While in son districts a man is prohibited taking more than one wife, in othe certain of the wealthy marry four, according to Mohammedan la spending a month with each.

According to Mohammedan custom a man is not allowed marry two sisters at the same time, a parent-in-law cannot marry child-in-law, nor a brother-in-law a sister-in-law while the spou is still living.

Previously native adat forbade a virgin contracting a marria with a man outside of her negari and to-day this seldom is don A woman who already has been married (orang rando) is allowe to marry a stranger.

Marriage. — As among the Bataks and other primitive people bachelors and spinsters are almost unknown in Minangkabau. spinster is said to receive the derisive nickname, apa guna, "what the use?" There is no reason for a Minangkabau woman to rema unwed, for her family finds a husband for her while she is still young girl; later when she becomes widowed or divorced she seel her own mate. In a later marriage a woman must receive the conser of her mamaq in order that she may be assured that her spouse wi be welcomed in the family house, but the man need consult no on

Only the first marriage is deemed of social importance in Minan; kabau. This is contracted without consulting either the boy or tl girl by the two djurai concerned in the matter. Boys are usuall married off at about the age of 15, the time of their circumcisio and girls at the time of their first menstruation. In spite of the soci; importance attached to this early marriage, it seldom has any lastir effect, and a woman not infrequently has changed mates five or s times before she arrives at the age of twenty. If the Batak woma may be said to enjoy her freedom before marriage, then her Minang kabau sister has her opportunity in post-nuptial days.

After all the older brothers and sisters of a girl have bee married off, the family decides on a suitable husband for this daughte and employs go-betweens to sound the feelings of the boy's famil If the consent of the latter family is obtained, the family of the gi sends small pledges (tandos) and receives tandos in exchange. Th heads of the sukus are informed of the engagement and it is mad public. If the affair be broken off later, either before or after marriag

e tandos are returned. Tandos are exchanged at the time of any
ontract with the same purpose as at a betrothal. Naturally if one
arty breaks a contract, the other party can claim possession of both
ndos, while if a contract is broken by mutual consent, tandos are returned.

Four or five days after the exchange of tandos the family of
e girl again sends presents and receives chickens, earthenware, and
oth. This is called the release from the selo (selo, sitting with
rossed legs). After this the two families can be more familiar with
ne another. If these presents were not given, the children born of
e marriage could demand help later from the family of the husband.

Engagements usually last but a short time. They may, however,
ast a year or two if the engaged couple is too young to marry,
hen important preparations have to be made for the wedding, or
hen an additional wing has to be put on the family dwelling. If the
ngaged couple are children and the engagement is of some duration,
ey live alternately in one another's house although they are not
llowed to come into contact. This is to maintain the bond between
e two families.

The actual wedding ceremony is conducted with great festivities
nd feasting, especially if the bridal pair come from prominent
amilies. In pre-Islamic times the mamaq of the woman and the mamaq
f the man performed the final ceremony. Now it is usually the father
f the woman who acts as her wali (guardian) and "gives her away".
s in southern India and everywhere in Indonesia the central act of
e wedding ceremony consists of the bride and bridegroom eating
ogether. Contrary to Mohammedan law the greater part of the expense
f the wedding is borne by the family of the bride. A symbolic
ffer of a bride-price in the form of a silver token is usually made
a deference to the regulations of Islam, but actually it is the groom
ho is bought, or, according to Willinck's phraseology, "rented".
his is done by means of the dowry, which amounts to from 25 to
0 guldens and which is brought from the house of the bride to that
f the groom. This small amount is called "ame" and is given back
t the time of a divorce.

Delayed consummation of the marriage occurs in the district of
gam, a custom which is also found in Java, Atjeh, and elsewhere
Indonesia. The bridegroom spends the night following the wedding
ith his wife in her bilik and there chats with her, but etiquette
emands that a pair of the wife's elderly relatives also be present

116

and that the newly-married couple enjoy no great amount
familiarity. The wife in fact acts quite coldly toward her husban
for five or six nights after the wedding, and when the husban
takes his departure in the mornings he has to do so without attractin
attention of the other occupants of the house.

A mock ceremony of bridegroom capture takes place the fir
morning, in a manner somewhat similar to that of the matriline
Garos of Assam. After the husband has chatted with his bride a
night he goes secretly to his own home in the morning. But a deputatio
of young men are sent by the family of the bride to round him u
and they bring him back by pretended force to the home of his brid
This ceremony is held in imitation of the actions of a bull, wh
not being used to a strange stall runs away and has to be led bac
Among the patrilineal Bataks the bride has to be led weeping to th
home of her husband; here among the matrilineal Minangkabau
is the husband who has to be led protesting to the home of his brid

In Batakland if a family is in danger of dying out a man
married into the family so that there may be male children to inher
the property. In Minangkabau the situation naturally is reverse
and when a family is in danger of dying out, a woman from the san
negari if possible is adopted so that her children may inherit.

Divorce. — The dissolution of a marriage while both parties a
alive is called batjarei hiduiq (to separate alive), while dissolutio
through death is called batjarei tambilan (separation by means
a spade).

At present, in portions of Minangkabau least influenced
Mohammedanism, divorce is conducted without any formality; former
this was so in all of Minangkabau. A man simply packs up h
things and leaves. He tells the motive to his family and his acquain
ances while the woman or her mother tell it to the mamaq. Th
panghulu has nothing to do with the divorce. If a woman wishe
to get rid of a man and has no grounds for divorce, she simp
furnishes notice by changing her sleeping quarters. The man tak
the hint and ceases coming to the house.

Childbirth. — During the birth of a child the husband must n
be present in the house. The husband and the midwife are suppose
to be ashamed of each other, and therefore practice avoidance. Th
afterbirth is placed in a purse woven from banana leaves and
buried under a certain pillar of the house.

Three days after the birth of the child the mother gets up to
erform light housework. If she is very weak, however, she is allowed
remain in bed fifteen days. During this time she is not allowed
eat red peppers, root vegetables, sweets, or condiments with her
ce. She lives on dried fish, salted dried rice and dried meat. The
oods tabooed are supposed to heat the blood; sweets cause pain.
o restrictions are placed on the father.

Treatment of children. — The children are not brought up by
ny particular member of the djurai but by the female relatives as
group, all of whom have the right of correction and all of whom
in in deciding on the child's career and marriage. The oldest
oman of the djurai has the most to say in these matters, together
ith her male representative, the mamaq. The father displays not
e least concern regarding his own children, although he gives them
mall presents from time to time. In the better families unmarried
irls are carefully guarded.

From the European point of view, the Minangkabau child
eceives a very faulty education. He is left almost entirely to him-
elf, and at an early age has to devote his energies to the economic
ursuits of the household. While still a boy he learns to read and
rite a little in the Arabic characters. In lieu of actual scientific or
terary training, he is taught to acquire manual dexterity and a
ractical knowledge of animal and plant life. The native industries
resently occupy his entire attention, such as the decoration of weapons
nd household utensils, the carving of buildings and the fashioning
f the precious metals. A girl while still young begins to weave and
ake baskets.

Puberty ceremonies. — Boys are circumcised and girls incised.
oys have a lock of their hair preserved to be ceremonially cut off
t puberty, while girls have their teeth filed before marriage and
heir ears bored while they are very young.

Both boys and girls are bathed in the river a few days after birth
nd are named at this time by the Mohammedan priest (malim).

Girls arrive at puberty at about the age of twelve or thirteen.
o ceremony takes place at this time, but from now on they are care-
ully watched and no longer allowed to play with the boys. During
eriods of menstruation (bulan, moon) the women avoid the use of
il in their hair, keep away from men, and bathe twice a day in
he river.

Boys become of age at fifteen, at which time they are entitle to manage their business affairs and hold office.

Names. — Children receive their names at the time they are fir bathed in the river, at the latest five days after their birth. Whi the names are actually bestowed by the malim, the parents offer number of names as choice. This first name is called a "little name (nama ketek). Later when the boys and girls marry they receiv their inherited titles, or little titles (galar ketek), and these satisf their vanity. Upon the assumption of titles the childhood names a lost. The only real titles are those of the panghulus (gala panghulu Names and titles are of Hindu origin, and their meanings are n understood by the present-day people.

With the assumption of the family title goes the right of pa ownership in the family property, such as rice fields. It is therefor just as great an offence to steal a family title as it is to steal th family property. Slaves had no rights to family titles but kept the childhood names.

The Minangkabau like the Bataks are loath to reveal their name and it is an insult to ask for the names of elder members of a famil Teknonomy, as before mentioned, is practiced, and a man names hin self after his nephews or children, a woman after her children o grandchildren.

Death and burial. — The dead always are disposed of by buria and this on the same day as that on which the death occurs. If man becomes sick at the home of his wife, word is sent to his relative If he dies, the body is handed over to his own family. The widov and her relatives have nothing to do with the burial.

The people have no outward sign of mourning. According Mohammedan law, the widow must wait four months and ten day and then if she is not pregnant, she can remarry. The Minangkaba widow, however, waits one hundred days, as the ghost of the dea man is supposed to wander around in the form of a bird in h own dwelling and in hers, for that period of time. Then a big feas for the dead is given and the ghost leaves for soul land, kampon achirat. The widow at this time pays her last visit to the famil of the deceased, and they visit the grave together. While no offering are put upon the grave, household implements, such as mats an baskets, and food, are given as presents to blood relatives. Dire offerings to the dead would be contrary to Mohammedan law.

In case a man loses his wife he can remarry at once, as there
no iddah, or mourning period, prescribed. However, he usually
aits a hundred days, as his wife is said to be hovering around in
rd-like form.

Children are not very much affected by the death of a parent.
the father dies they remain with the mother. If the mother dies
e father can demand one or more of the children. Usually, however,
: is content to visit his offspring from time to time.

The patrilineate and the matrilineate. — A study of two neigh-
oring but opposite systems of government and property ownership
. Sumatra furnishes convincing proof that both the patrilineate and
e matrilineate have developed from a common form of bilateral
amily and that in neither case has the system attained full de-
lopment. Government among the Bataks is entirely in the hands of
e men, and yet the voice of a woman is sometimes heard in the
uncil house. Women exert great influence on governmental decisions
. Minangkabau, but a woman never can be either mamaq or panghulu.
mong the Bataks, women own no property, and they themselves are
aid to be property, although they can be neither sold nor abused.
he Minangkabau women nominally own all the inherited property,
ut actual title to the property is in the hands of the men; the women
ave not the legal right to make a contract, not even to dispose of
emselves in marriage. Among the Bataks a woman is sold as a
ommodity into marriage, while in Minangkabau a fine pretense is
ade of hiring the husband by the family of the woman, yet both
ases yield on analysis to a substratum of wife exchange where a
oman from one family, sib, or moiety is traded for a woman of the
ther. Logically the Batak woman should be chaste when sold into
arriage, while her Minangkabau sister should merely hire a hus-
and after a long and eventful spinsterhood, yet the very reverse
f this situation is the case. Presumably both peoples at one time
racticed the common Indonesian custom of prenuptial sexual laxity.
f actual enslavement of one sex by the other, either among the
ataks or the Minangkabau, there is not a trace. The division of
abor is similar everywhere in Sumatra to that of Borneo or the
hilippines.

Evidently there has been some force which has created the two
pposing régimes in Sumatra; yet this force or influence cannot be
ought either in sociological necessity, in the functioning of local

customs, or in some accidental or deeply inrooted historical principle such as the levirate and sororate, the division of labor between the sexes, or patrilocal versus matrilocal residence.

The presumption therefore lies in favor of historical diffusion of custom. There is strong linguistic indication that perhaps somewhere between the first and second millenium B. C. Sumatra was subjected to direct Dravidian influence, and that certain sociological customs, including avoidance customs and joking relationships, cross cousin marriage, matrilineal and patrilineal sibs, moieties, exogamy and totemism, were imported from southern India into Sumatra and the Pacific.

Religion.

The religious beliefs of the Minangkabau are a mixture of paganism, Hinduism, and Mohammedanism. It sometimes is difficult to decide whether a particular belief is of Hindu or Mohammedan origin. The belief in seven heavens unquestionably dates back to Hindu days, for the Hindus had seven heavens and seven hells. The belief in seven heavens likewise is to be found in the Mohammedan religion, for Mohammed climbed to the seventh heaven. The fundamentals of the soul concept, or animism, however, are native Indonesian.

Cosmology. — The earth is conceived of as a flat disc resting on the horns of a huge bull. This animal stands on an egg, which is laid on the back of a fish, which slowly swims around on the surface of an immeasurably large sea. Under the sea there is but empty dark space. When some insect has the impudence to pick out a resting place in an ear of the bull, the animal shakes its head and the earth quakes.

High above the mountains and the woods extends the blue sky vault which hides the beauty of the heavens from human eyes. It is built up in seven layers, each more beautiful and costly than the others, until one arrives at the dwelling place of Allah, the High One.

The sun is conceived of as a ball of pure fire drawn through the sky by nymphs. Sun and Moon suffer ills the same as humanity and when they are sick they appear in a dark veil, i. e., an eclipse.

While Allah the Creator is the Supreme Being, there also are countless other spirits in the universe, both good and bad. The good spirits are called djihin Islam, the bad ibilih, Setan, or hantu. Spirit which appear to man, no matter under what form, are called hantu

Soul belief. — Corresponding to our idea of the soul, Maass
ates that the Malays of the Archipelago and Malacca have two
ifferent concepts and three expressions. 1. The Njawa (Minangabau njaò) is the soul in the sense of life, life bearer, life principle.
his is the real soul which leaves the body at the time of death.
his word and concept is the same as that of India proper, and has
een introduced into Sumatra and Java. 2. The Djiura (Minangabau djiò) from the Sanskrit djiva, life principle. 3. The Sumangat
Minangkabau sumange, Batak sumangot, Mentawei simagere) from
ıe Sanskrit sangat "strong" "very" with an "m" infix. This is the
ɔul in the sense of consciousness, life force, or health. It is this
ɔul which leaves in dreams and sickness, but which usually returns
gain to the body.

Toorn has made a special study of the Minangkabau soul
ɔncept. He writes:

"While the njaò is regarded as the source of life, the life or the
reath; the sumange is called the life force, the life fire, or con-
ciousness. The sumange is that which causes the impression of fear,
espect and wonder. It furnishes power, splendor and vivacity. It
ıakes itself apparent in the expression of the face, in the posture
nd movements of the body. Every healthy man may be called an
rang basumange by the Minangkabau, but this usually is said of
ome one who looks especially strong and healthy, who appears
ivacious and alive. If a man looks sickly, or has little or no expression
n his face, it is said that his spirit (sumange) is weak, or temporarily
as left him.

"The sumange, as well as the njaò, is immaterial. Between the
wo there exists an inner relationship; but so far as their material
ontainer is concerned, the concept concerning them differs. When
he njaò is gone, the body perishes, but it only is weakened by the
bsence of the sumange. Only when this permanently leaves the body
loes all life cease.

"The Minangkabau himself believes that the sumange is a being,
vhich has consciousness, which possesses a will, which has power
o think and feel, and which is entirely independent of the body.

"The sumange leaves the body either in suffering or in great
oy. This going away and returning of the sumange occurs both
oluntarily and involuntarily. The voluntary leaving occurs in dreams,
vhen the sumange lingers in places or by objects which have created

a deep impression. In some cases the dreamer speaks about the things
which the sumange encounters on his travels. From this kind of
journey the sumange returns of the free will. It is improper, however
to blacken or dirty the face of a sleeper, as this causes an aversion
in the sumange.

"The forced leaving of the sumange occurs in fright, anxiety
or sickness. Fright may be occasioned by the sudden meeting of
one sumange with another, which it did not expect, and which induced
it to leave its body. After this the sumange returns of its own free
will, after the unexpected stranger is gone. The anxious state of the
sumange also may be caused through worry, when the sumange
approaches a misfortune. We observe this in a criminal who is being
led to capital punishment, and whose palid face and quivering body
show that his sumange is gone. Sickness is caused when the evil
spirits torture the abstracted sumange. The suffering of the sumange
are felt by the entire body. The sumange, in this case, returns either
voluntarily or is forced back by the doctor (dukun)."

Animals and plants, like human beings, have souls (djiò). The
natives claim that when an animal dies or is killed its soul flies
away. But when a plant dies, there is no question of its soul
surviving after death. The plant dies, they say. An exception to this
rule, however, must be made in the case of rice. Among the Minang
kabau, as among all the rice raising people of the Archipelago, the
soul of the rice plant receives special treatment.

Rice Mother. — The Indonesian rice growing people not only
distinguish the nature of the rice soul from that of other animal and
plant souls, but often give the rice soul the same name as the human
soul. The Toradja of Celebes call the rice soul by the same name as
the human soul, tawuna. Among the Bataks the rice soul is called
tondi, and among the Javanese, Malay, Makassers and Buginese, it is
called sumange, sumangat, or semangat.

It can thus be seen that the rice plant is a thinking and feeling
being. Although the rice soul is in every rice plant and in every rice
kernel, yet this is especially true for the special plant which is ritually
taken out of the rice field. The rice soul is thought to be concentrated
in this plant, which is called mother, grandmother, grandfather or
uncle. The other rice plants of the field are called children or nephews

The Indonesians believe that the single rice kernels or plants are
persons who possess a power which can readily be lost at the time

hen the rice is cut, stamped, or cooked. For this reason a "mother
lant" is chosen, which is distinguished by a rich and powerful force
soul) and which contains the force of the rice field. The Rice Mother
lso attracts the soul of rice which has been lost to the crop, such as
aat which has been eaten by birds or mice.

One often finds that certain specific rites are performed, either
efore the crop has been taken in or afterwards, which have for their
urpose the gathering of the soul of the rice in the field and the
ringing of it into the granary. But the general purpose of all the
ce rites is to summon the highest good of the rice crop, the soul,
ad to lock it in the granary. The rites therefore assure a plentiful
op for the following year.

While the Minangkabau in general have lost the elaborate taboo
/stem common to the people of Assam and the pagan Indonesians,
ley have retained certain taboos (pantagan) in connection with rice
rowing. The Rice Mother must not be offended. It is forbidden:

1. To pull off one's coat in the rice field and cover one's head with it.
2. To draw the body of a woman who has died in childbirth past the
   growing rice. (The stalks would produce no blossoms).
3. A woman at certain periods is not allowed near the growing rice.
4. With uncovered head to uncover the upper or lower portion of
   the body in the rice field.
5. The unhulled rice can be brought into the house only by dragging
   it. It would be dishonored by being brought in otherwise, and
   would not remain in the cooking utensils.
6. To speak unchastely in the rice field. The rice would become
   ashamed and lose its odor and taste.

Eschatology. — The eschatological ideas of the Minangkabau,
ad the words used to express these ideas, are mainly Hindu. Moham-
edanism came to the archipelago from India and thus acquired
rtain Hindu concepts, but many of the beliefs no doubt antecede the
nversion of the people to Islam. The belief in the weighing of the
uls is interesting, as this idea originated in Egypt and came some-
hat late to India. Naturally the concept could spread no further
an the use of the scales. On the other hand, the judgement by the
idge of the dead is widespread in Oceania, occurring in prominent
rm in the eschatological beliefs of Fiji.

The Minangkabau believe that while the sumange goes away the

moment the body begins to feel sick, the njaò takes its departure aft
death. The angel Gabriel mounts with it to the heavens and allov
it to look down on the spot where it used to live. Then the ang
brings the soul back to earth. The dead still have the power of hearin
seeing, and feeling. Speech alone is lacking. On the way to the gra
the stretcher is set down for a few hours on the plain before t
dwelling, in order to give the soul a chance to ask forgiveness f
all the evil it has done, and to take departure from everything it h
loved. Further than this the soul has nothing to do with the boc
but goes back to its old dwelling place, where it rests in the gar
or on the ridge. The soul of a man visits daily the house of his wido
that of a woman the house of her husband. During the first hundr
days after the death the bed and chair of the deceased are beautifu
decorated. Nothing must be done which would annoy the soul, a
the dead person is spoken of with the greatest respect.

After the end of the hundred days a death feast is held and t
soul takes its departure to the land of the dead. It is believed t
the souls must run over a firm knife-edge wire, which is extend
over hell fire (called by its Sanskrit name, naraka). The evil fall
the good arrive at their heavenly abode, sirugo.

The good souls go to a place in heaven, where there is a t
tree (sadjaratu'l-muntaha). This is the racial tree of mankind, a
the souls abide there until the day of resurrection. At this time
good will inherit the earth and the evil remain in hell. The durati
in hell, however, is not eternal, but the good and bad deeds of the so
are weighed to determine the extent of the punishment merited. T
good deeds are called pahala (from Sanskrit phala, service, fru
and the bad deeds dosa (from Sanskrit dosa, sin).

Certain of the doctors (dukun) teach an esoteric doctrine
reincarnation for sin. This they doubtlessly learned from Mohamm
anized Hindu sources. The reincarnation of the soul takes pl
gradually and incompletely; for the animal, whether it be tiger, b
or snake, retains certain human body characteristics. This bei
which bears the name of djadi-djadian, places himself in
neighborhood of the dwelling of his family, where he receives fo
although attempts are made to banish him.

According to some doctors, the reincarnation from human bei
to animal, and from this animal into another, occurs seven times, a
then nothing remains from what formerly was a human being

earth. According to others, the metamorphosis takes place but once, and after the animal is dead the soul goes to soul land.

Doctors. — The Minangkabau doctor is called dukun or urang kapiturunan (turun, to descend, to come down). The dukun is either male or female. The women doctors, however, specialize in childbirth, the incision of girls, and massage. The male dukun's also have their specialists. Certain ones handle only internal sicknesses, others concern themselves with teeth filing, while still others circumcise or massage.

Insufficient knowledge has been obtained concerning the training of the dukun's. In general the position goes from father to son, or mother to daughter. The parent teaches the child orally, there being no written documents or formulae to hand down. The youth learns to gather herbs and witnesses the cures performed upon the sick. At the age of seventeen or eighteen the young dukun starts practicing for himself.

The dukun is greatly respected by the natives, not alone because of his medical knowledge, but also because of his command of magical formulae (mostly Mohammedan), by means of which he combats the evil spirits. He likewise is summoned to fight witchcraft, and in his capacity of medium, to enter into communication with spirits.

In spite of his title of kapiturunan, the dukun is a seer rather than a true shaman. Spirit possession is simulated beneath a blanket, but the dukun is not capable of giving a performance in the open, as is his Batak colleague. It is not known whether or not a neophyte dukun enters a vision quest in order to obtain a guardian spirit.

Toorn, however, states that a Minangkabau native goes into seclusion for the purpose of coming into contact with the spirits, from whom he wishes to learn one or more of the magical arts, as, for example, to make himself invisible. Usually he does this on the top of a high mountain, or in the thickest part of the woods. Here he remains until his wish is fulfilled, usually not longer than seven days. Presumably the prospective dukun undergoes this variety of vision quest. Maass mentions the fact that the dukun is able to see the ghosts of the dead at night. This visionary power is similar to that exercised in Mentawei by the seer.

The dukun cures by bringing back the soul, when it has been abstracted by the spirits. When anyone is sick the dukun is summoned, and certain herbs, flowers and rice are prepared by a woman who is not in her periods. The dukun brings these offerings to lonely high place and burns them in a dish. By this means h summons his friendly spirits (djihins). He then inquires thei purpose and urges them to aid in recovering the lost sumange an to bring it back to the dwelling of the patient. The dukun now lie down and is covered with a blanket. About fifteen minutes later hi limbs begin to tremble, an indication that his soul has left his bod and is on the way to the spirit village. Once there he tells the spirit (this is not heard by the human audience) the reason for his coming whereupon the oldest of the women djihin, Mande Rubiah, with som of her male and female followers, go to seek the sumange. Sometimes as in the case of serious illness, the evil spirits demand a sacrific for the return of the soul, as an armlet or kris. This is given t the dukun.

If Mande Rubiah does not succeed in recovering the soul, th patient is certain to die. If the djihins succeed in returning wit the sumange, the fact is made apparent by the trembling of the limb of the dukun, who remains unconscious, since his own sumange i still in the village of the djihins. The sound of voices which ar heard from under the blanket are said to be the voices of the djihin who have entered the body of the dukun. The djihins command tha benzine be burnt, so that the soul of the sick person can see wel enough to mount the ladder in the ghost house and partake of : feast. The soul then is escorted by the djihins back into its proper body

After all this has happened one usually questions Mande Rubial concerning further treatment for the sick person. The advice sometime is given that the patient should bathe for twelve hours, facing on or another of the neighboring mountains. In addition a sacrificia altar (ataran) should be constructed with gifts of cooked eggs, rice sirih and tobacco.

The dukun has still another method of curing. The patient surrounded by his relatives, is placed in front of a curtain. Th people are enjoined to maintain a deep silence, and the dukun step behind the curtain to confer with the spirits. One hears then th voices of the spirits and the voice of the dukun in conference. Finall the dukun comes back to the patient, tells him what has happened and what is required for a cure, spits on him, and recites a magica formula. In this manner of treatment there is no suggestion of spiri possession.

Maass, from his study of the Kuantan-district of Minangkabau, denies that the people in general have any concept of spirit possession, either shamanistic or as a sickness. Only a few, especially those who have been to Mecca, have learnt of the matter from the Arabs. The demons create sickness by tormenting the soul outside the body, not by entering into the person of the sufferer.

The bull-roarer (manggasieng) is used by the Minangkabau as a means of magically abducting the soul of a woman. This instrument is swung by a jealous lover who has been repelled in making advances. Some hair of the victim is made use of in the charm, and it is thought that the demons will steal the soul of the owner and reduce her to a state of madness.

CHAPTER III

THE ISLANDS WEST OF SUMATRA.

Introduction.

The more important islands to the west of Sumatra from the ethnographic point of view are Nias, the Mentawei islands, and Engano. Because of their geographical isolation, and the fact that the winds and currents are unfavorable to boats coming from Sumatra, the cultures of these islands are on a much lower level than those of Sumatra.

Most of the islands are surrounded by coral reefs and banks. The surf breaks heavily against these barriers, especially on the west coast, and this has rendered the landing of ships dangerous or impossible. The interior of the islands likewise presents an unfriendly aspect. The rivers are too shallow and full of sand banks for ships. The land itself is low, covered with dense jungle growth, and of a marshy, malarial nature. Small, uncertain footpaths lead through this wilderness. The natives themselves have contributed to the difficulties of exploration or annexation, fighting not only against one another, but also often uniting to confront foreigners.

The island of Nias has both the highest civilization and the thickest population; 200,000 people to its 650 geographical square miles. This island, however, was subjected to early pre-Hindu or Hindu influence, and has a megalithic culture, rice cultivation and the use of metals. These traits are lacking to the Mentawei Islands and Engano, which therefore present an interesting picture of Indonesian culture almost devoid of Hindu influence. The population of the four Mentawei islands: viz., Siberut, Si Porah, and North and South Pageh, together is estimated at not more than 10,000. It is well known that the Enganese, the most primitive of all the Indonesians, are on the point of extermination. In 1771 Engano was strongly populated, in 1868 there were still 6,500 Enganese, in 1909 there were only 372, and at present there are less than 300. Wars, epidemics and the barreness of the women are given as the main causes of the decrease in population.

All of the islanders speak dialects of the Malayo-Polynesian nguage, and are of the Malaysian race. Traces of Veddoid influence, shown by the presence of wavy-haired individuals, have been noted r Nias and the Mentawei islanders. In Nias there has been some ixture of type with the deutero-Malays from Sumatra, but the lentawei islanders have rigorously kept their women from contact ith foreigners. What is left of the Enganese is strongly tinctured ith Malay blood.

The animal life of the islands west of Sumatra is much scantier respect to mammals than on the islands of the Archipelago proper. lephants, tigers, rhinoceroses, panthers, and tapirs are absent. uffaloes are found in Nias, as well as wild boar. Boars are likewise be found in Siberut, but not in the southern Mentawei islands. eer are hunted in all of the western islands except Engano. The estern islands have an abundance of monkeys, including the gibbon, ad long tailed monkeys are found through the Mentawei group, but re lacking to the Archipelago. The rivers are rendered dangerous y crocodiles, and many varieties of poisonous and non-poisonous aakes lurk in the jungles.

The natives everywhere have dogs, chickens and domesticated igs. The chickens and pigs are eaten ceremonially at the time of asts.

PART I. NIAS.
Introduction.

Mention is made of Nias in the ancient Arabian and Persian ccounts of travels. The Persian merchant Soleiman (851 A. D.) rote about the head-hunters of Niyang (Nias). For many centuries ias served as a recruiting station for slaves, which were imported the west coast of Sumatra. In the 17th century the Dutch gained foothold in the island, since it became part of the domain of the ast India Company. In 1756 the English planted their flag in veral of the northern districts, but in 1825 the English posts again ere taken by Holland. By the beginning of the present century the land had been brought under a Dutch controller and Dutch civil w. Many of the natives have been converted to Christianity.

The native name for the island is "tano niha", land of the people. he word "niha" was converted by the Dutch into "Nias".

It usually is contended that the Nias people are derived from the

Bataks. The argument is based on similarities of language, physica
type, and customs of the two peoples. On the other hand, nothin
positive is known about the peopling of the island, and there are n
traditions on this matter. The people themselves, like the Polynesian:
trace their ancestry back to the gods.

The average height of the Niha is five feet, but in the south th
people are somewhat taller. The population is lighter in skin colo:
the cheek bones less protruberant, the lips thinner and the nos
narrower than the proto-Malays of Sumatra.

While there is great similarity in the forms of material cultur
social organization, religion and mythology between the Niha an
the Bataks-due to the fact that the common origin of both highe
cultures is Hindu-yet the Bataks lack a pronounced megalithic cultur
while the Niha have neither writing nor cannibalism. The linguist
resemblance likewise is not of a convincing nature.

Every writer on Nias points out the differences, linguistic, poli
ical, social, moral, intellectual and material, which exist betwee
North and South Nias. One striking difference is in the village
themselves. In the south these are large, well laid out, and furnishe
with an abundant water supply. In the north the villages are sma
and dependent on natural features for concealment and protectio
Hence they are usually removed from water supply. In the north th
people are apathetic physically and psychologically, due to poor foo
and uncleanliness, and as a reaction from the constant warfare an
insecurity of life in the past. In the south the people are energeti
and possess a high sense of order and artistic tendencies. Yet it
in the south that the natives have resisted foreign rule the mo
passionately, and even today practice head-hunting and huma
sacrifice.

Economic Life.

Villages and houses. — The Nias villages commonly are built
two rows of pile houses, with an open square in the center, pave
with stone. This form of settlement extends down into the Batu island

The common name for house throughout the island is "omo'
The houses are inhabited by one or more families. It is customar
for a father and his married sons to live in one dwelling, with perha
other related people as well. In the north the slaves likewise live
the family house, but in the south they have homes of their ow

All the social life of the village may take place in the famil

ouses. Guests are received, feasts celebrated, and all work, other
than agriculture, may be performed in the homes. The houses serve
as gathering places at night when there is no work to be done elsewhere.

In the north the houses are oval in form, while in the south they
are four cornered. The partitions of the houses, however, are everywhere similar. The main principle is that there should be a large,
fairly round room in the front, facing the village square, with a hearth
at the rear. Behind this room are the sleeping quarters. In the south
special rooms are sometimes erected here for married couples. In
the center of the island a few houses resemble Dayak communal houses,
with a gallery in front, and separate rooms for families to the rear.

Schröder has designated the most important house parts as
follows: 1. The under portion of wooden posts, between which are
the pig pens. 2. Steps or ladders. 3. The front room for public
life, cut off from the rear by horizontal lattice work. 4. A hearth
and private at the back of the living room. 5. The same arrangement
behind the sleeping room. 6. A double palm leaf roof. Smoke from
the hearths goes up to the top roof and out of the house.

The houses of chiefs in the south are of imposing architecture and
ornamentation. They are very much larger and made of better material
and workmanship than those of commoners. The height of the roof
is correlated to the splendor of the house. While it takes but a few
months to build the house of a commoner, that of a chief takes several
years. The house of one chief took five years to build.

When a new house is to be built drums are beaten to scare away
the ghosts and sacrifices are made by a priest. This is a time for
fasting. Special offerings are made to Lowalangi, the sky god, so
that the building will be firm. Pigs, also, are rolled from the roof
and killed inside the foundations of the building. Formerly human
sacrifices were made at the time of the erection of the pole, and
heads were hung before the idols. At the completion of the building
more heads had to be offered.

The house furniture is very simple. The people sleep on wooden
pillows, and have tables of stone or wood. Clothing and decorations
are kept in elaborately carved wooden chests. Stacks are attached
to the walls for lances and clubs. The floor is covered with mats
woven from leaves, and food is kept in rotan baskets. The skulls of
animals killed in the chase decorate the walls.

In the large villages the "bale" still is to be found. These ar
small primitive buildings in which wooden ancestral idols are kep'
In one village the bale consisted of a room made from four uprigh
pillars reaching from the ground to the roof. There were no sid
walls. In this bale seventeen heads were stored. The priests use th
bale when they wish to communicate with the ancestors.

The bale in Nias is no longer an assemblage place, although i
is thus mentioned in stories, nor is it a men's house. Stranger
coming to a village and having no other place to stay, howevei
sometimes lodge overnight in the bale. The bale of Nias is of far to
degenerate a form to be used for tribal council, as among the Bataks
The house of the most prominent village chief is used for this purpose

The villages of the south always were fortified by walls, ston
steps, and doorways, while the northern villages depended more o
natural fortifications. The stone steps leading up to a village ofte
remain after the houses themselves have fallen into decay. Near th
village is always the bathing place of men and women. This is
four cornered bath made of stone. Water is led into it by means o
stone gutters. In other villages water is conveyed to the bath b
bamboo carriers. Where a village is situated near a river this is use
for bathing. The smithy is situated either in or outside the village

Food. — The principal food of the Niha is vegetable. Othe
foods are eaten but rarely, excepting at feasts, when pigs are in grea
favor. On the northern coast, however, fish is eaten in quantity. Th
chief vegetable foods are rice, sago, maize, taro, and yams.

There exist a number of stories relating how rice was introduce
into Nias by the gods, but no historical account of its actual intro
duction. This cereal is used very much more at the present tim
than it was formerly. Both the wet and dry variety are grown. Th
usual Malaysian Rice Mother customs are observed. When the ric
is in blossom the Rice Mother is addressed by the priest. Then th
rice harvesting begins. At the end of the harvest three stalks of ric
are bound together and brought to an idol. The image is addresse
in prayer, and given a sacrifice of pigs and chickens.

Yams are eaten the greater part of the year. In certain localitie
maize is planted in the rice fields. Taro is eaten everywhere on th
island, and coconuts are important as food, especially in the south
There is an origin story relating that the first coconut tree sproute
after seven years from a boy who was buried in a sack. As else

here on the islands the natives chew sugar cane to obtain its sap. ago is prepared in times of food scarcity, and is used for food on shing trips. The tree, which grows in swampy localities, is cut down, e bark removed, and the meal washed and sieved.

Palm wine is partaken of, especially in the north. The men drink to excess at feasts, but women and children do not join in the inking. Betel is chewed throughout the entire island. The natives so smoke Javanese tobacco, and chew it with betel nut.

Salt is obtained from sea water, and traded inland.

The domestic animals eaten include chickens, goats, karabau, gs and ducks. Pigs, both domestic and wild, are the chief source animal food. The heathen and Christian people over the entire land, with the exception of the Mohammedan people on the coast, t pork. Pigs are killed at feasts, and the flesh when dried formerly rved as a medium of exchange.

The slaughter of pigs (bawi) takes place before the dwelling of e feast-giver or in the house itself. The animal is killed by stabbing, e body singed, and then cut into sections. The division of the rcass is a momentous occasion, since every person present has rights certain sections, and in former days a mistake would have caused uds and wars. The head of the pig goes to the foremost chief esent. The meat is cooked in native pottery or imported iron pots. oth pigs and roosters are castrated and fattened for feasts.

Chickens likewise are used chiefly as sacrificial animals. The vers and the feathers are given as food to the spirits. At feasts ndreds of chickens are decapitated by the partakers. The eggs of e fowl likewise are eaten. Most of the ducks consumed are of a ild variety found on the coast.

Karabau are as yet rarely to be found inland. On the coast they e killed for Mohammedan feasts. Goats likewise are of recent im- ortation.

The wild animals eaten include boar, apes, deer, civit, porcupine, a and land turtle, leguan, boa constrictor, birds, and a great variety fish. Mice and rats, the wild cat, snakes and frogs are not eaten. ice are avoided because they are thought to contain the souls of cestors. Women are forbidden monkey meat, the reason given being at a woman once turned herself into a monkey. While all wild imals belong to the brush spirits "bela", albino animals are pecially protected by these spirits and therefore are not eaten.

Hunting is conducted both for the purpose of getting rid of harmful animals and to obtain animals for food. Thus rats are caught in noose traps, and cats are highly esteemed for their mice catching propensities. Weasels are shot, and owls are hunted down in their nests to prevent them bringing rain to the island by their hooting. Crocodiles are highly respected, as elsewhere in Indonesia. In Nias they are thought to have been sent by Lowalangi. These animals are hunted only after they have stolen pigs. They are then either caught with a hook baited with chicken or they are speared. Their skins are used on festive occasions.

The chief food animals which are hunted are boar, deer and monkeys. Boar are sometimes hunted during rainy nights when they are unable to hear, or they are driven into bamboo traps, or nets. Dogs are used in the latter drive. Sometimes pointed lances are placed on the paths which the boars are accustomed to travel. Deer likewise are killed by this method. Monkeys are shot or are caught in traps which permit them entrance but not exit.

Birds are shot with a blow-gun or are caught in nets, traps or falls. Wild bees are smoked out for the sake of their honey.

There are a large number of ceremonials and taboos connected with the hunt. In the south the tree spirits must be propitiated with sacrifice before the hunt starts. A special language is employed on the chase, and the proper names of the wild animals avoided. It is believed that at one time the spirits (bela) had fire, but that man lacked it. Therefore it is forbidden to borrow fire from one's neighbor while a hunt is in progress. Other taboos arise from the fear of driving off the game. Thus it is forbidden to sweep out one's house, to break pottery, or to ring a gong at this time. In general all animals with the exception of cats, may be killed.

Contrary to the custom of the Mentawei islands, the true native Niha fishes without the aid of boats. In fact the Niha does not make use of boats at all. The rivers are not adapted to this form of navigation, and the natives fish only in the rivers, and not on the beach or in the sea. Fishing rights in the rivers belong to the village nearest the portion of the stream in question. Fish are caught by means of bamboo traps, drag nets, throwing nets and fish hooks. Fish also are poisoned or caught with nets behind artificial dams.

The people of the south eat three meals a day, while in the north two are eaten. Men, women and children eat together, but the slaves t apart. Eating is done with the fingers, but the people have pottery, conut shells and bamboo water containers as utensils. The oldest rm of fire making apparatus was the fire drill, but fire likewise was ade by percussion and by stone and flint.

Both dogs and cats are of importance in Nias. The dogs (asu) ve under the houses or by the hearths; as in Mentawei they live on e offal of man. Although they are not used as watch animals, they e useful in hunting. They bite the prey and hold on to it until the unters approach. Cats (mao) have somewhat of a sacred nature, as ready has been indicated. It is forbidden to kill or sell a cat, nce this animal serves as watch animal on the bridge to the land the dead.

Clothing and decorations. — The national clothing for men con- sts of a loin cloth and a cloth around the head to hold down the air. Cotton has rapidly replaced the non-washable tapa. Women ear a cloak, or at least a loin cloth, and a cloth around the head e same as the men. Hats are used by both sexes as protection om the sun. In the south tapa sandals are worn by people who alk on coral.

Costume varies according to the circumstance of the person, oseness to civilization, and the weather. Chiefs do not wear especially ch clothing, but assume gold ornaments at festivals. In the south ld ornaments are worn by the chiefs and important people at all nes. The loin cloth of men is usually red, blue or yellow. Young en try to wear as many different colors as possible. Poor people ssess nothing more than a short tapa loin cloth and coat. After death all decorations are taken off and only old clothing is worn.

Men wear their hair long and tied at the back of the head in knot. Women keep their long hair tied up with a head band.

Gold is the principal material used as decoration. Its name na'a (Sanskrit kanaka), shows that Nias had early trade connections ith either India or the Hindu colonies of Sumatra. Silver, copper, , brass, iron and lead are used in making the heavy Nias r-rings. Glass, earth or copper beads are worn. Other decorations ay include crocodile teeth, the teeth or tails of the tiger, and tortoise snail shells. Rotan often is coiled around the body, and fruit, orns, leaves or flowers thrust in the hair. The hibiscus flower is entioned in the earliest myths. It was worn by men and women to ep away the evil spirits.

The body is rubbed with oil, but is not painted. The Niha
not tattoo. Certain of the old people of the south are tattooed, but th
was done for the sake of visiting the Batu islands. The reside
Mentawei islanders of this group would have killed untattoo
strangers.

All the Niha have their teeth filed to a point, and formerly t
teeth also were blackened. The filing is done with a native file, a
the teeth afterwards are polished. The operation takes place betwe
the tenth and the fourteenth year of the child's life. Boys are c
cumcised as a sign of manhood between the 13th and 16th yea
The operation is performed by a layman, is without ceremony, and
merely the common Indonesian incision.

Trade and artifacts. — The Niha mined copper as early as t
tenth century A. D., as is shown by a Persian document, and probab
had gold long before. The civilization of the island is therefore
long standing.

In former times, however, slaves were the chief article of trad
and it was not until 1904 that the slave trade was ended, nor un
the last few years that slave holding was entirely abolished. T
people of Mentawei and Engano neither held slaves nor were th
themselves ever used either as slaves or servants by foreigners.

In 1836 the exports from Nias included coconuts, domestic fo
pepper, and many slaves. The imports consisted of iron, steel, copp
work, gold, grains, linen and Chinese wares.

There is no manufacturing for sale in Nias, but goods are ma
solely for home consumption. The chief industries of the island a
the making of idols, tapa making, woodwork and carving, clay burni
for pottery, metal working, netting, the manufacture of coconut o
rotan working, rope making, painting, matting, weaving and t
gaining of salt. Gold ornaments are made by the gold smith, a
helmets, hooks, shields and lance points by the iron smith.

Actually there are no true professions in Nias, since everyo
engages in pig raising and agriculture. The chiefs and importa
men supervise the work of their field slaves. The most honored
is that of the gold smith, and next, that of the carpenter and copp
worker. These trades are carried on by chiefs and the sons of chie
Even such an important trade as that of the gold smith, howev
is stopped at harvest time. Women do all the work connected w
pottery and weaving, while men do all the work in which cutti

nd hammering plays a rôle. The wives of the southern chiefs engage n no heavy labor whatever.

The division of labor appears more equitable among the Niha han among the Bataks. The man performs his part of the agri-cultural operations, takes care of the animals, goes on the hunt nd fishes.

Since almost the entire population is engaged in agriculture, early rising is necessary, and the people are awake at four or five in the morning. Unless the worker has slept in his field hut, the first hour is devoted to chores in the town. In the north the palm wine drinkers hen go to gather the sap which has flown during the night from he trees into the bamboo receptacles. The cattle food, which has been brought in the night before from the fields, is now given the cattle. At eight or nine o'clock, after the dew has dried, the people are engaged in field work, at certain times of the year in the rice fields. After the work in the fields, the men go home and the women gather food for the animals. Before eating the evening meal every one in he southern villages goes bathing. Food is prepared and eaten at about eight in the evening. Then comes an hour for gossip and story elling. By ten all are asleep. Rice season is the one of chief activity, after that is over, there is much hunting.

The facilities for trade within the island itself in pre-colonial days were favorable, especially in the south where the paths were well kept. The paths even to-day are laid along river banks, and one has to wade through water. Bridges are sometimes formed of a single rotan, with another above as guide. There is one suspension rotan bridge on the island. Goods are carried by hand, on the back, or on a stick suspended over the shoulder. Women have carrying baskets with straps over the head and shoulders. In time of war the women carry the baskets while the men travel unencumbered ahead, armed with lance and shield.

The musical instruments are of both percussion and wind variety. The most primitive instrument consists of two shells which are struck against one another. Various sized imported gongs form the native orchestra. The wooden xylophone used consists of three planks and is played upon with two sticks. The native harp is made of two bamboos between which slips are attached. The "strings" are struck with a hammer. The wind instruments consist of three kinds of flutes and a trumpet. A rice flute is made from rice stalks and is blown

at rice harvests. Small bamboo flutes also are used. Like the Pol
nesians the Niha have nose flutes, but these are found only in th
north, and are rare.

The weapons of offence consist of spears, swords, daggers, stone
and of recent years, fire arms. The spear is more used than th
sword. The spears are both thrown and held in the hand for thrustin
In head-hunting the victim is first thrust through with the lance ar
then decapitated. As in South Celebes, a warrior often creeps und
the house of his enemy and thrusts through the floor boards wi
his lance. Stones are thrown by hand, since slings are unknown. Th
Niha make no use of poisoned weapons.

Weapons are inherited and are not buried with the dead. The
rarely are hung up with the images of the dead.

Two forms of shields are used for protection. The first is ov
in form and is found throughout the entire island. It is held by th
arm and is used to guard off thrown lances and sword thrusts. Th
second form of shield is four cornered. The shields are made of woo
Warriors usually wear leather jackets made of crocodile or karaba
skin, and on special occasions helmets of thick leather ornamente
with crests of black hair, and artificial beards and mustaches
the same material.

Megalithic culture. — The megalithic culture of Nias has receive
wide-spread attention from scholars, due to its obvious connectic
with India and South Asia. Heine-Geldern, who has made the mo
thorough study of the megalithic complex, believes that megalith
and the sacrifice of cattle belong to the same historical layer
southern Asia. In Nias, as in Mentawei, the pig sacrifice replac
the cattle sacrifice. The main regions of well developed megalith
culture in Indonesia are the islands of Nias, Sumba and Flores, an
a part of Celebes. There also are prehistoric stone monuments in Ja
and Sumatra. Stone structures are entirely lacking in the Nicobar
Mentawei, and Engano.

There is the closest resemblance between the megaliths of Nia
and those of the Naga of Assam. Although the stone culture of Nia
is presumably of later date than that of the Naga, it is more ful
developed, and menhirs often assume the form of obelisks. In Nia
as among the Naga, there are stone fortress walls, paved street
and stone steps leading to the villages. Again, as among the Nag
the memorial stones are of two varieties: the monuments erected

e's lifetime, and memorials erected by survivors after the death of
person. A further resemblance between the two regions lies in the
ct that the erection of a memorial stone is accompanied by costly
asts, of which there are several grades. Furthermore, upright stones
present deceased males and lying down deceased females.

In every village of Nias one sees stone benches which originally
ere erected as seats for the ghosts of the dead. In the south the simple
nch is called daro daro, and those with a back attached, tedro hulu.
the north these benches are called behu and harefa. Benches are
kewise to be found in the woods, mountains and near bathing places,
rving the living as well as the dead. In many villages the skulls of
cestors are kept under the daro daro. The daro daro, or stone bench
sembly place of the Niha, corresponds to the assembly place, marae,
Polynesia.

Contrary to the customs of Sumatra and the other western islands,
ias is noted for its abundance of idols, usually of a phallic nature.
ese images are called adu, behelo or behu (adu from aitu, ghost;
helo from Malay brhala, idol; behu from beghu, ghost). All the
ols are called adu in the north. In the south this word is used for
ols not called behelo, these latter being idols made in the case of
ckness, as in the Nicobars.

Idols are made of clay, stone or wood, usually of the latter
bstance. In case of a death an ancestral idol is made and kept in
e house. Children, and men and women who have left no male
scendants, are given no idol. The sickness idols are very crudely
ade. The upper portion is forked with a bare indication of eyes and
se. The doctor uses these to summon the spirits who are to return
e soul of the patient.

The stone idols are called gowe, the same as the benches.
ey represent men and women with exaggerated sexual organs,
dicating a desire for children. The erection of these stones takes
ace with great festivities.

Time reckoning. — The people of Nias figure time from the
riod in which their ancestors came from the world above to the
rth. Every individual is able to give his genealogy from the time
at his first ancestors came to the earth.

The Nias year begins with the rising of the Pleiades, called zara.
ere is a native story that seven children (the Pleiades) went to the
y. The parents and a slave (Orion) followed. Planting is started

one month after the rise of the Pleiades. The year is reckoned betwe___
two consecutive risings in the same locality of this constellation. ___
one wishes to reckon in longer periods than a year, one counts t___
number of intervening rice crops, each crop representing six mont___

The year is divided into twelve numbered lunar months, and t___
month is divided into two parts, the waxing and the waning of t___
moon. The first part of the month is propitious to the beginni___
of undertakings, and the last part to their ending. The month ag___
is divided into days, some of them lucky and others unlucky. The d___
is divided by descriptive terms, such as "sun rise".

The sun is called si baja, which is also the name of the r___
spirit. It is believed that there were once two suns and no moon. T___
stars are thought to be the children of the sun and moon.

The Niha, like the Polynesians, reckon duration of time by nig___
instead of by days.

There are only two regions in the sky, the place where the s___
rises and where it sets. There likewise are only two directions, ___
stream and down stream. It is thought that the Bataks likew___
originally had but these two directions.

Games and dances. — The Niha, as is usual with the Indonesia___
make little use of artificial objects as an aid to their games. No gam___
of Hindu origin are played, and but one of Chinese origin, viz., k___
flying.

The few games in which artifacts are employed include footb___
playing with a lasso, throwing a spear at a target, and throwing sto___
along the water. In football the ball is made of rotan and the obj___
is to keep it as long as possible off the ground. Schröder believ___
that the ball may represent the sun which the people endeavor to ke___
from setting.

The games played without objects include those of strength ___
agility and those of wit. Among the first variety may be listed t___
swimming, standing on one's head, trying to pull one another ov___
with the hand, tug of war, and imitation pig stealing. Games of ___
include riddles and ring singing. Sometimes objects are conceal___
and children are sent to find them.

Games usually are played at the time of feasts, when the peo___
also amuse themselves with the native dances.

The favorite dance is the war dance in which warriors in f___
armor and with spears and shields engage in mock combat. A sna___

lance is found in Central and North Nias. This is enacted by men, with the women following with mincing steps. While the Niha are ot so much given to animal impersonating dances as the Mentawei, n the "chicken thief dance" a woman impersonates the chicken hawk. The clapping of hands represents the clapping of the hawk's wings s it descends. Family feasts are given at rice planting, harvests, louse building, the purchase of a gong, birth, betrothal and name giving. Chiefs give feasts to the entire village, and the circumcision of a young chief is an especially important event. While Nias feasts are not surrounded with taboos, as among the Naga and in Mentawei, yet they do represent a communion with the ancestors, and doubtlessly he dances and games enacted at the time were originally of religious significance. Drums and gongs furnish the music for dancing.

Society.

Government and classes. — The north and south of Nias was populated from the center. At the time of Marsden (1811) the population already was distributed over the entire island, and was divided into about fifty small districts. Each district was under a chief, and these were at constant war with one another. Schröder writes that there are at present thirty-seven districts and fifteen hundred and twenty-six villages in Nias.

The district (ori) was not the oldest unit of Nias government, but, as elsewhere in Indonesia, was doubtlessly due to Hindu influence. The government of the district actually rests in the hands of the village chiefs, and thus the village is the center of Niha rule. The sibs no longer have governmental functions in Nias, and it is only in the north that marriage is exogamous to the sib. The sole reason for the preservation of these patrilineal units is the desire for genealogical ancestor worship.

The laws and regulations of the island are in part determined by he district and in part by the villages. The district determines the ranking order of the village chief, the measures to be used in the region, the size of bride-prices, and the relative worth of gold, pigs, and rice. It is the district, and not the village, which has well recognized boundaries.

For practical purposes the highest unit of government is the village, with its own rule, laws, and property. The heads of the villages are called si ulu in the south and salawa in the north and

142

center. Ulu is head or upper course of a river; alawa means high, an si alawa that which is high. The chiefs possess their dignity b hereditary right, but only when their mothers too are of the sam rank. Otherwise the children belong to the rank of commoners. I the south the inheritance of the family rule, as well as that of chie taincy, passes to the eldest surviving brother (ama, a word used fo father or father's brother). In the north, however, the eldest so obtains the right of inheritance by catching in his mouth the dyin breath (soul) of his father. No doubt fitness for office counts a well as seniority.

In the big villages of the south where more than one sib liv together, there is always a main chief and lesser chiefs. The villag is divided into gana, or hamlets, and each hamlet is inhabited by sib and its respective chief. Each gana has certain duties and privi leges, such as the upkeep of paths and bridges. Only wealthy chief can have power, for these alone can furnish the necessary pigs t slaughter at feasts. There is the greatest jealousy among chiefs, eac attempting to outdo his rivals in the giving of feasts, and th attaining of rank.

The foundation of Nias wealth is agriculture and pig breeding So the principal chiefs are above all farmers and pig raisers. Fro the wealth they obtain in this manner the chiefs loan money and good to the commoners at high rates of interest, thus making them thei permanent debtors.

The chiefs assert their divine rank in various ways. They diffe from the commoners in apparel, for they alone, along with member of their family, wear golden ornaments, and they alone have the righ to hold slaves. The chiefs, according to the belief of most Niha, afte death go to a special place where they live in great state because c the sacrifices performed at their funerals. The ghosts of commo people, who received no great sacrifices at their funerals, canno become powerful spirits.

The Nias chief is regarded as a father by his subjects, and he i always spoken of as ama, father. His wife is spoken of as ina da, ou mother. The sons of chiefs are called achi, younger brothers.

Ranking next to the chiefs, in the south, are the si ila, chosen b the people from the commoners. These are really the village elder They provide the village chiefs with advice, and see to the prope carrying out of their orders.

Important matters are talked over in a gathering of the commoners, called by the chief. The gathering takes place in the town square, or at the house of the chief. The meetings are called to determine the proper interpretation of the adat. Variation from the adat would bring the living in conflict with the dead, who would punish the people by bringing strife and disease into the land.

The chiefs are thus law givers and upholders of the law. The people can exert influence through their formost men, but the ultimate decisions lie in the hands of the chiefs. The chiefs in Nias are far more important than the Batak chiefs, and in fact are thought to be the reincarnation of the forefathers who came down from heaven. Thus they are in a sense divine, and the course of events on earth depends on them. In this respect the Nias chiefs resemble those of Polynesia.

Between the chiefs and the commoners and slaves there is a great gulf. There is however, a peculiarity of Nias adat which compels the commoner, like the chief, to give a series of feasts before he can obtain his full rank.

Slaves are obtained either through war or debt. As among the Bataks, when a person is in debt up to the amount of the value of a slave, either he or a member of his family is enslaved. Also, as among the Bataks, the slaves are either house or field servants. The lot of slaves is not a hard one, and they wear no distinguishing badge. They are married off by their masters, who thus wish to increase the number of slave children. Due to the high cost of marriage among the free Niha, while almost all the slaves are married, a large proportion of the free remain single.

The master of a slave has the right to kill his servant, but this is seldom done, as it is a destruction of valuable property. Where human sacrifice formerly was called for, a slave of no value was sacrificed. As a rule only runaway slaves receive harsh treatment.

Law. — According to native Nias adat, a distinction is made between criminal and civil misdeeds. This clear cut distinction shows that the Niha have progressed well on the way towards state formation. In criminal matters, the affair is an infringement against the adat, and hence against the community. In former times criminals were invariably punished by death, and only at a later date could the matter be made good by a payment made to the chief. The classification of crimes is as follows:

1. Crimes against the forefathers (i. e. the adat).
2. Crimes against the authority (the chiefs).
3. Crimes against persons.
4. Crimes against property.

The law court of the Niha shows a further degree of developmen
above the most primitive stage in so far as "intent" entered into lega
decisions. When chiefs or their relatives are killed, however, n
distinction is made between murder and manslaughter.

A peculiarity of the Nias law consists in the severity with whic
offences against women are dealt with. A man might lose his han
if he be convicted of touching a woman on the breasts, and both th
man concerned and the woman might lose their lives if a woma
becomes pregnant outside of the marital state. Torture, such as th
use of burning pinchers, may be used on a woman to make her confes
the paternity of an illegitimate child. These laws may be explaine
by the fact that the Niha lay great stress on the prenuptial virgini
of their women, since the gods are concerned in the continuance
their own family lines. The sexual morality of the natives ha
diminished upon their becoming Christians. They fear punishme
in the next world far less than the pagan punishments of th
native adat.

The partitioning of the island into districts has considerab
ameliorated the law of blood revenge. Blood revenge is in confli
with the district adat, which requires that murder and manslaught
be punished by the chiefs of the region. This adat also extends, to
certain degree, to alien districts. Blood revenge mainly serves as a
excuse for head-hunting.

The Niha make use of the oath and ordeal. The ordeal is calle
tuna (Malay tenung). Among the ordeals practiced are the wat
ordeal, in which both parties dip under water, and the trial by battl
Oaths may be sworn to, individually or communially. There is
secular punishment for perjury, since the gods are supposed to punis
the perjurer. In order to avoid even this inconvenience, the native ha
a special god to whom offerings are made after he has perjured himsel

War. — The Niha had two varieties of wars before the days
Dutch control. The first variety was occasioned by a temporary disput
and often arose within a district; while the second was of the natu
of a standing feud, and was possible only between widely separat

stricts. All men capable of bearing arms fought, except the slaves, no were used as carriers.

Villages were attacked at night, and the weaker men, and the men and children were taken captive; all others were killed. The cestral idols were taken and placed beneath the house of the chief.

Schröder has listed the following causes of war, of which the st and the fourth were the most frequent incentive to combat:

1. The death of a person.
2. The rape of a woman.
3. Rape and theft.
4. The reception by a chief of slaves or fugitives belonging to another.
5. The non-payment of bride-price or other debt.
6. Disputes over territory.
7. Insults.

While head-hunting was an integral part of Nias wars, it seems obable that the basic motive behind this custom in Nias, as else-here in Southern Asia and the Pacific, was religious in nature. Heads ere required upon certain occasions, and they were obtained from ay foreign district with which the head-hunters were at feud. Heads ere never taken in Nias in connection with harvesting ceremonies. ney were procured in the south for the following reasons: 1. Blood venge. 2. At the building of a new village (the heads were offered the village stones). 3. At the building of the bale, where the village ods were housed. 4. At the building of an important chief's house. Upon the death of a chief, when the daro daro was placed before s dwelling. 6. At the big feast for the dead. 7. At the giving of ay big feast. 8. At the making of gold ornaments. 9. At the making irrevocable oaths. 10. In Central Nias heads had to be given ther-in-law as part of the bride-price. 11. In North and Central ias heads were provided in case of certain forms of sickness, in der to make the spirits release the soul of the sick man.

In one village the head-hunters were said to have eaten a piece of e victim's neck raw. It was the custom throughout the island to k the blood off the knife which had freshly severed a head. Schröder lieves that these survivals show that the Niha formerly were canni-alistic.

Like the head-hunters of the Philippines the warriors who had

taken a head were entitled to special forms of decorations. The
consisted of neckbands, kalabubu.

Birth. — The Niha practice a limited couvade. At the birth of
child the father cannot go into the brush, and until the child is
month old the parents cannot comb their hair. If they did this the chi
would fall from the house ladder. Neither parent is allowed to u
clay in his, or her, betel.

Cripples are killed at birth and likewise children whose moth
has died at childbirth. In the case of twins, one of the pair is hui
up in a sack and allowed to starve to death. Albinos bring great shan
to the mother, who is accused of having slept with a ghost. An albii
usually is killed at birth, but sometimes he is allowed to live until h
fifteenth year, in the hope that he will undergo a change of color.

Some days after birth, the child receives his name. A feast
held and the priest at the time predicts the future of the infant. Ti
father makes the choice of name, which is chosen according to co
temporary circumstance or some peculiarity of the child. A trivi
nickname often is picked out in order to deceive the evil spirits. Whi
Schröder states that the true name of a child is never mentioned,
also writes that teknonomy is practiced, and that the elders nar
themselves after their first child. Evidently children have true nam
and nicknames, and the parents call themselves after the nicknai
of the child. Women receive new names after marriage, and peop
change their nicknames in case of sickness. Chiefs assume honora
names after the giving of a feast, as, for example, "brightness
the sun".

Marriage. — The Nias adat concerning exogamy and kinsh
customs in general have been insufficiently reported upon. It appea
certain that originally the Nias had patrilineal exogamous sibs,
do the Bataks at the present time. These sibs still function to
certain extent. In the north they are called Orro, "children of".
the south there are the "Uri", family federations. Schröder writes tł
in the north marriage still is forbidden within certain lineages of t
sib, but that in the south marriage takes place by preference with
the family federation, of which there are three in number. Th
marriage is endogamous in the south, and exogamous to lineag
rather than sibs in the north. Cross-cousin marriage is found in Sou
Nias; that is, a man is supposed to marry his mother's brothe
daughter.

In the north an engaged couple must avoid one another. In the south, however, it is the custom for a man before marriage to aid the family of his bride in their work, and thus pay off part of the bride-price.

Marriage in Nias is always by purchase, and is binding not only on the grounds that it is a contract between two families, but also because it is connected with ancestor worship. The ancestral idols have to be notified before a marriage can take place. Polygyny is allowed, but is rare due to the high bride-price. The levirate is practiced with a lesser payment to the family of the woman.

The bride purchase is strongly patriarchal, and the woman passes over to the family of the man as a piece of property. Stress is laid upon the virginity of the bride, and widows and non-virgins are sold at half-price. In order to safeguard the unmarried women, they are not allowed to mix with the men at feasts, and they sleep together under the guard of an older woman.

The bride-price varies from 120 to 500 guldens, and is paid in instalments. Not only are the father and mother of the bride, and their respective relatives, entitled to a share, but a certain amount also has to be paid to the village chief and the people of the village. In the case of divorce this sum has to be returned.

It is commonly the custom to betroth girls, in receipt of a certain payment, at an early age, sometimes even before they are born. The marriages of the elder sisters are in this way arranged for before those of the younger sisters. If a girl is adult when betrothed she usually is not married off against her will. In all cases the desires of the mother are consulted, although according to adat the children belong entirely to the father. While all proposals of marriage are made through a third party, the prospective groom has the right to visit the village of the girl beforehand and see if she pleases him.

The village chief performs the marriage ceremony, which consists in part of the groom and bride eating and chewing betel together. The chief pours water over the feet of the bride, and offerings are made to the village god. The girl gets a new name at her marriage from her mother-in-law. After the marriage the bride goes to live with the groom. On entering her new home she is not supposed to touch the threshold, under penalty of infecundity.

Aside from the begetting of children, it is the duty of the women to tend the fields and the pigs. Only the women of the highest birth, who are married to important chiefs, are spared these duties. The women own as property their clothing, decorations and chickens. These are inherited by the daughters.

Divorce. — A divorce can be requested by either the husband or the wife. The family of the wife can demand a divorce only on one ground, that is, that the husband is remiss in paying his bride purchase instalments. A wife is not allowed to leave her husband for any other cause, and if she runs away she is sent back. A husband can send his wife back to her family, but only if she prove sterile which is considered her fault. For this, the consent of the chief must be obtained. The family of the wife then must either furnish a substitute, or pay back the bride-price.

If the husband dies and there are no children the woman can be taken back by her family. In this case the heir of the property of the deceased can claim the bride-price when the widow remarries. Or the widow can marry a son (through another wife) or brother of the deceased. If there are children the woman remains with the family of her husband. She can marry a brother of the deceased, but she is not in all parts of the island obliged to do this.

Death. — In Central Nias there are three main ways of disposing of the dead, depending on whether they are chiefs, commoners or slaves. The first are placed on platforms, the second buried, and the slaves are simply thrown into the jungle to be devoured by wild swine. The name of the coffins used for the dead is "owo", boats.

After death the corpse is washed with fragrant leaves, so that if it comes back to the house it will be recognized by its odor. If the deceased is a chief, he is dressed in festive clothing with golden ornaments. His mouth and nostrils are shut and his eyes closed.

After all this has been done, the wailing commences. During the evening the people from neighboring villages visit the death house. There is dancing and feasting, and gongs are struck to drive away the evil ghosts.

The first four days after the death are a mourning and taboo period. The body during this length of time is treated as if it were alive. Sharpened bamboos are placed around the dwelling, and no one is allowed to pass by, under penalty of death. Women sing mourning songs for these four days, and various sacrifices are made to the departed.

The body is taken to the graveyard on the third day and buried

roof is built over the grave, and implements for the dead deposited here.

On the fourth day the priest walks around the house to warn the ghost that it no longer is to enter the house and disturb the inmates. Prickly plants are placed to guard the house from its return. On this day also the wooden idol (adu) of the deceased is made and the ghost of the dead is summoned into it.

The reincarnated dead person is sought for this purpose at the grave. The deceased is thought to return as a spider (moko moko), so this animal is brought from the grave and applied to the idol. This besouling of the ancestral idol is done only for those who leave male descendants behind them.

It would appear that this particular form of ritual, which is derived from the Hindu belief in reincarnation, has diffused from India through Indonesia to Polynesia. Oldenberg states that in India in Veda times, if one wished to change the burial place of a body, and was unable to find the remains of the corpse, one merely had to spread a cloth by the side of a stream, call out the name of the dead person, and then bury the first insect or animal which alighted on the cloth as a substitute for the body of the deceased. In Samoa the soul likewise was thought to return as an insect which had to be wrapped in tapa and buried with the dead.

About two months after the death of a chief his bones are washed free from all flesh and a feast is held. The people of the south go head-hunting at this time, or rather did until very recently. There even existed in Nias professional head-hunters who sold heads to mourners, and who considered themselves under the protection of special gods of their own, as do the thugs of India.

At the death feast slaves are killed at the grave to serve their master in the next world, and the heads taken are rubbed against the coffin, while the deceased is implored to "rise up". When more than one head is obtained, they each bear different names. One, for example, is called a pillow for the head, another support for the arms and legs. All are called messengers for the dead.

The slave who has the duty of washing the bones of the dead is called "binu", the same name as that applied to the heads taken for the dead. He is very taboo, and has to sleep outside the village and have others cook for him. In former days the binu was finally tied to a stake and decapitated. His skull was put at the foot of the grave

as a "cushion" for the feet of the dead. As a mitigation of th
sacrifice, the binu at the present time has his left ear amputated.

The general feeling toward the dead in Nias as elsewhere is or
of fear. The ghosts of dead chiefs are especially feared, and likewis
the ghosts of women who have died in childbirth. To prevent th
ghosts of the latter from returning, the bodies of the women a
dragged out of the house through a hole in the wall.

Mourning consists in abstaining from certain foods, certain form
of clothing are not worn, and the mourners refrain from going o
of doors for the first few days.

Religion.

Introduction. — In the south an all-mother is placed at the b
ginning of things, while in the north a male principle is the originato
While in the south there is a hierarchy of personal gods, in oth
districts the wind gods are spoken of as the originators of all thing
and a world tree is mentioned from which everything developed. Th
idea of a world tree is not found in the south, where mankind i
thought to have sprung from a moon divinity. In the north the
likewise is a moon origin story. All the regions emphasize the fa
that twin gods married, and begot other gods and the human rac
This emphasis on incest, as well as the prominence of the world tre
in the mythology, is common to the Batak and Minangkabau belief
since all these peoples derive their mythology from Hindu, and ult
mately from Indo-European and Semitic sources.

Mythology. — The people of the south believe that the worl
originated as follows.

In the beginning there was no earth and no world, but Chao
was unnamed and unseen. Then this Chaos split and Ina-da Sam
hara Luwo was born. This goddess caused the world to be create

Then the stones split, and the following goddess, the Ancier
Mother of all races and gods arose: — Ina-da Samadulo Höse.

Although not married, this last named goddess begot fou
children, two pairs of twins, each time a son and a daughter. Th
pairs of twins which were born at the same time married one anothe
The youngest son afterwards was named Lowalangi and ruled th
skies, while the oldest, Latura, ruled the underworld. Strife aros
between these two, and Lowalangi threw stones down on the eart
for nine days.

Lowalangi married a second time, this time the twin sister of his elder brother, and this pair became the ancestors of the human race. This second wife gave birth to a child that was entirely round, without hands or feet. When the child was out in half, one half was female and the other half male. This couple married and gave birth to Hulu, the first person on earth.

The creation story as told in Center and North Nias relates of a dying god from whose heart grew the world tree. Lowalangi blew in the mouths of the first pair and thus gave them life. In some of the creation stories, account is made of the world river, which flowed round the edge of the earth, and the world snake underneath the earth. In all the stories the wind is featured as the creating force, and in all there was darkness in the beginning, since the sun and moon had not as yet been created.

The people of Nias believe that there are nine levels of heaven above the earth, in the uppermost of which lives Lowalangi. There are also nine levels below the earth. The story also occurs in Nias, as among the Bataks, the natives of Northwest Borneo, and in the Maui story of Polynesia, that the lowermost level of heaven once stood so near the earth that it reached to the roof-tops.

In the north and central portions of the island the conception is common that people are pigs kept by the gods. A person dies when his soul (noso, breath), first given him by Lowalangi, is finished. At the same time it is believed that death results because Latura has need of such a human being for his meal. In the south it is believed that people actually are the pigs of Lowalangi.

It is evident that the Nias god Lowalangi occupies somewhat of a middle position between the Hindu Brahma and the Polynesian sky god Langi, whose name is similar. In Polynesia, as in Nias, "langi" indicates the sky, heaven, or atmosphere. In Nias, Lowalangi is the god of the winds, and he gives people their souls or breath, which later returns to him. Thus the souls of the individuals are but part of the all-soul. Schröder believes that the word "lowa" in Nias indicates "breath".

Latura, who dwells in the underworld, is the Nias concept of a god of the dead. The situation was somewhat reversed among the early Aryans, where Yama was king of the dead. Yama lived with the gods in the highest heaven, under the "Cosmic Tree of Life", drinking soma which dripped from its leaves. He was surrounded by pitris, the souls of the righteous dead.

Both Lowalangi and Latura are otiose gods, since they receiv
neither prayer nor sacrifice.

The Niha believe in a number of tribal forefathers, or cultu
heroes. Most of the people relate about Hia, the father of mankin
He came to earth, when still a small child, lived there until a ful
grown man, and then returned to the heavens. From his attire ar
name it is certain that Hia is a moon god, and corresponds indeed
the moon goddess Hina of Polynesia.

A second culture hero is Daeli, who brought yams and polishin
stones to the earth. Some stories also relate that he brought fire
mankind. A third culture hero is Hulu. The origin of grass ar
trees are attributed to him, and it is said that they sprang from h
blood. The fourth tribal father is Sebuwa, who brought the prie
drum with him.

The Niha recognize as spirits the ghosts or forefathers (beghu
the wood spirits (bela or belada), and the gods. Certain natur
phenomena also are called beghu, as the spirits of evening glow, ar
the spirits which come out when the sun is shining through the rai
These nature spirits are very dangerous. In one locality it is thoug
that the giant snake under the earth causes earthquakes.

The soul and the afterlife. — According to Schröder the norm
Nias man is divided into the following parts:

1. The material body, boto. After death the body, with tl
exception of the bones, is thought to dissolve into the air.

2. The life-bringing breath, noso, which is borrowed from tl
wind and goes back again into the wind. Even the wooden idols, ad
have to be given noso in order to be efficacious.

3. The lumolumo (Cf. Fijian malumalu, the shade). Under lum
the Niha not only understands the shadow, but also the image as se
in the water. The lumo is thought to be a second person, an "eg
outside of the body. This is the soul which leaves the body and trave
in dreams and also in sickness.

The lumolumo is further divided, according to the eschatologic
ideas of the natives, into two parts:

1. The shadow. After death this goes to the underworld.

2. A likeness of the person, such as one can see in the wate
but which is split into:

a) A constant something, an image, which even after death is thought to be present near the grave.

b) The life-working principle of the likeness. (This cannot be thought of apart from "a".)

While in Nias the lumolumo as a whole turns into the ghost beghu), among the Olo-Ngadju of Borneo there is a division of the wo concepts. There the "liass" at once goes to the land of the dead, but he "karahang" goes only after the death feast, and then owing to the eads which have been taken, and which are demanded by the life-vorking principle of the likeness (2b).

Thus the Niha believe that in death the noso goes back to the gods. The body turns into what it was in the beginning, water and ir. There is no more lumolumo now, but the second of a dead person s the beghu.

After death the shadow ghost goes to the land of the dead, either n the heavens or in the underworld. The image remains near the grave. Spirits have to cross over a bridge in order to get to the sky vorld, below the bridge hell waits for the souls of the wicked. There s a watchman at the entrance of the sky world, armed with a shield nd spear, and having a cat as companion. The watchman examines he ghosts concerning their earthly life. According to Rappard, the hief sins of Nias are murder, poisoning, perjury, adultery and theft. Those who have led a wicked life on earth, and have given no feasts, specially death feasts, cannot pass over the bridge and are pushed ff into the water. This is done by the cat, the companion of the guardian of the bridge. The cat takes special pleasure in pushing nto limbo those who have harmed any of his own species during their ifetime.

According to Schröder, the Niha lay little stress on the idea of punishment in the afterworld, which is, in the main, a continuation of he present life. As already mentioned, chiefs who have had ample acrifices given them at their funerals enjoy a better lot than the ommoners. Day and night are reversed in ghost land, and the anguage of the dead is so reversed that only the priests can under-tand it. Members of this profession alone can see the ghosts, who ppear in the form of glowworms.

The belief is held that souls die nine times in the next world before hey become finally extinct. There is an idea that the dead likewise

are reincarnated on this earth in the form of various insects an
animals. The variety of insect or animal is determined both by ag
classification and the manner of death. For example, a drowned perso
turns into a white ant. Snakes and crocodiles especially are though
to be the reincarnated dead.

It may be noted that many of the Hindu ideas found in Nia
eschatology are strikingly like those of the Naga. The concept of th
bridge of the dead, the sanctity of cats, and the methods of reincar
nation are similar to the two regions.

After death the soul (noso) goes back to the gods. Lowalang
keeps all the noso in big pots, and certain portions belong to th
various tribes. Three gods rule over the destiny of men: Si Barasij
Noso, Ture Luluwo, and Lowalangi. The first gives out the soul
to the unborn babies, and the second gives out as much soul to eac
individual as demanded by Lowalangi. The amount of soul given ou
and thus the duration of life, depends on the demands made by th
unborn baby on Lowalangi. Thus we have the Hindu concepts of
trinity of gods and predestination.

Once a child is born its noso, or breath soul, lodges in the hear
The heart therefore enters into all Niha figures of speech as the se
of life and emotions.

Sacrifice. — There are two kinds of sacrifice in Nias: the sacr
fice to the ancestral spirits, and the sacrifice to the nature spirits an
gods. The first is in the nature of a communal meal and takes plac
at every feast. The ghosts eat the lumolumo of the slaughtered anim
and the people eat the meat. In offerings to the nature spirits an
gods, both the flesh and the lumolumo are given the spirits.

The various articles sacrificed included pigs, chickens, eggs, ric
palm wine, water and human heads.

Pigs alone are offered the highest gods. Before either pigs o
chickens are killed, some hair or feathers are singed in the fire as
presentation to the god to whom the sacrifice is to take place. Like
wise when a living person or a slave is to be sacrificed, some hair
first are cut off his head. In Mentawei pigs and chickens also ar
singed before being killed for sacrifice.

Eggs are broken over the object sacrificed to (as an idol), an
then no further use is made of them. While the sacrifice of eggs i
this manner is unusual in Indonesia, it is a prominent form of sacr
fice among the Khasi of Assam.

Priesthood. — The priest of Nias usually is called g-ere. This
ord corresponds to the Mentawei "si-kere-i", the seer and medicine-
an of the neighboring islands. Since the Nias medicine-man performs
e sacrifices, he is both priest and seer. The root "kere" used in the
o languages means supernatural power.

Both men and women may be priests. In the case of men, the
pernatural power runs in families, and the office is inherited from
ther to son. Young men of twenty have the right to practice medi-
ne. The period of instruction is eight days.

Whoever is destined to become a priests suddenly disappears,
ing carried off by the spirits. Usually the spirits let the young man
and he returns in three or four days to the village. When he does
t return the people look for him and often find him on a tree con-
rsing with the spirits.

Upon his return the novice seer is mentally deranged. It can also
ppen that he bears with him the animals representing his newly
und guardian spirits. For example, he may come back covered with
akes, which only the professional seers are able to see.

Sacrifices now are made to give thanks for the return of the
uth, and idols (adu) are constructed. These idols absorb the wood
irits from the youth, his reason returns, and he is competent to
rn the arts of sacrifice and healing.

The youth next is brought to the graveyard so that he becomes
own to the dead; to the river, to become acquainted with the water
irits; and to the mountains, to become acquainted with the mountain
irits.

When the novice returns from the mountains, he is not allowed to
at once to his own house, for that would bring him misfortune. The
osts who surround him would remain in his house and make his
lations and pigs sick. Therefore he goes to another town and remains
ere some days and nights in the hope of transferring the ghosts to
er people.

If the father is a priest he gives the novice instruction in magic,
orcism, and drumming. The other methods of curing the young man
rns from the other priests. He accompanies his instructor on
ofessional calls.

In the south the priests wear special clothing when in their
ofessional capacity, consisting of hair decoration and a cloth over
e shoulder.

Sickness. — The causes of sickness are as follows:

a) The absence from the body of the lumolumo.
b) The harming of the lumolumo, or the person himself.

The lumolumo can be taken away from the body by any one ‹ three causes:

1. By either one of the gods Lowalangi or Latura.
2. By evil spirits.
3. By the ghosts of the dead.

In the south it is always Lowalangi who takes the soul of t‹ sick man, for the people are considered the pigs of Lowalangi. In th‹ region it is chiefly Lowalangi who gives life, and Lowalangi w‹ takes life away.

Sickness likewise can be caused by old age, misfortune a‹ accident. In these cases it is the noso which is at fault. If a pers‹ dies of old age, it is because the noso which he asked for at birth ‹ used up. If a person dies from some accident other than head-huntin‹ it is because he asked for too little noso at birth.

The ghosts of people who have died of accident remain near t‹ spot of the misfortune, lamenting the fact that they had not been mo‹ foresighted at birth. The ghosts of drowned people, however, can ‹ brought to land by the proper sacrifice.

Curing. — Curing is entirely in the hands of the priests and t‹ dukun, laymen doctors who massage and suck. In cases where sic‹ ness is supposed to be caused by the spirit world, and these are in ‹ great majority, the priests are summoned.

People may be bewitched without the aid of the spirits. F‹ example, a sorcerer may project stones into a victim, causing him ‹ have rheumatism. The patient then is unable to urinate, and a duk‹ is called upon to suck red and white pebbles from his bladder.

In case of sickness due to soul loss, the priest must catch t‹ lumolumo in a cloth and apply it to the head and shoulders of t‹ patient. The priest knows when a ghost has taken the soul of t‹ patient, because the latter's body turns black. The beghu can abstr‹ the soul by frightening or biting a person.

In case of an epidemic the opinion is held that hostile demons ‹ catching pigs around the country. The remedy is to shut down t‹ settlement and keep out the spirits. People are allowed in, provid‹

1at they are not accompanied by evil spirits (i. e., have no con-
1gious disease). This is an effective quarantine, although the cause
f the disease is unknown.

The beghu also can make people sick by scattering ashes, &c.
round the country. They also place sickness in the water, and if a
erson drinks he becomes ill. But this great fear of the river water
1ust be attributed to the unclean habits of the natives. In Mentawei
1e people would be afraid to polute the rivers, lest the "Mother of
Vaters" become angry, and send sickness to the people.

When there are many cases of sickness within a village the priests
xorcise the evil spirits. They do this by going around the village
triking with their lances and hacking with their knives. A ghost, if
truck, stands a good chance of loosing one of its nine lives.

Often the ancestral idols (adu) are made use of for the purpose
f recovering the lumolumo of a patient. As an introduction, the idols
re decorated with fresh palm leaves. A chain of palm leaves, leading
rom the skull buried in front of the building to the adu representing
s original owner, serves as a trap for the lumolumo of the sick
atient. Along this chain the ghosts are led into the building where
1e idols are placed.

A big feast now is held and all the ancestors are invoked by
1e drumming of the priests. It is the duty of these doctors to scent
ut the evil spirits who have stolen the lumolumo and who seek
ntrance with the good ancestral ghosts. A present of a banana stem is
iven the evil spirits, who release the stolen lumolumo. This then is
rought by the ancestors into the building. It is placed upon the head
f the patient, who recovers. The priests can converse with the
ncestors by means of the idols. Priests receive their income from
resents. At sacrifices they obtain part of the sacrifice. The priests of
lias are seers but not shamans. They are never, except under Malay
1fluence, possessed by their guardian spirits.

The Batu Islands.

Intermediate between Nias and the Mentawei islands extents the
atu archipelago, consisting of fifty islands of varying size, sur-
ounded by coral banks and reefs.

The present population of the Batu islands is small, and in main
onsists of people from Nias. The Malays are located in trading

towns on the coast. The Mentawei people also are in the habit of coming to the Batu islands for the sake of trade. The culture of the islands is similar to that of South Nias, and hence it is probably that certain traits have diffused from Nias to Siberut via this archipelago.

The chief weapons of the archipelago are the sword, spear, and shield. The bow and arrow is not used. The people live mainly on sago and eat but little rice. Sirih chewing is common and but little tobacco is used. Palm wine is prepared upon occasion. There are three main professions: the gold smith, the iron smith, and the builder of large houses.

The government is of a despotic nature, and one or more villages are under a chief called siulu, whose rank is hereditary. Money is essential to the man who accedes to office, in order that he may give the necessary feasts. Slavery is similar in form to that of Nias.

Marriage is by purchase, as in Nias, and the marriage laws are as strictly kept, adultery being punished by death.

The Batu islands have a megalithic culture and idols, the latter being called adjuadju. These are of a phallic nature. The name for the medicine man, ereh, is of similar root to the word as found in Nias and the Mentawei islands, and doubtless this official has similar functions.

PART II. THE MENTAWEI ISLANDS.

Introduction.

The Mentawei islands consist of the northern island Siberut, the intervening island Si Pora, and the southern islands, North and South Pageh. The name "Mentawei" is derived from the native word for a man or a male, "si manteu". The natives call themselves, however, "sakalagan", or human beings. The name "Si berut" means "the mouse". Siberut and Si Pora were called originally Good Fortune because of their discovery by a Dutch sea captain at the time of shipwreck. These islands are later designated as one island under the name of Isle de la Fortune in a French Atlas of 1692. When it became known that the two islands were separate, the larger was called Big Luck Island, and the smaller Little Luck Island. On most of the English and American maps the two northern islands are called Mentawei, and the Nassau or Pageh islands are considered

eparate. Correctly, the entire group should be called the Mentawei
slands.

In spite of the great difference in culture between Mentawei and
aost of the peoples of Sumatra, the distance between the mainland
nd the western island group is not very great. In clear weather
ne can stand at the military station of Sawang-Tunku in North
'ageh and see the cloud bedecked peak of Kurintji, although the coast
ne of Sumatra itself remains concealed.

Culturally there exists a rather wide difference between Siberut
nd the islands to the south. Siberut, especially in the northern part,
ears certain resemblances to Nias, since the people make use of the
pear and shield, as well as the bow and arrow, practice head-hunting
nd have purchase marriage. Siberut, in contrast to the Pageh islands,
; as yet but little known, but from information lately published by
Virz, it appears not unlikely that the region has undergone late
iffusion from Nias. One of the villages of Siberut, called Simalegi,
'as settled by Niha coming from the Batu islands, and a variant
ialect still is spoken there, which shows relationship to the Niha
anguage. The customs of the village also resemble those of Nias.

Mentawei, Engano and the Nicobar islands have been classified
y Heine-Geldern as having a very archaic and primitive culture.
hey are alike in their lack of rice culture and grain. On
.ngano and the Mentawei islands sago and tubular roots, as taro,
re the chief nourishment. Weaving and metal work are unknown,
nd Mentawei and Engano likewise lack betel chewing. None of the
iree regions have the blow-pipe. Mentawei, as an exception to West
idonesia, has the bow. In certain aspects of material culture, as
ie round pile house, there is a relationship between Engano and
ie Nicobars, and the fish nets of Mentawei resemble those of the
licobars.

In respect to non-material culture, the islands of Mentawei and
ngano are lacking in sibs, and have a democratic form of govern-
ient, as opposed to the divine chieftaincy of Nias. Some trace of
Iindu influence may be seen, however, in the Mentawei customs of
iicken and pig sacrifice, the communal meal, and the arts of divin-
tion, especially that of hepatoscopy. On the other hand, the mythol-
zy of Mentawei has remained comparatively untouched by Hindu
ifluence, and there are neither creators nor creation stories.

Concerning the original home of the Mentawei people little is

known. It is generally supposed that the Mentaweians emigrate
from Sumatra to Nias, and thence to Siberut. From an account o
the year 1621, it seems clear that Siberut was the only one of th
Mentawei islands at that time inhabited. The Pageh islanders hav
retained traditions of migrations to the southern islands, and th
founding of the first village in North Pageh, Taikako. If, therefor
the Mentaweians represent an archaic Sumatra culture, maintaine
in isolation from Hindu influence, a study of the region should prov
of unusual interest. Naturally certain traits, as the elaboration o
the sacrifical or punen system, are of modern rather than archaic sourc

The Mentawei islands have never been a source of wealth o
great interest to the Dutch government. The first scientific accou
of the Pagehs was written by an Englishman, John Crisp, in 179
and utilized by Marsden. The group as a whole was nominally mad
a Dutch colony in 1864, and Dutch officials and Malay police s
in charge. It was not until 1904, however, that the Dutch actuall
placed a garrison on the islands. This was at the time of the Russo
Japanese war, and the Dutch did not wish a foreign power to utiliz
the islands as a naval station. The German missionary Lett attempte
to convert the natives in 1901. The Dutch made use of him as inte
preter. The people of Pageh believed that if they got rid of th
interpreter they would hinder the white colonization, and it was f
this reason that Lett was killed by a blow on the head in 1909. I
1915 the commander of the Malay police was shot and killed wit
a poisoned arrow when he attempted to arrest a murderer.

The present missionary, Börger, has for twenty years maintaine
amicable relations with the natives, who, on the whole, are a goo
natured and friendly people, when not molested in their native custom
and religion. He has converted two Pageh villages, Silabu an
Saumangamia. Individuals, apart from villages, can be converte
only under penalty of ostracism.

In the following description of Mentawei culture, an account o
the Pageh islands always is indicated, unless Si Pora or Siber
is directly mentioned. The Pageh culture not only is the best know
and the one directly investigated by the present writer, but it als
ist the purest culture: that is, the one least influenced by Nias. .
seems probable that a great part of the Nias influence came int
Northern Siberut after the Pageh islanders had migrated to th
southern islands.

The language of Pageh is somewhat different from that of Sipora, and greatly differs from that of Siberut. Natives of Pageh and Siberut are mutually unable to understand one another.

Economic Life.

Villages and houses. — The villages are always situated on streams, and at some distance inland from the ocean, so as to assure a supply of fresh water for drinking and bathing. Formerly the water courses were the chief means of communication between villages.

Each village consists of one or more uma (communal house) and the surrounding lalep (family houses). The uma and the surrounding family houses compose the Mentawei social, political, and religious unit. Like the Bontok Igorot of the Philippines the Mentawei village does not act as a unit. Each portion of the village has its own uma, and each portion is spoken of as an uma. Besides the uma and lalep there are houses for bachelors and widows in every village. These are called rusuk. While the uma and the lalep have altars, and sacrifices performed at the altars, the rusuk have none. In other respects they are like the lalep. All the houses of a village are built on piles, are without windows and are approached by a ladder consisting of a notched pole. The villages are always surrounded by a log wall which is designed to keep the pigs and chickens within their proper confines. These animals, before the days of Dutch hygienic measures, usually were kept beneath the houses.

Taikako is the oldest and largest village of the Pagehs. This village has four uma and a separate quarter for the rusuk. Elevated log sidewalks serve as communication between the houses. The people of Taikako regard themselves as the rightful owners of the Pagehs, and those who wish to found new villages must first ask their consent. If the people of other villages wish to plant coconut trees they likewise first must give presents to the natives in Taikako. When the inhabitants of Taikako are travelling they have the right to take coconuts from the trees belonging to other villages.

The village of Silaoinan (the name means "beside the river") is the youngest in the Pagehs. In 1908 the village of Taikako decided to oppose the Dutch. All the natives of the village did not agree to this action, and hence the village of Silaoinan was founded. Since the rimata (priest, chief) cannot be removed from office, those who disagree with his policies have to move.

The communal house or uma forms the center of Mentaw
social life. The rimata (priest) is the head of the uma, or divisio
of the village, rather than of the village as a whole. The men slee
in the uma at the time of punen (religious festival) rather than i
their own homes. This is to prevent their having sexual intercours
at the time. In Siberut the rimata sleeps in the uma, and in Page
several families may find sleeping quarters there. In the daytim
the front porch of the uma is used mostly by men, and the rear b
women and children.

The various uma of Pageh differ in size, but they all have th
same general plan. Both in front and in the rear there is a ladde
leading up to the main floor. A third, a spirit ladder, leads up
the front porch. Although this ladder is called a "monkey ladder"
it is intended for any of the wild animals hunted. During pune
the spirits of these animals are invoked to enter the uma. On th
first floor of the uma there is a porch in the front and rear. Th
first and largest room of the uma is called laibokat, or room to chatte
in. This room contains the hearth, the skulls of sacrificed animal
and along the sides are accomodations for the men who sleep ther
in time of punen. The center room is built in the form of a lon
hallway, and has loose boards on the ground. These are danced upo
on festival occasion. It is in this room that the two main altar
(buluat) are situated. One of these altars is supposed to be mal
the other female. Both sides of the center room are walled off, and c
each side are living rooms (lalep) for private families who dwe
in the uma. The rear room of the uma is called bagat uma, or th
interior of the uma. This opens off to the rear porch. The uppe
story of the uma (djaramba) holds the utensils, such as the hollo
log drum and large net for turtle fishing, which belong to the con
munity as a whole.

The center post of the uma passes through the center or dancin
room. On this post an altar is constructed, and upon the altar res
the katsaila. This is a bunch of leaves, including the sacred Dracaen
During punen the souls of the people are recalled, and they come
rest on the katsaila. The toraidja luima is a second sacred obje
hung on the center pole. This is also called punen and batu kereba
The center post takes its name from the batu kerebau. This fetis
includes sacred leaves, beads, and lead, all enclosed in a bambc
container. The toraidja luima strenghtens the life souls of the peop

f the uma and also the spirits of the uma, and ties the souls of
ie people to the uma. It may be hung either in the uma or in the
ouse of the priest (rimata). The priest first offers to the silimen
the sacrificial food itself), then to the katsaila, and finally to the
raidja luima. In reply to the questioning of the seer, the responses
f the katsaila and the toraidja luima must be in agreement.

The family houses, or lalep, are simple one story pile houses
intaining a single room and porch. Above each is a garret in which
shing, hunting, and food utensils are stored. The rusuk, or bachelor
ouses, are, as stated, similar to the lalep, only have no altars. For
iis reason the young men, who live in rusuk with their sweethearts,
re not allowed to eat there. Before every meal a portion of the food
ust be offered at an altar to the spirits.

Food. — The chief food of Pageh is taro. The taro fields are
iltivated by the women. The second most important food is bananas,
id this fruit is cultivated by the men. In Siberut sago furnishes
ie chief article of diet, but in Pageh it is used only as food for
ie chickens.

The only rice planted is that near the missionary station in
'orth Pageh, and in the two Christian villages. In respect to the
isence of rice cultivation, the Mentawei islands and Engano differ
om all other regions of Western Indonesia. The people of Mentawei
re unwilling to cultivate rice because in their long punen periods
iey are unable to work in the fields, and rice requires constant
ttention. The natives like rice, and buy it from the Malays at ex-
bitant prices before going on fishing trips, since it furnishes more
ourishment per mass than taro or sago. As Kruyt has pointed out,
ie opportunity to cultivate rice is the chief motive which impels
llages to turn Christian.

The taro fields are laid under water in loose marshy earth, and
ie women go to their work in canoes. These fields are owned
itirely by the women. It takes a year after the taro has been planted
ifore it can be eaten, but once cultivated a taro field is a permanent
quisition.

The banana fields belong to the men. Some are worked by one
 two families, and others by an entire uma. In preparing a field,
e underbrush is cleared off, and a number of the trees felled. Fire,
wever, never is used in the clearing operation. Sugar cane and
conut trees likewise are cultivated in the banana fields.

Many religious precautions have to be obeyed in the laying o of a new banana field, especially if it is to be communal propert If a tree falls, an earthquake is felt, or a snake is found, everyo has to go home. If a deer runs across the site, another deer mu be killed and punen held before work can be restarted. If a sna is found three times, the proposed site must be abandoned. Offerin must be made to the brush spirits everytime that a tree is felled.

Banana fields must be laid out anew every four or five year They have definite boundaries set off by bamboos, and the rima has jurisdiction over cases of trespass. When such a field belon to an entire uma, the rimata must initiate each undertaking connect with it. At its completion some of the fruit is brought to the um sprinkled with water, and laid upon the altar. Then a five month punen follows.

A large portion of the food supply of the people comes fro hunting and fishing. The chase of deer and monkeys is alwa connected with the punen system, and the meat has to be divid equally among all the members of the uma, and a portion sacrific in the proper manner.

The hunt is a communal affair participated in by all the m of the uma (excepting expectant fathers) under the leadership the rimata. Before the hunt the women bring in food from the field but during the time of the hunt they have to remain in the villag The hunt is conducted in daytime with aid of dogs, and bow a poisoned arrows.

When a deer or monkey is killed there is applause, "aile", thank the brush spirits. The fortunate hunter, the dogs, and also t booty are decorated with flowers and leaves. If the prey be a monke it is carried back whole to the uma; but if a deer, the animal cut up on the spot, and the flesh bound in leaves so that it c be transported in baskets. The blood is placed in bamboos and lat eaten by men and women.

The gong now is sounded in the uma, and all the men assemb The rimata enters with a peeled coconut and "gathers in" the sou of the deer and monkeys which remain in the brush. One of t men meanwhile beats on a skin drum. The flesh is cooked, and t rimata takes a piece of the heart and of the back for sacrifice on t altar. Then eating begins. The rimata finally takes the decoratio off the head of the animal, and feeds it with coconut meat, prayin

Come, come, spirits of the deer". This is done in order to insure plentiful supply of game by propitiating the slain animal.

The skulls of slain monkeys, deer, and large sea-turtles (iban ut) are hung up in the uma. The skulls of pigs are thrown away, ut rooster skulls sometimes are suspended on the roof, in order that ie roosters may crow and scare away evil spirits.

Sometimes during a punen the men engage in a monkey chase. n this case the monkey must be caught and not shot. The dogs hase the monkey up a tree, the men follow and shake the tree until ie monkey tumbles down, is bitten by the hounds, and takes refuge i another tree. Finally the animal is so exhausted from its flights nd wounds that it no longer is able to rise from the ground. If ie manner in which the monkey falls and the condition of its body re propitious, the animal is taken as prey to the uma.

Fishing is performed with nets, harpoons, hook and line, traps, ow and arrow, and fish poison. The women have a special crossed-tick net (panu) with which they catch fish while standing waist eep in the water. The casting net is a Malay innovation. Men refer to fish in the shallow water of the ocean with harpoon or ow and arrow. Both have detachable points. Fish are poisoned the shallow ocean with the roots of the Derris elliptica.

The catching of large sea-turtles plays an important part in the unen system. The djarik (net) in which turtles are caught resembles ie Andaman turtle net. The net is open, with floats attached to the pper portion and anchors to the lower. While the men are turtle shing the women and children at home are under severe taboos. 'hey are not allowed to plant, get wood, or gather coconuts. They iay not visit one another or borrow fire. Even the chickens are not llowed to set. For just as the young chicks emerge from their eggs, o will the turtle escape from the net. The fishermen are just as everely treated. They may not bathe, wash, or oil their hair. They iay not become angry, or even engage in conversation. They may leep at night, but they must do so with one leg extended, and one oubled up. All of these taboos have the double object of preventing ie djarik from becoming loose from its anchors, and the turtles rom the net. When brought home the turtle meat is divided equally mong all the members of the uma, but it itself is not considered acred, as is monkey meat, venison, pork or chicken, but may be hared by strangers who are visiting the uma.

The Pageh islanders have special months when they go in their large war ships (kalaba) to the uninhabited islands and catch crabs. Frogs and eels are likewise eaten by all, but not during times of punen. Frog hunting is done at night with the aid of torches.

Crocodiles are very sacred in Pageh, and are called "teteu" or ancestor. It is believed that an ancestor turned into a crocodile. The people of Siberut are said to eat the crocodile, but in Pageh neither the flesh nor skin of this animal may be used for any purpose what soever. The crocodiles are thought to be servants of the Mother of Waters, and it is believed that they are sent to punish taboo breakers as, for example, people who throw refuse in the water. When a person has been bitten by a crocodile, a trap is made in order to catch one of the species. When this has been done, the carcass and the trap are thrown into the river, so that no one further will be bitten by crocodiles. Then there is a two months' punen, in which every member of the uma gives a pig or chicken, and the livers are sacrificed to the slaughtered crocodile. In former times when a crocodile killed a man "punen lepa" was held, and a war expedition set out to obtain a human victim.

The flesh of the python is eaten in Siberut, but not in Pageh. The skin of the python, as well as deer hide, is used in drum making. The people believe that snakes are immortal because they yearly shed their skins.

In general, food is taboo in Mentawei if it is unfit to be offered in sacrifice. Women, children, and unmarried men are allowed to eat taboo food, but the spirits are considered averse to the practice. Squirrels, rats, most land and sea turtles, and spoiled fish, are taboo. The native will refuse all European food, such as beef, on the basis of this taboo. So there are no cattle on the islands.

Dogs play an important part in Mentawei life, although they are not food animals. There is no story to account for the way the people first obtained dogs. The Mentawei dogs are barkless. They bear no names, excepting where the custom of naming dogs has been borrowed from the Malays. Dogs are neither bought nor sold, but they are lent and a portion of the litter kept by the borrower. The killing of a dog forbidden, and if one kills a dog in a fit of passion because the dog has bitten someone, a three months' punen is held so that the ghost of the dog will no longer bite women and children. When a dog dies its carcass is simply thrown into the wilderness.

Cats are called mao, and are said to have been introduced by the alays. They are given away in friendship but never sold.

Men, women, and children are inveterate smokers. The excess to 1ich the Mentawei islander carries this habit may be attributed to e fact that betel chewing is unknown on the islands. No tobacco is own in Mentawei, and the people are entirely dependent on the alays for their supply. Tobacco is smoked in the form of cigarettes, e coverings are obtained from the leaves of the Nipa palm or the .nana tree. The word "to smoke" is "potpot", to suck.

The islanders have a national non-intoxicating drink called djurut. 1is is made of coconut milk, sugar cane sap, sliced bananas, and the eat of young coconuts. It is non-fermented. Djurut is drunk at mid- 1y as a regular habit, and also in the evening. It is not a sacred ink, but a few drops are always poured on the ground as libation ior to its being partaken of. It is always offered to guests as a ken of hospitality. Once a stranger has partaken of djurut with his ›st he feels assured of his safety.

Salt is obtained from the sea water. Little salt, however, appears be used in the preparation of foods.

Fire originally was made by boring into bamboo. The boring ›paratus is called gugudjut. Now Malay flint and steel is used. The :ople are afraid of fire, and will not use it to clear off the underbrush r a plantation. It is likewise forbidden to trample out a fire or to 'inate into one. Fire has the power of driving away sickness, and the er (sikerei) sways a glowing stick over his patient for this purpose.

Cooking and water carrying are performed entirely in hollow .mboos, since the people have no pottery. Every fire-place has a pply of these bamboos handy; some placed besides the hearth, and hers above to dry. The meat, fish, or taro, is placed inside the bamboo 1ich then is revolved above the fire to prevent burning. The result, ›wever, is unsatisfactory from the viewpoint of the foreigner, for the .tside of the food is burnt and the inside remains raw.

Clothing and adornment. — As customary apparel men wear a pa loin cloth made from the bark of the breadfruit tree. In times of .nen a yellow loin cloth is worn, dyed with the juice of the curry rry. Anything else which men wear is decoration rather than thing. Such decoration consists of bands of red colored rotan, glass :ads, and imported brass rings on the arms, fingers, and toes. The en often wear flowers tucked in their hair.

The clothing of the women likewise is simple. When they are home in the village they wear simply a strip of tapa (now usual imported cotton) around the lower portion of their bodies. When th go out they wear waists and skirts made from banana leaves. Ha are worn of fern, palm leaf, or, more seldom, of banana leaf.

The hair of both sexes is allowed to grow long. The men allo the hair to hang over the left ear and tie it in a knot at the shoulde It is decorated with many colored leaves, especially the croton. Tl males keep themselves close shaved, and both sexes pull out their faci hair and eyebrows. This deformation of the face is trying to the ey in the tropics, due to the glare on the water.

The most important decorations of the islanders, however, are the filed teeth and tattooing (titi). The latter is done by the aid of tv little sticks. On one of the sticks is a vertical needle. This stick tapped by the other stick. Small pricks are made in the skin in th manner, and the coloring matter, the darkened sap of the sugar car is inserted. A convex bow is started on the chin and comes down the shoulders. Lines also are made over the breast to the pit of t stomach. The hips, arms, legs, and fingers also are tattooed. T. tattooing on the women resembles that on the men, but is simpler form. The tattooing on the upper legs of the men is always done ju before marriage.

The tattooing on the calf of the leg, the back of the hands, and t sides of the body, is the final form of decoration, and formerly w always done at the time of a special punen, punen lepa. This pun was held to wipe out the evil influence of blood spilled in the villag as when someone was stabbed inside the village boundaries or kill by a crocodile. A special porch was constructed in front of the ur for the purpose of the tattooing, so that blood would not fall on t ground. In the words of my informant, "The blood that flowed fro the tattooing was for the purpose of covering the blood of t dead man".

Volz writes that every village of Siberut has its own pattern tattooing. After a war expedition the returning warriors were allow to put the picture of the beheaded man on their bodies.

While tattooing was compulsory under penalty of death, Kru claims that not every man had his teeth sharpened. Those who did n were mocked, but were able to marry. I, myself, never saw nor hea of any man with unmutilated teeth. When a boy's milk teeth fall o ey are simply thrown away, but when the second teeth (but not the sdom teeth) have arrived they are sharpened before they become o hard. The sharpening is done with an iron file, and the teeth e given three points. There is no ceremony or taboos connected with e operation, which any unmarried man can perform.

The Mentaweians have no form of circumcision whatsoever, and e tattooing and filing of teeth do not appear to be connected with any iberty ceremony.

Trade and artifacts. — The Mentawei islands have no division of bor, save that between men and women, and married men and the married. There are no professions save that of the seer (sikerei). ven the word "tukang" (Polynesian tufunga) is a recent impor- tion from the Malays, among whom it means one skilled in a craft.

Since there are no craftsmen or special occupations, there is practi- lly no intervillage trade. Each village, nay each uma or division a village, is self-sufficient. Still the word for trade exists, "pasaki", d the word to buy, "saki". The Mentaweians have no money, wever, and their only trade is that carried on with the Malays. It interesting to note the connection of these words with those having ligious significance. Thus "panaki" means to pray, or to request a ade of favors from the spirits. In the same way the noun "pasakiat" w means the Malay market place, but the original meaning was the tish stick placed in the field to which sacrifices were made.

In spite of the lack of intervillage trade, the Mentawei culture parasitic to the Malay. From these traders, whom they call by e general term for foreigner, sa-sareu (reu, far, hence those who me from far), the natives obtain all their iron tools, such as axes, ives and chisels. In return they give coconuts, rotan and brush pro- cts. Without these utensils the Mentawei could not build their elab- ate houses and war boats in a reasonable length of time. It is not probable, however, that in former days, when the natives still in- bited Siberut, they had but stone axes. The word "sikap" now eans a dull axe, but it probably formerly meant a stone axe.

There never was any trade between the various islands, and the ople of Pageh travelled to Siberut solely for the purpose of ob- ining human sacrifice for their punen.

The native weapon of the Mentawei islander is the bow and arrow. ll the varieties of knives and lances used are imported from the

Malays. An exception must be made in the case of the palite, a doubl[e] edged broad steel dagger contained in a sheath, which is native Mentawei. The original form of the dagger, however, as mentioned [in] the myths, was made of sharpened bamboo.

It often has been stated that the use of the bow is unusual [in] Western Indonesia. Heine-Geldern has mapped the distribution of th[is] weapon in Indonesia. It is used as a war and hunting weapon [in] Formosa and the Philippines, in Mentawei, and in Eastern Indonesi[a.] In Java it is used for target practice. The Toradja of Celebes use t[he] bow in ritual. But the word for bow (pana) is widespread in Weste[rn] Indonesia; the weapon itself formerely was used by the Bataks in wa[r] and now it is found widespread in Western Indonesia as a child's to[y.] Therefore I cannot agree that a strict line of demarcation can be mad[e] as suggested by Pleyte, between Western and Eastern Indonesia; t[he] former being the home of the blow-pipe, the latter of the bow.

The bows of Mentawei have a length of about four and a half fe[et] and are made of the black elastic wood of the Salap palm (Areng[a] obtusifolia). The string consists of the bark leaf rib of the Nipa pa[lm] (Nipa fructicanus), is very light and hollowed in on the lower en[d.] The arrows are of bamboo, the shafts of the hard wood of the Nibo[r] palm (Cariota urens), and are loosely attached. The arrow points a[re] poisoned with the sap of the Omai tree (Antiaris toxicaria), mix[ed] with an extract from the roots of the Tuba shrub (Coculus), tobacc[o] and lombok (Capsicum). The poison is dried on to the arrows ov[er] a fire, and is effective for several days. The arrows are carried in [a] bamboo quiver decorated with bead designs. The beads are thought [to] have the power of "sighting" the prey. The word for bow is rouro[,] the string, itek, the arrow case, bukbung, the arrows, logui. T[he] secondary grip is used in Mentawei.

The Mentawei have two forms of boats: the double-outrigg[er] canoe (abak), which is paddled, and the large war boat (kalaba) whi[ch] is rowed, and which also is outfitted with sails. The latter boat [is] ordinarily used for the purpose of catching crabs and gatheri[ng] coconuts in the small uninhabited surrounding islands, but is capab[le] of sailing to Siberut in fairly good weather. It has double outrigge[rs,] a rudder, a protecting roof, and two masts upon which the sails a[re] attached. As measured by Crisp, it is 25 feet long, with the prow pr[o] jecting 22 feet, and the stern 18 feet, making a total length of 65 fe[et.] Its greatest breath is 5 feet, and its depth 3 feet, 8 inches.

The canoes, which are used in the rivers and streams, but not in
e open sea, are hollowed out from single trees.

When a native travels in the interior he carries a hollow bamboo
ntainer for his tobacco, flint and steel, mosquito netting, and an
tra loin cloth. This container he puts on his head when swimming
vers. The people also make use of a variety of baskets for carrying
ro, chickens, and other objects. The women carry the taro home
om the fields in special rotan baskets called opa, which are strapped
their shoulders.

The utensils for eating are exceedingly primitive, and consist of
conut shells and wooden troughs (lulak). The natives always pour
ater over their hands before seizing their food out of the family trough.

The musical instruments consist of gongs, bells, mouth flutes,
in drums, hollow log drums, and wooden xylophones. The gongs
e said by Maass to have been imported by the Chinese, and by Kruyt
the Bugenese. The gongs and the tree drums (tudukat) are kept
the upper garret of the uma, and are struck by the rimata as a sum-
ons to a sacrificial meal, or when a deer is sighted. The skin drums
ateuba) are made from hollowed out sugar palms with deer or
thon skin at one end. They are the only instrument used in punen
the time of dancing. Small hand bells are used by the priests and
ers in sacrificing and performing works of magic. The word for
agic is, in fact, nunangnang, from nangnang, to tinkle a bell. The
lls are, of course, imported. The mouth flutes (pipian) are played
r pleasure in the fields. They are not used for courting.

There are actually two kinds of xylophones in Pageh, a large and
small variety. The log drums (tudukat) are really xylophones, since
ey consist of three logs of different size struck with a stick. The
all variety also are called tudukat, but they are small enough to
held on the lap. They are played in the fields for amusement.

In Siberut the log drums likewise are xylophones, and the three
rying sized logs have the same names as in Pageh: father, mother,
d child. Wirz writes that there is an actual language for these
ums, as in West Africa. The drums are kept in the uma, and usually
beaten by the rimata. According to the manner in which the drum
beaten, the people are informed when one of the following events
urs. An old man dies. An old woman dies. A child is born. An
my is killed. A house is on fire. A male ape is killed. A female
is killed. A boar is shot. A deer is shot.

War. — There are three causes for war in Mentawei: 1. blo‹ revenge, 2. the building of an uma, 3. the holding of punen lepa af‹ blood has been spilt in the village or a crocodile has killed someone.

In Pageh blood revenge is called luinun. If a man kills anoth‹ in a fight, the relatives will seek blood revenge. If a man kills anoth‹ for wrong doing, however, such as adultery, the relatives of t‹ murdered man are not allowed blood revenge.

Wars also are fought when a human sacrifice is needed for a ne‹ uma or for punen lepa. In Siberut the head of an enemy is obtain‹ as well as the arms and legs. Wirz writes that the flesh of the‹ members is eaten. The head is placed under the center post of t‹ new uma. Kruyt writes that the people of Sipora take the head, b‹ not the members, but Wirz claims that they are contented with the dea‹ of the enemy. It is certain that the people of Pageh never took hea‹ Some years ago, when they still were in the habit of going to Si Po‹ or Siberut on war expeditions, they conducted the affair in the follo‹ ing manner. They first lay in ambush and shot at those who we‹ fishing. The hostile uma was neither burnt or attacked. If t‹ warriors succeeded in killing one or more of the enemy, they hack‹ the bodies and decorated their own heads with plants and flowe‹ If not, they shot their arrows into the brush and went home. ‹ stead of a head, sacred flowers and leaves are placed under the cen‹ post of the new uma to appease Teteu, the earthquake god.

Head taking is (or was) very important in Siberut and there ‹ many taboos connected with the custom. The women at home have‹ remain quiet, and cannot cook. They spend their nights in the un‹ They abstain from fruits and certain fish. If they disobey these‹ junctions their men will come to harm.

When the warriors return with their trophies they utter a w‹ whoop at the mouth of the river. The parts are hung up in the u‹ for two days while the warriors dance around them. Then the pa‹ are buried, and the heads hung up in the bushes. The seers waft ‹ ghosts of the slain away with sacred leaves, and a taboo period‹ two months follows.

In Siberut when two parties make peace with one another‹ rimata of one side smears the head of the former hostile rimata w‹ oil, and then the action is reciprocated. Prayers are said at the ti‹

Calendar. — The year is divided into twelve months. The‹ ginning of the year is in June and is ascertained from the position‹

e Pleiades. This is crab season, and each of the four months of crab
ason (Agan) is named from the variety of crab caught in the month.

The next two months, October and November, are thought to
ring bad weather. The next four months are called Rura from the
ame of the prevailing southwest wind. Then come two more months
f supposedly stormy weather.

Society.

Introduction. — In Mentawei the concept of government and of
e family is so interwoven with the religion that it is impossible to give
1 idea of the native social organization without first summarizing the
ligious concepts. I will do this now, and later explain in greater
etail certain of the more important religious ceremonies and beliefs.

The religious festival of the Mentawei people is called lia or
unen. The lia is a family festival, is of shorter duration, and is ac-
mpanied by the sacrifice of chickens. The punen is the celebration
ttended by all the members of the uma, men, women, and children.
: is of longer duration, lasting sometimes for years, and both pigs
nd chickens are sacrificed. The house father (ukui) conducts the lia,
e priest (rimata) conducts the punen, aided by one or more seers
sikerei). According to Hansen, the Mentawei islanders are in a state
f punen, with its attendant taboos (takeikei), for about ten months
the year. The Mentawei concept of punen as a religious sacrificial
stival is known elsewhere in the cultural region of Southeast Asia.
hus the Bontok Igorot have their rest days. More strikingly similar,
owever, are the pena and attendant gena (taboos) of the Angami
aga of Assam. During these periods the unit of the village holding
e festival is rendered isolated and all work in the fields forbidden.
: is therefore only the severity of the Mentawei punen system, and the
xtent to which it has influenced all the institutions of the people, which
ake it exceptional.

Among the occasions on which punen are held may be included:
e building of a new communal house (uma), the choice of a new
riest (rimata), the making of a new communal field, the spilling of
lood within the village, an epidemic in the village, when a tree falls
the community, and after the killing of a sacrificial animal; monkey,
eer, or sea-turtle. The duration of a punen at the time of the founding
f a new uma or at the election of a new priest is so long (lasting at

174

least nine years) that these two events usually are held simultaneously
Family or personal punen, that is lia, are held at the time of sickness
in the household, marriage, adoption of children, the making of a boa
or family field, &c. It may be said that all children have to be adopted
but this is done in the family itself. In case the father is married t
the mother, he will adopt the children. Otherwise the father o
mother's brother of the woman will adopt the children. The ceremony
with all its taboos, lasts nine months. Adoption is necessary in orde
to give the child its legal rights in inheritance.

A punen is initiated by the ceremonial washing of the hair of th
participants, and the adoption of gala decorations. All work in th
fields is stopped, and strangers are denied access to the uma. Th
main ceremonial acts of every punen are the slaughter of pigs an
chickens, accompanied by the sacrifice of the livers and the taking
omens by haruspication. During the invocation accompanying ever
sacrifice, the souls of the people of the uma are invoked to return an
remain by their owners. During the first nights of the punen, th
seers dance. The dance serves the purpose of pleasing the spirit
and is held in imitation of various birds and animals. During th
latter part of the punen, hunts for monkeys and deer are made, an
the sea-turtle is sought for by placing large nets (djarik). Durin
the time of punen the men sleep in the uma, for all sexual intercours
is taboo. No special ceremony concludes a punen, but the men simpl
resume their fishing on the sea, the women their work in the field

At the time of any punen of importance, all the work of the peop
has to be initiated by the priest. Thus, no boats can be built until
first boat is constructed by the priest and his assistants and then cons
crated. The same thing is true of the first laying out of fields, fishin
djurut (the Mentawei drink) preparation, hunting, &c. This featur
of the punen system causes the prolongation of the ceremony, for i
case of any bad omen, such as an earthquake or sickness in the villag
the work of initiation is delayed. In the family lia (small punen
accompanying marriage or adoption, various kinds of work have to l
initiated and consecrated in much the same fashion. Finally, at the tin
of the erection of a new uma, all the youths who never have bee
initiated to an uma undergo initiation. The initiation of the youths
called eneget (from the root "sege", to arrive). This initiation is f
the purpose of placing the youths under the guardian spirits of tl
uma. It is a survival among these primitive Malaysians of trib

initiation, such as is found in Ceram, among most Negroid peoples, and many of the American Indians. For each youth taken into the uma, a pig must be sacrificed. Two pigs are sacrificed for each boy, and one pig for each girl. Adults who wish to join an uma different from their own are forced to give a pig for punen before leaving their old uma, and another pig upon entering the new uma.

Considering the Mentawei punen system from a theoretical point of view, it seems probable that the idea of animal sacrifice was taken up by the forefathers of the Mentaweians when they still were wandering family groups, and that the family lia thus preceded the more elaborate punen. That is to say, it was the oldest male (now the house father, ukui) who originally made the sacrifice, and this was done for the blood family, the original unit. Later, with the coming in of the communal house, the families became partially merged in the uma, or larger division, and the priest (rimata) became the officiating head, or father, of the community. The older lia, or family system, has never become lost. The word for sacrifice itself is lia, and the lia alone is the prevailing form of ceremony at ordinary family functions, births, adoptions, and mild cases of sickness. The lia also is an integral part of every punen, for at every punen feast and sacrifice there also must be a family sacrifice. That is, each house father must carry back a portion of the meat from the communal house, perform a sacrifice, and consume it with his own family, in his own home.

Another consideration which causes me to assume the priority of the family lia, is the prevailing spirit of communism among the members of the village unit (the uma). The members of the uma are, as it were, an enlarged family, with the rimata (priest) as their father. Just as in a family all goods are equally divided among the members, so in the uma, during punen time, all products of the hunt or fishing expeditions are equally divided, the priest receiving the same share as the others. Contributions for the sacrifice, moreover, when not for the purpose of expiating an individual fault, are equally levelled, and this again tends to create an equality in the ownership of domestic animals. With the exception of certain insignia of office, worn by the seers and priests when officiating (including chicken feathers worn by the priest), all clothing must be of the same kind during a punen period. During other periods, not much variation is shown in clothing or adornment, even at the present day.

It therefore seems probable that the punen system originated from a family method of sacrifice. Fastening itself upon a culture originally barren in ceremonial usage, it became extended under the guidance of the seers, who communicated many of the taboos from the spirit world, and presently permeated all aspects of Mentawei culture. Death, marriage, puberty, sickness, and the initiation of all methods of work, became mere aspects of punen ritual. Government, through a system of fines or ostracism, became a part of punen supervision. Communism, inherent in earlier family groupings, became ritually retained during punen periods. The punen system brings enforced idleness, prolonged abstinence from sexual intercourse for longer periods than are known perhaps to any other people on earth, intermittent periods of feast and famine, and an utter inability of the people to absorb foreign elements of culture, such as the rearing of non-sacrificial animals (as cattle), or the cultivation of rice, which requires steady labor. On the other hand, it has lasted because of the insistence of the seers, who play upon the credulity of the people. Likewise, it appeals to the group feelings of the people, keeping them united in a brotherhood of faith, a common ownership of material possessions, and an equality of rank and prestige.

In the discussion of Mentawei social organization I will hereafter use the following native words without explanation: rimata, priest, quasi chief of uma; sikerei, seer; uma, communal house, division of village; lalep, family house; rusuk, house without altar; punen, religious festival of people of uma; lia, family religious festival.

Government. — As among all very primitive peoples the Mentaweians have no true chiefs, laws, or government. The political unit (the uma) necessarily is very small, and public opinion enforced by the power of ostracism or death holds the natives to strict observance of the adat. In Pageh the largest village, Taikako, has about 160 inhabitants in its four uma, and the smallest village, Muntai, has but five inhabitants.

When the Dutch first started governing Mentawei, they selected the various rimata as the proper people to enforce their regulations such as path building, sanitation measures, &c. This was done in the belief that the rimata were chiefs similar to the chiefs of Nias or Batakland. The fallacy of this idea soon became apparent, for not only had the rimata no special authority over the natives, outside of punen periods, but their very characters prevented them from energetic enforcement of foreign edicts. The rimata are so taboo (suru, sacred) that they can do practically no work at all, and hence only lazy men will accept the position.

The position of rimata is not hereditary, although a son or brother of a former priest usually is chosen, since punen knowledge is likely to be handed down in the family. Some time after the death of a priest, the house fathers come together in the uma, and the oldest nominates a man. This choice is unanimously agreed upon. The priest need not be an old man. Any married man who knows the punen rules is eligible. In case there is any dispute concerning the choice, a new candidate is brought forward. Until this is done, the oldest member of the community makes the sacrifices. The election of a new priest usually is postponed, as has been explained, until a new uma has to be built. The helpers of the priest are chosen in the same manner as the priest, and are equally sacred or taboo. The helpers are called sikaute lulak (at the head of the trough) and sika muriat (at the end of the trough). The helpers divide the sacrifices among the people, and aid the rimata in giving punen advice. When the rimata is sick, or is about to become a father, the head trough man takes his place at the sacrifices. The rimata, his aids, and the sikerei, all have to be married men. This is to insure that they will obey all the taboos and eat no forbidden food, as is the custom of bachelors.

The rimata has charge of all undertakings of communal interest, since these are governed by punen regulations. He decides when the taro fields should be laid out, when a new building should be erected, and when the people should go to the fields and get food. The rimata drives away rain, takes the auguries, and obtains the needed herbs and leaves whose magical powers bring good luck.

The daily life of the rimata is much the same as that of the other married men. He gets no reward for his services, except when the choice bits from the sacrifices fall to him, as custom varies from village to village. On the other hand, he has the responsibility of seeing that the material for sacrifice is obtained and offered up in the proper manner.

The rimata and his assistants have all the taboos of other married men, plus certain others which arise from the fact that they have the souls of the people of the uma in their keeping. As married men they are not allowed to dig, plant, or kill any animals. They cannot eat taboo food, and above all, they cannot commit adultery. If they

committed adultery the spirits would kill both them and their childre
As priests they are spared most of the other work of the communit
such as carrying water and feeding the live stock. A priest will n
even light his own cigarette, but calls on an unmarried man for th
purpose. This is due to the taboo on holding fire in his hand. If
priest did this he would bring fever to the people of the uma.

Next to the rimata, the sikerei are the most important people in a
uma. The sikerei may either be male or female, and there is no ru
as to the number of seers an uma should have. For serious cases
sickness sikerei are summoned from other uma, with the consent of th
local rimata. The root of the word sikerei is "kere", invisible powe
and the more power a sikerei is supposed to have, the more is h
sought after.

Crimes may be divided into three catagories: 1. Injury to a
individual of the uma by violence; 2. Injury to an individual or a
the people of the uma by witchcraft; 3. Injury to all the people
the uma through breaking the punen rules.

If a man kills another person without due cause, and the victi
does not belong to his family, he is subject to blood revenge. If h
kills the victim inside his own village he likewise breaks a pune
rule, for he gives offence to the god Teteu by spilling blood on th
ground. In this latter case he will have to pay a ruinous fine in pig
and chickens to the people of the uma.

The importance of the seer in Mentawei society lies in the fac
that he is the person called upon to detect witches. If a case
sickness is said to be caused by witchcraft, and the patient die
the family asks the seer to name the murderer. The seer then goes t
an uninhabited island for the purpose of determining the culprit. Whe
he returns, he does not name the supposed culprit, but gives instea
a description of his appearance and clothing. The people of the um
then go to the rimata with the information. A council of the mor
influential men follows, and if the culprit is condemned he is at onc
captured and brought to the graveyard. There the sorcerer is hung
this form of punishment being used in Pageh to prevent blood flowin
on the ground. The body is buried without ceremony under leaves an
twigs. The family of the executed sorcerer are informed of the act, an
warned not to complain lest a similar fate overtake them. Sometime
a sorcerer is left on a deserted island, or simply expelled from th
village. The natives, however, claim that they execute this type o

iminal "for his own good". For as long as a sorcerer remains alive,
e cannot help dealing in the forbidden magic". The dead sorcerer
not able to gain admittance to the native land of dead souls. The
er has no obvious self-interest in his selection of the criminal, for
does not acquire any part of the possessions of the deceased. The
ealth remains in the family, and is not confiscated. Wars or feuds
not arise from witchcraft cases in Mentawei, for the accused person
always a member of the same uma as the victim.

According to native theory, it is usually the man or woman of
perior ability and abundant possessions who is bewitched. Thus, it
stated that a man is "poisoned" because he is diligent and has many
mestic animals. His family therefore wish to get him out of the way,
as to inherit his goods. Again, if a person is extraordinarily
ccessful in the hunt, or is merely long-lived, the sorcerer kills him
om jealousy. A frequent cause of supposed witchcraft arises from
dispute over the boundaries of fields, or jealousy on account of a
oman. Actually, it is the superior type of native who is accused of
itchcraft, and eliminated from the group. If a man is more success-
l in the hunt or in fishing than his neighbors, if he is more diligent
d acquires more possessions, he is the person picked out by the seer,
bears the onus of the group suspicion and envy. It is not by natural
eans, argue the natives, that So-and-so is long lived, or is rich in
ssessions. If he were not possessed of magical powers, if he were
t in league with the evil ghosts, he could not have been so successful.
itchcraft, then, is one of the methods by which the people of
entawei maintain their ideal of communism and equality.

The punishment for breaking a punen rule varies from the fine
a chicken or pig for sacrifice, to ostracism, exile to an uninhabited
and (which means death from starvation), or hanging. Naturally
th so many punen rules, the natives are bound constantly to break
me and thus incur fines. I, myself, kept breaking in on villages
ile they were holding punen. Since at this time no strangers are
owed, I always had to give the price of a chicken to the rimata.

Some years ago this punen rule was strictly adhered to, as well
the death penalty for both man and woman in case of adultery.
e natives also are greatly incensed if a woman becomes pregnant
ring punen times, when sexual intercourse is prohibited. I do not
ow the penalty for this breach of regulations. Usually the woman
mmits abortion before her crime is discovered.

When a man and his family withdraws from the uma, eith
voluntarily or as a punishment, he either can join another uma
live in a rusuk. In the latter case he is called a sipurusuk (one wl
lives in a rusuk, and does not join the punen of the people of the uma
While I was in Pageh, a native became converted to Christiani
and had to withdraw into a rusuk. A sipurusuk is not allowed to k
deer or apes.

Marriage and kinship. — In Siberut the marriage custor
resemble those of Nias, and doubtlessly have been influenced by t
natives from that island. While there apparently are no true si
in Siberut, Wirz mentions the fact that marriage is exogamous to t
"rara", which is an enlarged family group, or patrilineal genealog
Contrary to the custom of Nias, the natives of Siberut are stric
monogamous.

The father of the groom pays the bride-price, which may cons
of eight pigs, six knives, two taro fields, six durian trees, six cocon
trees, six chickens in chicken baskets, and one iron pan. The bric
price is divided among the members of the girl's family. The groc
must pay at least half the bride-price if he wishes to bring his w
to his own home. Contrary to the customs of Nias, the father of t
girl must give return presents. He gives a pig, and each of b
brothers gives five chickens. The father of the man receives two boa
full of coconuts, taro, and sago.

While in Pageh the women are allowed to live with men open
before marriage, in Siberut this must be done in secret, and in Ni
the women are presumed to have kept their prenuptial chastity. Lil
wise the women marry much earlier in Siberut than in Pageh,
fact at the time of puberty. If they become pregnant they are forc
to marry at once. Bastards usually are drowned.

Contrary to the customs of both Nias and Pageh, divorce
Siberut is allowed without difficulty, at the request of either par
If the woman is the guilty party, she must return the bride-pri
before she can remarry.

While in Pageh the woman own the taro fields, in Siberut t
women possess only implements and decorations. Marriage usua
is matrilocal in Pageh due to the desire of the men to share the fiel
of their wives; in Siberut it is patrilocal providing the man is al
to pay half the bride-price.

It appears probable that the bride-price was not the origin

orm of marriage among the Mentaweians. Purchase marriage is unusual among the more primitive peoples, and no mention of bride-purchase is to be found in the Mentawei stories. Further, the idea of rigid bride-purchase seems somewhat alien to Mentawei, where both strong patrilineal power is lacking, and the idea of purchase does not enter into other fields of social or economic life.

In Pageh the "rara" or embryonic sibs of Siberut are entirely lacking. On the other hand, the kinship terminology is similar to that of people with sib formation. Thus the mother's brother, kamaman, is differentiated from the father and the father's brother. In like manner, cross-cousins are differentiated from parallel cousins, although there is no customary cousin marriage. Address, however, is far more frequent by age classification than by kinship terms. I conclude, therefore, that the original kinship system of Mentawei was of the Polynesian type, with terms differing according to age status, and that marriage was forbidden within the blood group. All traces of sibs, and sib terminology, must have been borrowed from Nias.

Bride-purchase is practiced in but one village of Pageh, Saumangania. The name for the bride-price there is patalagaat, that which is placed in the middle. Of course, with the payment of a bride-price the peculiar feature of Mentawei marriage, the preliminary living together of the couple in a rusuk, is absent. In the same way, while marriage is patrilocal in Saumangania, elsewhere in Pageh a man either marries a woman of the same village or else settles down in the village of his wife.

Taking up now the regular mode of Mentawei marriage, we find that this can be divided into two periods. In the first period the man and woman sleep together, but are not allowed to eat together. For want of a better designation, I will call this betrothal. In the second period, after a marriage lia has been performed, the couple sleep and eat together. The husband then becomes an ukui, or house father. While the couple still are betrothed they must sleep together in a rusuk, since the man cannot visit his mistress at the home of her parents. Any children which are born are adopted (pipi) by the father of the woman, or if the father is not available, by the woman's maternal uncle. When the couple prepare to marry, the man first must lay out a banana field, and build a lalep (house) with the aid of his wife's family. Then after marriage, the children are readopted by the parents.

Girls often are engaged when quite young. The man goes to th mother and obtains her promise for the girl. No present is give however, at this time. When the girl is older, the man actually becom betrothed to her. He then gives some beads, cloth, and arm bands the mother. If the mother accepts, she sends her daughter the ne day to meet the boy in his field hut. Even if the mother does n accept, the girl is liable to go anyway. Both of these forms engagements are considered binding, and the mother is suppose thereafter to keep other men from her daughter. The first form occu only if the daughter is very young.

Either girls or men may be the owners of rusuks. It is in the forms of houses that the betrothed pair cooks and sleeps. They ea however, in the homes of their parents. Young men may visit eac other in the rusuk, provided they do it openly. Actually, as far adultery is concerned, the engaged pair are as good as married. man may desert his betrothed and take another girl. This, howeve is very much looked down upon by the people.

While a man is living with his betrothed in rusuk, he is suppose to do some work for the girl's parents in their field. He also supposed to keep the girl supplied with cloth, baskets, and ornament While the man is in rusuk he must avoid the father and mother his bride. That is, he must not speak to them. The girl must avo the mother of the man, but not the father. After marriage there a no restrictions of this nature. While marriage itself in Mentawei strictly monogamous, yet during the rusuk period a man may ha intercourse with all the sisters in a family. The keeping of a woma in a rusuk is not altogether an open affair. The man and the woma never enter together. Usually the woman goes in first, and the sometime after the man follows.

The rusuk period of marriage doubtlessly is a development fro the original Malaysian custom of prenuptial sexual promiscuity, whic in Pageh is prolonged by the fact that a man cannot afford ear marriage, due to the taboos on married men, which greatly hinder the economic activities. A man who keeps a woman in a rusuk has th advantage of a married man, insofar as he has a monopoly on h bride, but suffers none of the disadvantageous taboos placed c married men.

The most common reason given by the natives for marrying that the elders of the woman either died or left the village. The

ere remained no one to look after the children. The next most
important reason is the desire of the man to gain the use of the taro
fields of the woman. A third, and equally urgent reason, lies in the
desire of men to become priests or seers. As pointed out, these officials
must be married men.

It usually is the woman who desires a marriage to take place.
She does not, however, tell the man directly, as she would be ashamed
to do this. If she already has two or three children, she may say
to her friends, "I have so much trouble, it is almost as if my children
have no father". Then the man is told that he must marry the woman.
According to a census which I took at the village of Matobe, one
third of the children were born out of wedlock.

When it is decided that the young pair will marry, and after
the groom has the necessary house, domestic animals, baskets, &c.,
to render marital life economically feasible, a group of the relatives
of the man, under the leadership of the father of the groom or the
maternal uncle, go to the dwelling of the girl. Here a stereotyped
conversation follows. The father of the man asks for the girl for
his son, and the father of the girl accepts, depreciating meanwhile
the marriageable qualities of his daughter.

Then a date is set, and in preparation for the marriage lia, wood,
food, and grated sago as chicken food are prepared. After this the
people ceremonially wash their hair with lime juice (magiri). A preliminary visit which is held at the house of the girl takes place in
the evening. The next morning the actual ceremony takes place at
the house of the father of the groom, who performs the ritual. The
wife of this man brings in the bride.

The central feature of the Mentawei marriage is the eating
together of the groom and bride. Heretofore the couple had never
eaten together. After this ceremony the pair must always eat together
in their lalep. For a man or wife to eat separately would be a sin;
this sin has a special name, masoilo, and arouses the anger of the
spirits of the house altar. The exact manner in which the bride and
groom partake of their first food in common is the following: the
officiating brother divides a cooked egg from a white chicken in half,
giving one portion to the groom and one to the bride. After the
egg is eaten, a general feast follows. The name of the egg used
in the marriage ceremony is pasailiat kabei, "to change the house
hand".

184

After this marriage meal the men and women go separately
bathe in the river. On their way back they gather sacred flowe
for the house altar. Then the old flowers are removed from the hou
altar and scattered over the house, the new flowers being put
their place. Next the people oil their bodies, and make them yell
with powdered curry berry, as decoration of the lia. The officiatin
brother then sacrifices eggs and yam to the spirits of the alta
accompanied by a suitable invocation. Next he takes a white chick
and passes it over the heads of the married couple. This is call
lia-ake, to make lia. The invocation spoken is as follows:

"Here is our lia (sacrifice), a white rooster who can fly in the a
and who knows when it is morning. So may my wife and children be

In other words, the wife and children should be as clever as t
rooster. After the bird has thus been made use of, it is killed
having its neck wrung, sprinkled with water, singed over the fi
and the liver inspected for omen taking.

The remainder of the lia is performed by the married coup
aided by the brother. The affair lasts for a month or two. Eve
kind of food used must be obtained and sacrificed at the altar
the new house. Remnants from the new fields, boats, and new wo
tools also must be consecrated by being sprinkled with water in t
uma. Special foods that must be caught and sacrificed are shrim
and crabs. The idea is that these give the couple long life, due
their habit of changing their skins. The bouquet of flowers before t
altar also must be changed in the new home, since these sacred plan
are supposed to contain the souls of the dwellers of the lalep. Finall
the woman must be taken into the uma of the man, if the marria
takes place in the same village, or the man into the uma of the woma
if he be a stranger to the village. This involves a short punen perio
and the killing of a pig.

Since every married man becomes an ukui, or house prie
married life in Mentawei is in itself somewhat of a sacrament. Hen
it is not surprising to find that divorce is either absent, or at lea
very rare. The same statement naturally holds true for adultery
either side. Naturally the felicity of married life is no greater
Pageh than elsewhere, and wives, when displeased, are apt to r
away; husbands, to avoid their spouses. In the case of a wife's runnin
away at her own will, it is not in accordance with custom for t
usband to seek her return. She must do this of her own accord.

Mentawei nomenclature, as already stated, stresses age classes. ot only is a distinction made between children, youths above puberty, d married people, but a further distinction is made in cases of reaved persons, who while they are mourning, lose their personal mes. According to Pleyte, widowers can marry only widows. robably this rule is customary rather than obligatory.

The mother's brother, and not the father, is the natural companion boys in Mentawei stories. Kruyt writes that the father's sister is oser to the children than the mother's sister. A maternal uncle ust always allow his nephews and nieces the right to gather the oducts of his fields, along with his own brothers and children.

While thus there is a certain amount of influence felt from ighboring peoples who have sib systems and kinship customs in cordance with cross-cousin marriage and sib systems, the influence but slight. While, for example, the Bataks have a rigorous taboo the contact of brothers and sisters, the Pageh islanders allow em to eat and sleep together when small. When adult, however, others and sisters must sleep in separate houses.

The same rule holds true in the case of twins. Among many oples of the world twins are considered a public calamity, and e or both killed at birth. This custom perhaps arises from the ar that the twins, if of different sexes, have had incest in the womb. ich certainly is the belief and custom among the Bataks. In Pageh, wever, in the case of twins the lives of both are spared, and no reat harm is thought to have been done. Some people believe, in e case of boy and girl twins, that the pair will not live long, and ey make disparaging remarks concerning the prenatal morality the young pair.

Pregnancy and childbirth. — When a woman becomes pregnant e is relieved of all heavy work. She also is subjected to a number taboos. She cannot go near a dead animal, for fear of killing e foetus. She cannot sit or run in the sunshine, or sit with her ck to the fire. She cannot tie knots, plant taro, or wash sago. ertain foods likewise are forbidden the woman. No trace of the uvade appears, nor is the married man placed under many new strictions at this time. He is not allowed, however, to hunt.

While the woman is pregnant her husband must abstain from xual intercourse with her, nor can he again approach her until some ne after the birth of the child. During this period she is allowed

only to come into contact with married men. Even her own brother
if they be unmarried, are not allowed access to the house.

There are no midwives in Mentawei, but a number of women
aid at the time of a birth. They support the woman, who gives birth
to the child in a sitting position. When the event does not go off
smoothly, everything in the house is opened, and all knots are untied.
If in spite of these measures the child is late in arrival, the people
say that it is because the woman has broken a punen taboo. Then
if the condition of the woman continues to be serious, a seer is
summoned. Sacrifices are made, a half going to the seer as his
payment, and a cure affected in the usual manner. The seer brings
with him his bells, a basin of water, and plants with life-giving
qualities. The seer tinkles his bells, sings incantations, and urges
his guardian spirits to descend into the water. The plants are mashed
up and put into the water, and the woman is made to drink some
of it, the remainder being poured over her as a bath. Finally the
soul of the woman is invoked to return, and the cure is at an end.

After the child is born the navel string is cut with a knife by
the women. The placenta is covered with ashes, placed in a bamboo
cooker, and preserved above the fireplace. Children born dead are cast
out into the wilderness. If the mother dies in childbirth, the child is
strangled and buried with her. Otherwise the mother would come
back looking for the child.

The day after the birth of the child, the mother brings the
suckling to the river, and remains squatting in the water the entire
day with the child in her arms. She only goes home to eat. She
does this for three months, except when it rains. The child must
always receive the breasts of its mother in the river, never on land.
The mother, when not giving her child suck, binds her breasts with
rotan. Until the child is old enough to learn to walk, it is never
allowed to touch the ground. The word used for caring for children
is uka, which also means "to hold". Either the father or mother must
be in constant attendance on young children, holding them in their arms.

The adoption of the child. — After the birth of a child, the mother
can work as soon as her condition allows. The person who adopts
the child, however, must observe lia for at least ten months. If the
couple are married, it is the father who adopts the child, otherwise
the father of the woman. The delay caused by the adoption he
furnishes another argument against early marriages in Pageh.

One or two days after the child is born, the first lia takes place. his is called lia kabe-bela, "lia for the hand coming out". Chickens 'e killed in sacrifice, and the child is given its first talisman. The ther obtains wood, and cuts it as small as matches. These are rapped in red calico, and hung around the neck of the child.

After this the father has to initiate all kinds of his work in the ual ceremonial manner. For one month the father must only fish, e next month hunt, then make tapa, then start work on his fields, ially he either builds a boat or makes sago. Three months are spent preparing the decorations for the child, its brass wrist bands, arm nds, and tail of leaves. The brass ornaments are, of course, imported, t the time is spent in consecrating the ornaments. At the time of taching the final ornament to the child, the leaf tail, a special lia held, lia koirit alai. "The lia for the putting away of the hair." t the beginning of this lia, the hair of the child is cut, especially ound the neck and behind the ears. This hair then is wrapped in leaf of the sacred plant bobolo (Dracaena) and placed in a bamboo oker. In this cooker the hair of all the children of the family is pt and the cooker is inherited in the family. After this lia the hair the crown of the head can never be cut, for fear of losing the soul.

When the child is five months of age it receives its second isman, ngalou panake, the shutting talisman. From then on, it n eat all kinds of food without injury to itself. The talisman is lled "shutting", because it is supposed to close in the soul to the dy of the child. At this time the child also is given further corations, including strings of glass beads, and the hair of its head ain cut. In order to strengthen the power of the second talisman, o monkeys have to be obtained. The first monkey killed is called et, or to entice. The skull of this monkey is hung up in the uma usual. This skull, as well as all other deer and monkey skulls in uma, are supposed to lure the wild animals of the jungle, so t they can readily be caught. At time of punen, the souls of the d animals are summoned. They then come up a special ladder, the rit ladder, and enter the uma. The second monkey shot is called katnia, the cooked one. The cooked flesh of this monkey is rubbed the child, "in order to warm the talisman". Finally after the ld has been taken to the field, and a lia held there, and after all ms of work have been properly initiated, the lia for adoption is at end. The ordinary time for this lia is ten months, but if the

188

child is taken sick in the meantime, the affair will last longer. Duri
the course of the lia, the man holding it, and his wife, are una
to have sexual intercourse, or to attend to their ordinary work.
a result, their fields run to weeds. Still, the proper form of lia is h
to be a necessity, for without it the child is not regarded as legitima
and cannot inherit.

Personal names. — Personal names are changed frequently
Mentawei, as in Polynesia. If a person dies, the survivors of
same name must change their names. When a person becon
bereaved by the loss of a near relative, he or she goes into mourni
While the bereaved person is in mourning he loses his name, bei
called teteu, or some similar title. During the period of mourning
bereaved person must lay aside all ornaments, and abstain fr
attending punen. The ghost of the dead is believed to render
bereaved person unclean. At the end of the period of mourning
bereaved person is ceremonially washed, a lia is held, and the per
assumes a new name. A man or woman who loses a spouse mou
until he or she marries again. In case there is no remarriage
person retains the title teteu. A man or woman who becomes a s
assumes a new name. He will however frequently change this na

A child is given its first name before its fourth month. Either
father or the mother gives the name. A nickname also may be giv
A person's family cannot be inferred from his names, although th
may be ancestral. The name of a forefather or grandfather is
quently assumed, provided the member of the older generation alre
is dead. A person who is about to die will change his name, so as
to carry it down into the grave with him. The name which a d
person bore can never be used or mentioned again. To do this i
curse, since the name is ghost-contaminated. In former days it wo
have occasioned a fight. To further illustrate the close connect
between ghosts and names, it may be added, that elders not o
change their names at the death of a child, but also in the event t
subsequently a brother or sister of the dead child becomes sick.
seer then is summoned who gives the elders new names. The c
cause of sickness and death in Mentawei (outside of visible nat
causes and some forms of witchcraft) is soul-abstraction by gho
Hence name-changing here is fundamentally a form of ghost avoida

It is difficult to tell sex by Mentawei names. Women, howe
are more apt to be named after flowers. A half dozen names is li

elow taken from a list collected in Pageh. No guarantee can be
resented that the names are not nicknames. The Mentawei people
re reserved about giving their names, since these can be used in
itchcraft. The first three names are those of men, the latter three
f women.

Ngena-katiri	He who waits on the upper river.
Telu-malainge	He who is three times beautiful.
Manjang	An eagle.
Itjo-tubunia	She who looks at her own body.
Ta-anai-si-ake-nia	She who has no one to give her anything.
Ogo	The flower.

It finally may be remarked that no record is kept of the deeds
f ancestors nor of their names. Hence it is impossible to collect
enealogies or historical traditions. All the Mentawei stories have
ameless heroes. Either the hero simply is called a man, simanteu,
r else the name is descriptive of an achievement, as Segemulaibi,
he who climbs up (to heaven) on a rotan".

Death and burial. — Crying commences as soon as a sick person
as drawn his last breath. The body usually is carried to the
emetery on the same day. In Pageh the corpse is laid on a piece
f tapa cloth which previously had served as the sleeping mattress
f the deceased. A cloth is put over this, and the whole placed on a
ragbar. The body is brought, feet foremost, to the cemetery in a
oat. The body is carried feet foremost so that if it rises from the
rave it will have its back to the village.

There are numerous taboos on the day that the body is carried
▸ the cemetery. It is forbidden to pound sago, get taro from the
elds, or make a fire at the source of the river. If any of the taboos
ere broken, the ghost would come back to the village and bring
ckness. All work pertaining to a funeral must be done by unmarried
en and women.

The cemeteries lie upstream from the village. No care is taken of
ie places, and they are avoided as much as possible.

The body is washed at the cemetery before finally being disposed
. After the washing the corpse is clothed again and covered with
cloth. The washing is done so that the dead will join the other
eceased members of the family, and no longer trouble the living.

When a rimata is buried the pall-bearers cut his fingers, toes, a
thighs at the joints. This operation is necessary because the prie
is the caretaker of the sacred fetish, "the punen" of the uma, a
thus has the souls of all the inmates in his custody. Therefore
could bring the souls of the people with him into the grave. In t
words of the natives:

"If the souls of the people should say to the priest, or if t
punen should say, 'We follow you, father', then the dead priest wou
reply, 'Do not come, boys, do not come, girls, you cannot come to m
My hands and feet are wounded, my thigh also is wounded. I a
not able to take you and place you on my lap. Go back to the um
Your mothers will be there, your fathers will be there.' "

The usual method of disposing of the body is on a simple pla
form, from two to six feet above the ground. Other bodies, howeve
are buried in the ground. The pall-bearers do as they please in th
matter, perhaps following the previously expressed desires of t
deceased. The bodies of those who die in a punen period are n
buried at all, but are placed on a cleared off space of ground.
piece of wood is placed at the spot of such a burial as a warni
sign. A person who dies from a crocodile bite is placed in the branch
of a tree so that the sky spirits will see the body and take reveng

In Siberut the dead are disposed of in split-open tree trun
which are placed on platforms. In a manner similar to Pageh, t
unmarried must act as undertakers.

In Pageh at the time of a death the people of the village ho
punen for from three to six days. They are not allowed to go to s
during this time, and strangers are forbidden entrance to the villa
lest they become contaminated by the disease. The pall-bearers a
taboo for a certain period of time after the funeral. On returni
from the cemetery they must brush off the bad influence (gh
contamination, called badju) with sacred leaves. While taboo th
suffer the same restrictions as married people, and are forbidden
do heavy work in the house, plant, cut weeds, &c.

None of the property of the dead person is left at the gra
When a seer dies, however, all his sacred paraphernalia is tak
with him to the burial grounds. It is brought back again, howev
and inherited by a brother or son of the deceased. In former tim
it was the custom to destroy some of the fruit trees and crops of t
dead person, so that he would not take them all. This is still do

ı the village of Matobe. Elsewhere this is done only when there is
o one to inherit, or when the ghost of the dead (as seen by a seer)
omes back and demands his property.

The first act which the near relatives perform to indicate that
ıey are in a state of mourning is to cut one another's hair. This
. done upon the return from the funeral; spouses, and children and
arents, reciprocate in clipping one another. The widow and widower
ıy aside their names, and all ornaments until they remarry. As a
ırther token of grief the woman carries, if a widow or if she has
ost a child, a jacket of broad banana strips. This is worn for ten
ays. In the village of Silabu the men likewise wear mourning jackets.
hey stick their heads through large four cornered tapa cloths, and
ear large banana leaf hats.

While people are wearing mourning they are considered ghost
ontaminated, and are not allowed to mingle with the other members
f the village. For a month, likewise, a piece of the bark of a certain
ee is placed before the house of the deceased to show that it is
aboo. If one member after another of a house dies, the house is
onsidered "warm", and is abandoned.

If after a death there is a great deal of sickness in the village
ıe seer probably will say that he sees the ghost of the deceased, who
as come back. Then the people destroy all the property of the dead
erson, such as his banana and fruit trees. These are for the use of
ıe ghost. Perhaps relatives had promised a payment to the spirits
or the recovery of the sick man. They had failed to keep their word,
o the ghost returns seeking payment. Next a punen is held, and
acrifices made.

If sickness still continues in the village, special punen and sacri-
ces have to be made to the ghost. Fetish poles (kera) likewise are
ected at the mouth of the river to keep the evil ghost away. The
ack and kidney of a pig are offered to the ghost in punen. The
ack, so that the ghost will turn his back to the village, and the
dney (the seat of desire) so that the ghost no longer will desire
visit the village.

The rules of inheritance are very simple in Pageh. A house
ther often makes his will verbally on his death bed, at the same time
structing his family in native mythology and folk-lore. When he
es, the widow remains in the same house with the children. When
e widow marries she gives the house over to her son or brother.

Taro fields are handed down in the female line, as well as certai
house implements.

The dead linger three days near the burial place and then g
to soul land. In Pageh this is called "lagai sabeu, the large village
and is situated off the west coast of the island. The ghosts of th
dead come in a large war boat to fetch the new arrival, and whe
he arrives at the land of the dead a large punen is held to welcom
him. Life in spirit land is much the same as that here on earth. Th
ghosts fish, and have fields. They do not hunt, however. Seers alor
are able to visit the land of the dead, as well as the land of the sk
spirits. All ghosts are able to obtain entrance to lagai sabeu excep
the souls of those who have practiced sorcery while on earth. Th
souls of these wicked people remain outside the uma and cann
mingle with the others. So even in Pageh there is a test for admittan
to soul land.

Religion.

Spirits and souls. — The Mentawei people believe in natu
spirits, souls, and ghosts. The chief nature spirits are those in th
sky (tai-ka-manua), those in the sea (tai-ka-baga-koat), those in th
jungle (tai-ka-leleu), and those in the earth (tai-ka-baga-polak). Th
translations are literal. The spirits are not given individual name
nor are there higher gods, as elsewhere in Indonesia.

The earthquake god is called Teteu, or grandfather. It is becaus
of this god that human sacrifice formerly was made at the time
building an uma. If the god were not appeased, he would shake dow
the new uma. It is also because of this god that there is a tab
against the spilling of blood within the village. At the time of buildir
a new uma, however, blood purposely is spilt on the ground in ord
to summon Teteu up to witness the dancing.

Besides these spirits, the people of Pageh believe in two riv
spirits, Ina Oinan (mother of rivers, or water) and Kameinan, o
in translation, father's sister. The first of these spirits is propitio
towards the people, if properly sacrificed to, and providing they ha
committed no ritual sin. The custom of bathing the children in th
river, although a common Indonesian habit, is said to be due to th
necessity of acquainting the young with the water spirits, so th
they will not stumble in the rivers. The second spirit, Kameinan,
always spoken of as being evil.

The sky spirits are the most important of all, and the best seers
ve them as guardian spirits. Lesser seers are contented with the
d of the jungle spirits. The sky spirits, like the others, are considered
anthropomorphic beings; men, women and children, who live in
uses in a big village in the sky, and breed animals. They look
e same as the people on earth, only they are very much more
autiful. The Tai-ka-manua are often invoked for the purpose of
ding the growth of the banana trees and the taro, since they are
pposed to give rain and drought. In asking a favor of the sky
irits, one splits the upper end of a stick in three parts, places
od in this section, and rams the stick upright into the ground. This
called "pasi buluat" or making an altar. The seers are able to
imb to the sky on bamboos, or ascend in the state of trance, and
g favors from the sky spirits. There is a story that originally
eteu and the sky spirits were at war. Teteu shook the heavens,
d the sky spirits sent a flood down on him. Then a peace treaty
as made.

The Mentawei religion, in common with other Indonesian
ligions, hinges on the soul concept. The main purpose of the cult
Mentawei is to obtain health and long life. Disease is thought
be due to the temporary absence of the soul, death to be the
rmanent soul-loss. The soul that leaves the body in dreams and
ckness is called si-magere. The soul that leaves at death is called
tsat. It is this latter soul which turns into the ghost, sanitu. Ghosts
e always the bringers of disease, and are invariably malevolent.
hosts are never prayed to, except for the purpose of witchcraft, nor
they receive sacrifice except for the aforesaid reason, or when
ey return to the village to bring sickness. Avoidance is practiced
wards the ghosts, for they alone are primarily responsible for the
ring away of people's souls. In order to prevent this, kera or
tish sticks are erected at all the possible entrances to the village.
hese sticks prevent the approach of the ghosts, as long as the people
ave committed no ritual sin, have broken no taboo.

In Siberut alone is there a trace of ancestor worship. Wirz states
at there the ghosts of ancestors are honored under the title of sa-
kui, the fathers.

This leads to the necessity of another explanation. Not only have
l people souls, but all animals and plants likewise have souls. Thus,
hen a pig is sacrificed, the liver is placed on the altar for the

13

194

protecting spirits of the uma. But it is not the liver itself that th
spirits are supposed to eat, but rather the soul (ketsat) of the pig
and this ketsat resides in the liver. In one account of a pig sacrific
it is recorded that "the ketsat of the pig went squealing up to th
skies" as a sacrifice to the heaven spirits. There is still anothe
animating factor at the back of all things, both of the animate, an
of those, which to us, are inanimate. These are the spirits (kina
All objects have kina. Therefore it is not the fetish sticks (kera
themselves which keep the ghosts from the village, but it is th
spirits (kina) of the sticks which perform the office. For this purpos
the people give the fetish sticks thorns, spears, and daggers. Th
people also must sacrifice to the fetish sticks, or rather to the kin
of the sticks. Since everything in existence has kina, everything
considered anthropomorphic. Thus the uma, the houses, boat
bamboos, &c., speak, are spoken to, and act as human beings. On
of the most important taboos in Mentawei is directed against th
cutting of boats and work tools. The kina of these articles woul
object. Finally it may be suggested that the kina, or spirits, a
more fundamental than the souls of living beings. For while sou
are found only in living beings, spirits (kina) are found in all object
Even souls, si-magere, must have spirits, kina, to animate them! Th
the first line of an invocation made by the priest at the founding
a new uma reads, "Konan kina-si-magere-mai tatoga-ku". "Com
spirits of the souls of our children."

Curing and witchcraft. — The power to become a seer is acquire
through a vision, which comes voluntarily or involuntarily. Once th
seer has the magic power he gains the aid of guardian spirits, wh
assist him in his cures. The seer then is able to see and talk wit
the spirits and ghosts; he has, according to the native expressio
"seeing eyes and hearing ears".

A vision may come in the following manner. A man is sittin
for example, by his field hut. Suddenly some one comes and sits dow
beside him. They begin to talk, and the owner of the hut asks whe
the stranger comes from, and who he is. The stranger replies tha
he belongs to the place. The stranger offers the other man his tobacc
so that the latter may roll a cigarette. But the man notices that th
tobacco of the stranger never grows less as one cigarette after anoth
is made from it. The two start to go back to the village togethe
when suddenly the stranger vanishes. The man decides that th

isitor cannot be a human being. When the visitor comes a second
me to the field hut, he offers the man tobacco from a bamboo
ontainer. The container keeps rolling towards the man of its own
olition. Then the man again decides that the stranger must be a
pirit. The man talks the matter over with his father, and they decide
 ask the stranger to dinner. The guest arrives, but he is visible
 the clairvoyant alone. The stranger eats, but his dish never becomes
mpty. From this time on the man has the powers of a seer. He
en proceeds to take instruction from his fellow practitioners.

A man or woman may be made a seer by being bodily abducted
y the spirits. According to the story of Sitakigagailau, the youth
as taken up to heaven by the sky spirits and given a beautiful body
ich as theirs. When he returned to earth he was a seer, and the
ky spirits served him in his cures. In return he gave sacrifice to
e sky spirits at the time of punen held for healing.

The usual manner, however, in which boys and girls become
ers is by being summoned through sickness, dreams, or temporary
sanity. The sickness or dreams are sent by the sky spirits or the
ngle spirits. Malaria is the usual form of sickness. The dreamer
ay imagine that he ascends to heaven, or that he goes to the woods
oking for monkeys. In either case, dreams or sickness, there is a
mporary loss of soul (si-magere). Then a professional seer is
ammoned to make the sick boy or girl well.

The seer questions the spirits of the house altar concerning the
use of the sickness, and advises the youth (if a boy) to get married, so
at he will stop doing taboo things. If the seer is favorably impressed
y the youth, he advices him to go into training and become a doctor.
his advice naturally is said to have come from the spirits, who
reaten madness and death in case of disobedience.

The instructor first purifies the youth so as to eliminate all the
idju, or bad influence from his system, then the two gather plants
r the new balo-balo, the joint of bamboo, laden with sacred plants
id leaves, which every seer has before his house, and by means
 which he talks to his guardian spirits.

Next the instructor washes the hair of the youth (magiri), and
en he takes him to his house in order to aid him in acquiring his
sion.

When they arrive at the house of the instructor, the latter takes
 cup into which the required spirits are to be summoned. The

instructor charms, "let your eyes be clear, let our eyes be clear, so that we may see our fathers and mothers of the lower heaven". While the instructor sings, the two keep ringing their bells. After the invocation, the instructor rubs herbs on the eyes of the boy. For three days and nights the two men sit opposite each other, singing and ringing their bells. Until the eyes of the boy are clear, neither of the two men obtains any sleep. At the end of the three days the two again go to the woods and obtain more herbs, which they place in a half coconut. The purpose of the herbs is to make the bodies of the spirits shiny and beautiful, so that they will not be ashamed to reveal themselves to the boy. The instructor places the coconut between himself and the pupil and charms, "Here, make yourself shine for your father, my children (the wood spirits). Wood spirits, you are the owner. Shine in his eyes, so that your bodies are visible to him, do not conceal your bodies from him." This clears the eyes of the boy a little. In another two days, since neither the heaven nor the wood spirits have appeared as yet, the two men gather more herbs. If at the end of seven days the boy sees the wood spirits the ceremony is at an end. Otherwise the entire seven day ceremony must be repeated.

The next thing to be done is to make an outfit for the new seer which he wears while performing his office. First comes the hair ornament worn over the left ear. This is composed of chicken feathers wrapped around with bark twine. The twine is decorated with beads. The outer wrapping consists of bark, with an outer covering of red cotton cloth. Next, the breast band is made. This consists of brass spangles. The spangles are decorated with beads woven on coconut ribs and chicken feathers. Next, the brass arm bands are hammered out. Then rotan, of the black and red variety, is decorated with beads and wrapped around the candidate as a breech band. Three strings of beads are used as head bands (kirit). The head bands serve as telephone wires between the altar and the seer. It is through these that the seer talks to the spirits of the altar. Bamboo carriers to contain the oil used for anointing, brass arm and wrist bands are now made. Finally two bells are taken, and the handles wrapped around with red cloth. This is done so that the bells will cling to the hands of the seer. The bells serve to summon the spirits.

Nine days are taken up in the preparation of the outfit. Then the instructor gives the final charms to his pupil. He first asks, "Ar

ur eyes clear now, so that you can see your fathers, your elder and
ur brothers (the spirits)?" "Yes, I see them clearly", replies the
by. The instructor charms, "Boy! I am here when you are in need,
r I made you. You now will be able to give medicine to the people
Mentawei with cold (skillful) hands. You now will have seeing
es to see the wood spirits, hearing ears to hear the words of the spirits
whom we sacrifice at the altar. May your magic power secure you
ng life, may it enable you to visit continually the villages of men
d to cure the sick." The instructor next places the headdress on
e boy, who charms, "I take this headdress as decoration so that
may have magic power, that I have power in the villages of the
rangers. The people of the village will look on, the people of the
llages I visit will look on, the wood spirits will look on, the spirits
heaven will look on, the spirits of the sea will look on, the spirits
der the ground of the village will look on, the poles (kera) of the
llage will look on, all the children of the uma will look on. May
derive magic power from the seers of the other villages, so that I
ay question the altars of the other villages, that I may question the
irits of the other villages, that I may join my singing with that of
e other seers who also are powerful. May my spirits rule over other
llages, so that when I use my headdress as a means of knowing
hat to do I will be proficient in curing. I charm myself so that
be strong in body, that my magic power be enduring, that I have
ng life. Amen (bulatnia, may it be correct)."

Then the instructor places the breast band, the arm bands, and
leaf tail on the youth, and the magical outfit is complete. After
is the instructor blinds the eyes of the initiate, so that he is unable
see for two or three days. This is done so that the people will
lso be blind when the seer plays tricks on them. The seer puts the
ice of certain herbs in both eyes of the candidate, and charms,
Red laiga flower, make clear his eyes, may the faces of the spirits
ine that he may see them. May the eyes of the people be blinded
y this charm."

Next the instructor takes a bamboo container of a hand's length
nd open at both ends. He blows into both ears of the candidate,
arming, "I blow into your ears, my child, so that you will be able
hear the words of the wood spirits, and the speech of the altar.
cause you to have hearing ears, seeing eyes, and cold hands. I
use you to have magic power. I enable you to visit as a seer."

The new seer is now put upon a year's probation. During th
time he learns from the older man who has instructed him,
accompanying him on his visits to the sick, and also from the oth
seers by watching how they perform their tricks. During the ye
the new seer has certain taboos placed upon him, and if his wi
becomes pregnant in this period the people lose all confidence in hir

The power of the seer, unlike the power of the shaman, is n
necessarily a permanent acquisition. If the outfit, especially th
headdress, becomes ruined from age, or if the seer has not practice
for a long time and then wishes to recommence, he must renew h
power (masibaba kerei). This is also the case if the seer makes
mistake in his work, or breaks some taboo. In any of these circun
stances the seer becomes unable to have contact with his guardia
spirits, and the people refuse to call on him. In order to renew h
power the seer must have the aid of another man in the professio
and remake his outfit as in the beginning.

The necessity of adhering to professional etiquette as well as th
need for observance in order to learn the tricks of the trade, a
illustrated in the final advice which the instructor gives his pup

The words of the older seer, as here given, answer beyond dou
that well known question, to what extent is the primitive medicir
man sincere in the practice of his profession?

"Boy, you have indeed seen the spirits to whom we sacrifice, yc
have heard the voice of the altar, it has come to pass that you hav
spoken with our fathers the wood spirits. Now you are instructe
Those to whom we sacrifice do not wish that we should make mistak
in our work, they do not wish us to commit faults, to eat forbidde
foods. If we do these things the spirits will make us and our childre
sick, they will make trouble for us. When we go to our work,
we have committed any fault, we will not be able to see the spirit
If we have deceived the spirits of the altar they will pay no hee
to us. Do not be lazy. Watch our friends the other seers; part
our magic power comes from what we have learned, part from wh
we have seen."

When a seer is summoned to a village to take care of the cas
of sickness there, he first makes the rounds of the houses. In eac
house he talks to his guardian spirits by means of the house altar
and these spirits are supposed to inform him concerning the tabo
which the inmates of the house have broken. Naturally the peop

f the house hear but the voice of the seer, not the voices of the spirits. 'he seer has taken the precaution to ascertain beforehand from the eople of the village the particular "sins" of the inmates of each house, nd if they have broken none of the old taboos, the seer is forced to ivent new ones which he claims they have violated. It is in this ay that the taboo system becomes more and more intricate. As each ouse father is told about the taboos he, or the members of his house, ave violated, he promises to mend his ways. The sacrifices to the pirits and the actual curing comes later.

The seer goes out in the morning and gathers herbs in the jungle ear the village. They are chosen for their appearance and potency f name, rather than their therapeutic value. The seer scrapes and ixes them with water in hollow bamboo containers. These he puts side for future use in the treatment of patients.

In the early part of the afternoon the seer summons the souls of e people of the uma to return to their owners. This ceremony is alled sogai si-magere (the calling of souls) and is an essential of very lia and punen. Each person who is to be cured has to contribute s many chickens and pigs as directed by the spirits of his altar.

While the animals are being killed and brought into the uma by e unmarried men, the seer goes in front of the uma and invokes e souls of the inmates. He takes stems of the bobolo plant (Cordyline rminalis) to serve as receptacles for the souls of the people. One lant is taken for each household. The seer takes out his bells and ings, "Come, come, spirits of the souls of our children, do not go way. Do not leave us. Here is your food, chickens and pigs." The pirits see the seer, and enter the bobolo leaves. The seer stops ringing is bells, and taking the leaves, places them on the heads of his atients. The leaves are put above the fontanel. The object of this ct is to insure the safety of the life-giving soul (ketsat). The act is alled tutut ketsat, or locking in the ketsat.

The people now mount to the porch of the uma, where the priest nd the seer inspect the livers of the slaughtered pigs and chickens. f the tops of the livers are clear, and the veins in the region are not rossed, the sick people will recover. Liver sacrifices are then made t the altar by the priest, who meanwhile offers a formularized prayer.

After the sacrifice the meat is divided, one half going to the er, and one half to the people of the home uma. This food is placed bamboos and cooked at once, to avoid spoiling. The seer must

later surrender his portion to the inmates of the uma from which]
has been summoned. However, as payment for each cure which]
makes, he obtains an arm's length of cloth, ten strings of bead
one live chicken, a large basket of taro, and twenty-five coconu
This amount is paid for a "large cure". In money it is worth abo
five guldens, or two dollars. A "small cure" brings only half
much. The price of a cure depends on the seriousness of the cas
not on the wealth of the patient. Theoretically, at least, all the peop
of Mentawei are on an equal financial level.

In the afternoon following the sacrifice, the seer is ready to gi
the sick their medicine. He goes to the first house, in which a patie
lies, wearing his outfit, and bringing the herbs and implements. The
consist of the carrying baskets, thorn scrapers, bamboo holde
containing flasks of coconut oil and mashed herbs in water, and t]
bells. First the seer washes the head of the patient. Then he tak
some of the unscraped medicine and squeezes a portion on his han
and another portion into a cup. The latter he mixes with water
a hair wash. "Our children (the spirits) wash your hair so that ;
evil be thrown off from your body, so that all your sins be wash
away." Next the seer squeezes more medicine, and mixes the jui
in a cup with some water. The contents are poured over the patier
who also is given a sip to drink. The seer sings, "They, my childr
the spirits, wash you so as to throw off evil from your body. N
children wash you so that you be reminded of the correct mann
of living. This is your medicine".

If the seer is giving a very thorough treatment, he gives t]
patient seven kinds of medicine. The second type, like the first,
applied externally and internally as well. The third type is used
clean out the insides of the person, and thus cause the fever to depa:
The next three varieties of medicine are applied externally. In extern
treatment the Pageh seer does not make use of sucking, as does h
confrere in Nias, but he does apply massage. The magical meanil
of both varieties of treatment are the same, the extraction of diseas
bearing objects from the body of the patient.

The fourth variety of medicine is given for the purpose of makil
the patient's body mobile. An assistant sings, while the seer does t]
rubbing. "Fathers, the wood spirits, make powerful our hands .
we take hold of this medicine, for this sickness is very severe. [
this lest we be ashamed of our magic power, lest we be asham

f our visit. Here is medicine to make supple the body, we rub it
n the patient's body to make it supple." The fifth variety of medicine
s rubbed on by massage (porot). The medicine rubbed on is for the
urpose of "closing up the flesh". The seer sings while massaging,
Father, the wood spirits, make powerful our hands, so that we may
assage the body of the sick man. We massage the flesh so that
is bones become straight, that he may be able to obtain his breath
nd recover." While the seer is massaging with his hands, his
uardian spirits, the wood spirits, are massaging with theirs. Accord-
g to the account, if the medicine is correct, and the body of the man
pproves of it, the poison (from witchcraft) comes out at once in the
orm of a bone or some other object, and the flesh closes up. The
eer may pull out of the body some remnant of a taboo object which
e patient has eaten, the hair of a deer or monkey. Or, perhaps,
ecause of the man's sins, the evil water spirit (sikameinan) has
riven water into the patient's body. Then this comes out. Whatever
s in the man's body will come out, if the medicine is correct. If
e object does not come out, the man will die. For the next treatment
e seer opens his bamboo carrier and takes out his flask of oil. He
olds the mouth of the flask with his finger, and allows the oil to
rip out slowly. Then he rubs the oil on the body of the sick man.
Healing oil, make oily the sick man, make oily the sickness, make
ily the thing in the body of my child." The poison (tae) being well
iled, comes out readily.

The cure now is finished, and the seer and his assistant give a
ttle exhibition. They take out a short variety of bamboo carrier,
ance and sing. "We who are the fathers of the wood spirits make
spectacle for the people. We do it in order to make the sick man
ejoice. We make a miracle for the people of Mentawei. Reveal to
he people that we are your fathers, show them that we are in alliance
vith you. In this way we shall create confidence in our power, we
hall create confidence in our herbs, we shall show that our decorations
re worthy." While the two men sing, their medicine containers bob
p and down in their hands, keeping time to the song. At last the
novements of the containers become so violent that the doctors scarcely
re able to hold them. When their arms become tired the dancers make
n end to the performance. A final bath and sip is given the invalid,
nd the seer departs for the next house.

Dancing plays but a minor role in Mentawei religion, since it has been taken over as a part of the punen system. As already mentioned, the seers dance in the uma on the first evening of every punen, and each dance is an imitation of certain animals or birds. To add to realism the performers wear tails made out of leaves. The purpose is to lure the souls of the game, and thus insure success in the hunt. While I only saw male seers dance in Pageh, Wirz writes that female seers sometimes dance in Siberut.

When a punen is held for the express purpose of curing a village the seers hold a special dance (sairigi) in which they extract poison from the uma and its neighborhood.

First the seers sing to the uma, "Spirits of the uma, we make spectacle for our fathers the wood spirits. If there is any poison in your body, reveal it to us, so that we may find it, so that your children will not become sick." Then the people beat on the snake skin drums and the seers dance. One of the seers goes first to the front of the uma then to the back. He is looking for tae (poison). Anything he pretends to obtain he grasps in his hands and brings to the altar. "I have obtained this, spirits of the uma, reveal if there are any others." The spirits of the altar reply, "There is more poison on the roof." The people strike the drums again, and the seer again dances. He looks for poison on the roof, and obtains it. In the morning the same process is repeated, and all the fetish poles (kera) likewise are inspected and the poison taken from them. Then the village is clean.

Sometimes when the seers dance the sairigi they make the steps quicker and quicker. This is done for the purpose of falling senseless to the ground. It is by this means that the seer is able to communicate with the sky spirits. The seers say that they go to the sky in a boat and that the uma is their boat. It is the eagles who come and bear them up. When the seers arrive in the sky they visit the uma of the sky spirits. They make a speech there, and beg flasks of oil from the female sky spirits. The sky spirits are liberal, and give them oil. The seers claim that this is the kind of oil which gives them the most magical power.

If any of the people of the uma were lost in the woods, or had drifted off to sea, the seers look for them in their dance, and claim to find them. When the seers regain consciousness they tell the people where the lost ones are, so that they know where to look for them. If the lost people already are dead, the seers know this, for they learned it in their dance.

The art of healing in a primitive society cannot be described thout at the same time mentioning the art of bewitching, for the o arts are directly connected with each other, being opposite sides the same beliefs. If the sorcerer works by abstracting and harming e soul of the victim, then the doctor must recall the soul. If the rcerer works by injecting foreign injurious substances into the :tim, the doctor must remove them. Or, by a third method, if the rcerer curses his victim to the hostile spirits (in Mentawei the osts), then the doctor must remove the curse. This is done in entawei by aid of the helpful spirits. Naturally the doctor must ow the methods of the sorcerer, and in many places the two cupations are combined by the same practitioners. In Mentawei, wever, the seer is never suspected of witchcraft. On the contrary, is the person called upon to pick out the criminal. In Pageh the rcerer is called pananae, which means, he who places tae (poison).

One method of poisoning is to take some of the exuviae or operty of the victim and give it in sacrifice to the ghosts. This ethod may be considered either as harmful to the soul of the victim, else as working by a process of sympathetic magic. For example, e sorcerer will first steal some chickens from the victim. Then he ll steal some yams, eggs and cotton goods. He holds the stolen ods in the air, and striking them with certain poisonous plants, rses, "You ghosts, here is your food, your meat, your goods. I do t know the name of the owner of these chickens. But you know it. u look for him and aid my blow, so that he dies."

There are many ways in which the food, possessions, or exuviae n be worked upon by the sorcerer. The goods can be placed in a amp. Then as the goods grow mouldy, the owner becomes sick. e goods can be placed high up on the top of a tree. When the sun rns the goods, the owner becomes sick with fever. The goods can placed behind the hearth, so that they gradually become burnt. In of these cases the ghosts are invoked to aid the process of witchcraft. the sorcerer wishes to kill the small children of a man, he will take me of their decorations, toys, or food. These he will throw into the er and conjure the ghosts, "This is your dwelling place, spirits of food and toys of So-and-so. May the children become dark red with er. May they have coughs, asthma, &c."

Sometimes the sorcerer appears to work by sympathetic magic, led by the ghosts; at other times it is the souls of the victims which are directly attacked. As an example of witchcraft by sympatheti[c] magic, it may happen that the sorcerer will bury a "putput" fish in th[e] fields of the victim. This fish is able to inflate its body with air. Th[e] sorcerer curses, "This is your dwelling place, spirits of the putput. A[s] you swell up, may the body of So-and-so likewise swell up. Ma[y] fever and sickness come to him." Or a man may wish to harm [a] woman, because she has taken another lover. Then he takes some [of] her cloth and places it in a hollow bamboo on the fire. He conjure[s] "This is your dwelling place, spirits of the cloth of So-and-so. As yo[u] get hot, let the woman get dry inside, so that she never will be ab[le] to have children. As you close together, spirits of the bamboo, ma[y] the insides of So-and-so close together, so that she never will ha[ve] children." If, in spite of the curse, the woman becomes pregnant, th[e] sorcerer takes some of her cloth and puts it on the fork of a tree [or] on a thorn. He curses, "Here spirits of the cloth of So-and-so. In th[e] same way in which I hang you up here on a thorn, may the child [of] So-and-so hang up in pregnancy." In illustration of the way in whic[h] the soul of a person may be abstracted by the sorcerer, the followin[g] method is instructive. The sorcerer cuts open a bamboo between th[e] joints, and places inside the cloth and decorations of his victim. [He] then throws the bamboo into the river and allows it drift off to se[a]. He conjures, "This is your dwelling place, spirits of the cloth, spiri[ts] of the decorations of So-and-so. As you drift off, spirits of the bamb[oo] take with you what is inside. In the same way may the soul of S[o-] and-so, and the souls of his father, mother, and children, drift o[ff] and die."

Frequently it is only the property of a person which is damag[ed] by the sorcerer. Thus, the chickens of the victim may be killed. T[he] sorcerer will cut either his own chicken-coop, or else he will hold [a] knife in a threatening position directed at the chicken-coop of his enem[y]. He conjures, "You ghosts, incite the following animals to eat So-an[d-] so's chickens: the chicken weasel, the leguan, the eagle, the pytho[n]. The sorcerer may throw a piece of the "aileppet" plant (the nam[e] means "cold") into the chicken basket of his enemy. He charm[s] "You aileppet make the inside of the basket cold, and kill the chicken[s]. The sorcerer also may blind the hunting dogs of his enemy by takin[g a] bit of their meat and corking it up in a bamboo cooker. With the a[id] of the ghosts, the eyes of the dogs are thereby closed up. Even t[he] traps of an enemy may be bewitched. The sorcerer will spit on t[he] ap and charm, "I spit on you, spirits of the trap, so that the monkeys nd deer will have an aversion to you and you never will trap any ore animals".

In Pageh the seer is called upon to extract poison (tae) from bjects and people, as has been described. The foreign object could ave become lodged in a man by the spirits, because the man broke a boo, or it could have been sent by the ghosts. It usually is believed, wever, that a sorcerer has placed the object. Actually, there is but ttle witchcraft practiced. A seer finds the objects which he himself as brought with him, and which he produces from the walls of the na, or from the fields, by legerdemain. Often a man will wish to in an enemy. He then "salts" his own field with poison, and mmons the seer to find it.

To summarize. — The Mentawei seer acquires his guardian spirits ▪ a vision, either sought for or involuntary. The vision, if sought r, is obtained by a process of abnegation and purification. After the er has obtained his power he can see and talk to the spirits. He mains in special rapport with his own guardian spirits, who aid m in curing. Disease is caused primarily by the ghosts, who are lowed by the spirits to enter the village when a taboo is broken. The osts then steal the souls of the people. Disease also is caused by rcerers who work by sympathetic magic, by soul abstraction, and by acing "poison" in objects and in people. The seer cures by recalling uls, and by extracting poisons. He also is in position to conciliate fended spirits.

The Mentawei seer never is possessed by alien spirits, he never orcises spirits from the body of a patient, he never prophesies. The osest approach which the Mentawei seer makes to prophesy is in s "trip to the sky". In this case, however, the seer is gifted with pernatural vision rather than with a knowledge of the future.

Tribal initiation. — The people of Mentawei differ from other oples of Western Indonesia in having the vestige of a tribal initiation. becoming part of the elaborate punen system, however, this initiation s lost most of its original significance and ceremonies. While it one time probably was for boys alone, it now includes both the sexes. Siberut the ceremony takes place some time before puberty, and s as purpose the introduction of the youths into the rara, or enlarged mily group. In Pageh the ceremony is held at the time of building

a new uma, and all the boys and girls from surrounding villages who
never have been initiated come to the ceremony.

In Siberut the boys and girls receive their first loin cloths at the
time of initiation (enegu). The boys receive theirs on the first day
of the ceremony from the rimata, the girls from the wife of the rimata

According to the custom of this island, when anyone has a
sufficient number of pigs, he goes to the head of his family group, the
rimata, with the question as to whether or not an enegu can be held
A pig must be sacrificed for every child taken into the initiation. I
the father of the child has no pig, he buys one from a member of the
family. A ritual feast then follows. Following the initiation (which
Wirz neglects to describe) comes a ten day punen period, initiated by
a hunt.

In Pageh two pigs are sacrificed for each boy received into the
protection of the new uma, and one pig for each girl. The people dres
in their best yellow loin cloths for the occasion, and decorate them
selves with flowers. The priest who directs the eneget wears his custom
ary punen yellow tapa cloth, brass arm and head bands, and man
strings of beads strung around his neck.

When all is prepared, the priest strikes the gong in the uma, an
all the people come in. The parents bind the upper arms of the childre
who are to be initiated. The priest prays, "We have brought in th
katsaila (flowers on the altar) to our uma, we have brought in th
fathers to our uma, we have brought in the mothers to our uma, w
have brought in the children to our uma. We come in alive, we com
in with sound bodies. Bless us, spirits of the uma, bless us spiri
of our punen, watch our children, guard us."

Then the priest blows on the foreheads of the boys. Afterward
he takes two varieties of flowers and blows the petals on the neophyte
After this the neophytes blow on each other, and the parents on th
neophytes, but not on their own children. The children in turn blo
on the parents, other than their own.

The priest first blesses the boys. "I blow on you, my childre
May those of our children who look in the woods for food, who hun
be happy. May they succeed. May they be diligent in obtaining the
food, may they be faithful to their wives, may they not fight with oth
people of the uma. May they be strong in seizing pigs."

The priest blows on the girls with the leaves of a plant, and th
girls blow on each other. "This is why we blow on you, my childre

hat you be not irritable, that you be not angry with the people. That
ou be diligent in getting food, in fishing, and in scooping up fish
vith the panu (a triangular net used by women)."

The neophytes now are brought down to the river. When they
rrive at the water the priest takes a large-sized rooster and a large-
ized hen. He wets the feet of the chickens and lays them on the heads
f the neophytes. "I have made the feet of the chickens wet, so that
ou, my children, will never be irritable. Since water never dies, so
lso will you have long lives."

They mount to the uma, where each child has a bunch of Dracaena
eaves stuck in his or her girdle. In eating the feast of chickens and
ork which follows, the parents first eat out of the same trough as
heir own children, and then out of the troughs of the other children.
his establishes a bond between the elders of the uma and the children.
An uninitiated child is not allowed to eat with his elders the booty
aken in the hunt.

Conclusion. — In looking at the Mentawei religion as a whole, it
eems probable that the original important traits were those connected
ith witchcraft and curing, and tribal initiation. In this early period
t is likely that tattooing was performed solely at the time of puberty.
'erhaps the knocking out of incissors was likewise a sign of puberty in
Mentawei as in Engano, and that the filing of teeth came later.

The elaborate punen system developed from a more simple sacri-
icial stage. Its elaborateness is due to the isolation of the Mentawei
eople, their lack of economic competition and absence of alien mental
utlook. The system already is headed for decay. Once tobacco,
loth and oil for lamps were introduced, the natives of Mentawei had
ther aims to strive for, other work to perform, than that merely
rescribed by their religious rites. With alien goods necessarily came
lien and critical ideas. The Mentawei punen no longer is the same,
ither in length or in strictness of observance, as that of former days.
he natives themselves are well aware of this fact, and regard the past
s the Golden Age, when punen were real punen, and the amount of
acrifices furnished mighty feasts to the spirits.

PART III. ENGANO.

Introduction.

Engano is perhaps the most interesting of all the islands west o
Sumatra, since its population is, or rather was, the most primitive o
all Malaysians. In 1770 stone axes were still being used in Engano
whereas all other Malaysians had become addicted to the use of iron
At this time, however, the people of Engano already had learnt th
value of iron, and by "silent barter" with the Malays were exchanging
coconuts for old iron. Unfortunately for ethnology but little is know
about the social organization or religion of the Enganese, and with th
present practical extermination of this race, the chances of our ob
taining knowledge in the future are not favorable.

The name Engano is derived from a Portuguese word meaning
deceit or disappointment. The Portuguese may in some way have bee
deceived in discovering the island. They may, for example hav
thought that it was Java, or else that it was the gold island for whic
they were seeking. Engano was the first island which the Dutc
navigators discovered (June 5th, 1596). The island, however, stand
indicated on a map of Asia dating 1593.

The Malays do not know the name Engano, and call this islan
Pulo Telangiang, the island of the naked people. The Enganese ca
their largest and most inhabited island Chefu Cacuhia, the Big Islan
or e loppeh, the land. Marsden relates that the people of Lampon
before 1783 believed that Engano was inhabited solely by wome
and that these women obtained children from the wind, or by eatin
certain fruit. It is for this reason, and not because of any scientifi
proof that there is, or ever was, a matriarchate in Engano, th
Modigliani called his book of travels to Engano "L'isola delle Donne"
the island of women.

The island first was visited in 1645 by a Dutchman named Saa
The first scientific account of the natives was obtained in 1854 by Va
der Straaten and Severijn. A year before this scientific expedition a
English ship was stranded on the island and plundered by the native
Since then Engano has been periodically visited by Dutch officials, an
it is under the rule of the Dutch in West Sumatra.

The Enganese formerly were hostile to all outsiders, and when
ship was stranded on their shores, they blew on triton shell trumpe
to summon the people to plunder. Later, when they became accustome

o trade with foreigners, they brought their wives and daughters down o the ships to earn money from the sailors. Such a custom would have been unthinkable among the Niha or natives of Mentawei.

The people live in villages, called kaudaras, which are built along rivers or on the shore. Almost all the villages are surrounded by fortifications of tree trunks about five feet in height. These serve to keep wild pigs out of the settlements. Communication between villages takes place along poor paths through the jungle, or along the beach. There are no monkeys on the island, and wild pig and civit cats are the only game hunted. The people keep dogs and cats in the towns, but the latter certainly are not native.

Rice cultivation is of course lacking, and even the sugar cane is of recent importation. Unlike among the Mentaweians, however, pottery appears indigenous, and is of Neolithic type, with crossing lines. It is used in cooking. The people have crude double-outrigger canoes. The main weapon of the natives is the spear, and not the bow and arrow.

Economic Life.

Houses. — The villages consist of from six to ninety houses (uba) placed irregularly over the town limits. The shape of these houses is the most peculiar thing to be seen on the island. They are circular in construction, about three feet in diameter, and rest on ironwood piles six to twenty feet in height from the ground. The floors are made of planks. The walls run sloping to the roof and are made of wood or bamboo. The roof is woven from rotan leaves. A wooden image of a person or bird is placed on some of the roofs.

The house is entered by means of a notched ladder pole, the entrance being an eliptical hole in the wall just big enough to crawl through. The interior of the house is not divided into rooms. There is no other opening, so the interior would be dark were it not for the fire. The smoke attempts to escape through the doorway, unless this is shut with rotan leaves. There is no furniture excepting woven pandanus sleeping mats. Skulls of pigs and civit cats adorn the walls.

Only adult men and women sleep in these high houses. The other members of the family spend the night in huts and shelters less carefully built.

Each village also has a four-cornered communal house (kadiofe), which is built on piles, lacks walls, but has a rotan roof. This serves as reception hall and place of recreation. Affairs of government ar discussed in this house.

Heine-Geldern regards the round house as the oldest type i Indonesia. The most ancient form of the round house is built leve to the ground. This kind is found in Timor, and perhaps pre-date Malaysian influence. The Andamanese also have a round house bui on the ground, but it is constructed to accomodate more than on family.

More common than the ground-level round house, is the pile roun house. This dwelling is a mixture of the original round house an the later Malaysian pile house. This is found in parts of Timor, Engano, on the Nicobars, and as a young men's house in We Borneo. The oval houses of North Nias are modified from this forn The more modern, and more prevalent house form in Indonesia, four-cornered with semi-circular or oval pointed roof.

The tree house likewise occurs in Sumatra, the Philippines, an in the Moluccas. It is most likely that the Engano house is built a great height in substitution for actual tree dwellings.

Food. — The food of the people consists of taro, coconuts, yam bananas, birds, much fish, and when they are lucky, wild boar. Th domestic pig is eaten only at feasts, and chickens are said to be recent importation. The only drink is coconut water, and this whe coconuts are convenient. Ordinary water is partaken of with aversio

Taro and bananas are obtained from dry fields which are cult vated in the neighborhood of the villages.

The natives have a great distaste for salt, and originally thre away all food offered them by traders which tasted of salt. In 177 they did not know the use of rice, but by 1840 they had learned buy rice from the Malays and cook it themselves. In 1854 the peop still had an aversion to sirih chewing and tobacco smoking, but 1868 both men and women were inveterate smokers. The people al acquired the use of palm wine.

The Enganese cook the animals which they catch in the hunt burning off the hair or fur. The body then is cut open, the intestin removed, and the flesh broiled, or rather burned, over an open co fire. Taro and yams are cooked in bamboos as in Mentawei. Sm fish are eaten raw, but larger sea food is broiled over a fire.

Fire was made by drilling one piece of wood into another. It said that it took four men to perform this operation.

The pig and the dog formerly were the only domestic animals. he people take especial care of the pig, shut it up at night in a sty, nd keep it well fed and clean. In the daytime the domestic pigs ander around with the wild pigs, and can be distinguished only by eir cropped ears. The women suckle the young pigs as well as uppies. Every dog is named.

In hunting the wild boar the Enganese use big nets which are read out in the jungle and into which the dogs drive the quarry. The ars then are speared to death.

Fishing with hook and line is unknown. The people fish at low de on the reefs, and make use of imported throwing nets and three ointed harpoons. At the present time the barbs are of iron.

Birds are caught with nets, and snared on the trees with lime.

The crocodile never is killed. On the contrary, it is held in ighest honor.

Clothing and decoration. — Men as well as women went almost ntirely naked. The habit of going naked is unusual for Southeastern sia, but is still practiced by certain Naga; in some villages for men, others for women.

At ordinary times the men went entirely naked, or wore yellow eeved jackets made of tapa. But these jackets were worn solely for e hunt. The only daily clothing of the women was a strip of tapa oth, the size of the palm of the hand, which was tied on a string und around their waists. In field work and in fishing the women ore clothing made from finely shredded banana leaves. At feasts the omen wore vests of tapa, as did the men. In going out of doors the en commonly wore headdresses of tapa or fresh leaves as protection om the sun.

The fewer the clothing a primitive people wears, the more, as a le, do they decorate themselves. This is especially true of the Engan- e, who utilize external decorations and not tattooing. The deco- tions are assumed for feasts, and not for daily life. The men have ead decorations of broad strips of bark, lined with white coral. They so wear strips of bark around their arms and necks, to which mother pearl is attached, and stomach bands decorated with coral. The omach bands are solely for decoration, and do not cover the genitals. he women at feasts wear special headdresses, made from wood, on hich human images, or the heads of human beings, or perhaps birds, e carved. On the upper sides of the hats holes are punched to permit

the insertion of flowers and twigs. Furthermore the women wear ne
and arm bands lined with shell and beads, and very eloquent stoma
decorations of black bands with white beads. They also hang lar,
sea-shells around their necks, which serve as combs. Both men a
women are fond of sticking twigs and flowers in their ears.

The natives extend their ear lobes, as in Nias. Ear-rings are ma
of wood, or, in modern times, of tinfoil or buffalo horn. Flowers
feathers are inserted in the rings. The knocking out of the inciss
teeth of the women takes place before marriage. There is no fili
or blackening of the teeth of either sex.

Weapons and artifacts. — Spears appear to have been the origin
fighting weapons of the Enganese. They are about six feet in leng
and are made of nibong or other variety of hard wood. Some of t
lances have sharp bamboo points, and fish bones or shark teeth a
attached to these. In this respect the lances resemble those of Micr
nesia and Polynesia, rather than those of Indonesia. The more rece
spears have imported copper or iron points.

For defence the Enganese use shields about six feet high, a
three feet in width. The shields are stuck into the ground by their low
prongs, and using them as protection, the warriors throw their spea

The women of Engano have the reputation of Amazons. It
recorded that the wives, armed with long clubs, sometimes follow
their husbands to war and when the fight was going against their m
attempted to strike away the shields of their opponents. They a
used spears with barbed hooks for this purpose.

An early traveller (Hantmann, 1592) claimed to have seen t
natives of Engano hunting with bow and arrow. In the word li
of Franas, the word "piëko" indicates bow. Elsewhere there is
mention made of this weapon, and the natives themselves deny a
knowledge of it. Its use therefore evidently was at least limited, a
its disappearance early.

Through trade the Enganese have come into knowledge of oth
weapons and utensils, such as picks, knives and adzes. These we
already in abundance in the island before 1840. The natives boug
the knives, and then decorated the handles with their own designs.

Although the Enganese were constantly at war with one anoth
the fighting was never serious, due to the smallness of the grou
involved and the rules of warfare. The two sides remained at sor
distance, and if a member of one side was wounded by a thrown spe

he members of the party fled. Occasionally a man was killed in
his manner. Sometimes, however, a warrior put leaves on his back
and head as a sign that he would never flee, but would fight to the
death.

The causes of head-hunting are not known, but this was the
custom either in wars or private feuds. The wife of the "chief" wore
special festive clothing which had human nails on it. Every man of the
tribe" who killed or injured an enemy gave the woman a string of
beads with a nail attached to be placed on this robe. The robe was
called ulucawahe, the same name as that used for krises with human
heads on their handles. The latter were worn by women, suspended as
necklaces.

The heads of enemies were at one time kept under the houses and
perhaps in the communal house. When the first Chinese merchants
arrived, however, they persuaded the Enganese that the heads brought
sickness to the villages, for they feared that they themselves might lose
their heads. So the natives threw the trophies into the jungle and
ceased taking new ones.

The boats used by the Enganese are simple dug-outs with double
outriggers. The prows were carved in the likeness of human forms,
but bird figures are used at the present time. When a new boat is
placed in the water there is a great feast.

The people make use of rotan baskets besides their pottery, and
stone pestles. Water is carried in bamboos and coconut shell bottles.

The only musical instruments known are the jew's harp and
the nose flute, the former being of Malay importation. The women
dance at the time of a feast. They take each other by the hand
and form a ring. When they dance they move their shoulders and the
upper portions of their bodies to the sound of song and the nose flute.
At a death feast both men and women sing, and slowly sway their
bodies from side to side.

Society.

Government. — The accounts of Enganese social organization
vary to such a degree, and so little exact information is given, that no
reliance can be placed on any information concerning sibs or chieftaincy. According to Helfrich the people are divided into six sibs
(jahaauak) which are scattered through the country, and each has its
own chief. According to Oudmans, however, each village forms a large

family, and chiefs are unknown. The older men who handle trade between the natives and the Malays are called ama ama, or father, but they scarcely can bear the title of chiefs. Another account which relates of five maternal clans in Engano can be eliminated at once as impossible.

There certainly appears to be no other law in the land other than blood revenge. Differences between villages and districts, however often are settled by conciliation or by ordeal of war. That is, both sides line up for battle behind their shields, and when the first warrior falls, the side to which he belongs is held as guilty. Most of the disputes are said to arise over questions of land ownership or fishing rights.

Marriage. — Outside of the laws of family incest, there seem to be no artificial hindrances in the choice of mates. This fact renders the presence of either patrilineal or matrilineal sibs in Engano impossible. According to Modigliani and Helfrich, marriage is matrilocal and the man enters into the family of his wife, and works for the family. If the wife dies, the man continues working the fields of the wife's family until he remarries. Then he must pay a fine to the wife's family. Since the sororate and levirate are customary here, it obvious that the husband must pay a fine if he marries a woman other than his deceased wife's sister.

There is no strict purchase marriage, but the man gives presents to the family of the bride, and the bride brings a dowry into the marriage. Divorces are frequent, but they involve paying back part of the marriage price or dowry. A man can have two wives if he wishes. This is not done as a sign of wealth.

Oudmans speaks of two different forms of capture marriage Engano. It is not certain, however, that these are native. They may have been borrowed from the natives of Lampong. Certainly capture marriage is absent in both Nias and Mentawei.

In one of these forms, the groom takes the bride upon his back and in spite of the fact that the family of the girl already have given their consent to the marriage, they attack him with lances. If the groom comes out of the fight unscathed, he pays the bride-price and brings the bride to his village. In another form of marriage, the man elopes with the bride, and is followed by the father and male members of her family. The father threatens to pierce the man with his lance. The groom capitulates and pays the bride-price. It is to be noticed

the factory provides the

chcock's claustrophobic

berty and the villain's fatal

s expulsion of the Nazi

the world suddenly exploding

iticism of United States'

st effective use of the

is in _Lifeboat_ (1944). What

hes provides the crux of

d of different, disparate

Cathryn
Sjarudji

Hold until

3-22-89

at both of these marriage forms indicate patrilocal residence after marriage rather than the customary matrilocal.

Childbirth and names. — Childbirth formerly took place in the brush. If the woman gave birth to the child in the house, and she died during delivery, the entire village had to be abandoned. At ordinary deaths the house simply is taken apart and moved to a new site. At the time of delivery the woman is roasted over a fire.

Names are changed frequently, and a person is fined if he calls someone by a former name. It is said, that in taking a new name, one frequently takes the name of one's dog. A father calls himself after his child, thus, ama of so-and-so. Names are added in indication of mourning, as in Mentawei.

Death and mourning. — The dead are buried either in the center of the village or near the village. If a person dies from a contagious disease, however, he is thrown naked into the brush. If a woman dies as a consequence of pregnancy, she is wrapped in a tapa cloth, and buried in the brush. Children younger than three months are burnt after death, if older the corpse is wrapped in a fishnet and hung on a tree.

The customary form of burial for an adult man is to wrap him in tapa or in a fishnet, and put him in a grave in front of his house. The weapons, decorations and tobacco case of the man are buried with him.

If a man or a woman has a separate dwelling, then the house is moved from its former site, and two coconut and five banana trees destroyed. The widower or widow goes to his or her relatives. During the period of mourning, which usually lasts three months, the relatives of the deceased as well as the dwellers of the town can wear no clothing. The men wear only tapa caps on their heads, and the women headdresses of rotan or pandanus leaves, or a nipa leaf which has the form of a Phrygian cap. Modigliani writes that this cap is worn by the men, rather than the women, and believes that it is fashioned in imitation of the nautilus shell, which is much used for ornament.

Helfrich states that at the death of a man, the widow has her hair cut a little, but in the opposite case, the widower has his hair entirely shorn. Modigliani, however, states that the widow has her hair cut and is bathed in water, but that the hair of the widower is not touched.

The people of the town where the death has taken place are forbidden to sing, celebrate feasts, or enter into marriages.

People from other towns are not allowed entrance into th
mourning town. None of the natives of the island are allowed to hun
cut wood, or get water in the territory which belongs to the mournin
town, or fish in the sea on its coast. Anyone breaking these taboo
would be fined, half the fine going to the family of the deceased, an
half to the town.

Three months after the death a feast is given and mourning
laid aside. The relatives, however, do not as yet make use of the
decorations. If either husband or wife has died, the widower or wido
loses his or her name, and is called widower or widow. The mourn
is afraid to use his proper name because of fear of the ghost of th
departed. During the period of mourning neither a widower or wido
is allowed to sleep in a pile house, but builds himself a hut on the lev
of the ground.

The only other feast mentioned for the Enganese is that held
the founding of a new village. The people wear their ancient costum
at such a time; that is to say, the men go entirely naked.

Religion.

Gods and spirits. — The Enganese religion is doubtlessly simila
to that of Mentawei. However, it appears, as far as we known, b
little developed from a ritual standpoint. Helfrich gives but bri
mention on this point, and no other writers seem better informe

The people believe in spirits, both good and bad, who bear th
name of kowek. The Enganese have no idea of higher gods. Th
spirits inhabit the towns, the shores of the sea, the banks of the river
and the ocean. The worship of the spirits consists in the holding
sacrificial meals. Offerings are made at the time of sickness, and
long droughts. Sacrifices consist of taro, bananas, and fish.

The Enganese have the same concept of a world snake (Naga)
have the Bataks, the Dayaks, and other people of the Archipelag
The idea, as pointed out for the Bataks, is of Hindu origin. It is custor
ary among the Indonesians having this belief to appease the eart
quake god (i. e. the world snake or some substitute) at the time
earthquakes by some special cry. Thus the Bataks cry out "Swor
hilt, sword-hilt", because the Naga is held fast by a sword. T
Mentaweians believe that a powerful magician once was buried und
the center post of an uma, as the first human sacrifice, and since he

e cause of earthquakes, they call out at such calamities, "We are here :teu (ancestor), we are here Teteu".

The Enganese believe that earthquakes are caused by a great sea sh with fiery red eyes. There are special seers who are able to see is spirit, and these stand in great respect among the people. The atives also have a story of a man who was murdered by the people, ld placed in a hole. He became a powerful spirit, and to show his iemies that he still is alive, he causes earthquakes. Fish and palm ine are offered him at such times.

Sickness. — Disease is thought to be caused by ghosts (koe). Sick :ople may have the ghosts driven away from them by being struck by e leaves of sacred plants. The seers (ko hajo) may speak to the ghosts id inquire the cause of the sickness. This subject, however, is practially uninvestigated.

CHAPTER IV

NORTHERN SUMATRA.

PART I. ATJEH.

History. — The history of Atjeh before 1500 A. D. lies very muc‹ in the dark. However, about 500 A. D., according to the annals of tl Liang dynasty, a state by the name of "Poli" was situated in the nor‹ of Sumatra. This state possessed 136 villages. The account goes ‹ to say that rice ripened twice a year in Poli, that the people made a‹ wore cotton clothing, while the ruler wore silk. This same king w‹ wont to ride in a waggon drawn by elephants. At this time the peop‹ were Buddhistic. The Arabs with their Mohammedan faith enter‹ North Sumatra between 846 and 950. As we have seen from tl account of Marco Polo, the smaller states of the region had not as y‹ been converted in 1292, and the important kingdom of Samudr‹ located in the northeast at the mouth of the Pasè River, was convert‹ shortly afterwards.

The first sultan of Samudra founded also the sultanate of Pa‹ and finally the two kingdoms were united. In the middle of the 14‹ century Pasè, which had by this time been converted to Mohamme‹ anism, was under the sultan Malikuz Zahir.

In 1509 the Portuguese came to Pasè, and in 1521 they plac‹ a sultan of their own making on the throne of this country. Prior to tl coming of the Portuguese in 1509 we hear little of Atjeh. Atjeh befo‹ this period by no means indicated an entire land, but merely a harb‹ by this name, the present Kuta Radja and its neighborhood. Not on‹ was the harbor of little importance, but it was not even independer‹ being feudal to what was then the important state of Pasè.

The monopolistic policy of the Portuguese, especially in rega‹ to pepper and silk, was the main reason for the rise of Atjeh. Tl Portuguese tried to hinder free trade everywhere, and especially ‹ Pasè. In consequence of this restraint, trade sought free channel‹ Atjeh instead of Pasè, and the feudal kingdom was able to achie‹ independence. In 1524 Atjeh overcame Pasè in battle and drove tl Portuguese out of the kingdom. The puppet sultan of Pasè fled ‹ Malacca and the state was subdivided.

About 1520 the newly independent state of Atjeh obtained its first
ırbor king or sultan, Ali Mughajat Sjah. From this time on the
•wer of Atjeh continued to increase, so that the name of this harbor
ıgdom became extended not only to Great Atjeh, the northern tip of
ımatra, but to the provinces in the south as well.

Shortly after the rise of the kingdom of Atjeh it extended its sway
er the states on the east coast of Sumatra. In the middle of the 16th
ıtury the kingdoms of Aru (Langkat) and Gasip (Siak) fell to
:hehnese rule. At the end of the century, however, Siak was lost to
.jeh, and became part of the Minangkabau kingdom.

The first Dutch contact with Atjeh was established in 1599. A
w years later there commenced the so-called "Golden Era" of Atjeh
607—1636), under the renowned Sultan Iskandar Muda. At this
riod Atjeh extended its influence over the present dependencies in
ɔrth Sumatra, and also held various places on the mainland of
alacca.

Sultan Iskandar Muda was not friendly to the newcomers, the
ıtch. However, the following ruler, Sultan Iskandar Tsani, allied
ıself to the Hollanders, and helped them drive the Portuguese out
Malacca (1641). After the death of Iskandar Tsani, the power of
: Achehnese kingdom began to wane. First his widow ruled, and
ɛn three other women sultans. As a consequence of this female régime
ı anomaly in the Mohammedan world) the Achehnese Empire was
rupted by civil wars, and the vassal states attained virtual independ-
:e. In 1659 Atjeh was forced to sign an agreement with the Dutch
.st India Company giving the Company a trade monopoly.

The present day Achehnese are a very mixed people. Along with
: original population have mingled natives from Malacca and the
dang Highlands, heathen from Batakland and Nias (the latter
stly as slaves), Javanese, Hindus and Arabs. The final population
; been described as thinner, lighter, and more supple than the Malay,
h a darker skin color. They are more vivacious than the Malay. The
ginal Malaysian population probably was similar in appearance to
present mountaineers of Gajo and Alas lands. According to
last census the three peoples number as follows:

Atjeh	676,850
Gajo	35,000
Alas	12,000

Economic Life.

Villages and houses. — The Achehnese houses are in general similar appearance. They stand on sixteen piles, which are about feet in height. The house, from front to rear, is divided into three par these are separated from one another by doorways. A ladder lea up to the front gallery. Behind this is the middle or sleeping roo and to the rear of the house the back gallery. The sleeping roo which is the most sacred portion of the building, can only be enter from the rear gallery. Hangings separate the three sections of house from one another. The better houses have behind the ba gallery, as an extension, a separate kitchen with its own roof. This an advantage, as the smoke does not enter the house. Otherwise cooking must be done in the back gallery.

The homes of chiefs are sometimes bigger and more costly th those of lesser men, although there is no special difference between two. Many Achehnese chiefs now build their houses on the Europ model. In the native dwellings the floors are of planks or rotan, walls of planks, or bamboo and woven coconut leaves. Round or squ openings are left in the walls to admit light. These are closed at nig The roofs are made of sago or nipa leaf, with sometimes an ex roof of coconut leaf.

The front of the house is the least private part. Here uninvi guests are received, religious feasts are given, and general discussi take place. The back gallery is generally reserved for the wome daily work and cooking.

Members of the household, family members, and outsiders v are on intimate terms with the family, are likewise admitted. married pair sleeps in the very private center room. Here bride bridegroom have their first meeting on the evening of the wedd feast, and here corpses are washed.

Since marriage in Atjeh is matrilocal, when the daughter mar her father gives her a separate dwelling. Parents who are lack sufficient means to build a house in the neighborhood, erect an an to the left or right of their home, having a doorway leading to t back gallery. Wealthy people, however, have larger houses with ladders, two sleeping rooms, and two spare rooms on the sides. such a dwelling there is sufficient room for two married daught

The furnishing of an Achehnese house, while far more elaborate than of a primitive Malaysian, yet contains more in the way of ornaments and hangings than actual furniture. Outside of the cooking and the sleeping room, the household utensils usually are limited to some benches, chests, and mats, a number of which are laid on the floors of the galleries. A carpet is spread on the floor of the front gallery at times of feasts, and each guest receives a sitting mat.

The sleeping room is the most elaborately decorated portion of the house. The ceiling is covered with ornamented red cotton, and the floor entirely with mats. Elaborate hangings are placed on the walls. While actual beds are not used, the married pair sleep on mattresses and rest their heads on costly pillows. Curtains are spread between the sleeping room and the back gallery to prevent the son-in-law from coming into contact with his parents-in-law.

The Achehnese gampong (town) is composed of dwelling plots, rice and other cultivated fields, and the plains in the locality which have not as yet been cultivated. Often the houses are scattered in the plains without any special system.

On the north coast it is not the gampong, but the meunasah (men's house), which furnishes the smallest territorial unit. Each gampong consists of one or more meunasah's, each with a different name.

In Atjeh formerly, as is still true among the present Gajo, the members of a gampong were related by descent, real or fictitious. Thus each village formed a part of an Achehnese sib (kawōm). Naturally here, as among the Bataks, with patrilineal descent but matrilocal residence, the sibs lost their territorial aspect.

Besides the family dwelling houses, an Achehnese village contains a mosque (meuseugit or seumeugit) and a men's house (meunasah). The original form of Achehnese men's house (balè) still exists in survival form.

In Great Atjeh not every village is able to have its own mosque. According to Mohammedan law, the Friday service cannot be held unless attended by forty male, free, adult inhabitants of the locality. The Arabic word for such an inhabitant is "muqim". Hence when Mohammedanism first took root in Atjeh, it was found necessary to unite a number of villages (originally four as a rule) in order to establish a territorial unit which could support a mosque. Such a

territorial unit is called "mukim" in Atjeh. The mosque belonging
each mukim is to be found on the plains at some point between th
villages which support it.

Since the mosques lie outside the villages in Atjeh, and have n
minarets, the usual Mohammedan method of the call to prayer cann
be used. Hence the Achehnese make use of typical Indonesian drum
for this purpose. Such a drum (tambo) is kept outside of each mosqu
It is made of palmwood, and the hollowed-out side is covered with hid

The men's house (meunasah) is pre-Mohammedan, and commo
to Indonesia. As in Mentawei the smallest governmental unit of Atje
probably was originally a cluster of houses surrounding the men
house and forming a subdivision of a village. Such a house in paga
days was doubtlessly called balè, as it still is today in Java, and wa
built without walls.

With the introduction of Mohammedanism the men's hous
assumed the outward structure of the ordinary private house,
ostensibly became a house of prayer, and was called by the Mohamme
an name meunasah. In Malay this name is mandarsah, coming fro
the Arabic word madrasah, indicating a hamlet division of a villag

The meunasah is usually situated in Atjeh within the village.
is built like a common dwelling place, but without windows, an
without the customary interior tripart division. The men's house
similar in form, and serves the same general purposes in Atjeh, Gaj
and Alas.

1. The building serves as a house in which the men may spend th
night. Formerly it was the place in which all full-grown youth
gathered after sundown. Now this custom is going into discard, an
many villages at night have almost empty meunasah's.

2. The building serves as a house of prayer. The men's hous
became houses of prayer when Atjeh was converted to Islam. But th
houses at present are little used for this purpose except during th
Mohammedan fasting month.

3. The building serves as a place of social intercourse. The villag
male population gathers here when the day's work is finished. Whi
the main purpose of the gathering is harmless gossip; gambling an
chicken fights take place in villages where the elders are lax.

4. In the daytime the building serves as school. Here the youn
are taught the words of the Koran.

5. The building serves as village inn. Unmarried men from other villages pass the night at the meunasah.

6. In Great Atjeh the marriage contract is signed in the meunasah, where this is not done in the house of the bride.

In Atjeh, Gajo, and Alas the word "balè" is still used for an open structure without walls. In this respect it differs from the usual house and from the meunasah. The Achehnese distinguish various forms of balè, according to their use.

Balè meunasah. Where there is a meunasah there is usually also a balè. This serves as an annex to the meunasah, and common village matters are usually discussed in the balè.

Balè meuseugit. An annex to the mosque.

Balè rumoh. An annex to a chief's house. When a person comes to such a house he waits entrance in the balè rather than in the front gallery.

Balè kubu. A covered lodge near a holy grave where one places food with the object of averting sickness.

Balè pande. The smithy where the gold smith performs his work.

Clothing and adornment. — There is a certain amount of difference in attire between the coastal peoples and the mountaineers. Both wear trousers of great width. Outside of the trousers a loin cloth is attached, which is tucked in at the waist and extends to the knees. The coastal people usually wear jackets, while the mountaineers make comparatively little use of this garment, and wear in its stead a kerchief thrown over the shoulder, or fastened around the middle, or else laid on the head. The usual form of headgear, however, is the "kupiah", a cylindrical cap resembling in color the caps worn in Mecca.

A dagger and a folded kerchief alike are indispensable to an Achehnese man when he walks abroad. In the latter are placed all requisites for betel chewing and sundry toilet articles. Persons of position who are going on a journey carry, in addition, the Achehnese sword, which is the ordinary weapon used in fighting. It is carried in a sheath.

Women wear skirts over their trousers. On the coast the skirts hang to the feet, but in the mountains they hardly come lower than the kerchiefs of the men. Women also wear jackets and cloths thrown over their shoulders, in the same fashion as the Javanese scarf.

As decorations the women wear armlets, anklets, bracelets, meta collars and ear-rings. Rings too are worn on the fingers.

Food. — The Achehnese are essentially an agricultural peopl Rice culture is the main occupation of the majority. Sugar ca likewise is grown, and pepper culture is of importance in the province The main trees cultivated are fruit tees, although coconut and arec nut also furnish their products.

Rice is of both the wet and dry variety. The sawahs, or wet ri fields, when not laid in swamps, are irrigated by rain water which allowed to trickle down from the dams. Women plant the rice, but tl working of the fields is performed by men.

The chief food of the Achehnese, like that of the Malays, consis of rice, vegetables, and fish. Meat, as a rule, is only eaten on festi occasions. Buffaloes, oxen, goats, and sheep are seldom killed excej at the great annual festivals, or in fulfilment of a vow.

Society.

Government. — The government of Atjeh, its dependencies, an Gajo and Alas, are divided into six parts under the present Dutc rule. 1. The division of Great Atjeh. 2. The division of Pidie. 3. Tl division north coast of Atjeh. 4. The east coast of Atjeh. 5. Gajo ar Alas. 6. The west coast of Atjeh.

Atjeh was never an united kingdom under an autocratic sulta Even in the "Golden Era", the renowned Sultan Iskandar Muda wa more to be regarded as a harbor king than as a political power. H pomp and glory rested mostly on his trade monopoly. When later tl harbor monopoly commenced to give lessening returns, the bon which checked the activities of the feudal lords, the ulèebalang's, bega to weaken, and they in turn waged savage warfare upon one anothe Due to the commercial interests of Atjeh the sultans had always soug for conquests and treaties abroad rather than the proper subjection these robber barons at home, and such conquests as were affected the early part of the 17th century, as that of Gajo, were but incidenta By the end of the 17th century the power of the sultans had so falle that they were even in danger of losing their harbor kingdom.

When the Dutch entered Atjeh in 1873 the sultan no longer ha the dependencies under his political control, and was living in but shell of his former kingdom. Veth, as quoted in Kreemer, describ e fallen monarch. "In a dirty, half-fallen Kraton (palace) there yet ed a monarch who had entirely lost control of his vassals. Out of s small income, he barely managed to keep his court, which consisted a small group of opium addicts. In every circumstance this monarch s the poorest and most wretched ruler of the entire Archipelago."

In spite of the dismal political state of the sultan of Atjeh, he was ill the object of religious veneration. As Raffles expressed the matter, e sultan was "honored everywhere by his subjects, but obeyed where". This idea of a sacred king is also found in Minangkabau nong the Bataks, and elsewhere in Sumatra and the Archipelago, and not peculiar to the Achehnese.

After the Dutch had seized the Kraton the sultan fled to Pidië, d the last shadow of the former glory of the sultan of Atjeh nished. With the overthrow of the pretender Sultan Mohammet awot in 1903, the sultanate of Atjeh ceased to exist.

The political prerogatives of the sultans had been few in number; ne to be exact. Five of these had been but rarely used, and consisted various forms of punishment which could be inflicted on disobedient bjects. These were in brief: the looping-off of hands, impaling, a nd of crucifixion, slicing-off the flesh from the body of the con- mned, and the pounding of the head of the condemned in a rice ortar. Two other prerogatives were of but an honorary nature: the ivilege of firing a cannon at sunset, and the right of being accosted ith the expression "deelat". The remaining two prerogatives were of nportance. The sultans could issue written orders and letters of intro- ction, both of which were called sarakata, and the sultans alone had e right to coin money.

Outside of the actual province of the sultan, Great Atjeh was vided into three sagi's, or provinces, each named after the number mukim's (mosque units) which it originally possessed. Thus the mes of the sagi's were (and still are) called XXII Mukims, XXVI ukims, and XXV Mukims. Naturally the number of mukim's have creased in each of the sagi's since their foundation. The origin the sagi division is not certain. Snouck Hurgronje believes that iginally the sagi's were formed by ulёёbalang's who wished to aintain offensive and defensive alliances.

Each of the three federations was led by the most powerful ёёbalang in its midst. Such a chief alone had say in matters which ere of communal importance. The other ulёёbalang's governed their

15

territory as though there were no sagi's. The position of sagi head, a that of ulëëbalang, and other officials in general, was hereditary.

Originally it was the three sagi chiefs who elected the sulta They chose whom they wished, usually someone from the family of tl deceased monarch, but sometimes even strangers to Atjeh were electe The person chosen had to pay each of the chiefs $ 500 "as a marria present". The coronation of the new sultan was spoken of as a marria between the prince and his land. This system led to grave abuse ar bribery, so that at a later date the other ulëëbalang's shared in tl election.

According to the Dutch regulations for the government of Atje as drawn up in 1881, Great Atjeh was divided into distric (ulëëbalang's), the districts into mukim's, and the mukim's in gampong's. The heads of the sagi's in this way were dispensed wit although they later were also taken into the government as an act courtesy.

The ulëëbalang's were from ancient days the actual folk ar territorial chiefs. Each was governor, judge, and military leader his own district, in which he admitted no higher authority. The power was older than that of the sultan, and did not rest on roy instalment.

The ulëëbalang's are invested by their own people with the titl of teuku (from Malay tuan ku, my lord), or teuku pò, or teuku ampo By strangers they are called radja. They receive taxes when cattle a killed, and when they act in native law cases. They also recei salaries from the Dutch.

In Great Atjeh there are 15 ulëëbalang districts, of which tv are independent. The ulëëbalang has his aides. The chief of thes called banta, is usually chosen from one of his younger brothers nearest male relatives. The companions of the ulëëbalang are call rakan. These are people who live in his house or in the neighborhoo and receive food from him and his family.

Between the village governments and the ulëëbalang's come tl imeum's, the heads of the mukim's. Originally the imeum's were tl religious leaders (Arab imam, leader) of the Friday services held the mukim's. Presently, however, their posts became secular in natur and the imeum's were converted to hereditary chiefs of territori divisions, the mukim's. As such they were lesser ulëëbalang's, ar were made use of by these officials to announce and carry out order

The conduct of the Friday service went over to special mosque officials, the imeum meuseugit's.

The Dutch government, as already stated, has confirmed the mukim chiefs and has made them governing officials. Although the mukim's really are not governing territories, yet the people consider them as such, and as standing above the gampongs or towns.

The village, at present, is the smallest unit of government. The village population is depictured as a big family, consisting of four elements, the so-called four corners of the gampong.

1. The village chief, keutji (literally elder), or the "father" (koe or eumbah) of the village.
2. The village priest, teungku (meunasah), or the "mother" (ma) of the village.
3. The village elders, useuëng tuha (literally old members). These are the men of experience, wisdom, good manners and knowledge of the adat.
4. The remainder (ureuëng leu); thus the "children" of "father" keutji and "mother" teungku.

Matters of common importance to the village (as occasion of feasts) first receive approval after general consideration.

The religious head (teungku) is supposed to be literate, so that he can read in the Malay written Kitab Sirat, where he can find all the prescriptions for fastings, washing of bodies, public religious services, etc. Usually, however, the lack of knowledge of a teungku is proverbial. This is because the office of teungku, like that of the keudji, is hereditary. So many teungku's allow their office to be filled by more lettered members of the community, giving the substitute some of their pay.

The keutji has to look out for order and safety in his territory and the town. He has charge of all family law, the rice culture, housing, he regulates the distribution of the meat from slaughtered animals, he gives orders for the beginning and cessation of fasting, etc. The distribution of meat is an important ceremony in which everyone receives his due portion according to his rank and circumstances.

In regulating most events which occur in the village, the father keutji and the mother teungku confer together; the first because he is

responsible for the native customary law, the adat, the latter as sponso
for the religious law, the hukom (adat, Arabian for custom; hukom
Arabian hukum, to speak out).

The teungku receives in general the care of religious matters i
the village. Among the tasks of the teungku may be enumerated:

1. The care of the village mosque.
2. The collection of the religious tithes.
3. In normal cases the performance of the wedding ceremony.
4. The giving of a blessing at religious feasts.
5. Religious care of the dead and dying.
6. Oversight at the religious slaughter of animals.
7. Mohammedan blessing of children.

As elsewhere in Sumatra, the oldest divisions of the people wa
into sibs, and not into town or territorial units. Hence the territoria
governmental system which I have just outlined, for the greater par
at least, postdates the conversion of the people to Mohammedanisn

In Atjeh the common descendants of ancestors in the male lin
constitute a kawōm or sukeë (Arabian qaum, people or genealogy,
The kawōms at the present day are very degenerated, and are onl
maintained in the highland section of Great Atjeh, where politic
development is backward and blood feuds frequent.

The kawōm division splits the Achenese people, or at least par
of them, into four groups. The significance of the group names ha
been lost. The four sibs are: 1. Lhëë reutoih (the "three hundred")
2. Tjut-Dja- or To Sandan; 3. Dja-, or To Batëë; 4. Imeum penët (th
four Imeum's).

The members of each kawōm consider one another as bloo
relations, and have common rights and duties, especially if one of th
members is insulted, wounded, or killed. In case of such an even
blood revenge (bila) must be taken, or weregild (diët) obtained.

Usually representatives of each of the sibs may be found in ever
town. Where many members of the same sib live together, they hav
as leader a chief (panglima kawōm) who has charge of matters
communal interest, especially those connected with blood revenge. Th
ulëëbalang's confirm the choice of the people, and give the new officia
at his election, a particular steel weapon. A territorial chief is nev
chosen as panglima kawōm, for this double function might bring th
official into conflict with himself.

The Imeum peuët clan has always been more powerful, both in number and in ability to wage war, than any of the three other kawōm's. The remaining three therefore have more or less held themselves in confederation against it. When Atjeh transformed its governmental system from a genealogical to a territorial basis, the three confederate sibs held up their standing by shutting their rivals out from offices. While the three confederate sibs have furnished all the lëëbalang's and other high officials in the kingdom, none of the Imeum peuët sib have been able to rise higher than the rank of mukim chief. While at one time each of the three sibs elected its panglima separately, later they united in choosing these sib officials. Furthermore the three confederates aided each other in waging war for blood revenge.

At some prehistoric period all four sibs were probably exogamic, a man was prohibited marriage with a woman from the same sib, and all four probably had totemic restrictions. Snouck Hurgronje writes that at the period in which he investigated Atjeh, the sib Dja Sandan forbade its members the flesh of white buffalo and a certain salt water fish called alu-alu. It is common in India to find sibs, which originally were exogamic, later turn endogamic with the breakdown of primitive conditions. Such probably was the case in Atjeh, for Kreemer writes that the four kawōms originally were endogamous, but that later the members of the three confederates could intermarry, but they could not marry with the kawōm out of the confederacy.

The resemblance between the kawōm's or sukèë's of Atjeh and the suku's of Minangkabu is striking, since both have the division into four. It appears to me not unlikely that some form of dual division in early Atjeh, as in early Minangkabu, would account for the later rivalry between the three confederate and the isolated kawōm. However, in Atjeh there is no tradition that this ever was the case.

In Atjeh the people are divided into nobility, commoners, and slaves. Class distinction, while more pronounced than among the Bataks, is however less marked than in the southern regions of Sumatra, which at one time were ruled by Java. Class distinctions come most prominently to the fore on matters regarding competence to hold office, the formation of marriage alliances, and the amount of bride-price.

The nobility is composed of the sultan, his family, and the law-giving hereditary chiefs.

The commoners are usually subdivided into three levels, althoug it is difficult to find agreement as to the finer distinctions betwee the three.

1. The prominent people. These are relatives of the ulëëbalang" the imeum's, the members of the village government, the Mohamme an religious teachers, those instructed in writing, old notable familie and the rich.

2. The middle class. This includes the family members of th village rulers, the church elders, those who take their religious duti seriously, and, in general, those who, without belonging to th distinguished class, still enjoy a certain amount of prestige.

3. The common people, to whom may also be reckoned slaves an the descendants of slaves.

Slavery. Atjeh obtained most of its slaves from Nias, while th majority of the slaves in Gajo and Alas came from the Bataks. Th Achehnese prized the Niha very highly as servants, for they wei considered obedient, easy to teach, diligent, and trustworthy. Th women from Nias were thought especially beautiful.

A certain amount of slaves were obtained in wars, but th greater part were bought in Nias, or from the Malays and the Batak Furthermore there were some Chinese from the Straits and Africar from Mecca. Negroes were highly prized in Atjeh as house servant

In Atjeh, as among the Bataks and elsewhere, debtors who wei without means bound themselves to their creditors to work out the debts as pawns. Pawns were able to purchase their freedom, whi slaves could not do so unless their masters consented.

A man was prohibited by Moslem law from marrying his slav and this variety of marriage was unknown in Atjeh. The law, howeve permitted a master to live in concubinage with his slave. In Atje this seldom happened, for the Achehnese laid too much stress on the maternal descent. Moslem law states that the children of such union have all the rights of children born of a free woman. In Atj this seldom was the case; the legal rights were the same, but th social position was different, and one never forgot that such a pers had slave blood in his or her veins.

Islam does not forbid a freeman from marrying the slave another. It often happened in Atjeh that a freeman, while away fro

ome for some time, married a slave of someone in the neighborhood
f where he was staying. According to religious law, the children of
uch a marriage were slaves and belonged to the owner of the woman.
'he adat, however, treated the children as free, although of slave
escent.

After a shorter or longer period of time, slaves were amalgamated
y the free people. This accounts for much of the blood mixture in
tjeh. A slave was able to obtain his freedom in several ways, for
ere there were no legal means prescribed. Many masters made them
ree if they became permanently sick. Some acquired property, and
ith the consent of their masters, gave a feast, at which their freedom
as proclaimed.

Slaves, on the whole, were humanely treated and handled as
embers of the household of their masters. Kreemer quotes Dampier,
ho wrote in 1717, "The slaves in Atjeh have no hard lot, and many
re merchants and shopkeepers. They are able to purchase their
eedom. They hold markets, act as money-changers, and most of the
shermen are slaves. Some own their dwellings."

Raffles first attempted in 1820, as the governor of Benkulen,
put an end to the slave trade. The Dutch later gradually suppressed
. While this traffic in human beings lasted, it caused frequent
arfare in Nias, for the Achehnese constantly came to this island
purchase or steal slaves.

Marriage. — According to the renowned Dutch jurist, Van Vollen-
oven, and to the commonly accepted opinion of Dutch ethnologists,
e Achehnese relationship and marriage laws are based on the
lateral family, with survivals of the matrilineate and patrilineate,
d with Mohammedan purposes and insertions. The early writer
acobs also believes that the Achehnese went through three "stages";
e matrilineate, the patrilineate, and finally the bilateral family.

The main reason these ethnographers have for postulating early
natriarchate" in Atjeh, lies in the fact that the man must take up
sidence after marriage in the house and town of his wife. As we
ve seen, however, this form of matrilocal residence probably only
ose with the formation of the town system and the breakdown of the
iginal genealogical patrilineal sibs. There seems no doubt, however,
the transition from patrilineal to bilateral reckoning, for this has
curred in Atjeh in the past, and the transformation is still taking
ace at the present day.

The Achehnese marriage gives each of the parents equal right Descent is counted through both father and mother, and both man an wife possess their own goods.

In accordance with the so-called mother-right principle, the woma by her marriage, remains in her own house, or that of her parent while the children also are brought up there. If the man does not yet live in the village, he visits her in her house. This principle matrilocal residence is contrary to Mohammedan law, but is insiste upon by the village chief (keutji) as conforming to the adat.

No marriage can take place without the consent of the keut Only where the population is superabundant and the supply marriageable girls and women without husbands by no means excessiv will he agree offhand to a man of his gampong marrying outside it. "There are plenty of women here", he objects, "why should you and scatter your seed elsewhere?" On the other hand, the keutji h no objections to a woman marrying a man from outside the gampon as this increases the population of his town.

Due to matrilocal residence the closest relatives in a town a those who live closest to one another, and they usually are the d scendants of a woman in the female line. On the other hand, t descendants of a man can be found scattered around in the vario villages.

The patrilineal sibs no longer are of much influence in t Achehnese marriage, and, as shown, exist only as survivals.

Blood relations in Atjeh are called waréh, which is the Arabi word for a hereditary name (warith), although there is no sort hereditary right. The blood relations are distinguished, as t Achehnese express themselves, as of "own seed" or of "foreign seed Directly contrary to the Minangkabau idea on the subject, it is t man and not the woman who is supposed to propagate the speci The seed is thought to develop unaided in the womb, as the seed of plant in the field. While this is a Mohammedan concept, it is al pagan, as it is found among the Toradja of Celebes.

All the blood relatives of the older generation on the father's si are said to be of one's "own seed". They are all called wali (Arabi for guardian). The relatives of older generation on the mother's si are called karong. When both groups are merged together they a called wali-karong.

The Achehnese, like the Malays, have lost special terms in their inship terminology to indicate clan relationships, and merge the ther's brother and mother's brother with the father.

In Atjeh the Islamic marriage rules are followed excepting where ey conflict with native adat.

The marriage restrictions are similar to the Mohammedan. A man nnot marry more than four women at the same time. But polygyny rare with the man of ordinary means. When a wealthy man takes ore than one wife at a time, he does so at the cost of domestic anquility. Naturally a "harem" is impossible in Atjeh, since marriage matrilocal.

A man cannot marry a woman in the Mohammedan forbidden rades of relationship. According to the Koran a man is not allowed marry any blood relative on the mother's side with the exception of e descendants of uncles, aunts, great uncles and great aunts. But e adat goes even further. It is forbidden for brothers to marry omen who are sisters. This same rule holds for the Bataks and the ajo. It is also forbidden to marry a relation by marriage. This iminates the levirate and sororate, although they sometimes occur. t is forbidden both by civil and religious law to marry the children f a brother or sister.

Cousin marriage is found, as in the Mohammedan world. Thus e children of two brothers may marry, although this form of cousin arriage is forbidden almost everywhere outside of Islam. Cross-cousin arriage formerly was permitted in Atjeh; that is, the children of a rother and sister were allowed to marry. Cousin marriage, however, as limited to a certain extent, for marriage with the daughter of a ather's or mother's older brother or sister was regarded as incest. somewhat similar age status restriction is found among the Bataks, here a man should marry his deceased wife's younger sister but not er older sister. Naturally the Achehnese have different kinship terms or the older and younger brothers and sisters of the parents.

As is common elsewhere in the Archipelago and in Sumatra, the dat prescribes that an elder sister should marry before a younger.

Certain marriage restrictions are of a purely Mohammedan nature, nd as such are similar to those of Minangkabau. A woman is orbidden to marry for a certain period after her former marriage is lissolved. This is the Arabian iddah period, and a similar name is mployed for the period in Atjeh, Gajo and Alas. If the husband has died, this period is four months and ten days; if divorced, three months and ten days. If a divorced woman is pregnant she cannot marry until forty days after the birth of her child.

The Mohammedan law does not hinder child marriages, and girls formerly were brought to their husbands before they were mature. The average age of marriage for girls of the better class was ten years. Now this has been raised to between sixteen and twenty. Child marriage is contrary to primitive custom, and even in Gajo and Alas where little emphasis is laid on puberty, girls marry between fifteen and twenty-five.

The engagement. — Marriage in Atjeh, as has already been shown, is very much an affair of the gampong. Thus it is not a relative of the would-be bridegroom, but the keutji, the teungku, certain elders and the go-between, who undertake the presentation of the betrothal gift from the bridegroom.

First, however, the marriage proposal has to be made. This is done by the parents of the young man, after they have asked the consent of the authorities of their village. If both sides accept, an intermediary is sent by the parents of the boy and the bride-price is discussed.

If an agreement is reached, the betrothal gift is brought to the home of the bride, where it is accepted by the authorities of her gampong. The engagement present usually consists of gold ornaments whose value is about half of the bride-price. A feast is now held and the young couple are engaged. If later the marriage is broken off by the family of the man, the betrothal gift (which serves as a pledge) remains in the possession of the bride. If the family of the bride break the engagement they return double the value of the pledge.

The engagement lasts until the girl is considered of marriageable age. In Atjeh, Gajo and Alas, as in Minangkabau, the engaged pair must avoid one another. This is not surprising in these countries, for likewise before engagement there is no free mingling of the sexes. In spite of all precautions, however, and the fact that in Atjeh girls seldom leave the maternal house before marriage, secret love affairs are by no means unknown.

The wedding. — The date for the wedding is decided by mutual deliberation between the two families, some "lucky" day being decided upon. Among the Gajo the family of the bride hands the family of the bridegroom a knotted string, or quipus, on which there are as many knots as there remain days before the wedding. Among the man

eparations which have to be made for the wedding may be counted:
e bringing of the bride-price, the making of new curtains, pillows,
ats etc., the gathering of firewood, the shelling of rice, the preparation
sirih, and the borrowing or hiring of the bridal decorations.

So-called "gatja" evenings take place at the home of the bride
ring the three days preceding the actual wedding. No member of
e groom's family is allowed to be present at this time. The hand
lms, feet soles, and the finger tips of the bride are smeared with the
d sap of gatja leaves, thus giving the name to the festivities. Wealthy
ople give feasts to the entire village at one or more of these evenings.
om the first of these three days until the seventh day after the
arriage the young man is a bridegroom (lintō) and the young woman
bride (dara barō).

The actual wedding ceremony begins on the so-called andam day;
e day following the third gatja night. The day is so named because
e bride is clad entirely in her wedding outfit, and has the hair of her
rehead and a little of her eyebrows clipped (andam). The guests of
e bride and bridegroom all bring presents. The bride is purified at
s time, or, as the natives say "cooled", in order to exorcise evil
irits from her. An elderly woman (usually the wife of the keudji)
ews her with shelled and unshelled rice, sprinkles her with mead
ter in which is placed a gold ring, strokes her behind the ears with
fron colored rice, and places some of the rice in her mouth.

The wedding ceremony is a mixture of South Indian and
hammedan ritual, for primitive pagans are lacking in ceremony on
s occasion. The name for wedding is mampleuë, Malay mempilai,
m Tamil mapilai. The Gajo and Alas people use similar words.

On the evening of the same day, the andam day, there is a
cession in which the bridegroom in full costume is led to the
elling of the bride, where all the family members are gathered. The
degroom is on horseback and is accompanied by a native orchestra.

The members of the bride's village are lined up at the house of
bride ready to receive the guests. Jacobs writes that both sides are
d up as if for battle, and a verbal competition between the two
ties is reminiscent of capture marriage. This seems not unlikely, as
bolic capture marriage is still practiced among the Bataks and in
th Sumatra.

Finally the bridegroom is led up the house ladder, where he
ains standing half-way, in the meanwhile being pelted with rice.

Rice pelting is an ancient Hindu custom of perhaps fertility signi
icance. A man of the bride's family now gives the groom all kinds
instruction, in a more or less jocular vein, as to how he should tre
the bride, how he should work the fields, etc. Then the bridegroo
steps into the house.

The wedding ceremony proper takes place in the foregallery
the house, in Mohammedan fashion. Certain symbolic acts are pe
formed in the course of the ceremony, however, to signify the union
the couple and are Hindu rather than Arabian in origin, such as eati
together out of the same dish, and the sitting of the bride on the l
of the groom. At about two o'clock in the morning the bridegroom a
his party go back to their own village without further formalities.

The marriage as briefly described here (a fuller discription m
be found in English in Snouck Hurgronje's book on Atjeh) is t
complete ceremony as enacted for members of good families at the ti
of first marriage.

The bridegroom visits the bride every night for seven nights af
the wedding, but the marriage is not consummated until seven nig
after the wedding. We have seen that the Minangkabau also h
delayed consummation of the marriage, and the custom is widespre
in the Archipelago.

The bride-price. Actually there is no bride-price or purcha
marriage in Atjeh, for, according to Mohammedan law, the sum pa
is given by the bridegroom to the bride immediately after the weddi
service, and not to the family of the bride. This sum, according
Achehnese adat, must be paid at once. According to Mohammed
law the amount may be paid in instalments.

Since marriage is matrilocal, the so-called bride-price is necessar
low, and is compensated for by the fact that the parents of the br
furnish the house, and even food for a year, or until a first ch
is born.

As soon as the marriage is consummated and the wife no lon
is a virgin, the husband gives her certain jewels fashioned from sil
or gold, according to his circumstances. If the husband later divor
his wife, he can take back all that he has given, but not these jew
The Achehnese say that the jewels symbolize the fact "that the
has been climbed, and the fruit has been plucked".

Snouck Hurgronje has summarised the variations in Achehr
marriage from true Mohammedan law.

1. The power of the village chief (keutji) to prevent a marriage which is contrary to the village interests.
2. The adat law under which a woman can never be required by her husband to leave her home with him, and is even prohibited from so doing. The sole exception to this rule occurs where both her family and the local village authorities consent to her departure. This usually happens only when the woman's family is very inferior in rank or social position to that of the man, so that the customary gifts on his part are not reciprocated by her.
3. The betrothal gift (pledge) and its legal consequences.
4. The gift after the consummation of the marriage and the rules which govern it.

Avoidance. A husband and wife must treat one another with reat respect. While teknonomy is not practiced in Great Atjeh, and e husband and wife keep their own names after the birth of a child, t a husband and wife are forbidden mentioning one another's name. woman refers to her husband as "the father of my child", or "the an I married". A man never appears alone with his wife in public.

The greatest respect shown in Atjeh, however, is between parents-law and sons- and daughters-in-law. This commences with the gagement. The strongest avoidance is between mother-in-law and n-in-law, it is less between father-in-law and daughter-in-law, and ast between mother-in-law and daughter-in-law. The engaged or wly married man has to keep out of the way of his parents-in-law as uch as possible, in spite of the fact that he usually lives with them in e same house. When the son-in-law "comes home" to his wife, he tifies his return by coughing, so as to give the inmates of the house ne to get out of his way. Where the circumstances (as for example death, or a big sacrificial meal) make a meeting necessary, the son-law takes a very reserved attitude towards his parents-in-law and ats them with great respect. This respect is shown in the way in hich the husband greets and speaks to his parents-in-law, or when sits in their presence. The strongest forms of avoidance are shown st after the marriage, and the original timidity only begins to wane ter the birth of the first child.

An older brother, likewise, may seldom if ever be spoken to. A an must go out of his way to perform any command of an elder

brother which he considers just. He always speaks of the elder brothe
in the greatest terms of respect. Sisters are more intimate with on
another, but not to the same degree as among Europeans. None of th
writers mention the relationship between brothers and sister
Presumably there is no rigid avoidance between them here, as amon
the Bataks.

The avoidance customs prevent a firm family bond being forme
in Atjeh. The only strong family tie found is that between mother an
child. And yet in divorce a woman will separate from her childre
without feeling remorse. An Achehnese man seldom speaks of h
father, and then only in the same way he speaks of any other ma
It is his mother who gives him advice.

Marriage property. Everthing which the man brings into th
marriage remains his possession, even if it had the pretence of being
present to his wife after the seventh day of the marriage. If the fath
of the man still lives, he usually brings little else than his clothing

The chief gifts which belong to the bride are the bridal treasur
and the betrothal present. The jewelry gifts which the wife receiv
at the consummation of her marriage also belong to her. Everythin
which the wife receives from her husband up to the seventh day aft
her marriage, inclusive of the engagement and the virginity gi
remains property of the woman.

In marriage the man and the woman keep their property ful
apart. What the man and the woman earn through common wo
becomes joint property. This has special reference to field work.

At time of divorce, the property is divided into two parts, ar
each party receives back the portion he, or she, brought into marriag
The goods earned in marriage are divided into two, even if the m
did the earning.

At time of death, property is divided according to the Kora
with the above mentioned exceptions regarding the rights of t
spouses.

Divorce. In Atjeh divorces are obtained solely according
Mohammedan law. While Kreemer writes that divorces are less freque
in Atjeh than in most Mohammedan countries, due to matriloc
residence and the independence of the women, Jacobs claims that th
are very frequent indeed, due to child marriages and the fact that t
young couple scarcely know one another when engaged. The lat
writes that Achehnese who have married ten to fifteen times are

nomaly, and that he personally had met a young girl of thirteen who had just been cast aside by her third husband.

The three forms of divorce are: the one sided repudiation (taleuë, Arabian talaq) spoken by the man, the purchase of the repudiation (teuboih teleuë, Arabian choel') by the woman, and the divorce (pasah, Arabian fasch) by the judge.

A man can repudiate a woman at any time without showing cause, but a woman has to show cause, such as neglect, to the ulëëbalang and the tunku before she can obtain her freedom, that is, cause her husband to repudiate her, by paying double the marriage price. In case of divorce the man takes all the children. This is contrary to Mohammedan law, which allows the woman children who are too young to take care of themselves. But a man seldom divorces a woman who has a child which is not yet weaned.

The talaq, or simple repudiation, is common among the lower classes, but seldom used among the nobility, as it causes harsh feelings between the two families. The man is supposed to speak a certain formula three times, but usually simply makes one statement hold for the three. After the formula is spoken the third time, the man can never take back the woman. The formula used is, "I separate from you three times". Then the man takes the hand of the woman and lays it on three pieces of areca nut, and says, "Be thou before me as a sister, one, two, three!" While this formula has best be done before witnesses, it is often done without them. It cannot be repeated except for the actual purpose of divorce. The formula can also be sent by mail, if the man is away in another place.

As stated, a woman divorced this way can never be taken back again. However, as well may be supposed, a man may speak the formula in a fit of anger and then repent. So the Koran allows one loophole. If the woman marries and then is divorced, the original husband can take her back. In Atjeh, therefore, if a man wishes to take back the wife he has thus cast aside, he looks for a poor man and pays him to marry his wife. The man spends a night with the woman and then, in turn, divorces her. The first husband can remarry the woman after three months and ten days.

Law administration. Before the Dutch arrived there were no higher judges than the ulëëbalang's. In order to have a law case, an accusation had to be made by a private party in the court. Cases were decided on the merits of tokens (tanda), witnesses, Mohammedan oaths, and if need be, ordeals. Court usually was held in the balè of the ulèëbalang, but in serious cases, as theft or murder, the case wa treated in the mosque.

The oldest form of punishment was blood revenge (bila, a Hind word), taken by the members of one sib against those of another. Late weregild (Arabic: diët) was accepted by the aggrieved sib. The rig of asylum probably came from Hindu custom. Under Mohammeda rule the criminal could flee to the sultan's palace and become a serva of the sultan.

The manner of taking blood revenge differed from Moslem custor Among the Mohammedans blood revenge could only be taken in tl case of murder or physical injury, and then by the family of the victi after public authority had been given them. In Atjeh, blood reven; was taken under the leadership of the panglima kawōm by the membe of the kawōm, and the right of revenge extended to all the membe of the sib to which the victim belonged.

When the ulèëbalang's took over the administration of justice th considered adultery a crime, as an infringement of the right property, and even unchastity (sexual intercourse outside of marriag as a crime, being an offence against public morality.

In the time of the sultans, if a woman became pregnant out wedlock, or even if it became known that she went with a man, bo were put to death. They were half buried alive and stoned, or throw into a pit full of sharp spikes, or trodden under the feet of the sultar elephants. Women were tortured to reveal the names of their lovel If a woman belonged to an influential family, however, she w able to pay a large fine and marry her lover. If a man and a wom were caught in the act of adultery the husband had to kill both. ' have killed but one would have been regarded as a murder by t family of the deceased. The husband too could claim vengeance lat if he could produce a token, such as a piece of the man's clothing.

Kreemer writes, howèver, that while all forms of unchastity we common in Atjeh, its punishment was exceptional. The certainty of t punishment was far less than its severity, and hence the accusation unchastity was commonly made a method of blackmail by the office of the ulèëbalang's. Where fines were paid, they went into the pock of these officials.

According to tradition, when the state first took over punishment of crime, the original punishment for men was that rowning, for women that of strangling. Later the two punishments ere combined. The male or female culprit had his or her head held nder water, a bamboo rod was placed over the throat of the victim, nd two men, one on each bank, stood on the ends of the rod.

Moral Etiquette. The relations between men and women in Atjeh re very strictly governed, although the women do not veil their faces hen out of doors. No Achehnese woman or girl will uncover her reasts before a man, even though it be her own husband. A man will ot dare to address a woman who is walking alone, nor will a man alk alone with a woman, even though it be his own wife or mother.

In spite of, or perhaps because of, the strict manner in which tercourse between the sexes is regulated, prostitution exists as an stitution in Atjeh. It is well known that prostitution is rare or absent mong primitive peoples, and is the most prevalent just among those ivilized peoples who are the most prudish in regard to sexual ehaviour. In Atjeh prostitutes are recruited from the number of girls rom eighteen to twenty who are not married, and especially widows nd divorcèes who have not made a second marriage. Prostitutes are ooked down upon and not allowed entrance into some villages.

Childbirth. Counterconception and abortion are common in Atjeh, nd the families on the whole are small. Due to early marriages the rst child is born when the mother herself is scarcely adult, and at wenty-five the woman is worn out. When a woman wishes a child she ill utilize various magical means, such as sacrificing by graves, in rder to obtain it.

While usually in Atjeh but little attention is paid to a woman, he is made much of when pregnant, for now she has the fruit of the aan within her. After pregnancy is known by the cessation of the atural periods, at once both husband and wife take many precautions o avoid harm befalling the unborn child.

During the first five months of pregnancy the husband may kill o animals, not even a tiger or snake. If he killed an animal, the child vould assume the peculiarities of the animal, and birth would be ifficult. The man is not allowed to leave the house at night, but should emain at home to protect his wife from evil spirits. No one from a oreign village is allowed entrance to the house, for fear that evil ghosts nter with him. Or perhaps this is due to fear of the evil eye.

A pregnant woman is allowed to do no heavy work, nor see any nimal which might frighten her or cause a bad prenatal influence.

16

She is not allowed to kill an animal, and must abstain from certa[in] fruits which have the reputation of causing abortions, and from frui[t] growing too closely together, for fear of having twins. These are feare[d] from economic grounds, but perhaps the original fear of twins ma[y] have may have been of a superstitious nature, as in Nias.

After childbirth the woman is smoked over a fire. The placen[ta] is cut off with a bamboo knife, and buried in a pot before the hous[e.] A fire then is kept burning over the spot for seven nights. As amo[ng] the Bataks and elsewhere in the Archipelago, the belief exists in Atj[eh] that the afterbirth is the incomplete twin brother or sister of the chi[ld.] The ghost of the placenta is thought to come and play with the chi[ld] while the child is asleep. If the child has a stomach ache, it is thoug[ht] that the placenta is sick and curing herbs are laid on the spot whe[re] it is buried. If the child still howls, the placenta is dug up and buri[ed] in a drier or warmer place.

Infanticide is not allowed except in the case of malformed childre[n.] Sons, however, as in all Mohammedan countries, are preferred [to] daughters, and a female born out of wedlock is at once killed.

If the mother is unable to suckle the child, the grandmoth[er] performs the duty. It is claimed that the grandmother will produ[ce] milk even though she herself has not had children for years. It [is] thought best that a member of the family act as wet nurse, for thi[s,] according to Mohammedan law, establishes a blood bond between tw[o] families and forms a barrier to marriage. According to the Koran [a] woman is supposed to suckle her child for two years.

Women who come to visit a new born child are careful to speak [as] badly as possible about it. Otherwise the spirits would be envious a[nd] the child would die. For example, instead of saying that the child [is] nice and plump, one says, "What a fat puppy!" The child is likewi[se] given some opprobrious nickname.

The seventh day after the child is born is important, according [to] Mohammedan law. It is necessary on this day to give the child [a] name, to cut off his head hair, and to sacrifice to the child. Th[e] sacrifice, however, may be performed later when the child is grown.

In Atjeh name giving and the first hair cut are officially do[ne] on the seventh day, although they can be postponed. A feast is giv[en] and the hair of the head and the eyebrows of the child are shave[d] off. The sacrifice usually is delayed to the time of circumcision, [of] marriage, or even death.

On the forty-fourth day after the birth there is the ceremony of "the taking away of the oven". This is usually done on the 41st or 43rd day, since an even day is less lucky. A sacrificial meal is prepared and the midwife takes the oven on which the mother has lain and throws it under the house. Now the mother is bathed and under no more restrictions and may return to her husband's bed. The midwife goes home and takes away with her all evil influence from the house.

Before the midwife departs however, the child itself must be brought out of the house and made to touch the ground. This first contact of the child with the ground, the Hindu Mother Earth, is an important occasion for many of the people of the Archipelago. The child is smeared with red earth and chalk to secure it from the admiration of the public. Then it is carried out by the midwife and set with its feet on the ground. Afterwards it is usually brought to the grave of its nearest deceased blood relative, where it has its head washed.

Name giving. — A child receives its name by preference on the seventh day after its birth. The name may either be Arabian or native. Males often receive Arabian names, which on the advice of the teungku, are borrowed from a name divination book. Mohammedan male names include Ali, Amat, Mohammat, &c. Female Mohammedan names include Aminah, Remelah, &c. The native name, on the other hand, refers to one or another physical peculiarity of the bearer, or the day on which he was born, or the place in which he lives, &c. There can be no family or inherited name, due to a taboo on the names of the dead. Names are kept through life, although men receive additional nicknames.

The Achehnese have the following taboos on names:

1. A person is not allowed to mention his own name. If one wishes to find out the name of a man, one has to ask a friend or bystander. "Don't be like the turtledove", say the natives of Atjeh and Gajo, "who always is calling out his own name".

2. One does not call a companion by his own name, but calls him eumpië.

3. In conversation one does not call a person by his name, except in the case of very small children or very close relatives. An Achehnese refers to a person by his rank, position, or nickname. Relatives use relationship terms.

244

4. It is forbidden to mention the name of one's father, mothe uncle or spouse. To say to a native of Gajo, "In his you your father was called so and so", is an insult which wou lead to strife.

5. In Gajo and Alas, when a person has a child his former nan becomes taboo.

Puberty rites. Although not mentioned in the Koran, circu cision is the duty of every Moslem. This fact is so emphasized Malaysian India that to be circumcised is the equivalent of becomir a Moslem. Jacobs believes that the Achehnese had circumcision befo they became converted; however, the rite probably was incision rath than circumcision proper.

Boys are circumcised shortly after they have received elementa instruction in the Koran, otherwise between the sixth and tenth ye of their lives. Girls are incised somewhat earlier; usually about t time that they can walk, the second year. A Mohammedan prie circumcises boys, and a midwife girls, in Atjeh, Gajo, and Alas.

In Atjeh the circumcision has no special circumstances connect with it, and is attended only by the family. Sometimes, however, wh the boy has recovered from an illness, he is dressed as a bridegroo before the ceremony, and a ceremonial parade is made to an ancestr grave where his head is washed. Then a sacrificial meal is give Until the wound has healed, the youth is put on diet. He may e no vegetables, fruit, or sharp herbs, and in the main he must ex on dry rice. He may not set foot on the ground, but must we sandals.

After circumcision the prepuce is hung up in the house. If t youth is sick later on, the prepuce is taken down, washed in luk warm water, and the youth is given some of the water to drir Menstruating women, and those in general who are shedding bloc have no access to boys who have just been circumcised.

Circumcision here is all that remains of former tribal initiatio While among the Gajo boys are circumcised in groups, in Atjeh t rite is performed upon individuals. After the circumcision the boy treated as an adult. As soon as the wound has healed, until the ti of his marriage, the youth must sleep in the men's house. The o exception made is in case of serious sickness.

The incision of girls is done very secretly indeed, even the fatl oes not know when his daughter is incised. No celebration at all akes place at the time.

Filing of teeth is a pagan and not a Mohammedan custom. In act it is forbidden in a commentary on the Koran. However, the ustom is ancient to the Malaysian peoples, and among the pre-Hindu opulation of Bali, the Bali-aja, it was a prerequisite to marriage.

Due to Hindu and Mohammedan custom the filing of teeth is no onger required in Atjeh, and is falling into disuse. Still many of he population, both men and women, have their teeth filed. The peration is performed by a woman. Boys have their teeth filed as oon as their second set is complete (except for the wisdom teeth), irls have their teeth filed after marriage. Only the upper teeth are iled as a rule. The teeth are covered with a blackening substance, hich, however, is allowed to wear off.

The Achehnese girls have their ears bored when they are about ix years of age. The operation is usually done by the mother, and here is no further mutilation of the ear lobe.

The Achehnese girl has no special ceremony at the time of her irst period. As everywhere among Mohammedan people, a girl or voman at such a time, and upon each subsequent re-occurrence, is onsidered unclean. From the beginning of the period for seven days he can have no intercourse with men. She is not allowed to take art in prayer or any religious ceremony. The very orthodox will ot touch anything on which a menstruating woman has laid hands. After seven days the woman takes a purifying bath over which a ormula has been spoken.

Women are likewise forbidden coitus, according to Mohammedan aw, after childbirth, after eclipses of the sun and moon, and at a ater period of pregnancy.

Education. Everyone in Atjeh is instructed to read the Koran n the original Arabic characters. However, even the teachers do ot know what they are reading and would be unable to translate nto their own language. A fair facility in droning the sacred book can e acquired in two years time.

Boys also are taught to read Malay in Roman characters so that hey can read the Kitabs, a collection of religious writings written n Malay. They then re-tell these in Achehnese. Promising youths ontinue their education so that they can be religious teachers.

246

There are no actual scholars in Atjeh, and writing is not taug
in the schools. If Achehnese men know how to write, it is becau
they have learned it from one another.

Death. Four duties especially are enjoined on the survivors
a deceased Mohammedan.

1. The washing of the body.
2. Its envelopment in the shroud.
3. The ritual service for the benefit of the dead.
4. The burial.

These rules are generally observed in orthodox fashion amo
the Moslems of the Indian Archipelago. Coffins are exceptional amo
the Mohammedans, so that where they are used a little dirt is plac
beneath the body. In Atjeh only slaves and the poor are buri
without them.

In case of death in the family, a man observes mourning f
forty-four days. He wears no festive clothing, and goes neither
feasts nor to the market place. Except in emergency he neither worl
nor fishes. Women keep mourning in much the same manner, ar
neither oil themselves nor wear flowers.

There is no common burial place, but every family has its ow
burial grounds. A man who dies in the village of his wife is buri
in his own family burial grounds. Children are buried in the groun
of the father's family.

Religion.

The Achehnese are stricter in the observance of the Mohammeda
religion and customs than are any other people of the Archipelag
The Achehnese time reckoning is Mohammedan, and the feast an
memorial days of Islam are likewise celebrated in Atjeh. Man
Achehnese take part in the yearly pilgrimage to Mecca. Still the ol
or animistic belief in the power of spirits, natural forces, and loc
gods, survives in Atjeh no less than in other Mohammedan countrie
Certain of these survivals are sanctioned by Islam itself, especiall
the feasts to avert feared misfortunes, feasts held after the death
a relative, and after harvest. The saints honored and sacrificed t
are in part Mohammedan and in part local Achehnese.

Sickness is still generally attributed to the influence of ev
spirits, and methods of cure are connected with this idea.

Shamanism still holds sway in Arabia, and naturally also in
tjeh. The Achehnese shaman when first consulted eats a heavy meal.
hen he places a pot of boiling water near him, and keeps throwing
ood into the fire to keep himself warm. He chants louder and louder
ntil the sweat runs down his body. Finally he stops, seemingly
upified, and questions are put to him. The spirits inside of him
nswer questions concerning stolen property, the cure of sick people,
c. The shamans receive such high pay that resort is not put to them
ntil all other means failed. Both men and women are members of
is lucrative profession.

PART II. THE GAJO AND ALAS.

Introduction. Gajo and Alas are isolated inland countries of
orthern Sumatra. Outside of the southeastern region of Gajo, which
rders on Alas and Taniang, Gajo is everywhere surrounded by
tjeh, which acts as a broad girdle in separating the land from the
ean. Almost everywhere there extends between the Atjeh coast land
d the inhabited portion of the Gajo highlands a broad stretch of
ninhabited mountain land.

In the Golden Era of Atjeh at the beginning and towards the
iddle of the 17th century, the harbor sultans of Atjeh conquered
ajo and Alas and rendered the small patriarchal village republics
these countries vassal to Atjeh. Yet during the thirty years prior
the beginning of the 20th century, while the Dutch waged war in
tjeh itself, these interior countries remained unknown and unexplored.
ll that one knew was that behind the mountains of the north and
e west coast there lay highlands and a lake. It was also known
at the Gajo people lived there, that they had regular trade with the
chehnese and the coast of Minangkabau, and that they were ruled
er by radja's called kĕdjuron's.

In 1881 two magazine articles appeared on Gajo. But it was not
til Atjeh had been overcome (1898) that it was possible to obtain
curate knowledge of the interior. In 1902 four military expeditions
ent to various parts of Gajo. Snouk Hurgronje spent three years
thering information about the country and published a complete
scription in 1903.

Very much less is known about Alas than about Gajo. Most of
r information comes from Kreemer, who relies on an unpublished

memoir by the Dutch controller C. G. J. Christian, which appeared in 1915.

According to folk tradition, a number of heathen Bataks from Toba Lake came to Alasland under their chief Alas, from whom the people and the country have derived their names. After this repeated invasions took place into Alas, both from the Bataks and the Minangkabau. As these colonists all came to the original point of settlement, Batu Mbulan, the place became very thickly populated so that sections split off under their own chiefs, but still owing allegiance to the mother kampong. The Minangkabau colonists gained the ascendency and forced the remaining colonists to become converted to Islam. In 1912 the Dutch assumed the rule and converted the sil into townships, thus rendering territorial rule possible.

In my account I will necessarily speak mostly of the Gajo. must be assumed that the Alas have similar customs, unless other wise noted.

Economic Life.

Agriculture. The chief occupation of the Gajo is agricultur especially the growing of rice. Usually wet rice is cultivated, wate being obtained from the rivers. If there is a poor rice crop, as happen every twenty to twenty-five years, there is a great famine and mar people die.

The people also eat dried fish and deer meat. Cattle are bre but the flesh of buffaloes, goats, and sheep only are eaten at tim of feasts. These along with small horses serve as an aid to agricultur Buffaloes usually draw the plow.

Dry fields are mostly used for the growing of tobacco ar vegetables. Curdled karabau milk is used for food as among th Bataks and in the Minangkabau Highlands. Besides rice; maiz cotton, and sugar cane are staple crops in the region.

Houses and villages. The most important house that one e counters in Gajo is the dwelling house, umah. The house is bu on pillars, and is a communal dwelling; thus it is inhabited by number of related families. In this respect the house is similar that of Minangkabau, but the families are related patrilineally and n matrilineally. Aside from its greater length, made necessary by th number of indwelling families, the size corresponds with that of th Achehnese home. The house has two galleries, a front one (radi) f

en, and a back one (udjung) for women. The individual family
eeping quarters (bileq) are located in the center (lah).

A bileq serves as sleeping quarters for a married couple and
teir young children. Here, also, all the private family property is
ept. Each bileq has its own oven for heating at night and cooking.
herefore, as in Minangkabau, a family (lim) is called sara dapur,
one oven", indicating that the members of the family are oven
elatives, or sara kro, "rice relatives". Pine cones are burned in the
vens to furnish light at night. Cooking, however, is only done in
te ovens in exceptional circumstances, for the ordinary general
)oking place is in the andjong, a communal fireplace, which is some-
mes located in a separate building. This is a large oven with two
idividual fireplaces for every family.

The men's gallery is, as a rule, only used for feasts, and at other
mes is quite empty. It is likewise made use of at special festivities,
ich as circumcision and marriage. Some places are partitioned off
i this section of the house to serve as sleeping places for young
ten. These usually, however, go at night to the men's house, the
teresah.

The women's gallery extends through the entire communal house,
nd is used by the women when they are not busy with outdoor work,
ich as cooking, getting water, stamping rice and gathering wood.
he women spend their time here in spinning, patching worn out
othing, and weaving mats and mat work. Likewise the children play
i this gallery.

As in Atjeh, in the neighborhood of every communal house there
, a rice granary (kebon) built on piles.

In Gajo and Alas, contrary to the Achehnese custom, when a
aughter marries there is one inhabitant less in the house. The bileq's,
r sleeping quarters, can be subdivided when a man brings a wife to
is home, or the house can be made longer.

The men's house (meresah) is commonly separated from the
welling places, but it lies on the same village level. The meresah
; essentially the same as the Achehnese meunasah. A meresah has
lank floors and walls, and from one to five fireplaces for lighting
nd heating. A few meresah's have small side buildings (djodjah)
hich serve for religious purposes. But teaching by the village
eligious head, the imöm, likewise is done in the meresah.

The meresah is the customary place in which boys above eight years of age, unmarried men, widowers, and strangers spend the night. The married men also come to the meresah in the daytime when their out of doors work is finished, and sew or embroider here All the men must go to the communal house at meal time, for nothing is cooked in the meresah.

In Gajo and Alas the natives are grouped according to relation ship in a village. The village is called kampong in Gajo and kutö in Alas. Some villages contain only members of one sib, but usually a village contains three or four sibs with family subdivisions. Each sib inhabits a section of the village, or hamlet. The different sections are divided off from one another by some natural feature, such as streams, or by rice fields. Each hamlet may have its own men's house or one men's house may be used by several sibs.

In both Gajo and Alas the towns are built in the plains along the rivers. They are irregularly arranged.

Society.

Government. The Gajo division of the people is still rooted in genealogical rule, and has only gone over to territorial rule when compulsion has been used by the Dutch. The population is divided into patrilineal sibs (blah, suku, or kuru) inhabiting either a village or a portion of a village. In Alas the sib is called mĕrgö (Batak merga or marga) and the division of it is called suku or blah.

The smallest unit of government is a subdivision of a sib under its own family head, rödjö or pengulu. The subjects of a chief consider each other blood brothers, and call one another sara rödj (one rödjö), or sara inö (from one mother). This last appellation naturally is contrary to fact in an agnate society.

The subjects of a rödjö may at any time separate, and a part of them leave under a new ruler. The members of the two groups after the separation, no longer consider one another blood brothers and have no longer the old adat rights and duties towards one another Still the common descendants call each other wali (indicating agnate descent) and are not allowed to marry until both sides, with appropriate ceremonies, remove this last obstacle.

When a sib expands, it first forms separate hamlets, and then villages, but the authority of the rödjö is retained as long as possible

he patriarchal chief has his deputies (bödöl) who exert a somewhat
imited power in the various dwelling places of the sandörö (subjects),
ut the rödjö himself is called upon for important matters.

The position of rödjö is hereditary in the family. According to
he adat he is usually followed by his son, not necessarily the eldest,
ut by the one who is considered as mĕtuah, i. e., distinguished by
ucky marks. This choice is made by the sib mates, the sandörö's,
ided by a seer (guru) who is summoned. As among the Bataks,
he rule of ultimogeniture is followed both in inheritance and succes-
ion to office, and the choice first falls on the youngest son and then
n the eldest. If the youngest son is still immature, a guardian is
ppointed.

Just before the burial of the deceased rödjö, his name and rank
re assumed by his chosen successor, who is carried with the corpse
n the same litter to the burial place and then back to the house.
fter forty-four days the sandörö's have a gathering and the chosen
an is installed in his position.

The rödjö, like the Batak radja, is *primus inter pares* among
is people. The Gajo form of life is too simple to allow of much
omp. Usually the chiefs go about clothed as other men and without
ny special following. They themselves work in the fields. The ridge
f a rödjö's house is made of whole timber and is especially ornamented.
he rödjö also is entitled to a special coffin, while common people
imply are wrapped in cloth. Finally, the rödjö at the time of the
early feast is bathed and annointed in the presence of the multitude.
here follows a general rendering of homage in which the women
row rice at their ruler in order to cast off disease from the people.

Two authorities stand by the side of the rödjö to aid him in
overning. The tuö (or petuö), the "elder", or adjutant of the
ödjö, is usually of a safe age and noted for his knowledge of the
dat; furthermore there is the imöm, the religious head and guardian
f the hukom (the religious law). The latter has charge of religious
asts, the performing of marriages, and the burial of the dead.

The most important source of income of the rödjö is derived from
nes (called salah, the same as the misdemeanors for which they
e imposed) inflicted for violation of the adat. Abnormal forms of
arriage, as by abduction, are salah. Adoption marriage, adoption,
d the freeing of slaves also furnish an income to the rödjö. The
djö gets a certain sum for every marriage, and, in some districts,

for every burial. The rödjö likewise receives a share of every buffalo slaughtered at a feast.

The rödjö, imöm, tuö, and sandörö's form together the four natural classes which compose every Gajo society.

The only territorial chiefs are the kĕdjurun's, who were set up by Atjeh about two centuries ago when she controlled Gajo. According to tradition there were originally four kĕdjurun's, in order to conform to the Achehnese concept of the sanctity of the number four. At this time Gajo was divided into three provinces: Laut Tawar, the Döröt, and Gajo Luös. Two kĕdjurun's were chosen from Laut Tawar in order to make up the total four. The rulers of these districts received from the sultans of Atjeh certain insignia of office and their titles.

While the sultans of Atjeh had wished to create territorial chiefs who could be responsible for their lands to outside powers, they fell short of accomplishing their purpose. In the course of time the kĕdjurun's became less and less important, for they remained entirely outside the general scope of Gajo communal life. Since, however, the Gajo people themselves wished the kĕdjurun's to have some functions, they became the arbitrators of quarrels between the rödjö's, or between the subjects of different rödjö's.

When new settlements were founded, or when colonists came from a different territory, the consent of the local kĕdjurun had first to be asked. The blessing and consent of the kĕdjurun had also to be obtained at the installation of a new rödjö, whether his predecessor was dead, deposed, or chosen to head a new sib. Every kĕdjurun filled also the office of rödjö in his own sib, and the succession to the position of kĕdjurun was made on the same plan as that to rödjö.

When Gajo was annexed by the Dutch in 1904, the kĕdjurun's were raised again to importance as territorial chiefs, with the rödjö's subordinate to them.

Snouck Hurgronje has made a comparison of the Achehnese and the Gajo form of government. Due to the intimate knowledge which this writer gained of both regions, and the excellence of his exposition, the comparison deserves translation in full.

In Atjeh the ranks are as follows. The keutji is the kampong chief; under him are many ureuëng tuha (underlings), from whose number some are chosen as waki, who function like the Gajo tuö. The Achehnese teungku under another name performs the same office

the imöm of the Gajo. Finally there come the usual members of
e kampong whom the keutji calls his children (aneu). The Acheh-
se keutji rules over a territory, the kampong. All the people who
ter the territory and occupy land become the children of the keutji,
d when they leave and take up land elsewhere, his rule is broken.
Gajo a rödjö rules over so-called brothers, all of whom are sup-
sed to be of the same blood, and they cannot break this allegiance
less they enter another sib. This can only be done by adoption
by marrying in (the ambil anak, or adoption marriage), both of
ich methods are seldom practiced. In Gajo then it is the genealog-
l factor which counts; while in Atjeh the territorial factor comes
the fore, and the older sib unity remains, but in weakened form,
the kawōm's.

There is a great deal more solidarity between the sandörö's in
jo than between the people of a town in Atjeh; the latter only
ng fellow citizens who live together, but are not responsible for
:h other's conduct or debts. The Gajo sandörö's live as brothers,
l are responsible for one another in case of blood revenge, and in
e of any other debt or fine. Refusal to pay the debt of a fellow
dörö may lead to war. Contrary to primitive clan custom, but
ilar to Minangkabau adat, the Gajo have means of getting rid
an undesirable brother. His nearest blood relatives — who are
ones the most oppressed — petition the rödjö before the assembled
council to expel (menjeren, from tjere, to part) the undesirable
mber. The accusers have to pay the rödjö for this service. The
elled person can hope for nothing better than to be taken into
ther sib, for which service he has to give the new rödjö a money
sent for the privilege of being accepted, besides furnishing his
sib mates a feast. An entire family can even join a new sib if
s dissatisfied with its former rödjö. Such new members are for-
den marriage with women of their new sib, in the same manner
if they were born in it, while they may marry women of their
ner sib. But a man seldom or never makes use of this privilege
le the memory of the broken bond still exists. A person left over
not taken into a new sib lives on as a wanderer in the fields, or
uch towns where opium smoking and rooster fighting are the order
he day, or else flees to Atjeh.

The Achehnese keutji, although he is called the father of his
pong, and as such retains much patriarchal influence, is of far

less importance than the Gajo rödjö, who is really the head of a bloc
community. The keutji is limited in power by the imeum. Withou
the consent of this superior he is unable to handle important matter
in his gampong. The rödjö, on the other hand, is nearly independen
and need only call upon the other rödjö's when the affair involve
their subjects. He has almost no one superior to him in power. N
alone the regulating of all communal interests and the settlement
all differences, but also the judgement of all crimes, even capital, fa
to the rödjö, and all without direction from above.

Yet the personal power of the rödjö is small, in many cases le
than that of the keutji. The keutji, although his power is limited, ca
force the inhabitants of his village to do much which is by no mea»
agreeable to them. But the rödjö can only act when he is certain th
the foremost sandörö's will not oppose him. A decision against the
will simply will not be enforced. A command, also, that does n
correspond with the known adat will not be carried out. If the röd
attempts to cross the will of the majority a new rödjö is chosen. T
rödjö thus merely is the patriarch president of a little republic, who
members are jealous of their freedom, and his words are listened
only when they conform to the adat.

As among the Bataks, only married men have voice in the affai
of the sib, and they alone can act as witnesses and can be he
responsible for debts. In other words, a man is not considered adu
until married.

As everywhere in Indonesia, the adat (which is merely an Arabi
word for customary law) is supposed to remain unchanged fro
generation to generation, since it is supervised by the ancestors. T
primitive conceived the dead as jealous of the living and especial
antagonistic to innovation. A good rödjö, therefore, is a rödjö who
conservative and walks in the path of his forefathers. And yet the ad
does change, here as elsewhere among primitive or isolated people, ar
the rate of change is directly dependent on the amount of contact t
people enjoy with the outside world. Gajo is more isolated than Atje
but less isolated than Batakland. Hence the governmental system h
progressed to a point inbetween those of these two countries before t
Dutch took the rule.

War. Wars never were fought between two kĕdjurun's, as the
officials did not control territorial units. Commonly, wars were wag
between two rödjö's of the same district.

At the beginning of a war both sides fortified their towns with
ırth walls, pointed stakes, and bamboo slivers stuck into the ground
s traps. This was all done, however, without the kampong's really
eing in any danger, for it was against the adat to destroy dwelling
laces, and the actual fighting took place outside the towns. The fight
ısted until one side or the other was compelled to flee and take refuge
ı its kampong. Then peace was negociated by a neutral party.

During the war the ordinary rules of adat and hukom were not
ɔeyed. The rödjö chose another leader, called panglimo, to rule in
is place. The panglimo was supposed to be especially fitted for
adership in war. The panglimo, in turn, picked out an official called
emeter to act in place of the tuö.

The imöm either did not take part, or at least was not supposed
› take part, in a war between two Mohammedan parties. His place
as taken by the guru prang, a person skilled in reading omens, and
ı determing lucky and unlucky periods and days. If there were none
ı the district, a man was called in from outside.

Criminal law. The native concept that an infringement of the
lat, in order to be punishable, must be attested by a material token,
so holds among the Gajo. "Without a bendo no salah." (Without
token, no wrong.) A head cloth from a man committing adultery
the hand of the wife's husband is a convincing piece of testimony;
e attesting of witnesses without such a bendo is held as worthless.

Both the adat and the hukom are invoked for the punishment of
murder. Usually the guilt of a murderer is apparent, and no bendo,
' visible token of the murderer, is necessary for the purpose of
claring him guilty. If the murderer is unable to justify his deed,
is executed. Capital punishment takes the form either of strangling
drowning. In Alas beheading also is customary. A person is
owned by having his head held under water with a forked stick.
tis form of punishment, however, usually is reserved for thieves,
ile murderers are strangled.

Blood guilt is declared on a man who murders one of his own
› mates, as well as on a man who murders an outsider. In the latter
se the sandörö's from the afflicted sib come to the murderer's sib
if they were about to start war, but the rödjö of the guilty sib is
ıpowered to decide the matter according to the laws of god and man
ukom and adat). The rödjö's of the two sibs hold council together
d satisfaction is given.

Neither bela (blood atonement) nor diët (weregild) is given wh
a person is killed in war, or when a wronged individual persona
has killed a trapped thief or has avenged unchastity. In such cas
however, the theory of the bendo must be applied, and part of t
stolen goods must be found on the person of the thief, or the w
accomplice of the adulterous man must be given a wound. Later t
adulterous wife usually is strangled.

A guilty person, even though caught *flagrante delicto*, may
longer be killed by the wronged party if he has the good luck
reach the boundaries of his own kampong. A thief, if he escapes
flight, is punished by a fine and the forfeit of the stolen article.
tangible proof of the theft, not only is the stolen article necessary, l
the thief must also have received a wound in the course of his flig
Habitual thieves are drowned.

All unchastity, whether performed with an unmarried girl, w
the wife of another, or with a woman whom the culprit is unable
marry, is considered as not having had occurred where no token c
be produced. If such a token is produced, the matter is settled w
a fine, and the male relative (father, brother, or husband) is co
pensated. This is contrary to Achehnese law, which considers t
chastity as a crime against the state. In Gajo a woman is consider
the property of her father or husband, and hence the male owner
to be compensated for loss. Naturally the Achehnese law is but
development of the Gajo manner of thinking. With more civiliz
codes, unchastity, where punished at all, becomes again a civil rath
than a criminal matter.

Pregnancy is the best of bendo, and one does what one can
adjust matters. If the affair has not been settled by killing, the wom
is given to the man as wife. If this is not possible, because the wom
is already married, or because the marriage would be contrary
the Gajo laws of exogamy, both parties should be killed. Usual
however, the matter is adjusted by weregild, paid by the man or
the relatives of the woman, and the fruit in the womb is destroy
The woman then is forced into a marriage with a man of low ra

It must be noted that all officials (including the rödjö, tuö, a
imöm) are not liable to fine. If an official commits a crime he c
be deposed. A woman also, as among the Bataks, is considered
property and hence can own no property and pay no fines. The Ga

wishing to extol the position of woman, say that in this respect she
is like a rodjo, for she need pay no fines.

The adat prescribes besides the bendo, or tangible evidence, still
other means by which the truth may be arrived at: the oath and the
ordeal. Accusations for which there are no bendo, but which rest on
presumptive evidence, one names dowo soq, doubtful accusations. If
the evidence submitted is not sufficient even to be presumptive, the
accuser is fined for arousing false suspicion.

People who live in suspicion of theft, &c., may clear themselves
by oath. The simplest oath is sworn on the Koran or on the earth.
"May the earth not receive my body if I have sworn falsely." Perjury
is supposed to be severely punished in the next world. But since Allah
only punishes in the next life, and this lies a long way in the future,
and since his mercy is infinite, and he may pardon the offence of
perjury, more worth is laid on oaths where perjury will bring retribution
in the present life. Such an oath is made on some sacred object (stone,
tree, &c.), which acts as security for the truth of the assertion. The
object then is laid on some holy spot, as a grave. In case of perjury
one believes that material misfortune, such as heavy pecuniary loss,
sickness, or death will soon befall the culprit. This misfortune does
not come from Allah the merciful, but from the magic of the sacred
object.

The ordeals made use of are common in Indonesia. A reputed
poisoner is made to put his hand in burning oil. In case of dispute over
property, both parties duck under water, and the one who remains
under the longest is declared winner.

Marriage. — The Gajo family is patriarchal in form, and every
family is supposed to have one of four lines of descent. The fictitious
basis of sib descent is readily seen when one appreciates the amount
of foreign blood which has been brough in, either by outright
adoption into the sibs, or by the angkap marriage. This is the ambil
nak marriage of the Bataks and South Sumatra, where the man is
taken into the family of his wife.

Bataks and Achehnese only are adopted into a family when it is
apparent that they can be trusted. After the needed publicity has been
given by means of a sacrificial meal — at which, according to the
material circumstances of the adopting father, a buffalo or goat is
sacrificed — and after payment of the adoption fee to the rodjo, the
new member is taken as a sandoro, and from this time on belongs to

the sib. When a slave is adopted it is necessary to give a sacrifici
meal and thus get publicity, so that the man and his descendants r
longer will be treated as slaves.

The usual form of adoption is the angkap marriage, in which th
daughter does not leave her paternal house, but marries a strange
No bride-price is paid, and the man becomes a sandörö of the brothei
and tribal relatives of his wife. In order to satisfy the Mohammeda
law, the man gives a dollar to his wife as marriage present.

As in other forms of adoption, in this case also, the adoptin
man wishes a field worker and a procurer of children. He also wishe
to retain his daughter in his home, rather than sell her out. This
especially the case where the father has no sons.

No demands are made regarding the ancestry or position of
son-in-law acquired by this form of annexation, yet men who actual
were slaves are not very desirable, as they can be recognized by the fa
that both ear lobes are bored through. It usually is Achehnese an
other strangers, such as Malays and Kurintjiers, seldom Klings
Arabs, who are thus taken into the family. Sometimes, but seldor
Chinese are converted to Islam and married in.

Usually when a Gajo man marries in the angkap manner, it
but for a limited period of time. He cannot as yet pay the bride-pric
but he does not wish to postpone marriage. Such a man gives the be
of his working ability to the family of his bride so that he can brin
her to his own home as soon as possible. This kind of angkap marriag
is called angkap djandji. It is to the advantage of the father-in-la
to keep his son-in-law as long as possible, and often he will only gi
consent to the marriage when the latter has sworn not to pay the brid
price for a fixed period of time.

Once a Gajo man pays the bride-price he is entitled to bring h
wife and his children to his own sib. This payment may be made aft
the death of the man by his agnates. If the woman dies before th
entire bride-price is paid, the remainder of the debt is wiped out. Som
times a blood relative is given the man as substitute.

While a Gajo woman theoretically owns no goods and on
manages the possessions of her husband and children, yet a woma
married by the angak method is an exception to this rule. The husban
only possesses goods while he remains a member of the family. Fr
quently an Achehnese adventurer marries into a Gajo family and the

uns away, leaving his goods and children behind. The family considers such an affair an asset rather than a loss.

The customary form of marriage in Gajo is the purchase marriage.
Here the true form of purchase marriage is employed, and the woman
in consideration of the bride-price is purchased out of the sib to which
she belongs. Due to the Gajo respect for women, however, one does
not say that a man "buys a wife", but that he "fetches a wife". In
spite of this euphemism the bride-price is high, and other expensive
presents have to be given as well. So it happens not infrequently that
one finds elderly unmarried men and women in Gajo.

As a rule, with the exception of the sib restrictions, the Islam
marriage restrictions are adhered to. Yet it is not forbidden, although
it is not customary, for two brothers to marry two sisters from the same
mother. As is usual with tribes having sibs, the maternal uncle is
distinguished in relationship nomenclature from the father and father's
brother, and the children of brother and sister from the children of
two brothers or two sisters. No investigation has been made, however,
in the question of cross-cousin marriage either in Gajo and Alas. It is
safe to assume that this form of marriage occurs in both lands, in one
variety or another.

A man usually marries a woman who lives in his neighborhood.
The woman's family does not like to lose sight of her, and the man
wishes to know something about the woman he is marrying.

First marriages, which are the only ones of importance, are
arranged by the families on both sides. The engagement lasts from
one to three years, due to the necessity of the man acquiring the bride-
price, and the woman the dowry, such as cooking apparatus, decorations, clothing, mats, and even cattle, which she brings into the
marriage. In wealthy families the dowry sometimes is worth many
times the bride-price.

The wedding ceremony consists in part of the bride and groom
placing sirih in each other's mouths, and in plunging their hands into
water.

After the marriage the husband must remain in the house of his
father-in-law from four to seven days. During the period of his stay
he is subjected to hazing by the young girls of the bride's family. The
hazing is called "bersendo", meaning joking or play. It is very unpleasant for the groom, who in turn is covered with soot and chalk,

has water poured over him, and is made to sing and dance. If
performs badly he is fined. In the afternoons the groom bathes in th
river. At these times the young girls decorate him with emblems
his former occupation. If he was a tobacco planter, with all the im
plements used in planting tobacco; if a hunter, with weapons of th
chase and a dog bound to his leg.

Besides the angak marriage and the purchase marriage, the Ga
have marriage by elopement and marriage by abduction. The Gaj
however, do not practice marriage by elopement in order to lessen tl
costs of the marriage, although this form of wedding costs much le
for both families, but in order to surmount obstacles set by the paren

If the two young people wish to marry despite the wishes of t
parents, the girl goes to the rödjö of the man's sib and remains
his house. She bears with her certain tokens belonging to the ma
as his head cloth and sirih sack. The girl is entrusted to the guardia
ship of the rödjö. The relatives of the young woman send three tim
for her in a formal manner, and each time they are informed that s
has "come to live with her true companion". After this message h
arrived the last time, the male relatives of the girl pretend to be in t
greatest rage, arm themselves, and go to the house of the rödjö, whe
they once more demand the return of their relative.

The man now pays a certain sum of money and becomes engag
to the girl. The sum is only about the quarter of the regular marria
price. A marriage ceremony is soon performed, but the relatives
the girl pretend that they are still angry, and have nothing to do w
the wedding. A distant relative acts as guardian (wali) and gives
girl away at the altar. There are no festivities, and again the costs a
lessened. The pair remain a year with the relatives of the wom
(since such a small bride-price has been paid), and then, especially
a child is born, there is a reconciliation.

Actual abduction is handled in a far less lenient fashion.
some districts marriage is never allowed after abduction. There
abductor is punished either with death or a heavy fine, and the g
handed back to the parents. Where this rule is followed, abductio
are rare. In Gajo Luos the pair is allowed to marry, although
affair is a very severe breach of the adat.

Polygyny although everywhere allowed is seldom practiced.
ordinary man, once married, remains faithful to his one wife until
or her death. The bride-price is too high to permit the man of ordin

means to think of either divorce or polygyny. Very prominent and wealthy men, however, take a second wife. If the first wife has children the man pays her an indemnity. Both women live in the same house.

When a husband dies, the wife, especially if there are children, marries a brother or nephew of the deceased. In this case no bride-price is paid to the parents of the woman. Even if the woman does not marry another man of the same sib as her husband, as long as the family of the deceased husband takes care of her, her parents have no right to bring her back home or give her away in marriage.

If the woman returns to her home, and is given out in marriage a second time, her bride-price is but half of what it was the first time.

Children do not follow their mother in a second marriage, but remain with the father's family.

No avoidance or joking relationships among the Gajo are mentioned. Parents-in-law and children-in-law do not avoid one another. They do, however, avoid mentioning each other's names. The avoidance of names, in general, is very strict in Gajo. A husband and wife avoid each other's name entirely, and after the first child is born they lose their names, due to the practice of teknonomy.

Before closing our discussion of Gajo marriage, a word of explanation is necessary concerning the frequent occurrence of matrilocal marriage among these people. The usual explanation given is that it is a survival of the previous matriarchy. However, according to the theory held in this book, the bilateral family was the oldest form in Sumatra, giving place either to the patrilineal, or, in Minangkabau, to the matrilineal. Marriage then originally was an exchange between two families, and with the advent of the moiety and sib, between two sibs. With the breakdown of the exchange system, the bride-price comes in as compensation, as among the Bataks. Peoples with matrilineal descent, as the Minangkabau, or matrilocal residence, as the Achehnese, need no bride-price, because the family of the girl loses nothing by her marriage. As has been shown among the Bataks, and as is also true for the Gajo, when the marriage price becomes too high, marriages tend to become matrilocal. Among the Gajo, abduction is criminal because it provides neither for the payment of a bride-price nor its compensation, matrilocal residence. It is therefore a crime against property. Elopement is compensated for by a modified bride-price and a modified matrilocal residence. Even with actual bride-purchase, it is symbolically felt that money cannot entirely compensate the sib

of the bride for its loss, and hence the seven day matrilocal residenc
and the hazing of the groom.

Totemism. Since both the Bataks and the Achehnese had totemism
it is probable that certain, if not all, of the Gajo and Alas sibs like
wise were totemistic. Snouck Hurgronje merely states on this poin
that among the Gajo, as in Java, there are certain families to who
certain animals are taboo as food. This is attributed to the wish c
oath of the founder of the family, in consequence of an incident whic
is handed down in legend. Sickness or death would follow the in
fringement of the taboo.

Puberty ceremonies. In Gajo and Alas, as in Atjeh, the nam
giving and the hair cutting of the child take place on the sevent
day after his birth. The child is bathed in a nearby river on thi
occasion.

At the time of the haircut a lock is allowed to remain on th
crown of both boys and girls. At sickness or other misfortune thi
lock is cut off in the hope that the bad luck will be removed. Afte
circumcision the boy's hair is allowed to grow again. The girl allow
her hair to grow at the age of six. A girl has her ear lobes pierce
without ceremony. The ears then are artificially lengthened.

In Gajo, as already mentioned, a number of boys are circumcise
together some time before their sixth year. The festivities which occu
at this time are in the nature of wedding festivities, and the youth
are dressed as grooms. Girls are incised in Gajo when they are
few months old. This is done in Alas at about the age of five.

Boys and girls in Gajo have their teeth filed and permanentl
blackened by a male operator at about the age of fifteen. The teet
of both jaws are filed. In Alas the operation takes place at abou
the age of eight for both sexes.

Inheritance. Due to the peculier marriage regulations of Gajo,
would be impossible for the people to follow Mohammedan in
heritance laws. As a matter of fact the population is quite ignoran
as to what the regulations of Islam are regarding this matter.

The native rules of inheritance are not laid down in an exactin
manner, but there are general principles consistent with a patriarcha
society. While women in general cannot possess property, in practic
they possess as consorts of their husbands. As a widow, a mothe
possesses with her children, and thus she often manages the famil

roperty. Even the daughter possesses goods when, through an angkap
arriage, she is made a more or less permanent member of the
mily.

The father usually upon the marriage of his son gives him an
utfit consisting of part of a ricefield, one or more buffaloes, and
portion of the communal house. While all the elder sons usually
eceive an equal share, the youngest receives the most, sometimes
vice as much as any of the others. The youngest son is called bengsu,
nd has the duty of taking care of the elder brothers and seeing
at they are properly buried. When the father dies, the property is
ot divided further, but goes as a whole to the succeeding family head.
he making of wills is quite unknown.

If a man leaves only girls at the time of his death, and none
f these have performed an angkap marriage, then the youngest of
e elder brothers of the father becomes family head and takes care
f the family. If one of the daughters, however, has performed an
ngkap marriage, her husband receives the estate and becomes head
f the family.

When a man has sons and daughters and the daughters marry
the angkap fashion, it is usual for the father to give portions of
is estate to the daughters at the time of their marriages, concealing
e matter, however, from his sons. At the death of the father the
esidue of the estate goes to his youngest son.

Most Gajo men leave only enough property at their deaths to
ay the cost of the funeral, and there is little left over to give the
mily head. The privileges and duties of the youngest son can be taken
om him if he is not deserving of them.

Religion.

Due to the isolated position of the country, the natives know and
re very little about the Mohammedan religion. Few are hadji (have
ade the pilgrimage to Mecca), and even these have not remained
ng enough in Arabia to learn the customs.

The Achehnese must master a foreign tongue, Malay, in order
read religious documents, but they also have scattered writings in
eir own language. The Gajo have no written literature, and their
lk-lore consists only of legends and axioms.

It is therefore not surprising to find that the Gajo family adat is little influenced by Mohammedanism and varies almost as much from Mohammedan law as does that of Minangkabau.

The natives display little zeal in the performance of Mohammedan ritual, as is shown by the small number of mesegit's (mosques) in the land. Those who perform their religious tasks with any degree of regularity form a small minority, and are called by the Javanese title of Santri.

The people believe in friendly and unfriendly spirits and ghosts, and in saints, living and dead. All these have to be propitiated through gifts and cult practices. Some of these rites are condemned as being contrary to the laws of Islam, but the boundary is not very clearly drawn.

SOUTHERN SUMATRA.

PART 1. LAMPONG.

Introduction.

The people of Lampong, as stated in the introduction, are divided
) the mountain people, the Orang Abung, and the plains people,
Orang Pablan. The Orang Abung probably are the original
ple of the region, while the Orang Pablan are a mixture of these
Sundanese from Java. Certainly the lowland people have acquired
ay later Malaysian traits, as well as Sundanese culture. I will first
cribe the civilized plains people and then comment upon the
untaineers.

Little is known concerning the former trade and intercourse
veen Lampong and Bantam, which lies just across the Sunda
aits in Java. Bantam took an interest in Lampong because of the
per planted there, and gradually took it under control. The sultans
Bantam, however, laid no other obligation upon the people of
npong than the right to purchase pepper at a fixed price. The
ans of Bantam also conferred the title of punggawa, representative
he sultan, on the Lampong sib chiefs, and gave instructions for
settling of boundary disputes. Other titles as well were sold, for
Bantam sultans well knew how to turn the vanity of the people of
npong to their own commercial advantage. The titles conferred
e bartered in turn among the natives of Lampong.

The Dutch first established contact with Lampong at the time
1e East India Company. In 1864 the company received as monopoly
local pepper trade from Sultan Hadji of Bantam.

While Lampong is 500 square miles in area it has a population
ut 60,000 people. Van Hoevell attributes this scanty number to the
)wing causes:

1. The despotic nature of the chiefs and the rich.
2. The large sum of money which a man has to pay for a wife. This
Irance to marriage causes a large portion of the population to die
arried and childless.

3. The prevailing custom which forces a man to marry the wom‹
left by his deceased brothers, nephews and grandfathers. Due to th‹
custom there are Lampong children, and even sucklings, who ha
four, six, and more wives.

4. The amount of sickness prevalent among young children.

5. The number of people lost through murder or as victims
wild animals.

6. Van Hoëvell estimates that under Bantam rule one fifth of t‹
population was sold as slaves or captured by pirates.

Economic Life.

Agriculture. — The land in Lampong is unfavorable for irrig‹
tion, so that very little wet rice is cultivated. Formerly the soil w‹
trampled by karabau and the plow was not used. It has been recent
introduced by the Javanese. Several families own land together, t
planting and weeding being done by each family separately, wh
the families unite for the harvesting.

Cattle raising is not important in Lampong, but the people ke
karabau and a few goats as household animals. Fishing is one
the main industries.

The interior of the country is uncultivated and inhabited by wi
animals, chiefly by tigers, elephants, rhinoceros, monkeys, and wi
pigs, cats, and goats. The rivers are infested by crocodiles.

Villages and houses. — The villages of Lampong are on rive‹
and sometimes are far distant from one another. The houses (nu
are grouped around the communal house (sesat).

The family houses are built on piles, five to seven feet above t
ground. They are surrounded by fences, safeguarding the firewo‹
poultry, and other possessions. Each house is built one or more stori
high, and has a central section for the reception of strangers,
cooking place, and sleeping quarters divided into three sections f
the wives. If a man has more than one wife, they live according
the order of their marriages, the first wife in the first section, the seco‹
in the next, &c.; if a fourth wife is taken, a special section has to
built for her accomodation. The women whom a man acquires
inheritance must be taken into his own section of the house. T
concubines sleep in the third portion of the women's part.

The houses are built entirely of wood, or partly of wood and partly of bamboo or the bark of trees. The homes of people of middle rank are usually well decorated and thatched with palm leaf roofs. Most houses have a flight of steps with a veranda on top. The steps are used for drying goods, and the young daughters of the house receive admirers on the veranda.

In the oldest hamlet of every village the communal house, called sesat or balidana, is situated. The sesat is best constructed in the regions where Islam is of least influence. It is usually built on piles, and consists of one room with a number of subdivisions in which the people of different classes sit. The walls and floor of the building are woven bamboo.

The village government holds its meetings in the sesat, and the regulations of the authorities are here hung up for all to read. The sesat also serves for feasts and for lodging government officials, servants, and travelling Europeans.

Besides the village sesat, there is in every hamlet of the village a small public building called passeban, angung, or lungku, where the head of the hamlet with his oldest subordinates arrange minor matters of state which fall under his jurisprudence.

Among the wealthy people of Lampong elaborate use is made of silver for household utensils. Silver plates are used at feasts, and the sih is served in silver. Large porcelain and earthen ware are employed for storing goods, and trays are made of copper and wood. Water usually is stored in hollowed-out pumkins, although bamboos also serve this purpose. Far in the interior the people still manufacture their own pottery from necessity, but it is not of such fine quality as that found in Palembang or Java.

Clothing and ornaments. — While tapa cloth is made use of in the interior, the more civilised people clothe themselves like the Malays and Javanese.

Most of the decorations are assumed by unmarried women at the time of dances. The men use less elaborate ornaments. Besides their finger rings, the latter wear gold and silver kris cases. On festive occasions men of rank wear golden crowns, arm rings, neckbands, belts set with gold, and two or more krises. Married men wear silver ear-rings, which would be laughed at if worn by young bachelors.

The Lampong people are noted for the splendor with which young men of noble rank attire themselves for dancing. Besides their rich

clothing, they wear on their heads crowns made of pandanus leav
on their foreheads fillets of beaten gold, large horned combs in th
hair, and coral decorations around the head. Golden bands are li
wise worn around the neck. Each maid wears a gold or silver fin;
nail on the little finger of her right hand as a token of virginity. Coi
arm rings too are worn, worked with floral decorations. Slave gi
are not allowed gold finger nails, but are content with silver or copp

Economic life. — All excepting the nobles and the rich lead
regular life of work at agriculture or fishing. They rise at dawn a
bathe, or at least wash their faces in the river. Women wash th
children and fetch water at this time. The men and women bathe
separate places. Some of the people now eat a bit of rice for breakf;
and the well-to-do add coffee to their menu. Then every one goes
his daily task, which lasts an indefinite period of time. The poo
people work in the rice fields. The ordinary occupations of won
include fetching water, searching for firewood, threshing and cook
rice, spinning thread and weaving cloth, and mending their own ;
the men's apparel. At times the entire village is called out for wc
as when heavy loads have to be drawn or a communal house is to
built. The young people of both sexes aid in the work.

The midday meal, among the wealthy people, is eaten at
undetermined time, among the poor shortly before noon. The even
meal is taken before sundown. When people work in the fields tl
bring their food along with them. In the evening the men who do
remain in the fields go to the homes of their friends and relativ
in order to spend the time in gossip with them before going to l
Meanwhile the young men court the unmarried women.

The people of Lampong eat far simpler food than the Javan
The kapala marga, the person of highest rank, eats little else tl
rice and vegetables cooked in water. Those who live near the sea
rivers sometimes have a bit of fresh fish. Salt was formerly gi
to visitors as a special treat. Karabau meat is only eaten at fea
Both sexes chew sirih and are addicted to tobacco smoking.

Weapons of war. — In the days of Bantam rule, districts and ;
often fought against one another in boundary disputes. Distinc
weapons were the "knodsen", a pick tied to the end of a long st
and a long bamboo with a cobble stone at its end. With the latter
warriors displayed great skill in warding off the pick thrusts of
enemy, and in breaking the picks. Picks were also warded off v

hields. Another weapon, probably of Javanese origin, was a long
amboo with rotan thorns tied to its end. This was used to catch the
nemy or lacerate his skin. In Java the weapon was used to catch
ieves and "amoks".

Before the days of Mohammedan influence the people of Lampong
ere head-hunters, and this trait persisted until stopped by the Dutch.

Society.

Government. — The territory of Lampong is divided into five
rovinces whose names are taken from the rivers and bays of the sea
1 which they border.

Each of these provinces is again divided into smaller districts
lled mega (corresponding to the Batak word "marga"). Each mega
inhabited by a patrilineal sib under its own chief. The mega takes
s name from the sib which lives in it. The same system holds in
alembang, showing that the word "marga" originally had territorial
gnificance, and was not merely a genealogical term as it is at present
nong the Bataks.

The mega chief is called tuan ratu, datu, or sultan. Some take the
le of umpu. This alone is a Malaysian name, indicating a male or
male ancestor.

Since the people of Lampong compensate their proverbial laziness
assuming a vanity surpassing that of all the other natives of the
rchipelago (if such a thing is possible), they fell an easy prey to the
ltans of Bantam, who sold titles to the district chiefs in return
r yearly charges of pepper and other valuable gifts. Such chiefs
ho were recognized by Bantam are called pangerang or kjai aria.

The title of pangerang is still common among the people of
mpong of the present day, being handed down in the male line.
me of the possessors have sunk, however, to the lowest degree of
verty due to intemperance and loose living. In the present degener-
Lampong certain of the village chiefs also have assumed titles
ove those of the pangerang's, although this is flying in the face of
adat. Some of the titles are distinctly blasphemous, as Allah-bidjel,
he real God". Another title reads in bad Arabic: "Prince Gabriel,
favorite of the High God, who is accustomed to discuss his affairs
th God, to sleep with the angels, yes, and but a step further and
would be like God himself!"

At present inherited titles seldom are used excepting when chie‹ levy fines on guilty people.

Each district in Lampong contains a number of villages, ti‹ seldom more than ten. Each village is subdivided into hamlets, tumpu or suku. The hamlets may originally have been but four in numbe‹ but now count ten, twelve or more. The increase in the number ‹ hamlets is often due to the desire to rule of the elder brother of tl‹ kapala suku (the head of the old hamlet). When a man takes oth‹ members of his genealogy away from the old hamlet in order to for‹ a new, he has to obtain the consent of the village head, and mu‹ likewise pay the other hamlet heads. Hamlets exist which conta‹ only one house and a ruler who rules over his intimate family.

The village itself is governed by the head of the oldest suk‹ called kapala sukutoho. This ruler, however, is not independent, b‹ is under the orders of the mega chief, the tuan ratu.

The succession to office of a suku head goes to the next elde‹ brother. If there are no brothers, the office goes to the oldest son of‹ legal wife; or if such a man fails, then the son of an illegal wife will c‹ While the rightful ruler is alive, the man who is to succeed him h‹ the title of panjiembang, or secretary. On succession to office the ne‹ ruler has some karabau killed and gives a feast to the natives of t‹ village.

Succession to office for the sib or town chief is governed by t‹ same rule of seniority as for a hamlet head. In the same way t‹ oldest hamlet in a village furnishes the village chief, and the olde‹ village in the district the sib chief.

The tradition which accounts for the territorial and sib divisi‹ in Lampong runs as follows:

"The Lampong people are the descendants of a certain man nam‹ Lampong. He and his two brothers, Madjapahit and Sunda, lived ‹ the present site of Belalau. As the family grew larger it split u‹ and one part settled in Mura Dua and Kaju Agung (Palembang‹ while another portion spread over the present Lampong territo‹ A people called the Buwai Sumbing (descendants of Sumbing) we‹ met with in the Lampong district, and these were driven out.

"Gradually the chief tribes divided in the course of their wa‹ derings, forming new tribes (kabuwajan or buwai). The territe‹ occupied by a tribe was called mega."

Under Bantam rule the pangerang's or sib heads received at t‹

ime of their accession to office certain gifts and insignia from the avanese sultan. Among these gifts were patents of office (piagem) 1ade of copper, sometimes set with silver rims; outfits of Javanese lothing such as are worn at court; and weapons consisting of cannons, rises and pikes. All these gifts were handed down in the family.

Lampong chiefs also had outward insignia of office, the origin f which is not fully known. These insignia were the pepadon, the asako, and the lawangkori.

During their stay in Bantam the Lampong chiefs propably had oticed that the Javanese princes had the right to sit higher than the ommon people, so they copied the custom and introduced the throne-ke pepadon.

The pepadon is in the form of a four cornered bench, led up to y four solid steps, and made of a single piece of solid and very ubstantial wood. It is rarely more than nine or ten inches high, four et long and three broad. When chiefs are raised to this throne they re obliged to give a feast. When not in use the pepadon is kept in ιe communal house. It is used but once by its owner, and no one lse is allowed to sit upon it under penalty of paying a fine.

Not only the sib chiefs have pepadons, but in imitation the town nd hamlet chiefs also make use of these thrones. There is a difference 1 rank and privileges between owners of the various kinds of pepa-ons, and one can advance from one class of pepadon to another by urchase. If a chief inherits a pepadon he is able to ask a higher ride-price for his daughter, to receive part of the presents given by very new chief who wishes to buy a pepadon, and, under former ative rule, he received fines from breakers of the adat.

A few of the many minor privileges accorded to pepadon owners ιay be mentioned here. The owner of a sib pepadon has the right to se a white parasol with fringes. At festivals he may wear a white iece of cloth over his ordinary trousers. His female relatives on their ay to feasts have a piece of white linen in form of a half moon rried before them. The possessor of a town pepadon uses a yellow ιrasol and a yellow piece of cloth, while the owner of a hamlet padon uses red as his color. There are certain other rights which ry according to region, such as the right to push copper plates ong the ground at feasts. In one region the wife of the owner of sib pepadon has the right to stretch out her legs in front of her ιsband when she is being carried in a sedan chair to a feast.

The second of the insignia of chiefs is the sasako, a beautifull
carved armchair, which serves to distinguish those of lesser ran
from those who own a pepadon. The chiefs who have not sufficier
means to be raised to the pepadon are allowed to sit in such arm
chairs after they have given the required feasts. The sasako, like th
pepadon, is kept in the communal house.

The lawangkori is a variety of covered triumphal arch wit
beautifully decorated doors and woodwork. In some districts (
Lampong it is partially made of baked stones. Figures of porcelai
decorated with chalk are set into it. A person, usually someone less
than a chief, attains honor by possessing such an arch. The lawang
kori is placed in the neighborhood of the house of the possesso
Anyone visiting the house, and especially brides and bridegrooms, ar
allowed to use the arch if they pay a karabau or its worth in gold
the owner. The owner himself goes through it when he has performe
a "good deed", such as avenging a blood feud, or when he has con
back from Bantam and has received a new title or a memorial piec

The arches are said to antedate Mohammedan influence, an
Van Hoevell in fact saw one which was decorated with carved huma
heads made of wood.

There can be no doubt that the arch is older than the throne
chair, the latter insignia coming from Bantam. The arch, on the oth
hand, is a substitute for the megalith, which, as Heine-Geldern h
shown, is erected by the people of Southern Asia in connection with t
giving of feasts and the sacrifice of cattle. It is usually the most prim
tive Malaysians, such as the Mentawei Islanders, who lacked catt
sacrifice, megalithic monuments, and head-hunting. Feasts they h
in common with certain of the people of the Philippines, as me
sacrificial feasts, and not feasts for the purpose of social ostentatio

Feasts. In Lampong all important occasions are heralded
feasts. Feasts are held at the cicumcision of boys, at teeth filing, wh
a girl has her ear lobes pierced, when she marries, and when, if she
a woman of rank, she first leaves the house after marriage. Th
greatest of feasts, however, is held when a chief is elevated to t
pepadon. When a hamlet is new and has not as yet had a chi
promoted in this way, the chief upon his elevation is compelled to p
forty reals to the head of the village. This sum is divided among
those present at the feast and among the chiefs possessing pepador
The least number of karabau that a chief can have slaughtered on su

occasion is ten, if he gave less he would be made fun of for being ١or. Chiefs who have many subjects slaughter at least thirty karabau, ١d sometimes more, and give to each of the other chiefs present a live ١rabau as gift.

A chief whose ancestors had been raised to the pepadon can ١cceed to office with the mere giving of a meal at which one karabau slaughtered. But if his means permit he will slaughter at least one ٥re karabau than the man whose office he inherits, even though his ١edecessor was his own father. This is done to show that he is richer ١n his predecessor.

A large feast was formerly held when a person returned from ١ntam with a title and heirlooms. Usually a slave was bound to a ١ke and killed upon such an occasion. Likewise the recovery of a ١rson considered hopelessly sick was made a festive occasion.

Tournaments are held after feasts, and dancing which lasts to ١dnight. Then comes cock fighting and gambling.

The Dutch government at the present time is trying to modify the ١stom of "naik pepadon" (ascending the pepadon), because of the ١rge amount of time, money, and cattle consumed in the ceremony.

Laws. Mohammedan law is unknown in the region, in spite of the ١ct that the people are nominally Mohammedan. The native laws ١e founded on ancient customs, on regulations obtained from the ١ntam rulers, and on books of Madjapahit (Javanese) origin, called ١adjassu".

Punishments consist entirely of blood revenge and the payment of ١eregild, corporal punishment being unknown. Originally fines were ١id solely to the injured party and his sib, but under Bantam influence ١e chiefs obtained the privilege of levying fines for "the benefit of the ١te" (i. e. their own pockets).

If one man wrongs another he is fined and has to pay the injured ١rty a sum of money which is in proportion to the rank of the ١grieved person. This payment is called "penêpung", and is used ١ the purchase of a buffalo, goat or chicken. Then the animal is ١aughtered and a conciliation feast is held between the two parties and ١tween their families.

If a free person kills the head of his kawubajan or tribe, or a blood ١ative of this chief, the male relatives of the murdered person demand ١e life of the murderer from his near kin. But only among the wilder ١bes is this demand granted. Usually a chief from a neighboring

18

kabuwajan is called in as mediator. The guilty person, or his neare
relative in case the criminal has fled, is sentenced to pay the "bangu
to the relatives of the murdered man. In case the brother of the deceas
has succeeded to office, the weregild is set at 1,000 reals; if a so
800 reals. Besides the money a quantity of goods is paid as fir
including white linen, karabau, and two human heads, the fresher t
better. Likewise an "irawan", a living person, is bound to a stake a
killed by people who dance around him armed with picks and kris
Then the blood of the sacrifice is mixed with the blood of a buffa
and, diluted with water, is used by the wronged parties to wash the
selves free from the shame put upon them. The body of the slave wl
served as irawan is buried in the usual fashion. The two heads a
first used as foot stools for the injured parties at the time of a gr
feast at the communal house, and then buried at the feet of t
murdered man.

This description of the taking of weregild (as given by V
Hoëvell in 1852) clearly shows analogy to Batak custom, and substa
tiates the claim that the people of Lampong originally were of t
same origin as the Batak. Whether the bound prisoners actually ev
were eaten in Lampong, as among the Bataks, is a question that cann
be answered.

If a person of rank is murdered by a man of another tribe it lea
to war. The matter should be settled by the chief of a neighboring tri
If the murderer is of low rank, he sometimes is treated as "irawan
and his body, taking the place of the two heads required as weregil
is buried at the feet of the murdered man.

The greatest shame which can befall a family is to have one of
members murdered by a slave. In such a case the older members of t
family go to a distant place in order to purify themselves of the sta
This purification is effected through slaughter, often of unarmed me
women, and children. The heads are then brought home in triump
If the murder was done secretly, and the criminal not found, t
relatives further freed themselves from their shame by killing a sla
usually a decrepit one.

In regions near Bantam the people feign the irawan. They take o
of their own slaves and pretend to thrust and strike him dead. Th
they sell him to the highest bidder. They are afraid of Bant
punishment.

If the head of a hamlet kills one of his own subjects, he is broug o trial by the heads of the other hamlets in the village and fined ccording to the rank of the murdered person. If one kills a member f one's immediate family, however, such as parent, wife, or child, or slave for whom one has paid, there is no punishment. The person ho has done such a thing is reproached with the fact that he has amaged and brought shame on himself.

Incest and adultery are punished by beheading and drowning. here is no punishment for rape, however. The man either marries the oman, and, if necessary, keeps her as his slave, or else sends her to er parents and troubles no more about her.

In case of theft the injured party demands the simple or double eturn of the article stolen. But if the thief refuses to return the article, he case is brought before the chief. If a decision then is rendered gainst the thief, and he is unable to pay, he becomes the slave of the erson he has wronged.

The evidence of two people of unimpeachable honesty is sufficient or conviction of crime. While the witnesses testify under oath, the oran is rarely made use of for the purpose. Usually the oaths are worn to on the graves of forefathers.

Where there are no witnesses the spirits are called upon to decide y the use of ordeal. One method is to cut the head off a rooster and ee which of the two contending parties the chicken approaches in its eath agonies. Another method is to engage youths to dive under ater in order to see which can hold out longest. Or the accused erson can be made to pick out some object out of boiling oil or water, r pass his tongue over a glowing iron.

Inheritance. If a native of Lampong has more than one wife he ames as heir the eldest son born of his wife of noblest birth. The man able to give another son, not of noble birth, this position by holding a ast. The heir receives half of the movable goods of the father, while e other sons receive the remaining half. Immovable property, such fields, form the communal possessions of the family and every ember shares in their use. The right to alienate these rests with the dest son.

In general, if a man leaves no sons, the whole of his inheritance lls to his elders, or if these are dead, to his elder brother. Should is brother beget a son by one of the wives of the deceased, this son comes heir to the property. If the brother obtains no son through one the wives of the deceased, the son of one of his own wives succeeds.

When a son inherits, and he has wealth enough, he marries two women of equal rank. The son by first marriage he names heir of his deceased father, and the son of his second his own heir. However anyone may adopt a stranger, call him his legal father, brother, or child, and name him heir. A feast must be given at the adoption.

Thus a grandson is the natural heir of his grandfather. This is not altogether an advantage, for the estate includes the grandmother and other women left by the grandfather. The man does not marry his grandmother, however, and usually she dies a widow. Nevertheless the man often takes the remaining of his grandfather's widows (though not concubines) as wives. If there are no male descendants the property and wives go to the head of the hamlet in which the house is situated

If a man marries into a family in the ambil anak form, his wife and not he enjoys the property rights and the rights to the children

Marriage. According to tradition marriage was at first forbidden to all members of the same sib (mega). Later this prohibition only extended to members of the same village, and then to the same hamlet With the growth of civilization and the influence of Islam these rules became more and more lax, so that now only close blood relatives are prohibited marriage. We are not informed about the occurrence or non-occurrence of cousin marriage. Infringement of the marriage ada is punished by a money fine paid to the mega chiefs, and the transgressor must give a feast.

It is not easy to state the age at which it is customary for the people of Lampong to marry, as this depends mostly on the amount of wealth owned by the man's elders and relatives. If a man has no money with which to pay the bride-price the father of the girl demands, and there are no married brothers, nephews, or grandfathers by whose death he inherits wives, he usually remains unmarried, and dies without leaving children. This very often happens among the people of Lampong. Because of this fact the natives have the joking curse word "matlimahanai", "Die a bachelor!"

The conventional, though not the usual, form of marriage is that which is arranged beforehand by the parents of both sides and is publicly anounced to the inhabitants of the hamlet. This kind of marriage is called "mingan-mawaai", that is, "the good marriage".

In preparation for this form of marriage wealthy people sometime plight their children while they are still very young. This often is misfortune for the women, as divorce is unknown in Lampong. The room does not suffer if he is dissatisfied with the marriage, he takes one or more extra wives or concubines.

The bride-price, called djudjur by the Malays, is called serhoh in Lampong, while daw is the name of the gold and goods of which it is composed. After the payment of the bride-price the woman is accepted for good by the man and his family. She becomes the property of the man, and according to the adat, the marriage can only be dissolved by death. Under the levirate and sororate rules, even the death of the husband or wife does not put an end to the marriage contract, since this is a bond between the two families.

The bride must bring an outfit with her to the marriage. If she does not do so, the bride-price is reduced. In case of marriage between persons of highest rank, the dowry is worth about as much as the bride-price.

Van Hoëvell claims that purchase marriage probably was copied from the natives of Bantam under Mohammedan influence, and that the ordinary native practices elopement with the consent of the parents, this being the cheaper manner of tying the nuptial knot.

Marriage which is arranged by the parents, but is not publicly announced, is called "sabombangan kiempunan", that is, "abduction by previous arrangement". The preparations for the conventional form of marriage are observed, but some weeks or days before the wedding the girl is abducted by her lover. This saves the expense of a wedding feast.

The youth, after having eloped, conceals the girl in his father's dwelling or in the house of the chief person of his hamlet; the latter is the case if the girl is of higher rank than the man. After a few days or weeks have gone by, the father of the girl comes, at the head of a well armed band, equipped as for strife. The natives of the hamlet, being forewarned of the approach of the war party, go outside and entreat them to come to a temporary halt. The father, who pretends to be consumed with wrath, is offered a buffalo and goat as tokens of the price that will be paid for his daughter.

Then the father of the girl is taken inside the communal house, where he fights a sham battle with the father of the youth, or a substitute of equal rank. As an added touch, two roosters are made to fight at the same time. The rooster belonging to the bridegroom's father is defeated, and this is taken as a sign that the father should give in.

The two fathers finally enter the public room, where the bride-price is discussed. A certain amount of the money is returned, so that the father-in-law can supply clothing to his daughter-in-law. After this matter has been settled, the assembled people consume a meal, and the bridal pair are bound in marriage.

The wedding ceremony is conducted, in the main, in Mohammedan fashion. The village chief performs the rite. The bride and groom sit next to one another in the presence of their elders and relatives. Then the bridegroom lays his left leg over the knees of the bride. This is called "tiendes-siela", and comprises the entire manner in which the pair symbolically are bound together. The bride and groom also give one another marital names.

Capture marriage (nakat) can take place without the consent of the woman's family. The man then sends some presents by a go-between to the parents of the woman, so that they know where to find their daughter. In this case, if the offered bride-price is too low, or the abductor of too humble a rank, the father can take his daughter back. However, if there be doubt as to whether or not the daughter has still maintained her virtue, and there usually is some doubt, the marriage is allowed to stand.

In Lampong, especially where Islam has made little headway, the intercourse between the youths of both sexes is very free. This gives occasion for many elopements, particularly among people of lower class. After marriage, however, the women are very carefully guarded.

In the ambil anak form of marriage no bride-price is paid, and the man comes to live with his wife's family. The husband then receives a dowry which is in proportion to his rank, i. e. his pepadon. This variety of marriage usually takes place when the father has but one daughter and wishes to prevent the family from dying out. Frequently a relative is taken as son-in-law. If the husband receives no dowry he remains a member of his own family, but on receipt of the dowry he is adopted into the wife's family and is in position to inherit from his father-in-law.

After a man dies his wife is usually inherited by the elder brother, but if he agrees the widow may go instead to a younger brother. If the widow is childless the younger brother may either take her himself, or else marry her out. In the latter case he can ask only a small sum as bride-price.

If a woman dies, the man has the right to marry one of her

ounger sisters. He pays half the usual bride-price if his first wife died hildless, but the full price if his wife had left him one or more children.

While the sib system is very degenerated in Lampong, there is still vidence, such as the above, which shows that marriage here, as else-where, is regarded as an exchange between two families or sibs. Thus 1e bride-price is redeemed if the wife gives birth to a child. In the mbil anak marriage, the wife's family must pay, since they are urchasing a new member and the man's family losing a member. It is urther significant that when a woman marries outside of her village, ot only must the man pay the bride-price, but he must also compensate 1e village chief. Evidently, in this case, there is less hope of getting ack a new member into the wife's family.

The people follow Mohammedan law regarding polygyny, and a 1an is allowed four wives and as many concubines as he wishes. 'illage chiefs sometimes have as many as thirteen or fourteen wives nd concubines. The first wife is usually the chief wife, and rules over 1e others.

A marriage is only fully cemented when the wife has given birth) a child. Before this time the woman, if she be of noble birth, refrains rom showing herself to people other than inmates of the house. After 1e birth of the child the wife gives a feast and goes out in state. This s called "turun di wai", to go to the river.

Circumcision. — The children of wealthy people are circumcised ometime between their seventh and tenth year. Poorer people have 1eir children circumcised whenever they have enough money to hold a east, sometimes not at all. Girls are often allowed to remain without eing incised. The Orang Abung of the interior originally were not rcumcised, so the custom here may be entirely Mohammedan in origin.

Burial. — The dead are buried in Mohammedan fashion. The emetery of most towns is divided into as many plots as the town has amlets, so that each hamlet may have its own burial place.

Conclusion. — The civilization of Lampong appears a curious mix-1re of very primitive culture, similar to that of the Bataks, with an verlay of very much higher Bantam veneer. The higher culture is 1own by the clothing, house building, and the high development of eaving among the natives. On the other hand, the Lampong social rganization is in many respects similar to that found among the ataks. The people likewise have maintained their primitive Hindu art f writing, although this is merely used by the youth for the purpose

of writing love letters to one another. The religion of the region
nominally Mohammedan.

The Orang Abung.

The Orang Abung, probably the original natives of Lampon;
were once a wild nomadic people, without settled habitat or agricultur
who lived from hunting, fishing, and eating roots and herbs. The
first settled on the Abung River, and took their name from a mountai
in the region, Gunang Abung. Or perhaps the mountain and the riv
were named after the people. The language spoken by the Orang Abun
is a form of the Lampong language. These mountaineers were former!
much more numerous than they are at present.

At one time head-hunting was very prevalent here. It is said
have been the custom, that when a band of warriors returned from a
expedition, the young women met them on the way. Those who returne
with heads were courted by the women, but those who came back emp
handed were not even allowed to enter the village.

The skulls of the slain were put to double usage at the weddin;
The bridegroom placed the bride-price, of gold and silver, in a sku
and handed it to the father of the bride, and the couple drank pal
wine out of the skull. A marriage without this rite would not have bee
considered legal, nor would it have given the bride the status of
married woman.

The Orang Abung have kept longer than other Lampong peop
to the religion of their forefathers. The native religion, however, ha
never been described. It is known that pagan rites were observed
graves in the name of Mohammed.

In the main the people now have the same customs as the mo;
civilized natives of Lampong and are being absorbed by them.

The Orang Abung are divided into four tribes or sibs, and ma
riages take place much as on the coast. Before marriage there is fre
dom between the sexes, and a special corner is built in the family hou
where the young men can visit the girls and sing love songs. But th
freedom seldom leads to licentiousness. In the wedding ceremony th
groom lays his leg over the knees of the bride, and they give one anoth
marital names.

Polygyny is practiced, tokens of rank are bought, and feasts a:
held as in the lowlands.

PART II. PRIMITIVE PEOPLES.

The Kubu.

Introduction. — The Kubu live in the partly swampy stretch between the Musi, the Rawas, the Tembesi and the Batang Hari. At his date practically all the Kubu, willingly or unwillingly, are united and registered in villages (dusun's). In 1907 there were 7,590 Kubu distributed in five sibs (marga's). They are of a poor physical type, specially the women. While most of them have been converted to slam, this conversion has been in name only. They have not been willing to give up their former food habits, and remain omnivorous, eating all kinds of flesh, even though it be partially decomposed. Then also the males are not circumcised in the Mohammedan fashion, but are incised according to native custom. The girls are not incised at all.

The Kubu divide their history as follows: —

1. The ancient history. From the time of the Orang Bari to the coming of Ratu Senuhun.
2. The modern history. From the time of the coming of Ratu Senuhun until the Kubu came into contact with the government.
3. Recent history. From the time in which the government took charge to the present exploitation of the land for oil.

The Kubu relate that in very ancient times the coast of Sumatra was regularly visited by pirates, who brought their families with them. t once happened that a pirate brother and sister committed incest, and hat the sister in consequence became pregnant. The names of this pair are unknown, because the Kubu have a taboo on the names of ncestors. The pair was accursed by the pirates, abandoned in the rush, and founded the first Kubu settlement on the Lalan River.

The people who descended from this pair were called the Orang Bari, the "people of the good old times".

The modern history of the Kubu begins to be authentic, and takes lace in the first half of the 17th century, when Ratu Senuhun came to he people from Palembang. This prince made the wild people his ubjects. The copper "piagems" which he gave them are still handed own in families.

The Kubu at the time of Malay supremacy never came into direct ontact with the ruling race, but traded by "silent barter". That is, the

Kubu left products from the brush on the ground and retired, returning to gather up what the Malays had given in payment. Naturally the trade was never entirely fair to the more primitive population. This kind of silent barter lasted in the region until forty years ago. The Malays were seen, but never the Kubu.

The Kubu were ruled by their native chiefs, dipati. These were simply patriarchs who led the search for brush products.

In spite of their lack of direct contact with the more civilized race the Kubu picked up the language, the social organization, and the religion, of the Palembang Malay. They delayed changing their mode of life, however, and continued as wanderers in the brush until compelled to settle down and take up agriculture by the Dutch. Even now the Kubu is averse to regular work and to bathing.

This final change in the life of the Kubu started when the Dutch government in Palembang took matters in hand, and installed Malay tax collectors who acted under government supervision. Brush products were collected as taxes. In 1898 petroleum was discovered in Palembang, and since then the Kubu has learned the use of money.

The origin of the words Kubu, Lubu, and Ulu is unknown. Among the village dwellers, Kubu means people who eat everything, including unclean foods, who do not live in houses, and whose bodies are very unclean due to the Kubu's aversion for water: Thus people of the lowest character. On account of the stigma attached to their name the civilized Kubu do not like to be called by it, but prefer to be called Orang Dara or Orang Laut, land dweller or river dweller. In 1906 Van Dongen came into contact with isolated Kubus living in the swamps of the Ridan River who fully lived up to the title of "Kubu", as used by their more civilized brethren.

Economic life. — The primitive Kubu build pile houses, pondok consisting of small low platforms, without walls, and with leaf roofs. Four poles first are driven into the ground to act as corner posts. Four cross beams are then attached to these, and ten to twenty beams laid across as flooring. A loose leaf roof is placed as shelter about three feet above the floor. Rotan or liane is used as binder. No furniture, decorations, or amulets are made use of in the house. Men, women, children, and the invariable dog, creep at night into this scanty shelter.

Usually from three to five such houses are placed together in the brush in some high, dry place. This scattering of houses furnishes a Kubu village, and is called sirup.

The sole utensil kept by the Kubu in his house is the bamboo ooker, sometimes filled with water. When outside the house, at work the jungle, the Kubu carries the carrying basket on his back.

Men and women wear rolled up tapa cloth around their loins. hey neither decorate their clothing nor themselves in any way. hildren go entirely naked.

The Kubu uses a long wooden throwing spear as a weapon. With is he is able to kill all animals and catch his favorite food, the turtle abi). In catching turtles he uses the blunt end of the spear, on hich a long iron nail is attached.

Musical instruments of every kind, as well as the art of dancing, re unknown to this people.

The wild Kubu have no rice, and are unwilling to eat it. They ill not eat the flesh of cats, tigers, or elephants. They eat wild igs, all sorts of apes, and a turtle uneatable to the Malays. They are pecially fond of bananas, when they can get them. They further eat uits, earth roots, and worms, lizards, and snakes. The Kubu digs r worms and tubular plants with a splinter of sharpened bamboo, r a parang imported from the Malays. All foods are held above e fire, roasted a little and then eaten. The people do not use salt, ut the men have now learned to smoke tobacco.

The Kubu never comes into contact with water his life long, with e exception of a few raindrops which he is unable to avoid. Water cold and makes him sick. When he is dirty or covered with mud, e wipes off the mud with a parang or a bamboo stick. Owing to is aversion, he smells badly and constantly itches from skin disease. he Kubu is said to show great aptitude in avoiding all wet places hen going through the brush. Since he is accustomed to live in the rk brush, he also has a dislike for sunlight. Women never cut their air, but the men clip theirs with a parang. Neither sex comb their air or keep it in order.

A Ridan Kubu remains at the most a month in one place, some-mes only a week; then as the woods around his dwelling offers too tle food, or there is not enough fish in the river or swamp, and he is able to obtain his favorite turtle, he moves.

Along with the monotony and simplicity of their material culture, e Kubu have also a lack of social and religious development. What aboration they do have is of late Malaysian origin.

Social organization. While the settled Kubu are now divided in
sibs, in imitation of their neighbors, the wild Kubu have only tl
family organization. Nothing is known about their original laws
incest or relationship system. Schebesta writes that at present all b
closest relatives can marry, and that there are no avoidance custom

Young men and women run around together in the brush ar
make connections which lead to marriage. The girls marry short
after puberty. There is no ceremony about the matter, but the pa
simply goes to their elders and announce their intentions. The olde
man of the two families performs the marriage rite. The bridal coup
sit next to one another on the ground, the bride to the left of tl
groom. The old man asks the bride if she will have the groom, ar
she replies that she will. Then the old man makes the announceme
that if anyone should meet the pair together, he should not distu:
them, because they are married. After this the gathering is brok(
up and everyone goes his way. There is no acclamation or feastin
and anything like a bride-price is unknown. The Kubu say th
formerly the married pair took hold of each other by the little fing
of the right hand as a sign that they were united.

Among the more civilized Kubu, the Klumpang Kubu, marria(
also is performed by an elder member of the two families, and tl
elders have first to give their consent, but never interfere when ;
elopement has taken place. As a sign of marriage the couple ea
rice out of the same banana leaf dish.

Probably in imitation of the Malays, a Kubu is allowed as ma)
wives as he likes. Formerly some had three, but now none ha
more than two. If a Kubu has two wives, he makes his shelter som
what larger and sleeps in the center with a wife on either side.

Divorce is utterly without ceremony, and either the man c;
desert the women or the women the man. One young wild Kubu n
with by Van Dongen was deserted twice by the same woman. Neith
of the two, however, was able to find another mate, as there we
no more young Kubu left in the region. In case of divorce the childr
go with the parent they prefer, but young children naturally rema
with their mother.

When a woman is pregnant she is forbidden the sight of a de
body, an elephant, or a karabau. The birth must take place in t
brush. The woman is aided at this time by another woman or
her husband.

285

The new born child is not washed, but is cleaned with leaves
and tapa cloth. As soon as the mother can walk, which is sometimes
at once, and sometimes on the day following the birth, she goes to
seek food in the brush, either alone or accompanied by her husband.

A Kubu does not like it when his wife gives birth to twins or
triplets, as then he has to work harder for their support. He claims
that the woman is like a goat to produce so many offspring at once,
and, likely as not, he deserts her on the spot.

The children remain with their parents, dwell and dig roots with
them, until they are ten to twelve years of age. Then they are thought
capable of caring for themselves, wear their first loin cloths, and
build special shelters next to those of their parents. From this time on
they seek their food and no longer eat with their elders. The bond
between the parents and the children is now broken, and a child can
either wander off by himself in the brush or remain with his family
until he marries.

The Kubu have no incision or circumcision. In this regard they
are like most other Veddoid peoples, with the exception of the
Australians.

Every Kubu has a name, but the name is known only to the
people of the same "sirup". People of another family are not known
by name, and are referred to as "people of this or that little river".
The natives of one settlement come rarely into contact with those of
another, as there are no feasts, puberty ceremonies, or other communal
gatherings.

Naturally there are no wars between the various Kubu communities, or with outsiders. The civilized Kubu, however, have learned
from the Malays the art of extracting weregild by threat of blood
revenge.

If a Kubu suddenly dies, or if anyone is so sick that it is certain
he is about to die, the entire family runs away, leaving the dead or
dying person in his dwelling, and builds a new shelter in a distant
place. No more trouble is taken about the sick person. In like manner
if the Kubu find a spot where someone has died, or the remains of
a dead person, they run away as quickly as possible. The act of
running away from a dead person is called "melangan".

Even among the more civilized Kubu, when a person is sick, and
it is believed that he will not recover, the family flee to the brush.
If it is a child who is dying, only the parents remain with it. It is

thought that the sight of a dying person brings misfortune. Whe a sick relative has been abandoned, however, someone in the famil usually a brother, returns to the house after three days. If the sic person is still alive, attempts are made to cure him.

If the sick person is dead, the investigator gives immediate noti to the women and children in the brush. Then the family comes bac to the house and strews rice around it.

After this the body is wrapped in a customary cloth, laid on ladder and brought to the grave, which is about three feet deep. Foc is placed on the grave, and the ceremony is ended. Other means disposing of the body among the civilized Kubu include placing it a hollow tree, or leaving it in the hut and setting fire to the buildin

At the present time, after the death of her husband, the wido takes to the brush (melangan) for three months. After three montl in the brush the widow (or widower) may return and marry. If tl widow marries before this time she has to pay a fine to the relativ of the deceased for adultery.

Religion. — In spite of a rather considerable amount of info mation which has been gathered concerning Kubu religion, we actual know little about the original beliefs of this people. Kubu shamanis is of interest, as it shows that these people were capable of takir from the Malays a highly evolved practice and doctrine long befo they cared to adopt much in the way of material culture. Still the is nothing Kubu about the shamanism; it is Hindu and Malay.

Forbes, an English writer who visited the Kubu in 1885, write "They seem to have no idea of a state after death. They say, 'Wh we are dead, we are dead.'" Still Forbes knew that the Kubu avoid the dead, for he writes, "In their wild state they leave their de: unburied in the spot where they died, giving the spot ever after a wi berth." In like manner Hagen writes that the Kubu do not belie in a soul which survives after death, for the Kubu abandon th dead to the wild animals. Yet elsewhere this writer states that t Kubu attribute all sickness to evil ghosts!

At the present time the civilized Kubu shaman (malim) h acquired an elaborate Hindu philosophy of life. According to V Dongen, his belief is briefly as follows:

Every person is made up of sipat (material), roh (spirit, thinki matter), and njawa (health producing matter).

The material body is equated with sipat. The soul consists of njawa, or breath, which does not leave the body until the man dies, and of roh. Roh, the spirit, or power of thought, is able to leave the body and wander around, as in dreams.

At death the njawa and the roh go back to heaven (sorga) and are there received by God (Radja Njawa) for good or evil. Radja Njawa can be translated, according to Van Dongen, as All Spirit, World Spirit, or World Power.

The Kubu claim that the first shaman, called malim kujug, attained the title and powers of dukun, or ghost exorciser, by bringing his dog (kujug) back to life. Then every district sent a man to study under the malim kujug, so that each district acquired its own head malim. The present word "malim" is a shortened form of the phrase "dukun bermalim".

The office of head malim, as far as possible, goes from father to eldest son. At present the head malim is called pengasu (asu is dog). The head malim's act as chief officials at exorcisms, religious ceremonies, and important séances. The other people who assist (usually pupils) are ordinary malim's.

In the same manner as the malim kujug was assisted by his wife when he brought the dog back to life again (by stamping the evil spirits out of the animal), so now every malim pengasu has his wife assist him at ceremonies. She has the title of ulubalang.

When anyone is sick, the malim may be called upon to exorcise (bermalim) the patient. There are various kinds of exorcism formulae (songs, called saleh) which are used, but the séances do not differ very much from one another.

The day before the cure everything has to be prepared, and the necessary food obtained. All food is brought in "sevens", that is, seven articles at a time.

The malim, his assistants, and the ulubalang, eat nothing during the night of the exorcism, but merely smoke and chew betel while the cure is being enacted. When the others eat, they sit apart. The head malim, and usually his assistants as well, shut all the orifices of their bodies while they are performing their office. They may hear nothing, see nothing, neither yawn nor have stomach ache, while concentrating. It is also for this reason that the séance is held at night.

Towards sundown the head malim and his assistants purify themselves by bathing. Then they rub their bodies with lime juice.

The cure can take place in the house of the sick person if there is room enough, but often it is enacted in the balai, the communal house. Cylindrical drums, or tambourines, are used as music. These are struck with the open hand.

The séance comprises the rendering of thirty-three saleh's (songs) The final two are not strictly necessary, and are not given at smalle gatherings. A saleh is made in the following manner:

1. The malim's first recite the essential content of the saleh.
2. The tambourines are struck and the people stand up. This i followed by a round dance, in which all present at firs partake, but which is ended by the malim's alone.
3. The dance becomes wilder and wilder and the malim's fa into a swoon.
4. The malim's are awakened by being rapped on their hand The head malim then blesses the sick and the public, and give a philosophical account of the saleh which was given.

While the head malim is in trance he is able to see the soul the sick person in a tree, or on the roof of a house, entirely or partiall under the influence of the evil ghosts. The healing spirit (the sou of the first malim of the race, malim kujug) takes up his abod within the head malim after the twenty-fifth saleh, and remains the end of the cure. The ghost, however, does not speak throug the lips of the malim. Evidently the Kubu have gone as far as the could in their endeavor to imitate actual shamanism, but have faile in the crucial point.

Van Dongen writes that the Kubu have no folk-lore. In th respect they resemble the Veddas of Ceylon. These people also, acquiring Singhalese culture, have lost their original language an folk-lore.

In conclusion, it must be obvious that the Kubu are a degenera race. There is no reason to doubt that their culture at one time wa as complex at least as that of the Sakai of the Malay Peninsula. being pushed back into the marshy regions of Palembang, and being surrounded by Malaysians on whom they were in part parasiti and from whom they gradually acquired a foreign language an culture, they lost much of their original knowledge and arts. Whi at times it is dangerous to use biological analogies in dealing wi human culture, there is no doubt that a parasitic people are just

able to degeneration as a parasitic plant or animal. The Mentawei
Islanders are likewise parasitic on the Malays for iron. But these
latter people are geographically more favorable situated. Hence while
they acquired what they needed from strangers, they rigorously excluded
all that would endanger their own national existence.

The Orang Mamaq.

The Orang Mamaq are people of probable Veddoid origin who
live in the territory of Indragiri on the right side of the Kuantan
River, and are separated from the Kubu by the Sultanate of Djambi.
In 1880 there were 20,000 of these natives left.

About the middle of the 14th century, two sibs (suku's) of
Minangkabau people settled at the mouth of the Indragiri River. They
brought their matrilineal customs with them. The *jus connubii* existed
between the two sibs. At the end of the 15th or the beginning of
the 16th century, a prince from Johor in Malacca came to head the
Minangkabau people of Indragiri. Slowly the Johor influence spread,
and colonists from Johor came into the region.

Under Johor régime the matrilineal institutions of the region were
replaced by patrilineal; the democratic form of government by a
monarchy. The original Minangkabau dialect likewise changed to
Riouw-Lingga Malay. In the middle of the 16th century the conversion
of the people to Islam added its force in making the people patrilineal.
In spite of these strong patrilineal influences, however, the Malays
of Indragiri have maintained many matrilineal survivals in custom.
As Wilken has remarked, the "matriarchate" only occurs in its purest
form where Minangkabau Malay is spoken, and the Malays of this
region have lost this language.

While, therefore, the original Malay immigrants to Indragiri
have lost their matrilineal customs, they have transferred them to the
primitive Orang Mamaq, who have preserved both the original
Minangkabau language and "matriarchate". The Orang Mamaq
have not been converted to Islam. The name "mamaq" has reference
to the oldest brother of the wife, who is head of the family.

The entire people is divided into exogamous suku's, and descent
is counted in the female line from a tribal mother. All the members
of a suku live together in a family house, and are mutually responsible
for each other's actions. Marriage is monogamous.

A patih, or prince, heads all of the Orang Mamaq, while each su‍
is ruled by a panghulu. The patih formerly was responsible to Joh‍

The family houses of the Mamaq are pile dwellings. Rice ag‍
culture is practiced, but is said to be a recent innovation. The fo‍
eaten is mostly the product of hunting, fishing, or the jungle.

The lance and harpoon are used, but the blow-pipe is unknow‍
Spear and net are employed in fishing.

While weaving and pottery are unknown, the people are alrea‍
good workers in iron. They also work in rotan and weave baske‍
The bamboo flute, a Malay instrument, furnishes their music. Ta‍
is no longer worn, but cotton takes its place for loin cloths.

The Mamaq have more in the way of festivals than the Kub‍
A wedding is celebrated by a feast, and a large tribal feast is he‍
when the durian fruit is ripe. Cock fighting also takes place at th‍
time.

In religion the people resemble the settled Kubu. They ha‍
shamans like the Kubu, but the Mamaq shaman has learned to char‍
a fixed price for his cure.

The Sakai and Akit.

The Sakai live north of the Orang Mamaq, still however in t‍
alluvial coast plains, namely, in the Sultanate of Siak. They form t‍
large groups: the Batin Lima (the five tribes or sibs) and the Bat‍
Selapan (the eight tribes). The first group lives chiefly along t‍
upper stretches of the Mandau River, a tributary of the Siak Riv‍
while the second group lives on the upper Rokan River.

The Sakai are shy people, difficult to get into touch with. Mos‍
kowski has gathered practically all the information we have of the‍
They are of Veddoid origin, and in many respects similar to the Sak‍
of the Malay Peninsula. The Sakai of Sumatra, however, ha‍
received their language and matrilineal customs from the Minan‍
kabau who immigrated to the region in the 14th century. There is‍
tradition which relates that there was once a large Minangkab‍
kingdom on the Gassip River, a tributary of the Siak River, and th‍
the kingdom was overpowered by the Achehnese. The Sakai then fl‍
to the woods of the Mandau.

The Sakai do not like to be called by this name, but take‍
as an insult. They call themselves Orang Batin. The title Batin

orrowed from the Malays and assumed by a group of Sakai nobles
vith Malay titles.

Like the Mamaq the Sakai have borrowed freely from Malay
custom without being converted to Islam. They do not wish to give up
ating pork or dog meat, a favorite article of diet with them. They do
ot practice Mohammedan circumcision, but boys are incised at the
ge of thirteen, like the Bataks.

The tribes of Sakai are of nomadic culture, like all Veddoid
eople, and do not like agriculture. The Sultan of Siak has commanded
hem to plant rice, and once in a while punishes a man who has no
ield. It often happens that they sow rice, but do not reap it,
ince they are only commanded to sow, not to reap.

Each sib or suku has its own piece of land, however, where the
eople of the suku lay fields and gather brush products. The
3atin has a right to one tenth of the products. For their chief plant
f nourishment, the tapioca plant, the ground must be changed every
hree years. The Sakai also cultivate yams, taro, beans, pepper,
nelons, sugar cane, pineapple and bananas. Tobacco and betel they
uy from the Malays.

The only agricultural instrument used by the Sakai is the digging-
tick. In pre-agricultural times this stick was used to dig roots from
he ground. It is now used to make the holes in which the roots of
ultivated plants are laid.

In like manner the digging-stick was the primary form of the
pear. The Sakai still use the spear, but now they fashion a Malay
on point on its end. As among the Sakai of the Malay Peninsula,
o stone implements were made use of. Formerly wood and bamboo
vere used, and knives were make of bamboo splinters.

The Sakai have few domestic animals. They always owned the
og, and now they have a few half-tamed chickens.

The people support themselves mainly by hunting and fishing.
heir favorite food animal is the monkey, which they shoot with
low-gun and poisoned darts. Like the arrows of Mentawei, the darts
re poisoned with Antiaris toxicaria and a number of strychnine
lants. The wound is incised to make the animal eatable. While the
low-gun has almost disappeared from East Sumatra, it is the chief
eapon of the Dayaks of Borneo and certain tribes of the Malay
rchipelago, including the Sakai.

19*

Pigs, deer, and porcupine are usually caught in slings and trap of Malay construction.

Like the Mentawei Islanders the Sakai use the roots of the Tul plant (Derris eliptica) for fish poisoning. The practice still continue although, at the request of the Dutch government, it is forbidden t the Sultan of Siak. Fish poisoning kills the fish brood and mar young fish. Hook and line are seldom used. A common practi is to hang a fence across the river, with an opening in the center ar a fish trap in the opening. Or they use a net, with a platform abov on which the fisherman stands. All of these methods are borrowe from the Malays.

Formerly the Sakai wore the usual tapa girdle. Now they obta cotton goods from the Malay.

The house of these people is very simple, consisting of but single room, made of bark and dried palm leaves, and placed on a raf The people are constantly on the move, and can use no elabora dwellings. If their fields are exhausted, or the stream on which the live dries up, they migrate. Likewise a house is deserted at sickness death.

The marriage customs of the Sakai are somewhat confuse Originally the people had freedom of intercourse between the sexe which later led to a monogamous but unstable marriage. There wer no restrictions on marriage outside of those imposed by the bilatera blood family. The sib system was introduced by Minangkabau, and man was forced to marry a woman outside of his own sib. Later th Sultan of Siak introduced bride-purchase, and patrilineal inheritanc The latter, however, is intended for chiefs only. Since all these change took place in a few centuries, it is clear that social organization is by n means a stable institution.

At the present time marriage is forbidden within the sib. Whe a man wishes to marry a girl he first asks her mother. She in tur asks the maiden whether or not the suitor pleases her. If not, th matter is finished. If the girl replies in the affirmative however, he father is asked to give his consent. The man is not allowed to tak his wife or her children outside of her village.

If a young man is caught with a girl by her parents, he mus marry her and pay the bride-price, if able. The bride-price is usuall paid in goods, as the people lack money.

Among the Sakai of Rokan there is a peculiar form of capture
marriage. When a youth wishes to marry, he and the object of his
affections are placed on the side of a heap of dirt, and in the chase
which follows the youth must trap the girl. Since this chase is found
nowhere else in Sumatra, but also exists among the Peninsula Sakai, it
surely is original to the two peoples.

There also is a form of elopement marriage found among the
Rokan Sakai. When a man wishes to seduce the wife of another, he
hides with her seven days in the woods. If the husband can find his
wife within this period she must return to him, and the guilty pair pay
a fine. If the couple are not found, they come back and get married,
but without ceremony.

In marriage all property, both movable and immovable, belongs
to the woman. Chieftaincy is inherited through the mother. The
children follow the mother and not the father.

Divorce is very frequent. The wife can simply send her husband away. The children and the goods possessed in common remain
with her. A man too can leave his wife without formality, losing,
however, the children and the joint property. If he has not built a
house he must pay a fine to the family of his wife for the trouble he
has caused them.

The Sakai do not practice polygyny, and considerable stress is laid
on marital fidelity.

At the death of the wife all her possessions are divided into three
parts: one third goes to the husband, one third to her own family, and
one third is placed in the grave with her. At the death of the man,
everything which he earned together with his wife is divided between
his family and his wife's family. Very little is buried with a man.
Moszkowski found but a small knife and a copper coin in a man's
grave. The women have more to bury, for whatever ornaments are
used by the Sakai are worn by the women.

The burial customs are very ancient Malaysian in form and not
Veddoid. An exception may be made in the case of blood offering to the
dead, which is not found, so far as I know, excepting for the Bataks,
in Indonesia, but is found in Australia. A four cornered shelter is
erected over the grave. On the day of the burial the neighbors and
relatives come to the house of the deceased, cut themselves with knives,
and allow the blood to flow over the corpse. The relatives watch three
days over the grave of a commoner, and seven days over the grave of

a chief. This is done in order to frighten away the hantu kubur, th
evil spirit of the grave. For the same reason a fire is kept lit on th
grave. A large feast is given after a death.

Incision furnishes the only form of tribal initiation which th
people possess. All the boys of the sib are incised together, and a bi
feast is held at the time.

As has repeatedly been emphasized in this book, the so-calle
"matriarchate" does not necessarily improve the position of womer
Among the Sakai all hard work, as for instance the fetching of watei
is placed on the shoulders of the women. Moszkowski writes that th
rights which the women have *de jure*, are practiced *de facto* by th
male members of the family. The only difference between the mothe
right, as usual here, and father right, as customary elsewhere, consist
in the fact that the woman does not lie under the power of her husbanc
but under that of her elder brother, who, for a thousand reason, exert
a far more unpleasant mastery over her than her husband could o
would have done. Thus the most advanced theoretical rights are o
no avail if one has no power to enforce them.

Nothing is known about the original Sakai religion. The peopl
have no musical instruments, dances, or songs of their own. They hav
lost their myths, and when they talk at night it is mostly about fooc

In general the Sakai have the same beliefs as the Malay, fear th
same ghosts or antu, and depicture Batara Guru (Civa) as the wil
huntsman. The evil ghosts are the cause of all disease, and the mos
important function of the shaman is to drive them out of the body o
the patient.

The Malays believe that the soul leaves the body in the form o
bird, and is held in captivity by the evil spirits from whom the shamar
must wrest it.

The Sakai shaman intoxicates himself by dancing. In the dance h
holds a sword in his right hand and often also a bow and arrow. I
his left hand he holds an arm band lined with bells with which h
gives tempo to the drums. The shaman falls into a trance and commun
cates with the spirits, who, however, do not enter his body. When th
shaman comes to, he says that the patient need not fear as he has th
spirits in his power.

In a second performance the shaman sucks disease out of th
patient.

The Sakai, like all other primitive peoples, must at one time have had their own medicine men, or seers. They have lost these, and, as Moszkowski writes, they now imitate Malay hocus-pocus because they have nothing better.

There are two tribes of Akit in the Sultanate of Siak. Originally they were coast dwellers, but now they live on the Mandau and Siak rivers. Their name is said to be derived from their custom of building their houses on rafts. The physical culture of the Akit is interesting, for they are a very mixed race. Moszkowsky observed straight haired, curly or wavy haired, and even woolly haired individuals. Thus there is probably a strain of Semang or Negrito blood among these primitives.

The Lubu and Ulu.

The Lubu and Ulu are closely related peoples of probable mixed Veddoid origin who live in the central Sumatra mountain regions of the provinces of Padang Lawas, Ankola, and Mandheling; namely, in southern Batakland. The Ulu live south of the Lubu, in South Mandheling, and speak a Minangkabau dialect, having migrated from the Ran district of the Minangkabau west coast to their present abode. The Lubu have adopted, at least in great part, the language of their south Batak neighbors.

While both the Lubu and the Ulu formerly were migratory peoples with bilateral family and customs similar to the wild Kubu, they now have adopted sib systems and are being absorbed by the Bataks. Still the sib systems of the two peoples differ; that of the Lubu is patrilineal and in all essentials like the southern Bataks, while that of the Ulu is matrilineal and in all essentials like the Minangkabau.

The Lubu in 1891 consisted of 2,000 people, already semi-settled, and professing Mohammedanism. In 1856, Godon claims that they numbered 5,340. So this population is rapidly diminishing.

Willer and Netscher visited the Lubu in 1855, when these natives still roamed the mountains in a wild state, lived for the most part in tree houses, shot game with the blow-gun and poisoned darts, and existed on the products of the jungle, some of which they exchanged with the Malays. Their clothing was the simple tapa girdle. The people ate all kind of meat, even though it was badly decomposed, and cooked in hollow bamboos. The religion of the tribe was not described. They had as yet no sibs and had a simple chieftaincy.

As an example of rapid acculturation I will now describe the Lubu as seen by Kreemer in 1912.

The Lubu at present are poor, dirty people in tattered clothing. They are afraid of water, cannot swim, and seldom wash, although they live along rivers. They are lazy and timid before strangers. Although a harmless race, the Bataks mistrust them and suspect them of all kinds of witchcraft. They are utterly despised, and mingling of Batak and Lubu seldom takes place. In religion they are nominally Mohammedan, and are circumcised. While they keep no pigs out of deference to their religion, they are strongly suspected of secretly eating pork.

The Lubus are not very particular in their choice of food, and as special delicacies they eat the flesh of mice and bats and the larvae of wasps. They also eat monkeys which they shoot with their blow-guns. A short time ago maize was the main cultivated cereal, but now rice also is a common article of consumption. They are good climbers and earn money by climbing for the Bataks for coconuts.

The people have no buffaloes, cattle, or horses. They own a few goats and chickens. Hunting and fishing is done for their own consumption. They gather brush products for trade.

The national weapon is the blow-pipe (ultop). Only the priest and sorcerer (datu) is able to make the poison for the darts, as all kinds of formulae and a special language are required for its brewing. This must take place in the brush and not in the house. A number of people assist the datu and each of them has a special task in order to make the poison potent. One climbs a tree and pretends to falls from it, another pretends to vomit, while a third lies on the ground in assumed convulsions.

Besides blow-guns, the people use lances, knives, and guns on the hunt.

The musical instruments and songs of the natives are adopted from the Bataks. The people never dance, not even at feasts. The musical instruments are a few very simple toys intended to accompany the singing of songs by moonlight, or when they sit around the fire. The Lubu godang is a simple bamboo joint resounder over which a split string is extended; it is struck with a small piece of wood. Among the Bataks the godang is a variety of drum. The otuk also is a simple piece of bamboo from which pieces are cut. It is struck with a small stick. The Lubu likewise have a bamboo flute (tulika).

The Lubu compose songs in the depth of the night similar to the Malay pantuns, and both sexes join in them. In the so-called turi, the recitation of stories by the old men accompanied by the drinking of palm wine, only the males take part.

The Lubu no longer use tree houses. They now live in wretched huts built level to the ground. Larger pile houses are called umo. These people do not build rice granaries like the Bataks, but keep their rice in sacks in the house.

A group of houses forms a settlement (bandja), and a number of settlements form a district (kuria). There are eleven Lubu kuria in Mandheling. The chief of a bandja is called "na bodjo bodjo" and a district head "tuan diur". All the older male members of the community, i. e. the family heads, have voice in government and are called "nan tuho tuho". The Lubu unlike the Batak, have no nobles. At the death of a chief, his eldest son is usually chosen as successor.

Like the Batak, the Lubu are divided into sibs, called marga.

The ceremonies attending the life cycle of the individual Lubu are similar to the Batak.

The afterbirth is buried under the house, and is considered a second soul.

When the child is twenty days old it is bathed for the first time, and receives its first name. Teknonomy is practiced. If the child is called Sosok, the father is called amai Sosok (father of Sosok) and the mother bopo Sosok (mother of Sosok).

At the time of the name giving the child has its first haircut. The hair and the navel string are carefully kept. Incision, which consists in the splitting of the prepuce, is practiced for boys. Before marriage most girls have their teeth filed and blackened. This custom is rarely made use of by men.

The adat allows rather free prenuptial contact between the sexes, always providing that they belong to different sibs. In every village there is a special communal house for the boys and another for the girls. Both are called tawatak. Boys after the age of twelve live in the tawatak. Girls likewise pass the nights in a tawatak under the chaperonage of an old widow. Boys visit the girls in the evening and chatter, exchange witticisms, and spoon. But the young girls are supposed to remain chaste.

Marriage takes place when the girl arrives at about the age of fifteen, and is preceded by an engagement. The marriage is one of

purchase and is patrilineal and patrilocal. The bride-price is very low
only about one twentieth the amount of the Batak bride-price. In spi
of the bargain which the Lubu groom obtains, he usually finds it har
to pay the amount, and must work two years for his future parents-in
law while engaged to their daughter. In marriage the choice of th
young couple is more important than the wishes of the parents.

The adat prescribes that a man should marry his boru tulan
(mother's brother's daughter), because "the leech is always attracte
by an open wound".

The datu chooses a lucky day for the marriage, using a divina
tion book.

The most solemn moment of the marriage occurs when the brid
groom removes the decorations of the bride, for, according to adat,
married woman is allowed no jewelry. The woman now also loses he
name, and is called nama-bodju until the birth of her first child, whe
she is called after the child. The husband at the time of marriage ge
a new name related to the old name.

As among the South Bataks, at the bridal feast neither the fathe
of the bride nor the people of his sib are allowed to be present. Aft
the marriage the bridal pair is taboo (Batak robu, Lubu wobu) fe
seven days. During this time they remain in the house of the groom
parents. Avoidance is practiced between a man and his mother-in-la
and a woman and her father-in-law.

Marriage by capture is practiced by the South Bataks in orde
to avoid the expense of a wedding. This is not allowed among th
Lubu. Another frequent form of South Batak marriage (maniomp
the root sompo means "unexpected occurrence") takes place. In th
case the girl simply goes to the house of the parents of the boy ar
remains. This is often done when the girl is pregnant before marriag

After the death of her husband a woman is given to the young
brother of the deceased. But the younger brother is not obliged
marry the widow. He can hand her over to the next in line among h
family, or send her back to her own sib.

In inheritance the eldest son inherits first, and then the elde
brother. Women can own no property, but are considered the proper
of the man, his familiy, and sib.

Divorce seldom occurs, since marriages are made from the choi
of the young people, and the young man has to work hard for th

ride-price. If the woman wishes a divorce she returns the bride-price, and the children go to the man.

While, as I have said, the people nominally are Mohammedan, many of their pagan beliefs remain mingled with the pagan beliefs of their neighbors, the Mohammedan Bataks. Hosts of good and bad spirits are honored, and especially the spirit of Singa Tandang, the first tribal chief. Like the Bataks they believe in the power of tondi (soul), and in lucky and unlucky days.

Sickness is mainly attributed to evil spirits, especially ghosts, who work externally or internally on the patient. A person can perform magic by hiring a datu who has the evil spirits under his control. Black magic is very prevalent among the Lubu, and for this reason they are feared, although not respected, by their Batak neighbors.

Kreemer states that while some writers attribute unity between the Lubu and the Ulu who live in Mandheling, he himself doubts whether there can be the remotest connection between the two people, for in custom they are at the opposite ends of the pole from one another. The Ulu are matrilineal and have the adat kamanakan and the institution of the harta pusaka, etc. the same as the Minangkabau, while the Lubu have the patrilineal customs of the Batak. As I have shown, however, both these peoples have adopted unilateral reckoning in the course of a century, and both originally had the simple bilateral family of the Kubu. Therefore there is no reason to doubt the original unity of the Lubu and Ulu, as well as that of the Kubu and other Veddoid tribes of Sumatra.

The Orang Benua.

In the southern states of the Malay Peninsula, in the Riau-Lingga archipelago, on the island of Bangka, and in certain districts of eastern Sumatra, there are a number of primitive pagan communities who speak Malaysian dialects and who are of Malaysian race. In British Malaya they are known by names such as Bidwanda, Blandas, Mantra, Orang Benua; generically they are often described by the vague term Jakun. In the extreme south and on the islands they are likewise called by a number of names, including Orang Benua. If they live on the sea they are called Orang Laut, if on land, Orang Darat. The Malays contemptiously call these people Orang Utan, jungle dwellers.

Netscher (quoted by Hagen) described the Orang Benua of the island Rempang in 1854.

At that time the Orang Benua consisted of about 1,000 peopl
They were nomadic, wandering from place to place. As dwellings the
constructed rude shelters of bamboo sticks with leaf roofing. Potter
was used for cooking, but agriculture was completely lacking, and tl
people had but little commerce outside of the barter they conducte
for jungle products.

The Benua ate everything that the jungle offered; pigs, snake
frogs, leaves, and roots. In addition they obtained rice and sago l
trade. Both men and women wore loin cloths, originally of tapa.

The blow-gun and poisoned arrows were the chief weapons of tl
people. In addition, however, they used the Malay parang.

They carried all their possessions in a bamboo a foot long. The
goods consisted of blow-gun darts, a piece of poisoned wood on whic
they rubbed them, wood for making a fire, and perhaps a small knif

The Benua had as their constant companions little long hair
dogs with pointed ears. These were well taken care of, and were the
sole domestic animals.

The family relations were of a very loose variety, and sibs
purchase marriage entirely lacking. As soon as a boy was old enoug
to handle a blow-gun, he was set out by his parents to take care
himself. If he found a girl who pleased him, the pair returned to tl
boy's elders, if the latter still were to be found, and informed the
of the marriage. The boy received a blow-gun as wedding present ar
the girl some earthen pots. The marriage then was acomplished ar
neither of the wedded pair abandoned the other until sickness or dea
parted them.

Little is known about the Benua religion or medicine men. If
person was about to die he was abandoned in the woods. After tl
individual was dead he was given a superficial burial.

Wilkinson has shown that the various wild Malays of tl
Peninsula and East Sumatra, who are called by the collective title
Jakun, have the real right to be called Proto-Malaysian, although th
title is usually given to the people of the Archipelago other than tl
Malays, Javanese, and Minangkabau. The wild tribes speak a for
of Malay, but they pronounce the final "k", which is elided or slurr
by the Malays and Minangkabau. The fact that Proto-Malaysians a
to be found on the Peninsula explains why the Malay language can
traced there before the advent of the culture now associated with t
name of Malay.

The Jakun differ from the more advanced Proto-Malaysians culturally, since, as far as is known, they had assimilated no Hindu or pre-Hindu culture from India. They had, for example, no system of sacrificial feasts. On the other hand, they had pottery, but this was of ancient, presumably Neolithic, origin. The Mentawei Islanders lacked pottery, but probably the soil of the islands was unfavorable to its making, and they had lost the art.

The races and cultures of Sumatra.

In the preceding discussion of the various peoples of Sumatra it has been shown that wave after wave of cultural influence had swept over the island from the direction of India, bringing certain of the groups to a high state of civilization. This process had gone so far that the Dutch, gaining control, had little more to offer to the advanced groups than the idea of centralized political government, and with it security of person and property.

When the first Malaysians came to Sumatra they presumably found Negritos and Veddoids, who wandered through the jungles with their dogs, digging roots, fishing, and shooting game with bow and blow-gun. The people lived in rude shelters, were scattered in small family groups, and were led by their oldest and most experienced male members.

Judging by the Jakun, the primitive Malaysians of the Peninsula, it is doubtful whether the original Malaysian settlers were one bit more civilized than the indigenes they found on the island. Gradually, however, as the Malaysians received more and more cultural elements from further Malaysian settlers from the mainland, they became culturally superior to the wild tribes, and were able to exterminate the Negritos, and push the Veddoids back into the more desolate parts of the island. The peoples of the western islands left Sumatra before they had received the full benefit of these later cultural influences.

Thus, reckoning from the culture of Mentawei, the first traits which the Malaysians of Sumatra received included the use of pile houses, the out-rigger canoe and the sailboat, the domestication of tubular roots including taro and yam, the preparation of sago, and the domesticated pig and chicken. With the coming of pile buildings came the use of a men's house, and the people divided their villages into hamlets, each hamlet under its own leaders.

Before the actual intrusion of the Hindus in the early centurie A. D., the Malaysians had probably domesticated the karabau, and certainly had learned to grow rice, at least the dry variety. Rice wa called běras, however, or fruit, from its resemblance to other fruits the Malaysians already had. The Malaysians now also learned certain crafts, including iron working, and division of labor started among the male population. Megalithic monument making and head-hunting were early traits which were suppressed by the Hindus. The first because the Hindus introduced a different variety of large stone work; the second because it was too barbaric for the refined tastes of the conquerors.

Probably the most important of the pre-Hindu traits introduced was the idea of the sib. Once gathered into large sib units under sib chiefs, the Malaysians were better able to dispossess the Veddoids from the choice regions of the islands. The blood revenge or war group was now far larger than before, and these large groups were able to maintain their numbers and affiliations by intermarriage with one another. Probably even before the Hindu period the territorial aspect of the sib commenced to break down with the rise of towns, and the sib chiefs became town chiefs. The reason why all primitive peoples readily adopt sibs, and why all civilized people probably have gone through a sib stage, is because it enlarges the blood relationship group and thus gives security. With the further advance of civilization the territorial unit supersedes the genealogical, and sibs are no longer of advantage.

Once the sib is no longer of advantage, it becomes a disadvantage due to the onus of exogamy and collective liability. It is far easier to persuade desirable citizens to live in a town or cast undesirable citizen out of a town, than it is to admit or cast out members from a sib Properly speaking a sib should not be able to admit or release it members at will; a sib system in complete form has its members born into and die in its mother fold. In Sumatra we can find the sib in al stages of degeneration, and the various peoples passing into town an territorial units. As has been shown, first the Hindus and then the Dutch hastened this transformation.

The traits introduced by the Hindus were of much the same nature throughout the island and have been summarized for the Bataks. The included wet rice culture and the plow, cotton and the spinning wheel but more important were the Hindu concepts of life and religion.

bviously was due to Hindu influence that small Malaysian towns were
ble to strive with one another for vast commercial empires.

The question naturally arises as to why the Negrito of Sumatra
hould have become extinct and the Veddoid ruthlessly pushed out of
he way. Evidently these races were unable to assimilate traits of higher
ulture when historical chance gave them the opportunity. This would
eem the crux of the race superiority problem.

No people can be judged as to their capacities from a mere chance
tage of culture. To do this would lay one open to the historical blunder
f Tacitus, when he qualified the Germans as being unfit for mental or
hysical work (laboris atque operum non eadem patientia). Yet when
eople like the Vedda of Ceylon, who for centuries have been exposed
o a rich Buddhistic civilization, respond by taking to the jungles, it
ould seem certain that they lack some of the ambition displayed by
he Caucasian and the Mongoloid. The same charge may be laid to
he door of the Kubu and allied people of Sumatra. It is only within
ecent years, and at the insistence of the Dutch, that these races are
eing assimilated.

Finally, nothing in the history of Sumatra demonstrates that any
ace may gain superiority over its neighbors by maintaining its blood
ure from foreign infiltration. The Mentawei Islanders admit no
trangers in marriage, and in fact, formerly admitted no strangers at
ll on the islands, unless they were tattooed and accepted Mentawei
ustoms. The Malays, on the other hand, will welcome anyone who
ecomes converted to Islam. As a result the Malays, who are a
omposite of all races, are the progressive people of Insulinde. This
ame readiness to accept the new in all its forms and variations is in
act the true dividing line between the primitive and the civilized.

THE ARCHAEOLOGY AND ART OF SUMATRA
BY
ROBERT HEINE-GELDERN.

he stone age.

Diluvial human skeletal remains having been found in Java, it
tands to reason, that Sumatra, too, must have been populated by
uman beings as early as the Pleistocene period. However, no human
emains either artifacts or bones recognizable as belonging to this
eriod, have been found as yet in Sumatra. At the present moment it
eems quite impossible to ascertain the real age of any palaeolithic
ind made in this island, and it is not very probable that any of
hem date further back than the beginning of the Alluvium. There-
ore I wish to call attention to the fact, that I shall use the term
palaeolithic" in connection with the ancient cultures of Sumatra only
s denoting a cultural type, and not as implying a fixed time period.

Though our present knowledge of prehistoric Sumatra is rather
canty, we may discern two very different palaeolithic cultures: a
Flake Culture" and a "Hand-Axe Culture". Until now traces of the
lake Culture have only been discovered in two sites in Central Sumatra.
n a cave, Ulu Tjanko in Upper Djambi, the Swiss geologist, A. Tobler,
ound amidst shells of land and fresh-water snails, both of which had
erved as food, knife blades, points, and scraper-like instruments made
f obsidian (fig. 57). J. Zwierzycki found similar remains in another
ave of the same territory; but here, besides obsidian, other kinds of
tone had been used. The accounts of the discoverers, however, yield
o clue as to the age of these cultures. They may be related to the
lake Cultures of Ceylon and of the caves of Lamontjong in Southwest
elebes, and belong probably to the latest palaeolithic age. Some
emnants of human bones were found in the cave of Ulu Tjanko.
hey belonged to a delicately built race, probably of Veddoid origin.

We are far better informed about the Hand-Axe Culture. Its traces
ere found in the shell heaps in the northern part of the east coast

in the neighborhood of Medan and Seruwai, and in numerous spot scattered throughout the same territory and the hills beyond, as we as in the eastern parts of Atjeh near Seumaweh and Langsar. The she heaps have a diameter from 30 to 60 meters and are from 4 to 5 meter in height. They consist, for the greater part, of marine mussel an snail shells. No doubt the mounds originated in the immediat neighborhood of the sea coast. Today, however, due to the elevatio of the land, they are, in part, from 10 to 20 kilometers distant fror the sea. Besides shells and numerous stone tools, they contain bone of game animals, which were broken, so as to render easy the extractio of the marrow. The stone tools are roughly hewn and bear more c less the character of hand-axes, though differing from the typical old palaeolithic handaxes of Europe and India by being worked almos without exception, on one side only, whereas the reverse shows th untouched natural roundness of rubbles (fig. 58). The material used were quartzite, sandstone and different igneous rocks, such a andesite and others. There is a great variety of form. One can discer picks, tools of an oval or almond shape, short disk-like stone: longshaped ones, and others resembling laurel leaves in form. Som of them have straight-lined cut-off necks, similar to the "hache courtes" of the "Hoabinhien" of north-eastern Indo-China. There ar great quantities of unworked striking-stones, pounders, flat bow shaped grinding-stones and ruddel.

Schurmann, from geological considerations, came to the cor clusion that the shell heaps of Northeast Sumatra date from earl alluvial times. This theory is borne out by the cultural position c the remains concealed. The Hand-Axe Culture of Sumatra is doubtlessl related to the Hoabinhien and early Bacsonien of northeastern Inde China and the Hand-Axe Cultures of Siam and the Malay Peninsula Early traces of neolithic influence constantly appear in the middl period of all these cultures in the form of rough-hewn tools wit ground edges and of "rubble-axes", which are simple river pebble: ground to an edge on one side without being touched in any othe respect. It is evident therefore that all of these Hand-Axe Cultures c Further India can only belong to the final phases of the palaeolithi age. Though in Sumatra, the predominent part of Hand-Axe Cultur shows no traces of the Neolithic, nevertheless sporadic "proto-neoliths" tools with rough-ground edges, have also been found recently i that country.

Unfortunately, the human osseous remains found in the shell
heaps are of too fragmentary a nature to be of any help in ascertaining
the race of the people to whom they belonged. But considering the
analogy of Hand-Axe Cultures of Indo-China and the Malay Peninsula,
it seems very probable that the bearers of the Sumatra Hand-Axe Culture
also belonged to the group of Papua-Melanesoid races. We are not
as yet able to decide whether the two palaeolithic cultures of Sumatra
— the Hand-Axe Culture brought probably by Papua-Melanesoids and
the Flake Culture introduced probably by people of Veddoid origin —
existed side by side on the island or whether they succeeded one
another, and if so in which order. We may assume, that there were
still older palaeolithic cultures in Sumatra, but until now no remnants
of them have been discovered. Neither are we able as yet to distinguish
by archaeological methods the primitive Malaysian stratum, so
obviously present in the Kubu, Sakai, and some other tribes. It may
be possible, though not yet provable, that these primitive Malaysian
peoples were the transmitters of the afore-mentioned proto-neolithic
elements.

The fact that people with a very primitive agricultural civilization
are still living on the islands surrounding Sumatra — the Nicobars,
Mentawei-Islands and Engano — permits us to presume that early
neolithic cultures must have existed on the mainland of Sumatra.
Archaeological traces of these have not yet been discovered. We reach
firm ground only when dealing with a late neolithic culture, whose
most characteristic feature are different forms of adzes with four-
cornered cross-sections ("Vierkantbeile", quadrangular adzes, fig. 60).
This culture probably came to the Malay Peninsula and Indonesia by
way of China and central Indo-China (Laos and Siam) between 2000
and 1500 B. C. Its bearers introduced to Indonesia the Austronesian
languages, the outrigger canoe, rice cultivation, domesticated cattle
or buffaloes, head-hunting, and the custom of erecting megalithic
monuments. Beaked adzes belong to this culture as well as four-
cornered ones (fig. 59). Their gradual development can be traced
archaeologically along the trail of the Austronesian migration from
Upper Laos through the Malay Peninsula to Indonesia. Both, the
quadrangular as well as the beaked adzes of Sumatra, are very similar
to those of Java. The neolithic cultures of both islands show the
same preference for semi-precious stones and colored varieties of silex,
and the same wonderful perfection of stone cutting. Some of these

adze blades are real works of art. Not only is the close relationship between the Sumatrean "Quadrangular-Adze Culture" (Vierkantbeil-kultur) and the Javanese branch of this culture revealed thereby, but we can also perceive the high degree of craftmanship and the keen sense of beauty possessed by the Malayan population of Sumatra in the late neolithic period.

The art of Nias.

The joint application of archaeological and ethnological methods enables us to conceive an idea of the art of the neolithic Quadrangular-Adze Culture. It was closely connected with the megalithic system and still survives in many remote regions of Further India and Indonesia, especially among the mountain tribes of Assam and of northern Luzon, and in the island of Nias. It is predominantly plastic and monumental and serves primarily the rites of ancestral cults, eschatological beliefs, and magic aims. The simple aesthetic delight in fanciful decoration of houses, tools, and weapons, so exceedingly prominent in the Dayaks and many other Indonesian peoples, seems originally to have been completely lacking here. Thus, truely ornamental elements play a very inferior part in this art, and where they are found at all, are of a very simple and purely geometrical nature. However, we find a great many symbols in these regions of megalithic-monumental art, which to a certain extent serve as substitutes for ornaments. We may distinguish between magical symbols of fertility and wealth (as "women breasts"), and between "memorials" in the literal sense of the word. These memorials of success in war, hunting, and love, or of festivals and sacrifices (for instance "cattle heads"), are token which bring to him whose deeds they glorify, credit and honor. They are meant to bear witness of the religious and magical merit the person has achieved by the above mentioned deeds, therewith securing him happiness and wealth during lifetime, and thereafter protection against the dangers threatening the soul, being a warrant for his safe entrance into paradise. Actually, they serve the same purpose as the megalithic monuments. They are used on wooden buildings and monuments as well as on stone memorials. Besides this symbolic relief sculpture, plastic art, in the form of statues of the deceased and other ancestral figures, plays an important part in the megalithic-monumental style of Southeast Asia.

This style reached its culminating point on the isle of Nias. The amazing perfection of the stone buildings and stone sculptures is remarkable indeed. This does not mean that Nias is lacking in primitive megalithic forms! But next to primitive menhirs and dolmens we find exuberantly variegated and refined forms, and some which are quite new. This development had several different aspects in the various parts of the island.

In southern Nias, architecture is predominant. Stone village walls, stone-paved meeting places, stone steps leading up to more highly situated villages, all of them typical megalithic forms of Southeast Asia, have reached here an imposing height of development. Some of the stairs, built of carefully smoothed stones, the stone side-walls being decorated with relief sculptures, belong in their archaic simplicity to the most beautiful creations of Indonesian architecture (fig. 63). The stupendous technical accomplishment involved in their structure is shown by the fact, that the stairs leading from the village of Orahili to Bawomataluwo is built in four flights and consists of 700 steps.

In accordance with the artistic propensities of southern Nias, even the simpler megalithic forms, as menhirs and dolmens, erected by men for their own benefit or to the memory of their dead, have been transformed into architectural works of art. The simple menhir has been converted into an obelisk, a polygon pillar, or a low stela ending in volutes. The dolmen has become a round stone table or an artistically shaped bench, both called darodaro, "seat", intended as memorials for the dead whose spirits they are meant to serve as resting places, though they are also used by the living as seats at council meetings or festivals (fig. 35). Into the smoothed surface of the finest of these monuments, menhirs as well as darodaro, a few but charming artistic symbolic ornaments are chiselled, frequently in the form of the Nias rosette. On the Batu islands, and in one case in southern Nias, real thrones with armrests and backs have been found. On the outside of their backs are relief sculptures representing human figures or crocodiles. On the whole the people of South Nias seem to have a great preference for stone reliefs. We find them on monuments, side-walls of stone stairs, and even sometimes on simple pavements in the villages. Besides pure symbols and single figures we meet with whole scenes; in one of the largest darodaro four monkeys catching a shark are designed in a most lively manner.

In North Nias all of these larger stone buildings, steps, pave
squares, bathing places, bastions, &c. seem to be very rare or eve
lacking altogether. In Central Nias they have not changed much fron
the original megalithic form. Similarly the obelisks, stone pillars, an
stelae show a more primitive development in the Centre and the Nort
of the island. However, the development of the menhirs took here .
very different line where they were converted into hermae and ston
statues. In outward appearance, they are stone reproductions of th
wooden ancestral figures, but their significance corresponds to that o
the usual menhir. They, too, are erected as memorials of "feasts o
merit", or by mourners for their dead. And just as the menhirs, the
are meant to be back supports for the spirits of the deceased whe
they sit on the flat stone slabs lying before the statues. These slab
again, correspond to the darodaro of the south.

Unfortunately, little is known as yet about the stone sculpture
of Nias. Schröder has published pictures of stone hermae and of
more than life-sized statue found in the district of Moro'o in Centra
Nias. This statue in its straight, strictly frontal setting, with a fac
reduced almost to geometrical outlines, is in spite of all its shor
comings and primitive execution, still remarkable for its really monu
mental qualities. In other parts of the island we meet with mor
realistic and sometimes even grotesque forms. A characteristic sig
of the plastic tendency of the art of Nias is found in the horizonta
monuments sculptured as conventionalized figures of stags and horr
bills (fig. 62). Except for being hewn in stone they are copies o
wooden stretchers which are decorated with animal heads and are use
to carry around at rituals the hosts of "feasts of merit". Besides this
stone pillars with stone hornbill figures on the top, doubtlessl
reproduce wooden memorials.

Nias is exceedingly rich in wooden carvings of human form
for the greater part ancestral and guardian figures (fig. 37). It i
quite impossible to give here even an approximate idea of th
multiplicity of these images and of their form and meaning. Mor
over, this matter has never been thoroughly investigated and th
available reports are insufficient. The style of these figures varie
from a strictly naturalistic detailed rendering of human forms,
simple poles with a superficial indication of eyes and mouth. Accorc
ing to Schröder, the statues of the south are distinguished by roun
plastic forms and a polished surface. In Central Nias the image

seem to be more simplified, sometimes even to the point of mere geometrical forms. The carvings of the north are chiselled, according to Schröder, in a more level and less plastic manner. All of these images are naked, though they wear ornaments and frequently headgears. Many of the ancestral figures hold cups with both hands, thus calling to mind the megalithic beaker-statues of eastern Europe, the steppes of Siberia, and Central Asia. The hermae-like figures are mostly ithyphallic. Many of the full-length figures as well as the hermae have two horns, shaped like two-pronged forks, on their heads (fig. 37 left). These are anthropomorphic transcriptions, no longer fully understood, of the forked wooden poles used by the mountain tribes of Assam, of Further India, and of the isle of Flores as sacrificial stakes for cattle sacrifice and at the same time as memorials thereof. The carefully carved images, especially the ancestral figures and the household gods, are wrought by qualified artists, but the sketchy figures, hastily fashioned in case of illness and thrown away when no longer needed, are made by the priests. These more primitive images, in spite of their lack of craftmanship, sometimes succeed better in creating the impression of fervent feeling and animation than the laboriously executed ones, which invariably wear an expression of unperturbed calm.

The houses in northern Nias are built in oval shape, while they are quadrangular in the south. The marked inclination to create imposing architectonic forms which southern Nias displays in its megalithic art, expresses itself, too, in the architecture of the wooden houses of the chiefs. The dimensions of the latter houses are remarkable. The house of the Siulu of Bawomataluwo for instance is about 13 meters high (fig. 35). Probably in no other part of Indonesia has pile-building achieved such monumental style as here. Not only the outward appearance, the column-like pillars supporting the houses, the flaring construction of projecting walls, the audacious curves of steeply towering, powerful roofs, create a genuine artistic impression; but the disposal of inward space, too, is effected with high architectonic skill and artistry, and belongs to the best that has ever been achieved in architectonic art outside of high civilizations. The slanting light produces a most peculiar and attractive effect as does the contrast between the skillfully carved symbols — exceedingly tasteful images of combs, helmets, necklaces, &c. — and the simplicity of the well pro-portioned walls and columns, left without any other decoration. In some of the chiefs' houses there are chestshaped wooden thrones, decorated with relief carvings of human images, crocodiles, rosettes and geometrical ornaments, which may well be included among the best creations of Niassian art (fig. 61).

Unfortunately, our knowledge is not sufficient to attempt an historical analysis qualified to elucidate this remarkable bloom of the art of Nias. However, we may presume that the oval form of houses in North Nias, the use of images for averting evil spirits and illness and perhaps some stylistic plastical features, belong to a culture more ancient than the megalithic and probably related to the cultures of the Nicobars and the island of Engano. It was succeeded by the megalithic culture with its stone monuments and buildings, its ancestral figures and symbolic ornaments. The art born of the merging of these two heterogeneous layers must have been influenced in early times by Indian art, enabling it to rise far above its original niveau. Late influences of a high-culture, originating probably in Java, Sumatra or Further India, and presumably dating back till about the 14th century or earlier, manifest themselves in the carved figures of Niassian sword-hilts, showing motives similar to the Hindu-Javanese and Hindu-Sumatrean Makara and even motives from Buddhistic legends especially the Sutasoma-Jâtaka. Still more recent influences of Javanese or Sumatrean high-cultures become apparent in some chiselled works, such as the stone canopy of Hilisimaetano in South Nias. However, in spite of all foreign influences, the main character of the art of Nias is based on the megalithic culture, and it reveal with impressive lucidity the abundant possibilities inherent in the pre-Hindu megalithic art of Indonesia, ready to spring into full bloom once higher craftsmanship, a more thorough mastery of form, and higher spiritual aims offered the opportunity and inspiration.

The megalithic art of South Sumatra.

Traces of both, older and younger megalithic cultures are wide spread on the mainland of Sumatra. I refer to the stone village wall of the Bataks, the meeting places and squares for cock-fighting in Minangkabau — both surrounded by stone seats — to the erected stones and stone heaps in the same territory, the stone memorial and megalithic graves on the upper Rokan, the "stone canons" of South Kurintji and the stones — decorated with reliefs — at Bangk n Upper Djambi. Finally, as Prof. Loeb has pointed out, the Pepadon system of Lampong is rooted in megalithic culture and "feasts of merit".

By far the most important group of megalithic monuments is that on the plateau of Pasemah in Southwest Sumatra and in the adjoining districts. According to the investigations made by Van der Hoop, these monuments include menhirs — single or in groups — dolmens, stone troughs, stone cist graves, terrace buildings (said to be tombs), and above all stone images. These sculptures show distinctly two quite different sorts of style, the older one of which is primitive and indigenous. Squatting figures with hands folded around their knees or over their breasts belong to this older style (fig. 65). They are closely related to the primitive pre-Hindu stone sculptures of Java and, as these, certainly belong to the original megalithic culture. Among the sculptures of the second, more evolved style there are single statues as well as plastic groups. The latter represent men riding elephants or buffaloes (fig. 68, 69), one or two grown up people with a child astride on a buffalo, a man with two children riding an elephant, groups of two or three people, sometimes a man or woman with a child, groups of people standing next to an elephant or buffalo, a man fighting an elephant lying on its back (fig. 67), two men fighting a snake, two tigers pairing — the tigress clutching with her fore paws the head of a human being lying beneath her.

In Pasemah, as in Nias, we have to deal with a developed megalithic culture; but here the results have been of quite different nature. Instead of a static art, as in Nias, we are confronted with a thoroughly dynamic conception and rendering of the physical world (figs. 64, 66 to 69). Everything is full of movement, power and passion. The faces and all their features are conceived as powerful, animated masses. The protruding eyebrows, the round eyes, the large cheek bones and padded lips, the prognathism, and above all the huge lower jaws, give to most of these faces an expression of uncanny brutality. Clearly, in Pasemah, the sculptors have intended to bring forth a naturalistic rendering of native racial types. But the features are so exaggerated that some figures look almost like caricatures. This had the effect, that, erroneously, they were thought to be representations of negroid types. In contrast to the strictly frontal and column-like character of the sculptures in Nias most of the images of Pasemah, especially the groups, show agitated movement. Bodies are twisted; heads turned sideways, thrust forward, or thrown back;

the grip of mighty arms fights or masters some animal; bodies clutc[h] convulsively at each other. The exaggerated size of the human figure[s] in acute disproportion to that of the buffaloes or elephants they rid[e] or fight, increases the effect of brutal force.

While the Nias stone images are simple reproductions of th[e] wooden ancestral figures in stone and remain similar to these in ever[y] respect, it is very improbable that the Pasemah sculptures had woode[n] prototypes. Here, it would appear, we deal with an actual "ston[e] style". A very characteristic feature of these images consists in th[e] principle of making use as far as possible of the natural form of th[e] stone medium. This comes forth most noticeably in the Batugadja[l] group. Here the rock is adapted to the shape of an elephant flanke[d] on each side by a warrior in relief-work with the least possible alter[-] ation of its original form (fig. 64).

On the inner walls of two stone cist graves fragments of painting[s] have been found by Van der Hoop and De Bie. Two of these painting[s] in black, white, red and yellow, represent a man with a buffalo, [a] third one is probably intended to be a man with an elephant. The[y] deal obviously with the same subjects as the sculptures and depi[ct] them in the same style. The painted figures show the same violen[t] movements, the grotesque, almost caricatured faces, thus provin[g] with absolute certainty, that the sculptures and the stone cists origin[-] ated at the same period.

It is evident, that the sculptural art of Pasemah of the late[r] period, though not being devoid of primitive features, has been strongl[y] influenced by the style of some high-culture. This is obvious fro[m] marked naturalism, perfect freedom of movement, and a complete dis[-] cardance of the frontal restraints. The artistic reproduction of elephan[t] riders seems to indicate, if not the influence of Indian art on th[e] style of the Pasemah monuments, at least the influence of India[n] culture on their creators, as the elephant is tamed and put to us[e] as a riding animal in Asia, only in the range of Indian cultur[e.] Indian influence on the style of Pasemah art, though probably presen[t] in a few of the sculptures, is very slight indeed. In any case, eve[n] the faintest traces of Hinduism and Buddhism are lacking. Van de[r] Hoop has drawn attention to the fact, that on the stone of Batugadja[h] (fig. 64) two bronze drums of the oldest type, as were used in Ind[o] China about the beginning of the Cristian era, are represented an[d] that the swords, daggers, and helmets which are chiselled on Pasema[h] sculptures are very similar to bronze weapons belonging to the same period, which have been unearthed near Dông-son in North Annam and in Tongking. Moreover, Van der Hoop and other investigators found in stone cist graves of Pasemah, besides numerous stone and glass beads, a few fragments of bronze objects, a small golden nail, and an iron lance head. He infers from this that the creators of the Pasemah monuments had in the main a bronze age culture, though, as in Dông-son, they were acquainted with iron and occasionally made use of it. We may call this late bronze age culture, which probably began to penetrate South East Asia from the north not later than about 300 B. C., perhaps even as early as 600 B. C., and which must have lasted till about 100 A. D., "Dông-son Culture", just as we speak of a "Hallstatt Culture" or a "La Tène Culture" in Europe. That a vigorous wave of this culture spread over Sumatra is discernible from the traces it left in the ornamental art of the Batak and Minang-kabau (cf. pp. 319 to 322, 327 to 328).

As I attempted to demonstrate elsewhere ("Vorgeschichtliche Grundlagen der kolonialindischen Kunst"), the sculptures of Pasemah show far-reaching stylistic resemblance to the stone monuments of the tomb of the Chinese general Huo K'iu-ping in Shen-si province, erected in 117 B. C. The stone cist graves of Pasemah certainly do not belong to the older megalithic culture, which had come to Indonesia in the neolithic age. Wherever in Indonesia or the Malay Peninsula stone cist graves have been investigated, objects of bronze or iron were found. This fact allows us to presume that in the same way as the Pasemah sculptures are related to the Chinese sculptural art of the early Han period, the stone cist graves of Sumatra were related to the Chinese stone cist graves of this same time and that this form of tombs has been transmitted from China to Indonesia. Finally the paintings on the inner walls in Pasemah remind us, in spite of all stylistic differences, of the decorations of Chinese tombs of the same period.

Considering all this, we may well divide the monuments of Pasemah into two groups: an earlier one, comprising the menhirs, dolmens and the primitive squatting figures, and a later group, probably due to some colonizing movement coming from the mainland of eastern Asia between the years 200 and 100 B. C. This latter group includes the peculiar sculptural art of Pasemah and its stone cist graves. Some of the images, showing the characteristics of both groups, make it obvious, that both styles have met and merged in Pasemah. It is conceivable therefore, that some of the monuments of the older style may still have been erected at the same period as the more evolved bronze age sculptures.

The art of the Batak.

It has been mentioned that distinct traces of the northern in fluences to which the Pasemah sculpture owes its origin, have survived up to date in the art of the Batak. Art, as well as the entire civilization of the Batak, consists of elements of most heterogeneous derivation For the present the following four strata can be discerned: 1) the megalithic monumental style which, as mentioned above, derived most probably from the late neolithic Quadrangular-Adze Culture; 2) the style of the late bronze and early iron age Dông-son Culture; 3) Indian influences, and 4) Mohammedan Malay influences. It may be tha some motives originate in still more ancient neolithic civilizations prior to the Quadrangular-Adze Culture; but this we shall only be able t decide when the historical analysis of the art of Indonesia and Oceania which has as yet been scarcely begun, shall have advanced con siderably.

Apart from the cyclopean stone walls of the Toba villages, an some isolated and utterly crude and insignificant stone altars, mega. ithic monuments proper seem to be missing. Still, a very late an peculiar sepulchral sculpture seems to have developed here from originally megalithic roots. High and round stone urns with a ston lid and squatting figure on the top, and mainly the Toba stone coffins receptacles of the bones after the corpse has decayed belong to thi sort of plastic art. Into the front of the coffin a squatting figure i chiselled, and above it a large face with horns similar to those s prominent in the architectural sculpture and other carvings of th Batak. Sometimes there is another squatting figure at the rear en of the coffin. The whole is characterized by the sweeping lines an round forms peculiar to Batak art (fig. 23). This shape of coffin is said to have come into use only in the course of the 19th centur. During the last decades, under European influence, cement tombs wit inscriptions and decorations of horned heads (singas or stylized bu falo heads) were substituted — final and utterly degenerated epigon of the ancient megalithic tomb.

Batak sculpture on the whole seems to be rooted in the old megalithic art, although its significance, its motives, and to some extent its style have undergone many a change through influences from Eastern Asia and India. The ancestral effigies for instance, which belong to the megalithic culture, are receding in number and importance behind the magic figures. Winkler even maintains that the Batak possess no ancestral figures at all save those of the Debata group, the legendary tribal ancestors, to whom they pray for offspring. This surely is going too far. According to one of the native informants of Warneck for instance, wooden or stone effigies will be erected on a hill or near a spring for ancestors who have been exalted to the status of Sombaon. Volz, too, occasionally mentions ancestral stone figures. In some parts of the country stone figures, even life-sized ones, are erected on the graves or as monuments for the deceased. Some of these represent the dead man riding an elephant or horse, thus displaying Indian influence (fig. 74). Wooden boat-coffins, too, with human figures, are to be mentioned (fig. 25). But much more numerous than these eschatological figures are those devoted to magic. Among these are figures meant to avert evil spirits, and others, which, after having been "animated" by fixing some hair or nails, &c. on them, are offered to the illness-creating spirits as substitutes for the sick persons. But most important of all are figures "animated" by means of Pupuk ointment, extracted from parts of the corpse of a person specially killed for this purpose. Such figures become the seat of the victim's spirit, which has to serve his murderers as Pangulu-balang (see p. 87) i. e. protector and ally against human and demoniac enemies (fig. 30). The old form of the rigidly frontal squatting figure, or the figure standing with bent knees is maintained almost without exception. Though some of these figures are rendered with good craftsmanship (fig. 72) they hardly ever attain the artistic quality of Niassian sculptures.

Smaller objects, such as receptacles of magic medicine (Pupuk ointment, &c.) often are of greater artistic value and charm. As a rule these receptacles are made of buffalo or hill-antilope horns (fig. 73, 75). The wooden stopper frequently shows head and chest of the horned creature referred to in connection with the stone coffins. Sometimes the face is human, sometimes it is that of an animal. The sweeping curves of the profile betray Indian influence, but the row of human figures standing behind each other with bent knees on the

318

creatures back and head are wrought in the traditional style o
primitive sculpture. Thus, even such lesser subjects show clearly th
synthesis so very characteristic of the whole of Batak art. Moreover
figures of riders and rows of figures towering vertically above eac
other, similar to those of the magic wands yet to be mentioned, ar
sometimes to be found on the wooden stoppers of such receptacle

The figures of ivory, brass, horn, or wood, serving as hilts t
the Batak swords and daggers, are very similar to those of th
medicine receptacles (fig. 71). The significance of most of the motive
cannot be ascertained, as no research concerning them has as ye
been made. Unmistakable, however, is the Kalmâshapâda-Sutasom
motive, derived from a Buddhist Jâtaka story. The Batak, as th
Burmese and Shan, use two varieties of it. The first shows the ogr
Kalmâshapâda carrying king Sutasoma, whom he has ravished, o
his shoulders, while the second version depicts the giant animal-heade
ogre squatting behind the standing Sutasoma, ready to devour hin

The magic wands (p. 86) certainly belong to the most interestin
carvings of the Bataks (fig. 26, 27). They consist of a vertical serie
of human and animal figures — men, women, buffaloes, horse
crocodiles, and serpents — and strikingly call to mind the crest-pole
of the Northwest American Indians. Schurtz seems to be right whe
suggesting a possible genetical connection between both. It is mo
than probable that the various tales, told by the Batak about th
significance of these figures, are but late interpretations of a muc
older form, no longer understood. The use, too, of these staffs fo
magic purposes, as bearers of a Pangulubalang, is certainly n
indigenous. Apparently eastern Asiatic and Indian (tantric) influenc
affected this magical interpretation, as they did in the case of the inte
pretation of the ancient ancestral images into Pangulubalang figure
The Batak "magic wand", though preserving in the main its origin
shape, has undergone foreign influences with regard to some detail
There are even staffs plainly showing Indian influence in the
structure. Though a large number of them are artistically insignifican
there are some that excel by daring imagination, minute executio
and an excellent rendering of the magic-demoniac spirit of the
subjects.

Wares such as bangles, belt-ornaments, pipes, tobacco-cases, bete
boxes, and sword-hilts cast in copper, bronze, or brass, play an in
portant part with the Batak (fig. 18, 71). Even the above mentione

"magic wands" are sometimes made of brass. The casting is done in
he "cire perdue" method. Jewelry made of gold, silver, or suwasa
— an alloy of gold, silver and copper — often reaches a high degree
f artistry (fig. 12). Sometimes, for decorative reasons granulation-
echnique will be used. Double spirals and plaited bands belong to
he most frequently occurring motives. They both have their origin
n the Dông-son Culture. Besides these, other, more ancient motives
— such as buffalo-head and lizard — and more recent, Indian ones
— such as lion heads (singa) — have entered the metal art of the
Batak. Of special interest are the brass ornaments of the belts
fig. 70). They show an old Indonesian motive, a human figure
tanding on a buffalo's head, more or less assimilated to the horned
ion heads of Indian and Javanese art (Banaspati, Râhu, &c.).

We must still mention the objects executed in bamboo. The bamboo
oxes containing lime for betel chewers are decorated with the tumpal
triangle) motive, plaited bands, and double spirals interpreted as
reepers, and the latter two again bear evidence of the strong influence
f Dông-son art. Objects made of horn, show the same plaited band
n beautiful execution (fig. 75).

Domestic architecture and its decorations, show most distinctly
he fusion of the three chief stylistic strata, i. e. of the megalithic-
ymbolic style, the style of Dông-son, and the Hindu-Sumatrean one.
The most important and artistically significant house forms are those
f the Toba and of the Karo.

The Toba house is a rectangular building supported by piles,
ith walls slanting outwards, so that when, omitting the roof, a
ross section in any direction is taken, it will represent a trapezoid
esting on its smaller side. The saddled roof is lowered in the middle,
nd the pointed end of the ridge projects more acutely in the front
an in the rear of the house (fig. 23). This shape of house is rather
imilar to those represented on the bronze drums from Tonking at
e beginning of the Christian era, and originates possibly in the
ông-son Culture. The front of the house is lavishly decorated with
rved and painted ornaments. Double spirals, and scrolls derived
om them, are chiefly used (fig. 7). According to de Boer these latter
re supposed to represent a sort of sea-weed (siandor ni laut). Though
ey have obviously been assimilated to creeper tendrils through
dian and possibly Malayo-Mohammedan influence, they can decid-
lly be traced back to the old S-shaped double-spiral of the Dông-

son Culture. One beam of the front wall will often show paintings representing scenes of daily life, war, hunting, and festivals. These paintings of the Batak show plainly close stylistic connection with those of the Dayak of Borneo, and, as I have· explained elsewhere ("Vorgeschichtliche Grundlagen der kolonialindischen Kunst") both of them probably reach back as far as the Dông-son Culture. Of a more ancient origin are the female breasts in relief work on the front walls, a typical megalithic motive. The carved lizards, symbols of Boraspati ni Tano, deity of the earth, and probably some of the frequent circular motives, which are perhaps connected with the megalithic rosette, are also of older origin.

Heads of monsters, crowned with a sort of trident — two horns and a middle piece — are found as decoration of front walls, gables and corner posts (fig. 7). They are called Singa, a name borrowed from the Sanskrit, meaning lion, but sometimes, too, Gadja Dompak "elephant's head". The horned lion's head, so frequent in India and colonial Indian (Javanese, &c.) art seems to have supplanted the ancient indigenous buffalo head, or else to have been amalgamated with it. However, we must call attention to the striking resemblance of the Batak Singa to the trisûla-crowned human heads found a gable-figures in the South-Indian Pallava architecture, for instance on the Ganesa-Ratha at Mâmallapuram (7th century). This may lead to a more definite determination of the age and origin of Indian influence on the Batak.

The types of Karo houses (figs. 5, 8) show more variety than those of the Toba. Besides the houses supported by piles, there are other with a substructure of horizontal beams forming a sort of grill, resting on stone pillars. As with the Toba, the walls are slanting outward but the roof has still more become the form-deciding element. In its simplest shape it is a combination of a hipped and a saddle roof. About the middle of its sloping lower part rises a saddle-roof with projecting ridge-ends, mostly terminating in a likeness to a buffalo head. Except for the buffalo heads, this shape of roof is widely spread in eastern Asia and Melanesia. As early as the first centuries A. D. figures on a Japanese bronze mirror. It has possibly been transplanted to Sumatra along with the other components of the Dông-son Culture.

This sort of roof, in itself a compound of two different shapes has been further developed and complicated by the Karo. For instance the lower, sloping part was doubled, so that another, purely decorative storey arose, which in its turn bears the actual composed hip-saddled roof. Sometimes there are two saddled roofs crossing at right angles, a mode frequently occurring in Cambodian and Siamese architecture. Often a large pole will arise from the crossing point of the ridges. It bears a small reproduction of the whole roof and is finally crowned by a sort of sun-shade (figs. 5, 8). We may assume that this multiplication of roofs betrays the influence of the Hindu and Buddhist many storied roofs, like those of the merus of Bali and of Burmese. monasteries and palaces. The shade topping the roof is doubtlessly derived from the honorary shade on sacred buildings of the Buddhists. Among the ruins of the Buddhist temples at Bahal in Padang Lawas, thus in Batak territory, fragments of such stone umbrellas have actually been found. Here again we meet with the characteristic fusion of heterogeneous elements so typical of Batak culture.

The Karo as well as the Toba, paint scenes of daily life or legend on the walls of their houses, but the scroll motive is by far not as frequent and well developed as in Toba art. The Karo prefer motives of a simpler nature some of which are geometric. An almost never missing motive is a sort of geometrically conceived lizard, formed of the fibres of the Areng palm tree, by which the planks of the walls are fastened to each other.

Though the houses of the Toba and Karo are exceedingly attractive because of their phantastic roofs, beautiful proportions, and their lavish and tasteful ornamentation, no attempt whatever is made to dispose of their inward space. There are not even fixed walls separating the lodgings of the different families.

Finally we must mention the illustrations in the Batak books (fig. 28). Though the significance of the objects they represent is rooted solely in Indian magic and astrology, their style is obviously connected with the indigenous style of the wall-paintings.

We would consider it of great advantage if a more thorough analysis of Batak art, than was possible in this limited space, were made. This would bring forth, most probably, results of far more than local interest and would yield important indications for the history of Eastern Asiatic and even Oceanic civilizations.

The influence of late bronze-age Dông-son Culture will be found, as in the sculptures of Pasemah and the art of the Batak, in other parts of Sumatra. Even the ornamental art of the Mentawei Islands is rooted in the Dông-son style, with its spirals and plaited bands, quite contradictory to the otherwise primitive character of their culture. However, this style has also formed the basis of the art of a much more cultured people, the Minangkabau of Central Sumatra.

The archaeology and art of the Hindu-Buddhist period.

Suvarnadvîpa, "the Island of Gold", i. e. Sumatra, became known to the Hindus at the very latest about the first century A. D. Probably Indian colonies have been there about the second century A. D. if not earlier, though until now no archaeological traces of these first centuries of Hindu-Sumatrean history have come to our knowledge. The oldest Hindu-Sumatrean monument as yet discovered, is a stone torso of a Buddha statue, which has been found shattered to several pieces near Bukit Seguntang, a hill in the immediate neighborhood of Palembang. Krom has called attention to the fact, that this image has been influenced by the South Indian school of Amarâvatî. According to Mrs. Stella Kramrisch who kindly helped me in determining the dates and Indian affinities of the earliest remains found at Palembang and Djambi, it cannot date further back than the second half of the fifth century. But as it is presumably not younger than the sixth century, it may possibly belong to the time before the foundation of the empire of Srîvijaya, the existence of which is traceable only from the seventh century.

Other finds of sculptures made at Palembang may be ascribed to the time of greatest prosperity of Srîvijaya, whose capital must have been situated at about the same spot as the present Palembang. A stone Bodhisatva torso, having been found, too, on the slopes of Bukit Seguntang, and the more than life-sized statue of Bodhisatva Avalokiteśvara, found on the river Musi, are connected with the artistic style of the South Indian kingdom of the Pallava of the seventh century A. D., thus seeming to belong to the first period of Srîvijaya's rising power. Three very beautiful bronzes, a Buddha, an Avalokiteśvara, and a Maitreya, belong to the style of Central Java and must date from between the eighth and the tenth centuries (fig. 78 c, d, e). They were found in the Komering river not far from Palembang. Another find, made on Bukit Seguntang, is a bronze Buddha head with a flower wreath (fig. 78 a, b). Considered stylistically and iconographically it is quite unique, thus bearing witness to he existence of an indigenous Sumatrean style, besides the styles of South Indian and Javanese origin.

A point of great interest among the finds of the period of Srîvijaya is formed by four inscriptions written in the Old-Malay idiom interspersed with Sanskrit words. Three of these inscriptions are dated, being the oldest dated inscriptions from Indonesia as yet known, and moreover the oldest existing texts in Malay and even Austronesian language in general. The characters are very similar to those of the Pallava kingdom.

The oldest of these inscriptions, found near Palembang, is dated 605 of the Śaka era, i. e. 683 A. D. It gives details about an important event having happened in this year but which it was not as yet possible to elucidate completely. By some archaeologists it is even thought to refer to the foundation of the capital of Śrîvijaya. The second one, found at Tala Tuwo near Palembang, dates from the Śaka year 606, i. e. 684 A. D., and informs us of the endowment of a garden by the king, ending with a long Buddhist blessing (pranidhâna). We may infer from it that the kings of the Śailendra dynasty of Śrîvijaya, who later contributed so thouroughly to the propagation of Mahâyâna-Buddhism in Indonesia and on the Malay Peninsula, professed this religion in its tantric form of Vajrayâna as early as the seventh century. By far the largest part of Hindu-Sumatrean monuments of all times, belong to the sphere of the Mahâyâna. In contrast to Java, Sumatra is able to boast of only very few monuments of purely Śivaitic character, and Hînayâna-Buddhism has not left archaeological traces whatever, though according to the Chinese pilgrim Yi-tsing this was the predominant religion till about the end of the seventh century.

The third inscription, found at Kota Kapur on the isle of Bangka, dates from 608 Śaka (686 A. D.) and is a proof that this island was then subject to Śrîvijaya. It gives tidings of a campaign the king of this country undertook against Java. A fourth inscription, very similar to the one of Kota Kapur but not dated, has been found at Karang Brahi in the region of Djambi.

Besides this there are few monuments in Sumatra which can be recognized with some probability as belonging to the period of the kings of the Śailendra dynasty. Primarily we must mention two Buddha statues from Djambi (reproduced by T. Adam), whose style corresponds to the North Indian style of the seventh century and clearly is connected with the traditions of Gupta art. Near the remains

of a brick-building at Si Mangambat in Mandailing, Bosch found
several stones ornamented with reliefs (one of them with a Kâla head),
remnants of some temple showing undoubtedly Central Javanese
character, dating most probably from the eighth or ninth centuries
Some Sivaitic sculptural and architectonic remains of Central Javanese
character, too, thus also dating from the eighth till tenth centuries
have been found near the river Lematang west of Palembang.

In the Batak territory in the region of Gunung Tuwa in Padang
Lawas a bronze group dated from 946 Śaka (1024 A. D.) was dis
covered. It represents the Bodhisatva Avalokiteśvara in his four-armed
shape as Lokanâtha, "Lord of the World", between two Târâs. For
once, the inscription records even the artist's name, Sûryya. Though
this group was certainly cast in Sumatra, its whole style as well as
the characters of the inscription show decidedly Javanese influence
again. We know by a Nepalese manuscript from the eleventh century
that Lokanâtha was highly worshipped in Sumatra about this time
and that one of his sacred images, erected in the capital of Śrîvijaya
was famous throughout the whole Buddhist world.

Among the various remains of the Hindu-Sumatrean period we
must call attention to four beautiful Makara heads, found at Kampong
Solok near Djambi. One of them bears the date of 986 Śaka (1064
A. D.). As usual with the Sumatrean Makaras a figure of a warrior
is standing between the monster's gaping jaws.

A prominent group of ruins is to be found in Muara Takus on
the upper Kampar river, remains of brick-buildings, among them
three stûpas and a terrace. A slender tower-like stûpa is the best
preserved of all (fig. 79). Bosch assumes, from the Nâgarî character
found on a stone and on a small gold plate, that these monument
can not be more ancient than the twelfth century. The brick stûpa
of Tandjong Medang in Upper Padang dates probably from the same
time. The marked prevalence of brick buildings as compared with
stone architecture, as well as the prominent part of the stûpa, are
characteristic traits distinguishing Hindu-Sumatrean from Hindu-
Javanese art.

The sculptures and buildings of the biaras of Padang Lawas
belong to the most interesting ones of the island. Biara, from
sanskrit vihâra, i. e. monastery, is the name by which ruins from the
Buddhist period are known in Central and North Sumatra. Excepting
one small secondary temple built of stone, there are only brick

buildings. The Biara Si Topayan near Gunung Tuwa consists in its present condition of two terraces, and between them a little courtyard. Two inscriptions refer to the foundation of the sanctuary. Some details of their ancient Javanese characters rather recall the characters of the Batak script. It may be that the latter originates from these parts. All the other biaras of Padang Lawas consist of a walled-in square with the principle temple surrounded by smaller temples, stûpas, and terraces, in the middle. A staircase, in its lower part flanked by Makaras, leads up to the basement of the rectangular cella. The corbelled roofs of two of the biaras of Bahal near Portibi, on the river Panei are still partly existing. They imitate the form of a stûpa and like it were crowned by a shade of honor. The basement of one of the biaras was ornamented with brick reliefs respresenting dancing Râkshasas and squatting lions. The principal sacred image of the Biara No. 2 of Bahal, yields interesting information concerning the history of religion. It represents Heruka dancing on a corpse, one of the most terrible gods of Vajrayâna-Buddhism, who was offered bloody sacrifices, probably even human ones, and among the rites of whose worship, the drinking of human blood and eating human flesh played a part. This worship of Heruka formed a point of contact between the Indian and the indigenous rites — since Padang Lawas is inhabited by a branch of Bataks — and gave impulse to the transformed interpretation of Batak cannibalism into a magic rite of degenerate Buddhism. And just this Buddhist interpretation, though forgotten again in the course of time, possibly was one of the essential reasons why Batak cannibaslism was able to survive for so long a period.

On account of these obvious traces of late tantric Buddhism, Bosch assumes, that the biaras of Padang Lawas must have been built during the period between King Krtanagara's accession to the throne of Tumapel-Singhasâri (1254 A. D.) and the death of King Adityavarman of Malayu (after 1375 A. D.). From a number of monuments and inscriptions we may infer that tantric Kâla-Cakra Buddhism with all its aberrations — a religion combining Buddhist and Śivaitic elements — was predominant in Central Sumatra, in Malayu (Djambi), as well as in Minangkabau, during the above named period. King Krtanagara of Tumapel-Singhasâri (East Java) invaded Sumatra in the year 1275, and Malayu (Djambi) became a tributary state to his empire. Now Krtanagara was a fervent partisan of Kâla-Cakra Buddhism, so that, if this religion was not actually brought to Sumatra by the Javanese invasion, its development was certainly much favoured by it.

Near Sungai Langsat, on the left bank of the Batang-Hari river, Westenenk discovered a stone bearing an inscription, obviously the base of some idol. The characters are the usual Javanese Kavi characters and the language is Kavi interspersed with numerous Malayisms. The inscription records that in the year 1208 Śaka (1286 A. D.) King Krtanagara ordered an image of Bodhisatva Amoghapâśa Lokeśvara — a gift of prince Visvarûpa — to be brought from Java to Sumatra by four dignitaries, and to be erected at Dharmmâśraya on the Batang-Hari to the gratification of the whole population and of Maulivarman, king of Malayu, then vassal to Krtanagara. The image itself, representing the Bodhisatva surrounded by Dhyâni-Buddhas, Târâs, and other Buddhist deities, was brought some sixty years later to Rambahan, another place in the Batang-Hari region, where it is still to be seen. Conforming to the period and the land of its origin, its style is the same as that of the empire of Singhasâri. Probably it is essentially a replica of the principal image of Tjandi Djago in East Java, the latter being a portrait of king Krtanagara's father, King Vishnuvarddhana — whose sepulchral temple Tjandi Djago had been — in the shape of Amoghapâśa. Another image found at Sungai Langsat is a more than life-sized statue of the god Bhairava. This sculpture, too, belongs to the sphere of Singhasâri art, and was probably brought from Java to Sumatra about the same time as the Amoghapâśa.

The doctrines of tantric Kâla-Cakra Buddhism seem to have fallen into fertile soil in Sumatra. This is disclosed by the inscriptions of King Adityavarman who ruled Malayu and Minangkabau during at least three decades. He ascended the throne probably between 1343 and 1347 and died sometime after 1375 A. D. In the year 1347 A. D. he ordered Krtanagara's statue of Amoghapâśa to be taken to Rambahan, established it in a Buddhist sanctuary there and had it sanctified anew. By his orders a detailed record of this was engraved on the back of the image. It has been deciphered by Kern and interpreted by Moens. From this as well as from other inscriptions we learn that the king was ordained to the highest tantric orders. The Sanscrit language used in the inscriptions is exceedingly faulty and deficient, an obvious sign of the decay of culture since the seventh century, at which time Śrîvijaya had been a centre of Buddhist learning to which Chinese pilgrims travelled from afar to study Sanscrit.

Finally, we may mention that the close relations between Sumatra and South India, specially with the Cola empire, leading to the foundation of a Buddhist sanctuary on South-Indian soil by a king of Śrîvijaya about 1000 A. D., and on the other hand, to the temporary conquest of Śrîvijaya by a king of Cola in 1023 A. D., have left archaeological traces in Sumatra. For instance, an inscription was found at Lobu Tua near Baros, written in Tamil, dated from 1088 A. D. and originating from a South Indian commercial partnership. From the 13th and 14th centuries we have a few inscriptions written in South Indian characters, and in one of the biaras of Padang Lawas a female bronze image, of decidedly South Indian origin, was found.

Mohammedan archaeology and the art of the Moslem poeples.

Older Moslem monuments are, with few exceptions, practically limited to tombstones, many of which were not even made in Sumatra, but were imported from Cambay in Gujerât (India). From an historical point of view their inscriptions are of great value. Some of these tombstones date as far back as the first period of Islam in Sumatra, as for instance the stone of Sultan Malik al-Saleh, the founder of the empire of Samudra-Pasè, who died in 1297 A. D. Besides the tombstones a few older cupolas in Atjeh ought to be mentioned as well as a curious little building at Kota Radja (Atjeh), the Gunongan, i. e. "mountain", erected by Sultan Iskandar Thani (1636—1641) as a sort of pleasure tower.

Here I ought to give at least a brief sketch of the more recent arts of the Mohammedan peoples of Sumatra, such as weaving, metal work, and carving in horn, ivory, or wood. However, although much valuable work has been done by Dutch ethnologists concerning the technical rudiments of these applied arts, no preliminary historical research in style has as yet been done. It is naturally quite impossible to attempt any such work in this limited space, as a thorough research would have to reach far beyond Sumatra. I shall have to content myself, therefore, with the statement that the stock of ornamental themes of applied art, as practised among the Mohammedans of Sumatra, though belonging seemingly to a single style only, is in reality a conglomerate of elements of heterogeneous origin. The basis is still in many a case the old bronze-age Dông-son style, as is easily conceivable, for instance, from the plaited bands and S-shaped double spirals so prominent in the art of Minangkabau (fig. 76). Later on, Hindu, Hindu-Javanese, and finally Moslem motives were assimilated, and even Chinese influence may have had its say in the development of Malay ornamentation.

Special attention ought to be bestowed on the architecture of Minangkabau. The Minangkabau house form is related to that of the Toba and to the houses figuring on the oldest bronze drums of the Dông-son Culture. The shape of the roof is repeated, though not in the vertical direction as with the Karo, but the different parts are shoved into each other horizontally (figs. 31, 33, 34). This form of roof is also to be found in Cambodian and Siamese architecture. There is certainly a connection between the latter and that of Minangkabau, but it is not possible as yet to ascertain whether this sort of structure originated in Indo-China or in Sumatra. Sometimes both ends of a Minangkabau house will graduate to a kind of oriel, thus giving it the curious aspect of a sailing boat of the midde ages with fore and aft-castle (fig. 33). The walls are lavishly decorated with scroll motives and other ornaments, mostly of Indian or Mohammedan origin, though in a few cases still betraying the old Dông-son rudiments. The application of glass mosaics in wall ornamentation again intimates some sort of connection between Central Sumatra and Siam.

The balai, or communal houses, are very similar to the domestic dwellings, but the wings only are enclosed by walls, the middle part being left open (fig. 34). Among the most charming buildings are rice granaries, built on piles, with richly decorated walls slanting outwards, and a saddle roof lowered in its middle (fig. 31 left).

Very little research has been done with regard to the old Sumatrean mosques built of wood. It seems that throughout the greater part of the island, at least in Atjeh and Minangkabau, the Indian form of roof ascending in steps like the roofs of the meru of Bali and of Burmese monasteries and temples, has been adapted to Mohammedan architecture.

Conclusions.

Let us attempt to sum up the different cultural strata that we were able to ascertain.

1. The late palaeolithic Flake Culture; its bearers being probably Veddoids.

2. The late palaeolithic Hand-Axe Culture; its bearers being Papua-Melanesoids.
3. The protoneolithic elements of the later phases of the Hand-Axe Culture (implements with rough-ground edges, rubble-axes), introduced perhaps by Proto-Malaysians.
4. The earlier neolithic civilisations, still recognizable in Engano and in the Mentawei Islands, though not traceable as yet archaeologically.
5. The late neolithic Quadrangular-Adze Culture (Vierkantbeilkultur) which was brought from Further India to Sumatra by the original Austronesians ("Malayo-Polynesians"), probably between 2000 and 1500 B.C. (quadrangular and beaked adzes, the technique of sawing stone, cultivation of rice and millet, cattle raising, outrigger boat, megaliths, ancestral figures, headhunting, &c.).
6. The late bronze and early iron age Dông-son Culture which reached Sumatra probably before or about 300 B.C. (socketed bronze celts, daggers and lances of bronze or iron, bronze drums, spiral and plait-band ornaments, figurative painting, and probably the form of the Toba and Karo houses). It was brought to Sumatra probably by merchants and colonists from northeastern Indo-China (Tongking, Annam) and South China.
7. The Chinese influences of early Han times, coinciding partly with the later phases of Dông-son Culture (stone-cist graves, Pasemah sculptures, the latter being closely related to the plastic art of the early Han period).
8. The Hindu-Sumatrean culture which took birth at the very latest during the second century A.D. under the influence of Hindu colonists and Brahman and Buddhist missionaries; continual influences from different parts of India and Greater India (Java, and probably Kambodia, Siam, and Burma) lasting at least till the fourteenth century A.D.
9. The Mohammedan culture, prevalent in North Sumatra from about the middle of the thirteenth century, in the greater part of the island since the fifteenth or sixteenth centuries; transmitted by Mohammedan traders from India, specially from Gujerât, and later also from Arabia.
10. The later Chinese influences, dating back at least as far as the end of the fourteenth century A.D.

This provisional list, no doubt, falls far short from the actual facts. For instance, there must have existed in Sumatra more ancient palaeolithic cultures, not yet known to us. Bronze age influences, too, probably reached the island before the Dông-son Culture, but we are not, as yet, able to prove this.

Of course we must not imagine that the cultural strata enumerated above, have each been brought to Sumatra by a single strictly circumscribed cultural or invasional wave only. On the contrary, we deal here with exceedingly complicated proceedings. This will easily be confirmed by the investigation of such civilizations as reached Sumatra in historical times. Certainly Sumatra first came into touch with Hindus and Hindu culture at the very latest during the first two centuries A. D. But from this time the intercourse between India and Sumatra never wholly ceased. I need only point out the Buddhist establishments founded at Nâlandâ in the ninth century and at Nega-patam about 1000 A. D. by kings of Śrîvijaya; the reproduction of Sumatrean Buddhist idols in a Nepalese manuscript of the eleventh century; the prominent part played by Śrîvijaya in the history of later Buddhism, and the manifold threads of Buddhist activity and learning spreading from Sumatra to China, India, and even Tibet. The invasion of Sumatra by a king of Cola in the eleventh century, the Tamil inscription of Lubu Tua from the year 1088 A. D., and the Dravidian tribal names still to be found among the Batak are also not to be forgotten. So we can safely assert that Sumatra has not only once been colonised by Hindus, but that, owing to more than a thousand years of close connection, it became an integral part of the Greater Indian cultural area. It is natural that other cultural elements reached Sumatra from the Tamil region and Malabar, than those that came from Bengal, and again, influences coming from South India in the time of the Cola kings of the eleventh century, must have differed remarkably from those of the Pallava period in the seventh. More-over, material as well as spiritual influences did not take their way always directly from the Indian mother-country, but were also trans-mitted by way of various Indian "colonies", specially by Java, thus being subjected more or less to changes and assimilations, before reaching the island.

The history of Sumatrean Buddhism is exceedingly characteristic of the continual participation of Sumatra in the development and trans-formation of Indian religious life. Consider the tremendous difference between seventh century Buddhism, when Yi-tsing came to visit the island and the Buddhist scholar Śākyakîrti wrote his books in Śrîvijaya — it was the time of the prevalence of Hînayâna, Mahâyâna with slight tantric influences just beginning to gain ground — and the extreme tantric Kâla-Cakra Buddhism during the days of Krtanagara, Maulivarman, and Adityavarman in the thirteenth and fourteenth centuries!

Similar historical layers are discernible in connection with Sumatrean Islam and Mohammedan culture. While Islam was imported from India, more accurately from Gujerât, and owing to this had primarily a more or less Shiite tinge, it was subjected from the seventeenth century to steadily increasing Arabian orthodox influence. With the Gayo we even find some decidedly Ottoman weapons and garments, a sign that even Turc influences have pushed far into the interior of the island.

We may assume that what we recognise to be valid for historical civilizations, will in all probability hold true concerning prehistorical periods, though we are as yet not able to prove it. Could we but discern different sub-strata of the neolithic Quadrangular-Adze Culture, we should perhaps be able to dissolve many an apparent disagreement between archaeological and ethnological results. I need only refer to the fact, that we are not yet able to discern a coincidence between the distribution of prehistoric culture-layers and such fundamental social forms as for instance the father-right of the Batak and the mother-right of Minangkabau.

Finally, intending to exclude any possible misinterpretation, I want to assert once more that, naturally, most of the spiritual and material contributions of foreign origin have been developed in Sumatra in original, and often even in a very ingenious way. We need only think of the artistic creations of Nias and Pasemah.

We are still at the beginning of archaeological research in Sumatra. But though still an immense amount of field work will have to be accomplished, we may hope that this island — owing to its position on the way, primitive man must have taken from Asia to Australia and the Southseas, and on the way for the seafarers of later periods, between India and China — will yield us facts of most fundamental importance for the history of mankind.

BIBLIOGRAPHY

Abbreviations of Names of Journals in Bibliography.

A	Anthropos
AA	American Anthropologist
AfA	Archiv für Anthropologie
AMZ	Allgemeine Missions-Zeitschrift
BTLV-NI	Bijdragen tot de Taal-, Land-, en Volkenkunde van Nederlandsch-Indië
G	Globus
IAE	Internationales Archiv für Ethnographie
JAI	Journal of the Royal Anthropological Institute
MNZ	Mededeelingen van wege het Nederlandsche Zendelinggenootschap
NI	Nederlandsch Indië oud en nieuw
OV	Oudheidkundige Dienst in Nederlandsch Indië, Oudheidkundig Verslag.
TBB	Tijdschrift voor het Binnenlandsch Bestuur
TI-TLV	Tijdschrift voor Indische Taal- Land- en Volkenkunde
TNI	Tijdschrift voor Neêrland's Indië
TNAG	Tijdschrift van het Nederlandsch Aardrijkskundig Genootschap
UC-PAAE	University of California, Publications in American Archaeology and Ethnology
ZE	Zeitschrift für Ethnologie
ZvR	Zeitschrift für vergleichende Rechtswissenschaft

Bibliography.

Sumatra, its History and People.

Introduction.

BEYER, H. O., STEIGER, G. N., and BENITEZ, C. A History of the Orient. New York, 1929.

COLLET, O. J. A. Terres et Peuples de Sumatra. Amsterdam, 1925.

FERRAND, G. L'Empire Sumatranais de Crivijaya. Paris, 1922.

HEINE-GELDERN, R. Urheimat und früheste Wanderungen der Austronesier. A 1932. Südostasien in G. BUSCHAN, Illustrierte Völkerkunde. Vol. II. Stuttgart, 1923.

KLEIWEG DE ZWAAN, J. P. De Rassen van den Indischen Archipel. Amsterdam, 1925.

KROEBER, A. L. The Peoples of the Philippines. American Museum of Natural History, Handbook 8. New York, 1928.

KROM, N. J. Hindoe-Javaansche Geschiedenis. s'Gravenhage, 1926.

LEKKERKERKER, C. Land en Volk van Sumatra. Leiden, 1916.

LOEB, E. M. Patrilineal and Matrilineal Organization in Sumatra. AA 1933—34. Die soziale Organisation Indonesiens und Ozeaniens. A 1933.

MARSDEN, W. The History of Sumatra. London, 1811.

MARCO POLO. The Book of Ser Marco Polo.

ZONDERVAN, H. Das Völkergemisch Sumatras. ZE 1930.

Encyclopaedie van Nederlandsch-Ost-Indië. 4 Vols. s'Gravenhage and Leiden. 1917—1921. Article, "Banka". Encyclopedia Britannica. 14th Ed. Article, "Sumatra".

Bataks.

ALKEMA, B., and BEZEMER, T. J. Volkenkunde van Nederlandsch-Indië. Haarlem, 1927.

BOER, D. W. N. DE. De Toba-Bataksche Grondrechtsbegrippen, ingeleid met eene uitenzetting van daarmede samenhangende andere adatvormen. TBB 1914.

BRENNER, J. Besuch bei den Kannibalen Sumatras. Würzburg, 1894.

COLLET, O. J. A. Terres et Peuples de Sumatra. Amsterdam, 1925.

HEYTING, TH. A. L. Beschrijving der Onder-Afdeeling Groot-Mandeling en Batang-Natal. TNAG 1897.

HOËVELL, G. W. W. C. Baron VAN. Iets over 't oorlogvoeren der Batta's. TNI 1878.

JOUSTRA, M. Het leven, de zeden en gewoonten der Bataks. MNZ 1902. Karo-Bataksch woordenboek. Leiden, 1907. De Bataks. Uitgaven van het Bataksch Instituut, no. 7. Leiden, 1912. Batakspiegel. Uitgaven van het Bataksch Instituut, no. 21. Leiden, 1926.

336

JUNGHUHN, F. Beschreibung der Battaländer. Vol. 11. Berlin, 1847.
KÖDDING, W. Die batakschen Götter und ihr Verhältnis zum Brahmanismus. AMZ 1885.
LEKKERKERKER, C. Land en volk van Sumatra. Leiden, 1916.
LOEB, E. M. Patrilineal and Matrilineal Organization in Sumatra. AA 1933—34. Shaman and Seer. AA 1929.
MARSDEN, W. The History of Sumatra. London, 1811.
MEERWALDT, J. H. Wijzen de tegenwoordige zeden en gewoonten der Bataks nog sporen an van een oorsprongkelijk matriarchaat? BTLV-NI 1892. De Bataksche tooverstaf. BTLV-NI 1902. Gebruiken in het maatschappelijk leven der Bataks. MNZ 1904.
NEUMANN, J. B. Het Pane en Bila-Stroomgebied op het eiland Sumatra. Studien over Bataks en Bataksche landen. TNAG 1886.
NEUMANN, J. H. De Smid. MNZ 1903. Een en ander aangaande de Karo-Bataks. MNZ 1904. De tendi in verband mi Si Dajang. MNZ 1904. Kemali, Pantang en Rebu bij de Karo-Bataks. TI-TLV 1906.
OPHUIJSEN, C. A. van. Der Bataksche Zauberstab. IAE 1911. Kijkjes in het huiselijk leven der Bataks. Uitgaven van het Bataksch Instituut, no. 4. Leiden, 1910.
TIDEMAN, J. Simeloengoen. Het land der Timoer-Bataks. Leiden, 1922.
VOLZ, W. Nord-Sumatra. Vol. 1. Berlin, 1909.
WARNECK, F. Das Eherecht bij den Toba-Batak. BTLV-NI 1901.
WARNECK, J. Tobabataksch-Deutsches Wörterbuch. Batavia, 1906. Die Religion der Batak. Göttingen, 1909. Das Opfer bei den Tobabatak in Sumatra. Archiv für Religionswissenschaft, 1915.
WESTENBERG, C. J. Aanteekeningen omtrent de Goddienstige Begrippen der Karo-Bataks. BTLV-NI 1892.
WIJNGAARDEN, J. Iets over naamgeving en eigennamen voornamelijk bij de Karau-Bataks. MNZ 1894.
WILLER, T. I. Verzameling der Battaksche Wetten en Instellingen in Mandheling en Pertibie: Gevolgd van een overzigt van Land en Volk in die Strekken. TNI 1846.
WILKEN, G. A. De Verspreide Geschriften. 4 vols. s'Gravenhage, 1912.
WINKLER, J. Die Toba-Batak auf Sumatra in gesunden und kranken Tagen. Stuttgart, 1925.
YPES, W. K. H. Bijdrage tot de kennis van de stamverwantschap, de inheemsche rechtsgemeenschappen en het grondenrecht der Toba-en Dairi Bataks. s'Gravenhage, 1932.
"Bataks" and "Huwelijk" in Encyclopaedie van Nederlandsch-Oost-Indië.

Minangkabau.

ALKEMA, B., and BEZEMER, T. J. Volkenkunde van Nederlandsch-Indië. Haarlem 1927.
COLLET, O. J. A. Terres et Peuples de Sumatra. Amsterdam, 1925.
JOUSTRA, M. Minangkabau, Overzicht van Land, Geschiedenis en Volk. s'Gravenhage, 1923.

KOHLER, J. Über das Recht der Minangkabau auf Sumatra. ZvR 1910.

LEKKERKERKER, C. Land en Volk van Sumatra. Leiden, 1916.

MAASS, A. Durch Zentral-Sumatra. Vol. 1. Berlin, 1910.

VAN EERDE, J. C. Een Huwelijk bij de Minangkabausche Maleiers. TI-TLV 1901. De Volken van Nederlandsch Indië. Vol. 1. Amsterdam, 1920.

VAN HASSELT, A. L. Volksbeschrijving van Midden-Sumatra. In Midden-Sumatra. Reizen en Onderzoekingen der Sumatra Expeditie, onder Toezicht van Prof. P. J. VETH. Third Part. Leiden, 1882.

VAN DER TOORN, J. L. Aanteekeningen uit het Familieleven bij den Maleier in de Padangsche Bovenlanden. TI-TLV 1881. Het Animisme bij den Minangkabauer der Padangsche Bovenlanden. BTLV-NI 1890.

WESTENENK, L. C. De Minangkabausche Negari. Mededeelingen van het Bureau voor de Bestuurszaken der Buitengewesten, bewerkt door het Encyclopaedisch Bureau 17. Weltevreden, 1918.

WILLINCK, G. D. Het rechtsleven bij de Minangkabausche Maleiërs. Leiden, 1908.

ZWAAN, J. P. KLEIWEG DE. De Verhouding tot de aangetrowde familie in den Indischen Archipel. BTLV-NI 1918.

Articles "Minangkabau" and "Sukus" in Encyclopaedie van Nederlandsch-Oost-Indië.

Islands West of Sumatra.

NIAS.

ALKEMA, B., and BEZEMER, T. J. Volkenkunde van Nederlandsch-Indië. Haarlem, 1927.

HEINE-GELDERN, R. Die Megalithen Südostasiens und ihre Bedeutung für die Klärung der Megalithenfrage in Europa und Polynesien. A 1928.

HORNER, L. Batoe-Eilanden. TNI 1840.

KLEIWEG DE ZWAAN, J. P. Die Heilkunde der Niasser. s'Gravenhage, 1913.

RAPPARD, TH. C. Het Eiland Nias en Zijne Bewoners. BTLV-NI 1909.

SCHRÖDER, E. E. W. Gs. Nias, 2 Vols. Leiden, 1917.

VAN EERDE, J. C. De Volken van Nederlandsch-Indië. Vol. 1. Amsterdam, 1920.

MENTAWEI.

CRISP, J. An Account of the Inhabitants of the Poggy, or Nassau Islands. Asiatic Researches. Calcutta, 1799.

HANSEN, J. F. K. De Groep Noord en Zuid Pageh. BTLV-NI 1915.

KARNY, H. H. Auf den Glücksinseln. Natur. 1925.

KLEIWEG DE ZWAAN, J. P. Bijdrage tot de Anthropologie der Mentaweiers. TNAG 1917.

KRUYT, A. C. De Mentaweiers. TI-TLV 1923. Een bezoek aan de Mentawei-Eilanden. TNAG 1924.

LOEB, E. M. Mentawei Religious Cult. UC-PAAE 1929. Mentawei Social Organization. AA 1928. Shaman and Seer. AA 1929. Mentawei Myths. BTLV-NI 1929.

338

MAASS, A. Bei liebenswurdigen Wilden. Berlin, 1902.

NEUMANN, J. B. De Mentawei-Eilanden. TNAG 1909.

PLEYTE, C. M. Die Mentawei-Inseln und ihre Bewohner. G 1901. Sumpitan and Bow in Indonesia. IAE 1891.

ROSENBERG, H. Der Malaiische Archipel. Leipzig, 1878.

TEN KATE, H. F. C. Eenige opmerkingen betreffende de Anthropologie der Mentaweiers. TNAG 1918.

VOLZ, W. Zur Kenntnis der Mentawei-Inseln. AfA 1905.

WIRZ, P. Het Eiland Sabiroet en zijn bewoners. NI 1931.

ENGANO.

HELFRICH, O. L. De Eilandgroep Engano. TNAG 1888.

MODIGLIANI, E. L'isola delle Donne. Viaggio ad Engano. Milano, 1894.

OUDMANS, A. C. Engano, Zijne Geschiedenis, Bewoners en Voortbrengselen. TNAG 1889. (Compiled from older accounts.)

WALLAND, J. Het Eiland Engano. TI-TLV 1864.

"Engano" in Encyclopaedie van Nederlandsch-Oost-Indie.

Northern Sumatra.

HURGRONJE, C. SNOUCK. Het Gajoland en zijne bewoners. Batavia, 1903. The Achehnese. 2 Vols. Leiden, 1906.

JACOBS, J. Het familie- en kampongleven op Groot-Atjeh. 2 Vols. Leiden, 1894.

KREEMER, J. Atjèh. 2 Vols. Leiden, 1922.

LEKKERKERKER, C. Land en Volk van Sumatra. Leiden, 1916.

VOLZ, W. Nord-Sumatra. Vol. 11. Die Gajolander. Berlin, 1909—1912.

Encyclopaedie van Nederlandsch-Oost-Indie. Article, "Acheh".

Southern Sumatra.

BOERS, J. W. De Kubus. TNI 1838.

COLLET, O. J. A. Terres et Peuples de Sumatra. Amsterdam, 1925.

DONGEN, G. J. VAN. Bijdrage tot de Kennis van de Ridan-Koeboes. TBB 1906. De Koeboes in de Onderafdeeling Koeboestreken der Residentie Palembang. BTLV-NI 1910.

FORBES, H. O. On the Kubus of Sumatra. JAI 1885.

GODON, A. P. Bijdrage tot de kennis der Lubus van Sumatra. TNI 1864.

GRAAFLAND, A. F. P. De Verbreiding van het Matriarchaat in het Landchap Indragiri. (The Orang Mamaq.) BTLV-NI 1890.

HAGEN, B. Die Orang Kubu auf Sumatra. Frankfurt am Main, 1918.

HOEVELL, W. R. VAN. De Lampongsche distrikten op het eiland Sumatra. TNI 1852.

KERCKHOFF, CH. E. P. Eenige opmerkingen betreffende de zoogenaamde "Orang Lubu" op Sumatra's Westkust. TNAG 1980.

KREEMER, J. De Loeboes in Mandailing. BTLV-NI 1912.

LEKKERKERKER, C. Land en Volk van Sumatra. Leiden, 1916.

MOSZKOWSKI, M. Auf neuen Wegen durch Sumatra. Berlin, 1909.

Neumann, J. B. Het Pane en Bila-Stroomgebied op het eiland Sumatra. TNAG 1886.

Ophuijsen, C. A. van. De Loeboes. TI-TLV 1884.

Schebesta, P. Orang-Utan. Leipzig 1928.

Skeat, W. W. and Blagden, C. O. Pagan Races of the Malay Peninsula, London 1906.

Veth, P. J. Het Landschap Aboeng en de Aboengers op Sumatra. TNAG 1887.

Willer, T. J. and Netcher, E. Iets over de Lubus en Ulus in de Binnenlanden van Sumatra. TI-TLV 1885.

Wilkinson, R. J. A History of the Peninsular Malays. Singapore, 1923.

Encyclopaedie van Nederlandsch-Oost-Indië. Article, "Lampong".

The Archaeology and Art of Sumatra.

Stone Age.

Erb, J. Ein Fund von Steinwaffen in Süd-Sumatra. IAE 1904.

Heine-Geldern, R. Urheimat und früheste Wanderungen der Austronesier. A 1932.

Hoop, A. N. J. Th. van der. Megalithic remains in South-Sumatra. Zutphen 1932.

Kleiweg de Zwaan, J. J. Wat weten wij van den voorhistorischen mensch in den Indischen Archipel en op het naburig Aziatisch Continent? TNAG 1928.

Küpper, H. Paleolithische werktuigen uit Atjeh. TNAG 1930.

Maass, A. Ein Steinbeil aus Kerintji. ZE 1914.

Sarasin, P. Neue lithochrone Funde im Innern von Sumatra. Verhandlungen der Naturforschenden Gesellschaft in Basel 1914.

Schürmann, H. M. E. Kjökkenmöddinger und Paläolithicum in Nord-Sumatra. TNAG 1931.

Stein Callenfels, P. V. van. Rapport over een dienstreis door een deel van Sumatra. OV 1920. Het eerste palaeolithische werktuig in den Archipel. OV 1924. Bijdrage tot de chronologie van het neolithicum in Zuid-Oost Azie. OV 1926.

Stein Callenfels, P. V. van, and Evans, I. H. N. Report on cave excavations in Perak. OV 1926.

Vaufrey, R. Découvertes d'industries préhistoriques à Sumatra et dans la presqu'île de Malacca. L'Anthropologie 1927.

Witkamp, H. Kjökkenmöddinger ter Oostkust van Sumatra. TNAG 1920.

Zwierzycki, J. Een vondst uit de palaeolithische cultuurperiode in een grot in Boven-Djambi. De Mijningenieur 1926.

Pre-Hindu Archaeology.

Berg, E. J. van den, en Neumann, J. H. De Batoe Kemang, nabij Medan. BTLV-NI 1908.

Bie, W. P. de. Verslag van de ontgraving der steenen kamers in de doesoen Tandjoeng Ara, Pasemah-hoogvlakte. TI-TLV 1932.

340

Bont, G. K. H. de. De Batoe's Larong (kist-steenen) in Boven-Djambi, onderaf-
deeling Bangko. NI 1922/23.
Bosch, F. D. K. Een bronzen vat van Kerintji. OV 1922.
Heine-Geldern, R. Vorgeschichtliche Grundlagen der kolonialindischen Kunst.
Wiener Beitrage zur Kunst- und Kulturgeschichte Asiens 1934.
Hoop, A. N. J. Th. van der. Megalithic remains in South-Sumatra. Zutphen
1932.
Stein Callenfels, P. V. van. De Batu Kemang. OV 1924.
Vonk, H. W. De "batoe tatahan" bij Air Poear (Pasemah-landen). TI-TLV 1934.
Westenenk, L. C. Uit het land van Bittertong (Zuid-Sumatra). Djawa 1921.
De Hindoe-oudheden in de Pasemah-hoogvlakte. OV 1922.
Witkamp, H. Drie "steenen kanonnen" in Zuid-Kerintji. TNAG 1922.

Archaeology of the Hindu-Buddhist Period.

Adam, T. Oudheden te Djambi. OV 1921, 1922.
Bosch, F. D. K. Verslag van een reis door Sumatra. OV 1930.
Brandes, J. Bijschrift bij de door den heer Neeb gezonden photo's van oudheden
in het Djambische. TI-TLV 1902.
Coedes, G. Les inscriptions malaises de Crîvijava. Bulletin de l'Ecole Francaise
d'Extrême-Orient 1930.
Kalff, S. Sumatraansche oudheden. NI 1920/21.
Kerchoff, Ch. E. P. van. Aanteekeningen betreffende eenige der in de afdeeling
Padang-Lawas voorkomende Hindoe-oudheden. TI-TLV 1889.
Kern, H. De verspreide geschriften. Vol. 6, 7. 's-Gravenhage 1917.
Kern, R. A. Enkele aanteekeningen op G. Coedès' uitgave van de Maleische in-
schriften van Crîvijaya. BTLV-NI 1931.
Krom, N. J. Een Sumatraansche inscriptie van koning Krtanagara. Verslagen
en Mededeelingen der Koninklijke Akademie van Wetenschapen, Afdeeling
Letterkunde 1917. De inscriptie van Karang Brahi. TI-TLV 1919. In-
leiding tot de Hindoe-Javaansche kunst. 's-Gravenhage 1923. Hindoe-
Javaansche Geschiedenis. 's-Gravenhage 1926, 2nd. edition 1931. Kunst
van Crîwidjaya. NI 1929/30. Antiquities of Palembang. Annual Biblio-
graphy of Indian Archaeology 1931.
Maass, A. Durch Zentral-Sumatra. Berlin 1910.
Moens, J. L. Het Buddhisme op Java en Sumatra in zijn laatste bloeiperiode.
TI-TLV 1924.
Neeb, C. J. Het een en ander over Hindoe oudheden in het Djambische. TI-TLV
1902.
Nilakanta Sastri, K. A. A Tamil merchant-guild in Sumatra. TI-TLV 1932.
Ophuysen, van. Oudheden te Si Mangambat en Bonan Dolok. Notulen van
het Bataviaasch Genootschap van Kunsten en Wetenschappen 1888.
Perquin, P. J. Oudheidkundig onderzoek te Palembang. OV 1928.
Pleyte, C. M. Over een paar Hindoebeelden van Padang-tjandi. TI-TLV 1907.
Ronkel, Ph. S. van. A preliminary notice concerning two old Malay inscriptions
in Palembang. Acta Orientalia 1924.
Stein Callenfels, P. V. van. Rapport over een dienstreis door een deel van
Sumatra. OV 1920. Verslag over zijn inspectiereis door Sumatra. OV 1925.

VERBEEK, R. D. M., en DELDEN, E. TH. VAN. De Hindoe-ruinen bij Moeara-Takoes aan de Kampar-rivier. Met aanteekeningen van W. P. GROENEVELDT. Verhandelingen van het Bataviaasch Genootschap van Kunsten en Weten-schappen 1881.

WELLAN, J. W. J. Crîvijaya, 1250 jaren geleden gesticht. TNAG 1934.

WESTENENK, L. C. Eenige opmerkingen naar aanleiding van "De Hindoe-ruinen bij Moeara Takoes etc. door Verbeek en van Delden". TI-TLV 1913. Uit het land van Bittertong (Zuid-Sumatra). Djawa 1921. De Hindoe-Javanen in Midden- en Zuid-Sumatra. Handelingen van het Eerste Congres voor de Taal-, Land- en Volkenkunde van Java. Weltevreden 1921. Boekit Segoentang en Goenoeng Mahameroe uit de Sedjarah Melajoe. TI-TLV 1923.

YZERMAN, J. W. Beschrijving van de Boeddhistische bouwwerken te Moeara Takoes. TI-TLV 1892.

Inventaris der oudheden in de Padangsche Bovenlanden. OV 1912.

Voorloopige lijst van oudheden in de Buitenbezittingen. OV 1914.

Mohammedan Archaeology.

BOSCH, F. D. K. De inscriptie op den grafsteen van het gravencomplex genaamd Teungkoe Peuet Ploh Peuet. OV 1915.

DJAJADININGRAT, Raden Hoesein. De stichting van het "Goenòngan" geheeten monument te Koetaradja. TI-TLV 1916.

GOLDIE, W. Het een en ander over oudheidkundige monumenten in de XXVI Moekims (IX Moekims Toengkoeb) in Groot-Atjeh. TI-TLV 1911.

KREEMER, J. Atjèh. Vol. I. Leiden 1922.

MOQUETTE, J. P. De datum op den grafsteen van Malik Ibrahim te Grissee. TI-TLV 1912. De grafsteenen te Pasè en Grissee vergeleken met dergelijke monumenten uit Hindoestan. TI-TLV 1912. De eerste vorsten van Samoedra-Pasè. Rapporten van den Oudheidkundigen Dienst in Nederlandsch-Indie 1913. Verslag van mijn voorloopig onderzoek der Mohammedaansche oud-heden in Atjèh en Onderhoorigheden. OV 1914. De grafsteen van Kloem-pang (Deli). OV 1922.

MOQUETTE, J. P., en DJAJADININGRAT, R. A. Hoesein. Een merkwaardig, ingewikkeld raadsel op een Pasè'schen grafsteen. OV 1923.

The Art of the Present Population.

BOER, D. W. N. DE. Het Toba-Bataksche huis. Mededeelingen van het Bureau voor de Bestuurszaken der Buitengewesten bewerkt door het Encyclopaedisch Bureau XXIII 1920. Het Niassche huis. Ibidem XXV 1920.

BOSCH, F. D. K. De rijkssieraden van Pagar Roejoeng. OV 1930.

BRENNER, J. FREIHERR VON. Besuch bei den Kannibalen Sumatras. Würz-burg 1894.

ENTER, J. Het wichelboek der Bataks op Sumatra. NI 1933.

FISCHER, H. W. Planggi-Tücher aus Atjèh. IAE 1912.

GOSLINGS, B. M. Roodgekleurde Djambi-batiks. NI 1930/31. Heeft er te Palembang een door de eigen bevolking uitgeoefende batikkunst bestaan? NI 1931/32.

HAMER, C. DEN. Beschrijving van de twee krissen, als rijkssieraad verbonden aan het Sultansgezag over Djambi en het Pangeran Ratoeschap aldaar. TI-TLV 1906.

HEINE-GELDERN, R. Eine Szene aus dem Sutasoma-Jâtaka auf hinterindischen und indonesischen Schwertgriffen. Jahrbuch für prähistorische und ethnographische Kunst 1925. Die Megalithen Südostasiens. A 1928. Vorgeschichtliche Grundlagen der kolonialindischen Kunst. Wiener Beiträge zur Kunst- und Kulturgeschichte Asiens 1934.

HELBIG, K. "Sichtbare" Religion im Batakland auf Sumatra. ZE 1933.

HUENDER, W. Het Karo-Bataksche huis. BTLV-NI 1929.

HUYSER, J. G. Ornament van Indisch koperwerk. NI 1916/17, 1917/18. Koperwerk uit Midden-Sumatra. NI 1925/26. De Sumatra-tentoonstelling te Rotterdam in Maart 1926. NI 1926/27. Nog eens: oud koperwerk uit Siroekam. NI 1933.

JACOBS, J. Het familie- en kampongleven op Groot-Atjeh. Leiden 1894.

KLEIWEG DE ZWAAN, J. P. Het eiland Nias en zijn bewoners. NI 1926/27. L'île de Nias et ses habitants. Revue Anthropologique 1930.

KREEMER, J. Atjèh. Vol. I. Leiden 1922.

LOEBÈR, J. A. Geillustreerde beschrijvingen van Indische kunstnijverheid. Amsterdam 1903/16.

M., D. v. d. Wij willen Batakkers blijven. NI 1925/26.

MAASS, A. Durch Zentral-Sumatra. Berlin 1910.

MODIGLIANI, E. Un viaggio à Nias. Milano 1890. Fra i Batacchi independenti. Roma 1892. L'isola delle donne. Milano 1894.

Beschreibung einer von G. MEISSNER zusammengestellten Batak-Sammlung, mit sprachlichen und sachlichen Erläuterungen versehen und herausgegeben von F. W. K. MÜLLER. Veröffentlichungen aus dem königlichen Museum für Völkerkunde 1893.

NEUMANN, J. H. Karo-Bataksche offerplaatsen. BTLV-NI 1927.

NIEUWENHUIS, A. W. Die Veranlagung der malaiischen Völker des Ostindischen Archipels. IAE 1913, 1914.

OPHUIJSEN, CH. A. VAN. Der bataksche Zauberstab. IAE 1912.

SCHRÖDER, E. E. W. Gs. Nias. Leiden 1917.

STEIN CALLENFELS, P. V. VAN. Rapport over een dienstreis door een deel van Sumatra. OV 1920.

VELTMANN, T. J. Nota betreffende de Atjèhsche goud- en zilversmeedkunst. TI-TLV 1904.

VOLZ, W. Hausbau und Dorfanlage bei den Battakern in Nord-Sumatra. Globus 1899. Nord-Sumatra. Berlin 1909/12.

WARNECK, J. Die Religion der Batak. Leipzig 1909.

WINKLER, J. Die Toba-Batak auf Sumatra in gesunden und kranken Tagen. Stuttgart 1925.

WIRZ, P. Nias, die Insel der Götzen. Zürich 1929.

Katalog des Ethnographischen Reichsmuseums, Leiden. Vol. 4, 6, 8, 10, 12, 14.

INDEX.

350